INTERNATIONAL BUSINESS FINANCE

FINANCE SERIES

CONSULTING EDITOR:

DR. GEORGE C. PHILIPPATOS

C. H. Butcher, Sr., Chair of Banking & Finance
University of Tennessee
Knoxville, Tennessee

Finance Principles: An Introduction
Suk H. Kim, University of Detroit, and
Henry J. Guithues, St. Louis University

Financial Markets: Instruments and Concepts
John R. Brick, Michigan State University

Interest Rate Futures: Concepts and Issues
Gerald D. Gay, Georgia State University, and
Robert W. Kolb, Emory University

Interest Rate Futures: A Comprehensive Introduction
Robert W. Kolb, Emory University

International Finance
Gerald D. Gay, Georgia State University, and
Robert W. Kolb, Emory University

International Business Finance
Suk H. Kim, University of Detroit

INTERNATIONAL BUSINESS FINANCE

Suk H. Kim
UNIVERSITY OF DETROIT

Robert F. Dame, Inc.
511 Research Road
Richmond, Virginia 23235

ISBN 0-936-328-30-4

Library of Congress Catalog No. 82-74195

PRINTED IN THE UNITED STATES OF AMERICA

Designed and typeset by Publications Development Co. of Crockett, Texas, Developmental Editor: Nancy Marcus Land, Production Editor: Bessie Graham

PREFACE

International Finance is a field with great promise of growth. Enrollment at colleges and universities in this discipline has expanded rapidly. Furthermore, a truly phenomenal growth in interest in the subject by practitioners and governments has occurred in the 1970s, a trend which should continue.

The reason for the interest and growth is not hard to find. Although some foreign business operations have existed for centuries, the world has entered an era of unprecedented global economic activity with worldwide production and distribution. International finance has become more important as it serves increasing world trade and foreign investment.

The international business community is experiencing dramatic fluctuations and keener competition because the international economic environment has changed radically in the last ten years. Since 1973, a predictable international monetary system has changed to a volatile exchange system. The creation of OPEC has shifted wealth from the major industrial countries to the major oil exporting countries. New institutions and markets such as the Eurocurrency markets have integrated segmented national capital markets. Governments have taken a more active role in regulating both domestic and international financial markets. These factors have made it necessary for managements to become much more aware of the international financial environment.

Most large and many medium-size companies in the United States have international business operations of one type or another. In recent years, it has become clear that even companies without foreign investment can be significantly affected by events in the international environment. If business school graduates understand the basic elements of international finance, they will be at an advantage to move their companies forward.

The formal recognition of the importance of international business was slow in the United States. It was not until the later 1960s that awareness of the problems associated with international operations began to have a clear impact on business education. By this time, it was recognized that existing theories and techniques of finance based on business experience within the United States were neither general nor universal. The teaching of international finance began to appear in business school curricula in the mid-1960s and it was markedly accelerated during the early 1970s.

In recent years, more and more individuals have been urging business schools to meet this challenge. They argue that all business school graduates must have a comprehensive grasp of international business and its environment. The American Assembly of Collegiate Schools of Business (AACSB) has responded positively to this challenge. Since 1974, the AACSB has taken a series of steps to alter its accreditation standards in order to include a requirement that the international dimension of business be added to the curricula.

This book can be used in international finance courses at universities, company management development programs, and management institutes. In writing this book, it was my intention to provide an operationally useful analysis of the international financial system to international business managers. Three special features of the text are conciseness, readability, and practicability. The book should motivate the reader to seek out additional knowledge and courses to upgrade his or her understanding in the field of international finance.

This text consists of five major parts. Part One (Chapters 1 and 2) discusses major environmental differences and the motives for both world trade and foreign investment. Part Two (Chapters 3 through 5) deals with the forces that affect the relative prices of currencies in international markets. These forces include the balance of payments, the international monetary system, and the foreign exchange market. Part Three (Chapters 6 through 8) covers sources of international finance. One major facet of financial management is to raise funds on favorable terms. In the case of international finance, this involves those sources of funds to finance world trade and foreign investment. Part Four (Chapters 9 through 12) discusses the management of assets. The second major facet of financial management is the efficient allocation of funds among assets. The decision to invest abroad must consider various environmental differences such as disparities in exchange rates, differences in taxes, and differences in risk factors. Part Five (Chapters 13 through 15) describes techniques for controlling the operations of a multinational company. Accurate financial data are especially important in international business where operations are typically supervised from a distance. Multinational taxation is an important part of international finance because it has a pervasive effect on all aspects of multinational operations. Once the company establishes foreign subsidiaries, international transfer pricing becomes an important dimension of pricing strategies.

I wish to thank those individuals who have provided the constructive advice critical to the successful development of this text. I would like to express my thanks to Dean Donald Byrne (University of Detroit) for his support and encouragement. I gratefully acknowledge many comments and suggestions from my friends: Raj Aggarwal (University of Toledo), Gerald Cavanagh, S. J. (University of Detroit), William George (University of Detroit), Henry Guithues (St. Louis University), Seung Kim (St. Louis University), George Philippatos (University of Tennessee), Robert Redlin (University of Detroit), Charlton Schoeffler (University of Detroit), and S. Srinivasulu (Eastern Michigan University).

In addition, a number of my students at the University of Detroit deserve special acknowledgement for their contributions: Howard Brubaker, Chris Danowski, Sandra Drought, Kim Kellar, and Janice Misiewicz. My special thanks go to Herbert J. Marr, Duk J. Park, and Sue Park. Dean Marr (Evening Business Administration Program of the University of Detroit) has stimulated my thinking through his counsel and guidance. Dr. Duk Park and Mrs. Sue Park, as my in-laws, helped me complete my doctoral program through their generous financial and moral support.

Finally, I cheerfully acknowledge my foremost debt of gratitude to Susan Mary Nickerson for her exceptional contributions to every aspect of the book. Susan Nickerson, as my student assistant, carefully read the entire manuscript several times and made numerous suggestions for improving the clarity of the text. In addition, she did a multitude of miscellaneous chores with absolutely no complaint that helped to make my work much easier and more enjoyable. One could not dream of a better assistant.

Suk H. Kim
Detroit, Michigan

ABOUT THE AUTHOR

Dr. Suk H. Kim, an Associate Professor of International Business Finance, is the Acting Chairman of the Department of Accounting and Finance at the University of Detroit. He received his MBA from Pepperdine University and his Ph.D. in Finance from St. Louis University.

Dr. Kim's expertise is documented by his record of publication and the recognition of the academic community. He has published four college textbooks and 30 articles on international business finance and capital budgeting. Recent articles have appeared in such prestigious journals as the *Columbia Journal of World Business*, the *Journal of International Business Studies*, the *Engineering Economist, Management Accounting, Internal Auditor*, the *Journal of Financial Education*, and the *Collegiate Forum*. Several current finance textbooks cite his earlier findings and researchers from this field refer to his work when establishing the groundwork for further exploration.

Dr. Kim is an active member of the Academy of International Business, the Financial Management Association, the Midwest Finance Association, the National Association of Accountants, and the American Institute for Decision Sciences.

CONTENTS

PART ONE

Motives for International Transaction

$£¢

ONE

INTRODUCTION

Although some business operations in foreign countries have existed for centuries, the world has recently entered an era of unprecedented global economic activity with worldwide production and distribution. There are many examples of the increasing importance of international operations. U. S. firms such as IBM, Gillette, and Pfizer earn more in international than in domestic operations. Multinational companies such as Mobil Oil, British Petroleum, IBM, and Gulf Oil do business with more than 50 countries around the world. U.S. exports and imports have increased more than ten times in the last two decades. By the same token, international finance has also become increasingly important as it serves world trade and foreign investment. International earning assets for the Bank of America, for example, represent more than half its total earning assets. Citibank maintains more than 250 overseas branches in over 100 countries. Simply stated, each nation is economically related to other nations of the world through a complex network of international trade and financial relationships.

What are the differences between multinational companies and domestic companies from a financial manager's point of view? The efficient allocation of funds among assets and the acquisition of funds on favorable terms are conceptually the same for both types of companies. However, these two types of companies derive their differences from the fact that they do business in different environments. A basic understanding of these differences is essential if the international manager is to function effectively within the international environment.

ENVIRONMENTAL DIFFERENCES

Successful international operations require adequate information about the environmental factors that affect business operations in foreign countries. In conducting foreign business operations, U.S. methods and techniques should be adjusted to accommodate the customs, attitudes, economic factors, and political factors which prevail in the country of operation.

How do management principles in one country differ from those in other countries? In principle, concepts in the functional business areas of accounting, finance, management, and marketing are as relevant to business management in one country as they are in another country. However, when a business crosses national boundaries, the environment in which these concepts are applied is different. The three types of environmental differences to be described in this section are (1) types of risk, (2) conflicts of interest, and (3) multiple environments.[1] It is important to recognize that these three types of differences are neither mutually exclusive nor exhaustive.

Types of Risk

The three major types of risk confronted in international business operations are political risks, financial risks, and regulatory risks. Political risks range from moderate actions such as exchange controls to extreme actions such as complete confiscation of all assets. Financial risks involve varying exchange rates, divergent tax laws, different interest and inflation rates, and balance of payments considerations. Regulatory risks are differences in legal systems, overlapping jurisdictions, and restrictive business practices against foreign companies.

If a company plans to invest heavily in foreign countries, it must consider all of these risks for many years ahead. The conduct of busi-

[1] For details, see Stefan H. Robock, Kenneth Simmonds, and Jack Zwick, *International Business and Multinational Enterprises* (Homewood, Ill.: Richard D. Irwin, Inc., 1977), Chapter 3.

ness across national boundaries involves extra dimensions of risk which are rarely confronted in domestic business operations. Ideally, a company should analyze these extra risks to understand underlying causal forces. Then it should develop some specific measures to handle them effectively.

Conflicts of Interest

Various conflicts of interest may occur in international business operations for a variety of reasons. Owners, employees, suppliers, and customers may have different national identities. The interests of sovereign national states may be divergent. The goals of multinational companies and their host countries may be contradictory. Some conflicts of interest may exist within the multinational company. Furthermore, other conflicts may exist in the relationship between the multinational company and the external environment.

Many multinational companies desire to have home-country nationals in key positions for their foreign operations. They tend to hire local persons for nonmanagerial positions. Thus, disparities in salaries and wages are almost inevitable. Most developing countries require multinational companies to hire and train local people for management positions in exchange for local business operations. Many external conflicts relate to profit-motivated decisions which involve the transfer of funds, production, exports and imports, and employment from one country to another. For instance, the desire for foreign exchange remittances by the multinational company and the desire for the local government to restrict these remittances frequently create a serious problem.

Multiple Environments

In addition to the elements of risk and conflict just discussed, multinational companies have a wide variety of operational problems due to the multiplicity of environments in international business. These environmental diversities require different concepts, analytical methods, and information. Hence, multinational companies should identify, evaluate, and predict all the environmental variables. Some important environmental variables are the form of business organization, different institutional settings, and cultural differences.

THE ORGANIZATION OF THE BOOK

This book consists of five major parts. Part One (Chapters 1 and 2) examines environmental differences and motives for both world trade and foreign investment. Most textbooks for financial management courses are written as though the world stops at the borders of the United States. Most finance courses are also taught in that way. Recent statistics, however, indicate the growing importance of world trade and foreign investment. Hence, it is important to understand the economic basis for world trade and foreign investment.

Part Two (Chapters 3 through 5) deals with the forces that affect the relative prices of currencies in international markets. These forces include the balance of payments, the international monetary system, and the foreign exchange market. Prices of products and investments across national boundaries are expressed in international money. Commercial transactions between countries were once handled under the relatively rigid gold standard. But pursuit of national economic goals—healthy economic growth, full employment, stable prices, and the favorable balance of payments—has led to many changes in the international monetary environment under which business must operate.

Part Three (Chapters 6 through 8) describes sources of international finance. One major facet of financial management is to raise funds on favorable terms. In the case of international financial management, this involves those sources of funds to finance world trade and foreign investment. These funds can come from either internal or external sources. Internal sources of funds such as earnings and depreciation are the major sources of funds for most multinational companies. But external sources of funds such as bank loans and Eurodollars are important as well.

Part Four (Chapters 9 through 12) covers the management of assets. The second major facet of financial management is the efficient allocation of funds among various assets. This part describes the management of current assets, capital budgeting, and risks associated with foreign investment. The objective of current asset management is to protect the purchasing power of assets and to maximize the return on investment. The management of current assets is extremely important for the multinational company. Thus, the complicating international factors and approaches for resolving them should be analyzed carefully. Financial management literature on capital budgeting has expanded rapidly in the past decade. As a result, relatively sophisticated techniques exist to analyze how foreign investment decisions are made. Investment decisions affect the value of a company's stock by influencing both the size of the earnings stream and the riskiness of the company. This risk factor in foreign operations takes on a new dimension of importance because it is rarely encountered in domestic business operations. Risks associated with foreign operations can be divided into two categories: political risk and foreign exchange risk. This part describes the nature of these risks and some techniques to minimize them.

Part Five (Chapters 13 through 15) describes techniques for controlling the operations of a multinational company. Chapter 13 discusses multinational accounting theory and practices. It may be too early to recognize multinational accounting as a separate field of study. In recent years, however, substantial amounts of resources have been devoted to further development and refinement of international accounting. Meaningful financial reports are the cornerstone of effective management. Accurate financial data are especially important in international business where operations are typically supervised from a distance. Chapter 14 considers the significance of national tax systems on international business operations. Perhaps multinational taxation has the most pervasive effect on all aspects of multinational operations. Where to invest, how to finance, where to remit liquid funds are just a few examples of management actions affected by multinational taxation. Chapter 15 covers international transfer pricing. Because transfers between related business entities account for approximately 40 percent of all international trade, the multinational company must try to satisfy a number of objectives. This chapter examines some of these objectives, such as taxes, tariffs, competition, inflation rates, exchange rates, and restrictions on fund transfers.

SUMMARY

There are many indications that the scope of financial management should be expanded for multinational companies. Some of them are the increased world trade, the increased movement of both human and financial resources between countries, the growth in the number and size of multinational companies, and the improved ability for the collection and analysis of information. Moreover, most large and many medium-size companies in the United States have international business operations of one type or another. In recent years, it has become clear that even U.S. companies without foreign investment can be significantly affected by events in the international environment.

Essentially, the concepts of business management are equally applicable to multinational and domestic companies. However, these two types of companies are subject to environmental differences. These differences include taxes, the economic system, the political system, inflation, and interest rates, and many others. Thus, the financial manager must know the institutions and environmental conditions in all foreign countries in which his company has subsidiaries and affiliates.

APPENDIX 1A
INTERNATIONAL BUSINESS: STRATEGIES FOR THE '80s[1]

According to Alvin Toffler in his book, *The Third Wave*, from the end of World War II to the early 1970s, the corporation functioned in a relatively stable environment. The dollar was king. Currencies remained stable for long periods. The postwar financial and economic structure was solid. The escalator to affluence was still ascending and economists were so confident of their ability to predict and control the economic machine that they spoke casually about "fine tuning" it.

In spite of our preoccupation with Vietnam in the late 1960s, we were enjoying economic growth, a healthy stock market, a hard dollar and favorable expectations about our future and our ability to influence events. What happened in the 1970s to change all of this?

THE ECONOMY

Although we grew two and one-half times in GNP, from $953 billion in 1969 to $2.5 trillion in 1979, this figure included about $1.1 trillion of inflation. Real growth went from $1 trillion in 1969 to $1.4 trillion in 1979. In 1969 the U.S. produced about 47 percent of

[1] This is Block's speech made at the annual meeting of the American Assembly of Collegiate Schools of Business in Philadelphia in May 1981. Reprinted with permission from the AACSB's monthly newsletter, *Newsline*. This also appeared in the Fall 1981 issue of the *Collegiate Forum*.

the total output of the top 20 industrial nations. Today, that figure has slipped to 35 percent and is continuing to slide.

What else happened in the 1970s to disrupt economic growth? We went from energy rich to energy poor, from real growth to no growth or to negative growth. Consumers moved their investments from stock and bonds to hard goods and collectibles. We went from nominal to substantial unemployment, while at the same time the price of money soared. We hit new highs and new lows, both in the wrong direction.

THE GOVERNMENT

During the 1970s, the position of the United States as a world leader diminished. Since Watergate and Vietnam, the role of Congress has increased, the role of the executive office has diminished and the federal machinery of the regulatory agencies has become even more cumbersome and bureaucratic. Major cities have begun to strain under the threat of bankruptcy.

The paradoxes are astounding; our efforts to increase and improve our Social Security system now seem to contain the seeds of insecurity, as we struggle to finance our obligations. Our new sensitivity to environmental and social issues created such new agencies as EPA, EEOC, OSHA, ERISA, ERDA, and FEA which have increased the cost of doing business in the private sector.

Businessmen, and the public in general, have become increasingly frustrated with the sluggish response of the bureaucracy to troubles in our economy.

THE INTERNATIONAL SCENE

The United States has taken a beating in this arena also. We lost much of our technological lead, went off the gold standard and our dollar has substantially devalued compared to 1970. We've witnessed the rise of major international competition to U.S. business and have seen European and OPEC nations invest heavily in U.S. industry, real estate and the stock market. Who would have believed 10 years ago that the highest executive salaries, or the highest standard of living would be outside the United States.

Twenty years ago two-thirds of the world's largest industrial organizations were U.S. firms. Today less than half are. Nine of the 15 largest world banks were U.S. banks, now only three are in that group. Eleven of the largest world steel companies were U.S. firms, now only five are.

LABOR

In the 1970s, wages rose faster than productivity, while union power slipped. Work ethics in the United States changed rapidly. Toffler sees this as a result of the movement in the United States from mass society values to a greater emphasis on the diversity of jobs and the people who perform them. In his words, "Refusing to be treated as interchangeable, people arrive at the workplace with an acute consciousness of their ethnic, religious, professional, sexual, sub-cultural and individual differences." So, in short, the predictions for the 1970s were not realized; we saw the "happiness curves" ultimately turn into turbulence and chaos and we experienced consolidation and concentration.

Why this gloomy review of the past 10 years? The simple fact is that the world is not the same as it was in 1970. "Conventional" business wisdom no longer applies. It's not only a brave new world–it's a world only for the brave. Management must learn to deal with enormous complexities, scarcities and uncertainty; static models are inadequate for dealing with rapid change–change related to gyrating currencies, revolutionary information systems, transnational production, global banking, erratic energy supplies and prices, social welfare pressures, high unemployment, new attitudes among workers and consumers, imbalances of trade and an alarming incidence of growing militancy in the non-industrial world. Executives are simply not used to operating in such an unfamiliar and explosive environment. Any one of those is bad enough; taken together they are frightening.

ISSUES FOR THE 1980s

So, what about the 1980s? Yoshi Tsurumi of the City University of New York predicts that the business environment of the 1980s will be characterized by twin phenomena: (1) the management of industrial growth given a scarcity of managerial, natural, technological, and financial resources; and (2) the globalization of markets, which will erase any distinction between which national corporations serve any foreign and domestic market.

Scarcity of Resources

Resources will be scarce in the 1980s with increased competition for those which exist, not only from the industrialized nations but also from the industrial and commercial corporations of other countries, but they are establishing factories in our country–310 in 1978-1980 alone, and are competing head on with us in our own domestic markets.

Another issue for the 1980s is the necessity for continued technological development by government and U.S. industry. Our investments in research and development have declined recently on a real basis. Our new American products today are spinoffs of earlier technological achievement. The major markets and products of the 1980s will be different from what we have seen in the past. Technology will be a strong force for these changes and we must encourage research and development as never before in order to compete successfully in world markets.

The major issue for America in the 1980s is growth, or the lack of it. We have a whole generation of management that has never operated in a no-growth economy. Yet, the solution is not just the obvious one of finding a growth industry or a growth market. Everyone will be attempting to do this. Further growth requires cash. It eats up profit. It requires a long-term investment commitment. And, long-term perspective is not a traditional American trait.

Growth Overseas

An article from *The Chicago Tribune* on February 4, 1981, printed the results of a survey that showed that 70 percent of the 1,000 largest industrial companies in the United States expect their international growth to be greater than their domestic growth in the next five years. John Mathis, an international economist for Continental Bank, cites the technical capability of the United States and the devaluation of the dollar as encouraging this trend. Many U.S. clients use our European and Japanese offices to develop growth and market penetration strategies as well as reduce cost and improve their operations. Yet, a company must be careful about foreign investments. Six out of ten of the companies surveyed claimed to have suffered from unstable business environments overseas in the past five years. Only one-third of the companies formally evaluated these risks in their investment decisions overseas. One country cannot solve its problems at the expense of other nations. Gain for one is loss for the other–and the result is a zero-sum game. A restrictive posture will only delay technical advances, decrease our competitiveness and increase the cost of servicing the market.

Growth Through Increases in Productivity

The greatest problem facing U.S. business today is the decline in the growth of productivity. The most recent study by the American Productivity Center showed that productivity in the manufacturing sector declined 1.9 percent in 1980. This problem stems from many facets in the business community today and is a broad strategic issue. I submit to you there are five fundamental changes or challenges which we will have to come to grips with if we hope to make a dent in the productivity problem.

The first is the vast growth in the service sector of our economy: growth in government; growth in financial and service institutions; and growth in the number of indirect and non-production jobs. This factor will continue since predictions call for some 90 percent of the employed population to be in non-production jobs somewhere between 1990 and the year 2000. The real problem isn't only that the type of work is changing, but rather that we have not developed effective management tools for measuring, managing and motivating this type of work force. Direct and indirect work standards, time studies, ratio delay, work sampling and many other traditional management tools and approaches which we and other management consultants have used for years to help clients with these types of problems aren't entirely applicable.

A second great challenge to productivity improvement opportunity concerns resource scarcity and availability. It is not particularly reassuring in a world of great instability, international terrorism and tenuous alliances to note that 80 percent or more of selected critical mineral resources for the U.S. are outside our borders. We need to find ways to become more independent in controlling selected resources over which we cannot achieve independence. We need to think through new forms of economic alliances and secure longer term arrangements. We need to offer still greater incentives for existing resources. Ultimately, we need to consider developing international resource sharing arrangements, perhaps through an international resource bank similar to the International Monetary Fund or World Bank.

A third challenge to increased productivity is the ever-increasing role which the federal government has assumed as a regulator of industry. We need new approaches to evaluate the trade-off benefits to society of more safety, environmental, consumer, drug, minority, antitrust regulation, etc. It is no longer a question of virtue or moral value, but how much can we afford or how fast. We must drop the unnecessary aspects of regulating and move to a philosophy of sponsorship of business, one that rewards investments which create jobs in areas of growth and opportunity and not simply take from the strong to subsidize the marginal, the weak and the unhealthy.

Ideally, the government should encourage and help provide skill and capital to the industries of the future—the winners—the industries that will eventually absorb the industrial jobs now connected with failing industries. In short, we need a reindustrialization policy. The government should provide tax incentives that stimulate industries to grow and modernize, fund research and development and support training programs to increase the efficiency of the job force.

Fourth, one of the greatest sources of productivity drain in this nation is our traditional adversary philosophy: Management vs. union; industry vs. government. The cost of living in this kind of world is horrendous. These concepts of checks and balances are a luxury we no longer can afford. We find ourselves in a constant state of confrontation with unions. We must come to grips with the need to go from a lose/lose philosophy to a win/win philosophy for all the critical parties involved.

Finally, perhaps the greatest source of productivity loss in the United States is the short-term orientation of management. When social critic Tom Wolfe named the 1970s the "Me" decade, he was bemoaning the rise of a basic self-centeredness that is coloring our social fabric. In a similar vein, the same lack of commitment implied in this expression is now permeating the business world. Growth in U.S. industry is often stymied by demands for immediate earnings per share and dividends.

Before we close, we must emphasize a "sharpening up" and increasing use of some of the most successful internal management approaches of the past—the kind of actions required to respond to changes in the marketplace, to compete effectively and to achieve low cost production. Survival and profitability will go to the corporations who direct their resources to growth businesses, who adapt to the needs of the marketplace, who innovate to fulfill special needs and who produce at lowest cost with the best utilization of assets.

SUMMARY

In summary, profitable growth is the strategic issue of the 1980s and the solution is to think globally and act locally, versus thinking locally and acting globally. In its simplest terms the "global approach" says, with respect to business strategy and markets: "Plans to go to the Pacific Basin had better fit into a total strategy (synergy). And when you go, you had better be prepared to "go local" (people, laws, customs, distribution).

The global solution requires us to deal with the totality of productivity improvement not just in the plants, but in all of the general and administrative areas of business operations including managerial.

The global solution requires us to look at the tradeoff value of regulatory change in a broad economic rather than a specific interest group sense. Global views must prevail over protectionist interest groups; we must consider the international consequences of local and national actions.

The global picture requires us to look at our resource dependency and scarcity and seek new solutions to prevent blackmail or at least minimize the economic consequences of such in the future.

And finally, we must develop and utilize systems and approaches which will enable management to make the proper decisions for the short-term consistent with a long-range strategy.

In the 1980s, American businessmen will have a lot of choices to make with respect to how to compete successfully internationally. Tomorrow's management will be held to be accountable, not just for its national economic performance, but also for its global performance–politically, economically and socially.

Corporations will ultimately be judged not only on profitability, but on how they contribute to the solution of the broader problems of our society in a world of change.

The judgment will be based on those who survive and whether they have reconstructed a growth environment for the 1990s. It's a brave new world and U.S. businessmen need a new game plan.

TWO

MOTIVES FOR WORLD TRADE AND FOREIGN INVESTMENT

Human desires are unlimited while resources are limited. Thus, one of the most important tasks for man is to seek new knowledge necessary to bridge the gap between desires and resources. The traditional concept of economic man assumed that man allocates his scarce resources between competing uses in the most economic manner. Robinson Crusoe's world, for example, would involve allocating his labor time between alternative uses. He would use one level site on the island as either the location for a hut or as a vegetable garden. Of course, the real world consists of many persons and nations that are interdependent for sociological and economic reasons. Most societies face problems similar to those faced by Robinson Crusoe but in more complex forms.

The advantages of economic interdependence between persons center mainly on the efficiency of specialization. Specialization of function or division of labor allows each person or nation to utilize any peculiar differences in skills and resources in the most economic manner. There are a number of reasons why specialization produces a greater amount of goods and services. (1) Natural talents between people are different. If intelligent people specialize in mental tasks while physically strong people specialize in physical tasks, the total amount of output becomes greater than if each person tried to do both for himself. (2) Even if the natural abilities of two persons are identical, specialization may be advantageous because it creates the opportunity for improved skills and techniques through repetition of tasks. (3) The simplification of function through specialization leads to mechanization and the use of large-scale machinery. (4) Personal specialization avoids the loss of time that occurs in shifting from one task to another.

MOTIVES FOR WORLD TRADE

The theories of comparative advantage and factor endowments have been suggested as two major motives for foreign trade.

The Theory of Comparative Advantage

The classical economic theory of comparative advantage explains why countries exchange their goods and services with each other. Here the underlying assumption is that some countries can produce some types of goods relatively more efficiently than other countries can. Hence, all countries are better off if each specializes in the production of those goods which it can produce relatively more efficiently and buys those goods which other countries produce relatively more efficiently.

Why Comparative Advantage Occurs. The theory of comparative advantage depends on two points. (1) The factors of production, such as land, labor, and capital, are unequally distributed among nations. (2) The efficient production of various goods and services requires combinations of different economic resources and different technologies. For instance, Canada has vast amounts of fertile land resources and relatively few people. In contrast, Japan has little land and abundant skilled labor. Thus, Canada may produce such land-intensive goods as wheat more economically than Japan, while Japan may produce such labor-intensive goods as cameras more economically than Canada.

However, it is important to recognize that the distribution of economic resources and technology can change over time. This change may alter the relative production efficiency. In the last 10 to 20 years, some developing countries have considerably upgraded the quality of their labor forces and have substantially expanded their stock of capital. Therefore, they now produce such capital-intensive commodities as steel, machinery, and automobiles.

Example 2-1 The world consists of two nations (Canada and Japan) and two commodities (wheat and cameras). For a fixed amount of $1,000 in land, labor, and capital, Canada and Japan can produce either of the following two commodities:

Country	*Wheat*		*Cameras*
Canada	180	or	6
Japan	80	or	8

The optimum product-mix in Canada involves 90 bushels of wheat and 3 cameras while the optimum product-mix in Japan contains 50 bushels of wheat and 3 cameras.

It is clear from the above table that under full employment conditions Canada's exchange ratio for the two products is one camera (C) for 30 bushels of wheat (W) or 1C = 30W. Japan's exchange ratio for the two products is one camera for 10 bushels of wheat or 1C = 10W. Thus, Canada's comparative advantage is greater in the production of wheat, whereas Japan's comparative advantage is larger in the production of cameras. In other words, these two countries produce both products but at different levels of economic efficiency. If they specialize according to comparative advantage, Canada must produce wheat only while Japan must produce cameras only. If they trade with each other, larger outputs of both wheat and cameras are available to both nations because specialization results in a more efficient allocation of world resources.

The exchange ratios for the two products differ in the two countries. This difference becomes the basis for mutually beneficial specialization and trade. Trade requires a new exchange ratio between the two products so that Canada may obtain one camera for less than 30 bushels of wheat and Japan may obtain more than 10 bushels of wheat for one camera. Thus, the terms of trade must lie somewhere between 1C = 30W and 1C = 10W or 30W > 1C > 10W.

The actual exchange ratio will depend on world supply and demand conditions. However, assume that the international exchange ratio for the two products is 1C = 20W. The quantities of the two products available to both countries after specialization and trade would be greater than the optimum product-mixes before specialization and trade.

Table 2-1 shows the gains to the two nations from specialization

Table 2-1 The Gains to Both Nations from Specialization and Trade

Country	Before Specialization	After Specialization	Exports (−) and Imports (+)	Outputs After Trade	Gains from Specialization and Trade
Canada	90W	180W	−80W	100W	10W
	3C	0C	+ 4C	4C	1C
Japan	50W	0W	+80W	80W	30W
	3C	8C	− 4C	4C	1C

and trade. If Canada exports 80 bushels of wheat (out of 180 bushels) for 4 cameras, it would enjoy 100 bushels of wheat and 4 cameras. Hence, Canada would have 10 more bushels of wheat and one more camera than the optimum product-mix that existed before specialization and trade. If Japan trades 4 cameras (out of 8 cameras) for 80 bushels of wheat, Japan would enjoy 4 cameras and 80 bushels of wheat. Thus, Japan would enjoy one more camera and 30 more bushels of wheat than its optimum product-mix.

Specialization and trade permit the two-country model to obtain a total of 180 bushels of wheat and a total of 8 cameras. It is important to note that the two countries had a total of 140 bushels of wheat and a total of 6 cameras before specialization and trade. Thus, larger outputs of both wheat and cameras are available to the two countries from specialization and trade.

The Theory of Factor Endowments

Countries are substantially different in their endowments of economic resources. This explains why Brazil is more efficient in the production of coffee and why the United States is more efficient in the production of steel. Brazil has the soil, weather, and abundant supplies of unskilled labor necessary to produce coffee more economically than the United States. The United States possesses the raw materials, facilities, and ample supplies of skilled labor necessary to produce steel more efficiently than Brazil.

Differences in national factor endowments explain differences in comparative factor costs between the two countries. Capital costs are lower in the United States than in Brazil because the United States has relatively more capital than Brazil. Labor costs are lower in Brazil than in the United States because Brazil has relatively more labor than the United States. Simply stated, the more abundant the supply of any factor, the lower the cost of the factor.

According to the theory of factor endowments, a country must specialize in the production and export of any good that uses large amounts of abundant factors. The country must import those commodities that use large amounts of scarce production factors at home. Most developing countries have a comparative cost advantage in the production of labor-intensive commodities. Most industrialized countries enjoy a comparative cost advantage in the production of capital-intensive commodities. Thus, specialization and trade could be mutually beneficial if industrialized countries specialize in the production and export of capital-intensive goods and if developing countries specialize in the production and export of labor-intensive commodities.

Product Life Cycle Theory

All products have a certain length of life. During this life they go through certain stages. A product's life begins with its market introduction, its market grows rather rapidly, its demand reaches maturity, its market declines, and finally its life ends.

This theory attempts to explain both world trade and foreign investment patterns on the basis of stages in a product's life.[1] In the context of international trade, the product life cycle theory assumes that certain products go through four stages. (1) A large company introduces a new product in response to some change in the home country market. After a time lag, this home country establishes itself as an exporter with a monopoly position. (2) Increasing transportation and tariff costs make it less attractive to export the product. Thus, the firm begins to produce its product in some foreign countries. This international production replaces home country exports in certain foreign markets. (3) Some foreign companies begin to compete in third markets. This competition leads to a further reduction in home country exports. (4) Some foreign companies export the product back to the home country. Many factors such as low labor costs, economies of scale, and government subsidies make it possible for foreign companies to invade the home country market.

[1] Raymond Vernon, "International Investment and International Trade in the Product Life Cycle," *Quarterly Journal of Economics* (May 1966), pp. 190-207; and Rita Maldonado and Anthony Saunders, "International Portfolio Diversification and the Inter-Temporal Stability of International Stock Market Relationships, 1975-1980," *Financial Management* (Autumn 1981), pp. 54-63.

Other Motives for World Trade

We have seen that differences in comparative costs explain why specialization and trade are mutually beneficial. Another important cause of international trade is the fact that costs may fall as outputs expand. If each country specializes in a limited number of products in which it has a comparative advantage, economies of mass production could be realized. Mass production and mass marketing improve skills and technologies. Opportunities to eliminate duplicate facilities occur. There are also opportunities to consolidate the functions of production, marketing, and purchasing. These types of operating economies and improved skills can lead to larger outputs of goods and services even if no differences in comparative costs between countries existed.

Even if differences in comparative costs between countries and economies of scale were absent, international trade might take place due to differences in tastes. Suppose that both Canada and Japan produce fish and meat in approximately the same amounts. If Canadians prefer meat and Japanese prefer fish, then a mutually beneficial export of meat from Japan to Canada and fish from Canada to Japan would take place. Both countries gain from this exchange, because the sum total of satisfaction derived from the trade is greater than would be possible under isolated self-sufficiency without trade.

Free Trade Versus Protectionism

It should be emphasized that the possibility of foreign embargo on sales of certain products and national defense needs may cause some countries to seek self-sufficiency in some strategic commodities. Political and military questions constantly affect international trade and other international business operations. Conflicts between multinational companies and host countries historically occurred over such issues as political ideology, national sovereignty, control of key industries, balance of payments, and control of export markets.

Tariffs and import quotas are the two primary means of protectionism. Tariffs on imported commodities may be imposed for purposes of revenues or protection. When tariffs are used to increase revenues, they are usually modest. However, when tariffs are employed to protect domestic companies from foreign competition, they are typically high. Although protective tariffs do not eliminate the importation of foreign products completely, they clearly put foreign sellers at a comparative disadvantage. Here consumers must pay more for foreign goods. Thus, the consumers reduce their consumption of imported commodities. Domestic companies do benefit from such tariffs, but they kill all the advantage of specialization and trade.

To shield domestic producers from foreign competition, import quotas may also be used. They specify the maximum amounts of certain products to be imported during a given period of time, usually one year. Import quotas are sometimes more effective than tariffs in reducing the importation of certain products. Although tariffs are high, certain commodities are imported in relatively large quantities. In contrast, low import quotas totally prohibit imports beyond the quota.

Free trade, based on the principle of comparative advantage, leads the world to achieve a more efficient allocation of resources and a high level of material benefits. But strong arguments for protectionism have been made. They include the protection of domestic industries to establish themselves, military self-sufficiency, the increase in domestic employment, and the diversification for stability. Although arguments for protectionism are very popular in many countries, they fail to overshadow the importance of free trade. World leaders have long recognized that the reduction or elimination of artificial barriers to trade is one of the necessary conditions for the expansion of world trade. A General Agreement on Tariffs and Trade (GATT), the European Common Market (EEC), the Kennedy Round, and the Tokyo Round are just a few developments that have emerged to liberalize world trade.[2]

[2] A General Agreement on Tariffs and Trade was signed in 1947 by 23 nations. It contained three important rules to liberalize world trade: (1) nondiscriminatory trade policies for all member countries, (2) the reduction of tariffs by multilateral negotiations, and (3) the elimination of import quotas. The European Common Market was established in 1957 to remove trade barriers among the member countries. The Common Market consists of Belgium, Denmark, France, Ireland, Italy, Luxembourg, the Netherlands, the United Kingdom, West Germany, and Greece. Turkey is an associate member. The Trade Expansion Act of 1962 allowed the United States to enter into the Kennedy Round of tariff negotiations which was concluded in 1967. It calls for the reduction of trade barriers between the United States and the Common Market. Negotiators from the 99 countries concluded the Tokyo Round of multilateral trade negotiations in 1979, which calls for the reduction of nontariff barriers. The most important part of these agreements is a series of detailed codes spelling out permissible and nonpermissible "good" behavior by governments in almost all nontariff measures.

MOTIVES FOR FOREIGN INVESTMENT

Many companies have been induced to enter into new and profitable markets abroad since World War II. The economic and political forces in the host countries, along with their desire to sell more abroad, are largely responsible for the expansion of foreign direct investment. Companies find it increasingly easier to reach foreign markets through the establishment of local manufacturing facilities than solely through exportation. Increased tariff restrictions and more restrictive import quotas have made it very difficult to reach foreign markets solely by exportation. Increasing transportation and import duties have caused the prices of exported goods to increase sharply, thus reducing the competitiveness of many companies' exports.

The theory of comparative advantage and its corollary, the theory of factor endowments, have provided a foundation for the justification of world trade. However, similar theories for foreign investment are yet to be fully developed. Nevertheless, the product life cycle theory and the portfolio theory have been suggested as a basis for explaining and justifying foreign investment.

Product Life Cycle Theory

The theory of product life cycle explains changes in the location of production. When new products are introduced in home country markets, their sales and profits tend to increase sharply until they reach maturity. Competition increases rapidly as these products approach their maturity point. This competition narrows profit margins. At this stage, companies may utilize foreign manufacturing locations to lower production costs and sustain profit margins.

This theory assumes that larger companies in highly advanced countries have a comparative advantage in new products. But companies in developing countries have a comparative advantage in the fabrication of mature products. Highly advanced technologies, highly educated labor resources, and abundant capital are essential to develop new products. They are readily available to larger firms in advanced countries. Larger markets and necessary alteration requirements in early production stages are additional reasons why larger companies in the developed areas of the world first introduce new products in the home country markets.

As products become mature, product defaults and technological imperfections, inherent in new products, are ironed out so that the method of production becomes standardized. Competition begins to appear during the stage of market growth and becomes highly intensive during the stage of market maturity. At this point, some companies begin to shift their standardized manufacturing method to developing countries for a number of good reasons. (1) The standard production method requires many unskilled workers. (2) Most developing nations have the relatively abundant supply of unskilled labor. (3) Labor costs are much lower in developing countries than in the United States.

Portfolio Theory

The portfolio theory is another economic rationale for foreign investment. This theory lies on two variables: risk and return. Risk is the variability of returns associated with an investment project. Two projects may have the same long-term average rate of return. But one project may fluctuate widely in annual return while the other may have a stable return. A project whose returns fluctuate widely is said to be more risky than the other whose returns are stable.

Typically, only a few financial variables are known in advance. Businessmen and investors are basically risk averters. Thus, they desire to minimize the overall degree of risk for their investment projects. Fortunately, there are many business situations where the risks of individual projects tend to offset with each other. As a consequence, successful diversification makes it possible for investors to have the risk of a portfolio less than the sum of the risks of the individual projects in the portfolio.

A study by Levy and Sarnat indicated that a company is often able to improve its risk-return performance by holding an internationally diversified portfolio.[3] The key element in the portfolio theory is the correlation coefficient between projects in the portfolio. When projects with low degrees of correlation are combined with

[3] Haim Levy and Marshall Sarnat, "International Diversification of Investment Portfolio," *American Economic Review* (September 1970), pp. 668-675. For other useful references, see Vihang R. Errunza, "Gains from Portfolio Diversification into Less Developed Countries' Securities," *Journal of International Business Studies* (Fall-Winter 1977), pp. 83-99; and William P. Lloyd, et al., "International Portfolio Diversification of Real Assets: An Update," *Journal of Business Finance and Accounting* (Spring 1981), pp. 45-50.

each other, a company is able to reduce its risk in relation to expected return. The Levy-Sarnat model assumes that foreign investment projects tend to be less correlated with each other than domestic investment projects. The economic cycles of different countries, *i.e.*, the United States and Saudi Arabia, do not tend to be totally synchronized. On the other hand, most domestic projects tend to be highly correlated with each other because they depend on the same state of economy.

Oligopoly Model

Oligopoly exists where there are only a few firms whose products are usually close substitutes for one another. Because a few firms dominate a market, each of these firms has a large share of the market so that its policies have repercussions on the other firms.

The oligopoly model offers a rationale to explain why multinational companies invest in foreign countries.[4] The model assumes that business firms make foreign investments to exploit their quasi-monopoly advantages. The advantages of a multinational company over a local company may include technology, access to capital, differentiated products built on advertising, superior management, and organizational scale.

Horizontal investments for foreign production of the same goods in the home market are made to produce operating economies of scale. The horizontal investment may reduce the number of competitors, eliminate duplicate facilities, and expand the firm's operation in an existing product line. Vertical investments for foreign production of raw materials are usually made to control input sources. The control of input sources may make it possible for companies in an oligopolistic industry to raise barriers to the entry of new competitors and to protect their oligopoly position. Some defensive investments are made by some companies to prevent the others from getting an unanticipated advantage.

Other Studies of Motives for Foreign Investment

Many foreign investments are motivated by strategic decisions. Although these strategic considerations are many and varied, we may

[4] Fred T. Knickerbocker, *Oligopolistic Reaction and the Multinational Enterprise* (Boston: Harvard Graduate School of Business Administration, 1973).

group them into two categories: those from the standpoint of host countries and those from the standpoint of investors.

Nehrt and Hogue suggested that companies invest abroad to seek: (1) new markets, (2) raw materials, (3) production efficiency, and (4) new knowledge.[5] Many companies, whose products are at a saturation stage in the home country markets, attempt to preserve or expand their markets for these products through foreign manufacturing locations. A subset of the market strategy falls within the context of the product life cycle theory. Oil companies, mining companies, and lumber companies find it difficult or costly to obtain raw materials at home. Hence, they invest their money abroad to obtain these raw materials. Some production-efficiency oriented companies look for low costs of production such as low labor costs. This is one of the most important reasons why multinational companies choose some countries in Africa, Asia, and South America for their overseas investment. Not many companies invest abroad to seek new knowledge because multinational companies tend to have superior knowledge over local companies. However, some companies may desire to dig out news of technical developments in foreign countries through foreign investment.

The National Industrial Conference Board surveyed a sample of 60 nations and found that many developing countries have various incentive programs for private foreign investments.[6] They include tax incentives, tariff exemptions, financial assistance, remittance guarantees, administrative assistance, protection against competitive investments and imports, and protection against nationalization and political risk. These and other incentive programs would undoubtedly motivate multinational companies to invest in those nations offering such incentives.

Aharoni studied the foreign investment decision process.[7] He surveyed 38 American companies which had invested in Israel. This survey found that the motives for their investment in Israel were outside proposals such as those from foreign governments, strong competition from abroad in the home market, fear of losing a market, and the band wagon effect. The term "band wagon effect" is used here to mean the fact that successful foreign operations reported by a

[5] Lee Nehrt and Dickerson W. Houge, "The Foreign Investment Decision-Making Process," *The Quarterly Journal of AISEC International* (February-April 1968), pp. 43-48.

[6] The National Industrial Conference Board, *Obstacles and Incentives to Private Foreign Investment*, Vol II (New York: Conference Board, 1969), pp. 1-6.

[7] Yair Aharoni, *The Foreign Investment Decision Process* (Boston: Harvard University, 1966), Chapter 3.

company induce its competitors to go abroad. It also found a number of auxiliary motives for direct foreign investment, such as utilization of old machinery and capitalization of know-how.

SUMMARY

This chapter has examined motives for both world trade and foreign investment. The theory of comparative advantage and its corollary, the theory of factor endowments explain why countries exchange their goods and services with each other. The theory of competitive advantage depends on two assumptions. (1) Economic resources are unequally distributed among nations. (2) The efficient production of various products requires combinations of different economic resources and different technologies.

Both the product life cycle theory and the portfolio theory provide a conceptual rationale for foreign investment. The product life cycle theory assumes that a country uses foreign manufacturing locations when products approach their maturity point. The portfolio theory states that the company invests overseas because an internationally diversified portfolio of assets improves the risk-return performance of the company.

PROBLEMS

2-1. Assume that production possibilities data for the United States and Taiwan are as follows:

		Production Alternatives		
Country	Product	A	B	C
U.S.A.	Clothing	0	30	90
	Food	30	20	0
Taiwan	Clothing	0	20	60
	Food	15	10	0

a. What is the comparative cost of clothing and food in the United States?

b. What is the comparative cost of clothing and food in Taiwan?

c. Identify the product that each country should specialize according to the comparative advantage.

d. Assume that both countries decided to specialize in a product according to the comparative advantage. With 1 food = 3½ clothings terms of trade, the United States exchanges 10 tons of its food for 35 units of Taiwanese clothings. With the assumption that B is the optimum-product mix, prepare a table such as Table 2-1.

e. With a fixed investment of $10,000, the United States produces more in both clothings and food than Taiwan. Does it mean that specialization and trade do not provide any benefits for the United States?

REFERENCES

2-1 Agmon, Tamir, and Donald R. Lessard, "Investor Recognition of Corporate International Diversification," *Journal of Finance* (September 1977), pp. 1049-1055.

2-2 Aharoni, Yair, *The Foreign Investment Decision Process* (Boston: Harvard University, 1966).

2-3 Baldwin, Robert E., "Determinants of the Commodity Structure of U. S. Trade," *American Economic Review* (May 1971), pp. 126-146.

2-4 Bettis, Richard A., and William K. Hall, "Strategic Portfolio Management in the Multinational Firm," *California Management Review* (Fall 1981), pp. 28-38.

2-5 Blackhurst, Richard, Nicolas Marian, and Jan Tumlir, "The Issues of Further Reductions in Barriers to International Trade," *Trade Liberalization, Protectionism, and Interdependence*, GATT Study No. 5 (Geneva: General Agreement on Tariffs and Trade, 1977), pp. 21-42.

2-6 Dince, Robert R., and Peter N. Umoth, "Foreign Exchange Risk and the Portfolio Approach: An Example for West Africa," *Columbia Journal of World Business* (Spring 1981), pp. 24-28.

2-7 Eichengreen, Barry J., "A Dynamic Model of Tariffs, Output and Employment under Flexible Exchange Rates," *Journal of International Economics* (August 1981), pp. 341-360.

2-8 Errunza, Vihang R., "Gains from Portfolio Diversification into Less Developed Countries," *Journal of International Business Studies* (Fall-Winter 1977), pp. 83-99.

2-9 Grubel, Herbert G., "Internationally Diversified Portfolios," *American Economic Review* (December 1968), pp. 1299-1314.

2-10 Helpman, Elhanan, "International Trade in the Presence of Product Differentiation, Economies of Scale and Monopolistic Competition: A Chamberlin-Heckscher Ohlin Approach," *Journal of International Economics* (August 1981), pp. 305-340.

2-11 Johnson, D. Gale, "Comparative Advantage of the United States Agriculture," pp. 221-230 in Robert E. Baldwin and J. David Richardson, eds., *International Trade and Finance* (Boston: Little, Brown, and Co., 1981).

2-12 Kim, Seung H., "Financial Motives of U. S. Corporate Investment in Korea," *California Management Review* (Summer 1976), pp. 60-68.

2-13 Knickerbocker, Fred T., *Oligopolistic Reaction and the Multinational Enterprise* (Boston: Harvard Graduate School of Business Administration, 1973).

2-14 Levy, Haim, and Marshall Sarnat, "International Diversification of Investment Portfolio," *American Economic Review* (September 1970), pp. 668-675.

2-15 Lloyd, William P., Steven J. Goldstein, and Robert B. Rogow, "International Portfolio Diversification of Real Assets: An Update," *Journal of Business Finance and Accounting* (Spring 1981), pp. 45-50.

2-16 Maldonado, Rita, and Anthony Saunders, "International Portfolio Diversification and the Inter-Temporal Stability of International Stock Market Relationships, 1957-1978," *Financial Management* (Autumn 1981), pp. 54-63.

2-17 National Industrial Conference Board, "Why Industry Invests Abroad," in *the Multinational Corporation: Studies on U. S. Foreign Investment*, Volume 2 (Washington, D. C.: U. S. Department of Commerce, 1973).

2-18 Nehrt, Lee, and Dickerson W. Houge, "The Foreign Investment Decision-Making Process," *The Quarterly Journal of AISEC International* (February-April 1968), pp. 43-48.

2-19 Rabino, Samuel, "Tax Incentives to Exports: Some Implications for Policy Makers," *Journal of International Business Studies* (Spring/Summer 1980), pp. 74-85.

2-20 Rugman, Alan R., "Motives for Foreign Investment: The Market Imperfections and Risk Diversification Hypothesis," *Journal of World Trade Law* (September-October 1975), pp. 567-573.

2-21 Vernon, Raymond, "International Investment and International Trade in the Product Cycle," *Quarterly Journal of Economics* (May 1966), pp. 190-207.

2-22 Wind, Yaram, and Susan Douglas, "International Portfolio Analysis and Strategy: The Challenge of the 80s," *Journal of International Business Studies* (Fall 1981), pp. 69-82.

PART TWO

International Monetary Environment

THREE

THE BALANCE OF PAYMENTS

The balance of payments records all transactions between a given country and the rest of the world during a specified period of time. It includes receipts and payments for both private and government economic transactions, whether these transactions involve cash or credit.

The ability of multinational companies to move money across national boundaries is critical. Multinational companies depend on this ability for exports, imports, the payment of foreign debts, and dividend remittances. Many factors affect a firm's ability to move funds from one country to another. In particular, a country's balance of payments affects the value of its currency, its ability to obtain currencies of other countries, and its policy toward foreign investment.

This chapter has three objectives: (1) to discuss the balance of payments accounts, (2) to define and explain the balance of payments, and (3) to explain the means for correcting a balance-of-payments disequilibrium.

DOUBLE-ENTRY ACCOUNTING

The balance of payments depends on the principle of double-entry accounting. Each transaction is recorded as debits and credits of equal amount. Increases in assets and decreases in liabilities or net worth represent debits or uses of funds. Decreases in assets and increases in liabilities or net worth represent credits or sources of funds. However, it is important to recognize that the balance of payments is neither an income statement nor a balance sheet. The balance of payments is a sources-and-uses-of-funds statement that reflects changes in assets, liabilities, and net worth during a specified period of time.[1] Sources of funds within the context of international transactions include exports of goods and services, investment and interest earnings, unilateral transfers received from abroad, and loans from foreigners. Uses of funds include imports of goods and services, dividends paid to foreign investors, transfer payments abroad, loans to foreigners, and increases in reserve assets.

Some illustrations of selected transactions might help us understand the effects that these transactions have on the balance of payments.

Example 3-1 Merchandise Trade An American company sells $50,000 worth of machinery to a British company. This British company pays for the machinery in 60 days. These merchandise exports are credited because they provide the United States with an increase in its claims on foreigners. At the same time, the American exporter should increase its short-term investment abroad, *i.e.*, an increase in its accounts receivable. This short-term investment represents a use of funds or a debit entry.

Liquid short-term capital	$50,000 (debit)	
Exports		$50,000 (credit)

Example 3-2 Services Services represent nonmerchandise transactions such as tourist expenditures. Consider an American woman who visits her husband in Japan. She cashes $5,000 worth of her U.S. traveler's checks at a Japanese hotel. Before she returns to the United States, she spends the $5,000 in Japan. In this case, the United States received travel services from Japan in the amount of $5,000. In return for these tourist services, Japanese banks now have $5,000 worth of dollars. The services provided by Japan are clearly a use of funds. The resulting increases in deposits of Japanese banks in U.S. banks represent a source of funds. This transaction will appear in the U.S. balance of payments as follows:

[1] For details, see Suk H. Kim and Henry J. Guithues, *Financial Management: An Introduction* (Richmond: Robert F. Dame, Inc., 1982), Chapter 5.

Tourist expenditures $5,000 (debit)
Liquid short-term capital $5,000 (credit)

Example 3-3 Unilateral Transfer This account covers gifts by domestic residents to foreign residents, or gifts by the domestic government to foreign governments. Assume that the U.S. Red Cross sends $20,000 worth of flood-relief goods to Chile. The term "transfer" reflects the nature of the transaction: the United States receives nothing in return. Because the United States sends its goods to Chile, this transaction reduces the real assets of the United States. Thus, these transfers should be debited. The sale or unilateral transfer of products by the United States represents exports and these exports are credited. The flood relief shipments appear in the U.S. balance of payments as follows:

Transfer payments $20,000 (debit)
Exports $20,000 (credit)

Example 3-4 Long-Term Capital This account shows the inflow and outflow of capital commitments whose maturity is longer than one year. It covers investments in financial assets without significant control of the real assets. The account also covers investments in real assets or financial assets with significant control of real assets. Assume that an American purchases $5,000 worth of French bonds and pays for it with a check drawn on a Los Angeles account. The United States now owns a French bond, while France owns U.S. dollar deposits. Since the acquisition of the French bond increases U.S. portfolio investments in foreign countries, the portfolio investments must be debited. At the same time, the dollar balance, owned by the French, represents an increase in U.S. liabilities to foreigners. Hence, the U.S. liquid short-term capital should be credited. This transaction will appear in the U.S. balance of payments as follows:

Portfolio investments $5,000 (debit)
Liquid short-term capital $5,000 (credit)

Example 3-5 Nonliquid Short-Term Capital Nonliquid short-term liabilities are flows of funds that are not normally resold. Bank loans represent nonliquid short-term liabilities. Suppose that a U.S. bank lends $10,000 to a Canadian firm. Since this loan reduces U.S. purchasing power, the U.S. nonliquid short-term liabilities must be debited. At the same time, the bank creates or increases a deposit balance for the foreign firm through its loan. Because this loan increases U.S. short-term liabilities to foreigners, the liquid short-term liabilities should be credited. In the U.S. balance of payments, this transaction will appear as follows:

Nonliquid short-term capital	$10,000 (debit)	
Liquid short-term capital		$10,000 (credit)

BALANCE-OF-PAYMENTS ACCOUNTS

The double-entry accounting principles presented in the previous section apply equally to the United States and to other countries in the world. These countries systematically summarize all the financial transactions between their residents and the residents of other nations on the basis of these double-entry accounting principles. The balance-of-payment statement records all sales and purchases. This statement also accounts for any differences between receipts (sales) and expenditures (purchases). Because all transactions are recorded as both debits and credits, total debits must equal total credits.

The balance of payments is typically listed in three sections:

1. Current account
   Merchandise exports
   Merchandise imports
   (a) The balance of merchandise trade
   Services
   (b) Balance on goods and services
   Unilateral transfers
   (c) Balance on current account
2. Capital account
   Long-term capital
   (d) Basic balance
   Nonliquid short-term capital
   Miscellaneous items
   (e) Net liquidity balance
   Liquid short-term capital
   (f) Official settlement balance
3. Official reserve account

It is important to recognize that a balance-of-payments statement has many forms in current literature and statistics. In order to understand the interrelationships involved in the balance-of-payments statement, three concepts need to be analyzed in further detail: the current account, the capital account, and the official reserve account.

The Current Account

The current account includes merchandise exports and imports, earnings and expenditures for invisible trade items (services), and unilateral transfer items. Entries in this account are "current" in nature because they do not give rise to future claims. The balance of payments on the current account is the broadest measure of a country's international trade because it includes financial transactions as well as trade in goods and services. A surplus on the current account represents an inflow of funds, while a deficit represents an outflow of funds.

The Balance of Merchandise Trade. The balance of merchandise trade refers to the balance between exports and imports of physical goods such as automobiles, machinery, and farm products. A favorable balance-of-merchandise trade (surplus) occurs when exports are greater in value than imports. An unfavorable balance-of-merchandise trade (deficit) occurs when imports exceed exports. Merchandise exports and imports are the largest single components of total international payments for most countries.

Services. International trade involves exports and imports of both goods and services. Services include such invisible items as military expenditures, interest and dividends, travel and transportation, plus fees and royalties. A country's purchases of services represent imports with debits recorded. A country's sales of these services to foreigners represent exports with credits recorded. The balance between exports and imports of goods and services is called the balance on goods and services.

Unilateral Transfers. Gifts and grants are included in the unilateral transfers by both private parties and governments. Private gifts and grants include personal gifts of all kinds, philanthropic activities, and relief organization shipments. For example, money sent by immigrants to their families in their native country represent private transfers. Government transfers include money, goods, and services as aids to other countries. For instance, goods and services provided by the United States government to other countries as part of a drought-relief program represent government transfers.

The Capital Account

U.S. residents and businesses may choose to invest in foreign countries. Of course, foreigners may engage in similar capital transactions. They may buy real assets in the United States. They may also invest in U.S. government securities. The capital account consists of loans, investments, other transfers of financial assets, and the creation of liabilities. Unlike current account entries, entries in the capital account indicate changes in future claims. Loans and their interest should be paid, dividends on investments should be paid, and so on. The capital account covers long-term capital, nonliquid short-term capital, and liquid short-term capital.

Long-Term Capital. Long-term capital flows represent claims that have a maturity of longer than one year. They include direct investments, portfolio investments, and loans. Private flows are characterized by direct and portfolio investments. Government flows are characterized by loans.

Direct investments are equity investments such as purchases of stocks, the acquisition of entire firms, or the establishment of new subsidiaries. The U.S. Department of Commerce defines direct investments as investment in either real capital assets or financial assets with a minimum of 10 percent ownership in a foreign firm.[2] Portfolio investments are purchases of foreign bonds or other financial assets without a significant degree of management control. Desires for return, safety, and liquidity in investments are the same for international and domestic portfolio investors. However, international portfolio investments have additional risks such as changes in exchange rates, wars and revolutions, and expropriation. Portfolio investments in utilities and government agencies are active because risk of loss in these fields is less than in other fields.

Government long-term flows include loans, financial support in economic development projects overseas, subscriptions to various regional development banks, and participation in other foreign projects

[2] *The Balance of Payments Statistics of the United States,* Report of the Review Committee for Balance of Payments Statistics to the Bureau of the Budget (Washington, D.C.: Government Printing Office, 1965), pp. 62-63.

either directly or through international institutions. In particular, the U.S. government makes substantial loans to many nations for purposes of economic development. The U.S. Export-Import Bank also extends loans to other nations in order to promote U.S. exports.

Short-Term Capital. Short-term capital represents claims with a maturity of less than one year. Such claims include demand deposits, short-term loans, and short-term securities. Two types of short-term capital flows are nonliquid and liquid short-term capital. Nonliquid short-term flows include bank loans and similar short-term funds that are very difficult to liquidate quickly without loss. Liquid short-term flows represent such claims as demand deposits and short-term securities that are easy to liquidate quickly with minimum or no loss.

Changes in the short-term capital accounts take place for two general reasons: compensating adjustments and those independent of such transactions. Some short-term flows occur due to changes in the current account or changes in long-term investments. More specifically, short-term capital changes due to merchandise trade, services, unilateral transfers, and investments. Short-term capital movements, induced by such transactions, are sometimes called compensating or accommodating adjustments. These compensating accounts change only in order to finance other items in the balance of payments. In contrast, some other short-term flows are attributable to differences in interest rates among nations and to expected changes in foreign exchange rates. Short-term capital movements caused by such changes are frequently called autonomous adjustments. These autonomous accounts change for purely economic reasons.

Miscellaneous Items. Miscellaneous items consist of the allocation of special drawing rights (SDRs) and statistical discrepancy. SDRs are rights to draw on the International Monetary Fund (IMF) and are sometimes called "paper gold." At its 1967 meeting in Rio de Janeiro, the 106 members of the IMF adopted a plan to create new international reserves in the form of SDRs. In 1970 SDRs went into use as a supplement to gold and dollars in international reserves of nations. SDRs can be used as a means of international payment. When a country receives its SDRs allocation, the balance of payments entry involves a debit to the reserve asset with the corresponding credit to the SDRs allocation.

Because all debits are offset by credits and vice versa, the balance of payments should always balance in theory. But it rarely does balance in practice for a number of reasons. In the balance-of-payments statistics, data are incomplete, gathered from many different sources, and lend themselves to different interpretation by various people and agencies. Thus, the debits and credits may not balance at the end of the year. This is why the statistical discrepancy is treated as a "plug" item to keep the accounts in balance. Although this item could be placed anywhere in the balance of payments, it is typically placed close to the short-term capital account because the Department of Commerce believes that more errors and omissions occur in that account than in other accounts.

The Official Reserve Account

Official reserves are government-owned assets. The official reserve account represents only purchases and sales by official monetary authorities such as the Federal Reserve System of the United States or the Bank of England. The changes in official reserves are necessary to account for the deficit or surplus in the balance of payments.

Official reserves are composed of gold, SDRs, and convertible foreign exchange. For most countries other than the United States, the principal convertible currencies are the U.S. dollar and the British pound. But such hard currencies as the German mark, the French franc, and the Swiss franc have become increasingly important as reserve currencies. An increase in any of these reserve assets represents a use of funds or a debit entry in the balance of payments. On the other hand, a decrease in reserve assets indicates a source of funds or a credit entry.

THE ACTUAL BALANCE OF PAYMENTS

The IMF compiles balance-of-payments results for its member countries and presents them in its *Balance of Payments Year Book*. The U.S. Department of Commerce compiles U.S. balance-of-payments statistics and publishes them in its *Survey of Current Business*.

The Volume of World Trade

The volume of world trade increased by 8.5 percent per year from 1963 to 1973, but its growth slowed to 4 percent per year from

1973 to 1980. The volume of world commodity output increased by six percent per year from 1963 to 1973, but its growth slowed to three percent per year from 1973 to 1980. These statistics indicate a strong correlation between world trade and world production. Cyclical downswings in the major industrial countries and the lower long-term growth path since the early 1970s have combined to keep the growth in the volume of world production and world trade to a minimum in 1980. Both figures recorded the third lowest gains in a quarter of a century in 1980.[3]

The value of world trade was well below $1,000 billion in 1963, but it reached almost $2,000 billion in 1980. In 1963 the commodity composition of world trade was manufacturers (55 percent), agricultural products (29 percent), fuels (10 percent), and minerals (6 percent). On the other hand, in 1980 the commodity breakdown of world trade was manufacturers (55 percent), fuels (25 percent), agricultural products (15 percent), and minerals (5 percent).[4] These statistics tell us that the percentage share of world trade for fuels increased very sharply for the last two decades, while the percentage shares of world trade for agricultural products and minerals declined.

Table 3-1 shows the regional composition of world trade. The industrial countries' share in world exports declined from 68 percent

Table 3-1 Regional Composition of World Trade
(percentage shares in world exports and imports)

Region		1973	1976	1978	1979	1980
Industrial areas	EXP	68	63	65	63	61½
	IMP	69½	66½	65½	67	66
Traditional oil exporting developing countries	EXP	7½	13½	11	13	15
	IMP	3½	6½	7½	6	6½
New oil exporting developing countries	EXP	1½	2	1½	2	2½
	IMP	1½	2	2	2	2
Other developing countries	EXP	10½	10½	10½	10½	10
	IMP	13	12½	13½	14½	15
Least developed countries	EXP	*½*	*½*	*½*	*½*	*½*
	IMP	*½*	*½*	*1*	*1*	*1*
Eastern trading area	EXP	10	9½	9½	9	9
	IMP	10	9½	9½	9	8½

Source: IMF Survey (October 26, 1981), p. 336.

[3] *IMF Survey* (Washington, D.C.: International Monetary Fund, October 26, 1981), p. 333.

[4] General Agreements on Tariffs and Trade, *International Trade*, 1980/81 (1982), Chapter 1.

in 1973 to 61.5 percent in 1980, the lowest level in two decades. The industrial countries' share in world imports decreased from 69.5 percent in 1973 to 66 percent in 1980. On the other hand, the share of the traditional oil exporting countries in the value of world exports reached a new peak of 15 percent in 1980, double the share in 1973. The share of these countries in the case of world imports increased from 3.5 percent in 1973 to 6.5 percent in 1980.

During the past few years, significant changes have occurred in the current account balances of the major industrial countries. Not only has the aggregate balance worsened, but the distribution of balances among these countries has been altered substantially. Table 3-2 shows that the major industrial countries experienced a sharp turnaround in their current account, from a surplus of $18.4 billion in 1978 to a deficit of $36.8 billion in 1980. Two major contributing factors to this dramatic swing have been the 140 percent increase in OPEC (Organization of Petroleum Exporting Countries) petroleum prices and the decline in the exports to oil-exporting countries. The growth rate of exports from the major industrial countries to OPEC fell steadily from 1976 to 1979 before exhibiting a small increase in 1980. An interesting feature of the adverse movement of current account balances from 1978 to 1980 has been its concentration in the accounts of countries which had relatively large surpluses at the beginning of this period. At the same time, the country with the largest deficit in 1978—the United States—was among the few that experienced marked improvement in its current account balances over this period.

For countries other than the United States, the impact of recent OPEC actions has been exacerbated by the appreciation of the U.S.

Table 3-2 Current Account Balances (billions of $)

Country	1977	1978	1979	1980
Canada	– 4.0	– 4.4	– 4.4	– 1.3
France	– 3.0	3.8	1.5	– 7.8
Germany	4.1	9.2	– 5.3	– 16.0
Italy	2.3	6.2	5.1	– 10.0
Japan	10.9	16.5	– 8.8	– 10.7
United Kingdom	– 0.5	1.2	– 3.5	5.3
United States	– 14.1	– 14.1	1.4	3.7
Total	– 4.3	18.4	– 14.0	– 36.8

Source: The Federal Reserve Bank of St. Louis, *International Economic Conditions* (October 21, 1981), p. 1.

dollar. Because the price of imported petroleum is denominated in dollars, the rise in the domestic prices of petroleum resulting from a rise in the dollar price of oil has been compounded by the appreciation of the dollar. From the beginning of 1979 to the middle of 1981 the dollar price of Saudi Arabian petroleum rose by 141 percent, but the German mark price of Saudi Arabian petroleum rose by 219 percent, the Japanese yen price increased by 183 percent, and the French franc price rose by 230 percent.[5]

The U.S. Balance of Payments

The balance of payments always balances to the extent that debits equal credits. However, countries always have either deficits or surpluses. This seeming conflict arises due to the methods used to interpret balance-of-payments results.

Essentially, analysts focus on those transactions that occur because of self-interests. These so-called autonomous transactions include exports, imports, unilateral transfers, and investments. The arithmetic sum of these autonomous transactions is sometimes called "above the line items" and represents the balance-of-payments surplus or deficit. The balance-of-payments surplus occurs when autonomous receipts exceed autonomous payments. By the same token, the balance-of-payments deficit takes place when autonomous payments exceed autonomous receipts. On the other hand, compensating transactions occur to account or compensate for differences between international payments and receipts. These compensating items are frequently called "below the line items" and are used to eliminate international disequilibrium.[6]

> ***Example 3-6*** Assume: (1) U.S. exports are $10 billion; (2) its imports are $20 billion; (3) it receives remittances of $5 billion; and (4) its public grants and loans to other nations are $2 billion.
>
> The payments associated with these autonomous transactions are $22 billion, while the receipts are only $15 billion. Thus, the United States has a $7 billion deficit in its balance

[5] The Federal Reserve Bank of St. Louis, *International Economic Conditions* (October 21, 1981), p. 1.

[6] For details, see John Hein, *Understanding the Balance of Payments* (New York: The National Industrial Conference Board, 1970).

of payments and must undertake $7 billion worth of compensating transactions to make up the difference. These compensating transactions involve sales of its gold, reductions in its balance of convertible currencies, or increases in the balance of its dollars held by other nations.

It should be obvious that a nation's deficit or surplus will vary according to the definition of autonomous transactions. The balance-of-merchandise trade designates only exports and imports of merchandise as autonomous transactions. Hence, a nation's surplus or deficit depends solely on merchandise trade. The current account includes merchandise trade items, services, and unilateral transfers as autonomous transactions. The basic balance considers current account items and long-term capital items as autonomous items. Finally, the net liquidity balance designates basic balance items, nonliquid short-term flows, and miscellaneous items as autonomous items. A clear definition of autonomous transactions is essential to isolate the most probable causes of imbalances and then to determine alternative courses of action to be taken by government officials in remedying these imbalances.

An Advisory Committee on the Presentation of the Balance of Payments Statistics suggested that the United States discontinue its publication of the basic balance, the net liquidity balance, and the official reserve balance. Its publication of these balances was discontinued in June 1976. This discontinuation occurred mainly due to floating exchange rates, the accumulation of large amounts of dollars by oil exporting countries, and increasing difficulties of distinguishing between long-term and short-term flows.[7]

Table 3-3 summarizes U.S. balance-of-payments figures for the 1960-1981 period. Balance figures appear in the memoranda lines 76-79. However, none of these balances includes any capital account. The table does not present the net balance of lines 80 and 81, but these two lines as a whole coincide with the old official reserve balance. The level of aggregation in the capital accounts makes it impossible to compute the old basic and net liquidity balances.

A careful examination of the most significant figures in Table 3-3 could allow us to develop a fairly clear understanding of U.S. performance, problems, and responses over the last two decades. The United States is the world's largest trading nation. In 1981, it exported $236 billion worth of goods (line 2) and imported $264 billion worth of goods (line 18). Both figures represent more than ten percent of the world total. The U.S. balance on merchandise trade (line 76) was

[7] *Wall Street Journal* (May 17, 1976), p. 2; and *IMF Survey* (June 7, 1976).

Table 3-3 U.S. International Transactions (Millions of dollars)

(Credit +; debits −)[1]	Line	1960	1961	1962	1963	1964	1965	1966	1967	1968
Exports of goods and services [2]	1	**28,861**	**29,937**	**31,803**	**34,214**	**38,826**	**41,087**	**44,562**	**47,314**	**52,363**
Merchandise, adjusted, excluding military [3]	2	19,650	20,108	20,781	22,272	25,501	26,461	29,310	30,666	33,626
Transfers under U.S. military agency sales contracts	3	335	402	656	657	747	830	829	1,152	1,392
Travel	4	919	947	957	1,015	1,207	1,380	1,590	1,646	1,775
Passenger fares	5	175	183	191	205	241	271	317	371	411
Other transportation	6	1,607	1,620	1,764	1,898	2,076	2,175	2,333	2,426	2,548
Fees and royalties from affiliated foreigners	7	590	662	800	890	1,013	1,199	1,162	1,354	1,430
Fees and royalties from unaffiliated foreigners	8	247	244	256	273	301	335	353	393	437
Other private services	9	570	607	585	613	651	714	814	951	1,024
U.S. Government miscellaneous services	10	153	164	195	236	265	285	326	336	353
Receipts of income on U.S. assets abroad:										
Direct investment	11	3,621	3,823	4,241	4,636	5,106	5,506	5,260	5,603	6,591
Interest, dividends, and earnings of unincorporated affiliates	12	2,355	2,768	3,044	3,129	3,674	3,963	3,467	3,847	4,151
Reinvested earnings of incorporated affiliates	13	1,266	1,055	1,197	1,507	1,432	1,543	1,793	1,756	2,440
Other private receipts	14	646	793	904	1,022	1,256	1,421	1,669	1,781	2,021
U.S. Government receipts	15	349	383	473	499	462	510	599	636	756
Transfers of goods and services under U.S. military grant programs, net	16	**1,695**	**1,465**	**1,537**	**1,562**	**1,340**	**1,636**	**1,892**	**2,039**	**2,547**
Imports of goods and services	17	**−23,729**	**−23,591**	**−25,778**	**−27,047**	**−29,222**	**−32,801**	**−38,599**	**−41,606**	**−48,800**
Merchandise, adjusted, excluding military [3]	18	−14,758	−14,537	−16,260	−17,048	−18,700	−21,510	−25,493	−26,866	−32,991
Direct defense expenditures	19	−3,087	−2,998	−3,105	−2,961	−2,880	−2,952	−3,764	−4,378	−4,535
Travel	20	−1,750	−1,785	−1,939	−2,114	−2,211	−2,438	−2,657	−3,207	−3,030
Passenger fares	21	−513	−506	−567	−612	−642	−717	−753	−829	−885
Other transportation	22	−1,402	−1,437	−1,558	−1,701	−1,817	−1,951	−2,161	−2,157	−2,367
Fees and royalties to affiliated foreigners	23	−35	−43	−57	−61	−67	−68	−64	−62	−80
Fees and royalties to unaffiliated foreigners	24	−40	−46	−44	−51	−60	−67	−76	−104	−106
Private payments for other services	25	−593	−588	−528	−493	−527	−461	−506	−565	−568
U.S. Government payments for miscellaneous services	26	−313	−406	−398	−447	−535	−550	−644	−691	−760
Payments of income on foreign assets in the United States:										
Direct investment	27	−394	−432	−399	−459	−529	−657	−711	−821	−876
Interest, dividends, and earnings of unincorporated affiliates	28	−220	−194	−185	−223	−202	−299	−372	−381	−388
Reinvested earnings of incorporated affiliates	29	−174	−238	−214	−236	−327	−358	−339	−440	−488
Other private payments	30	−511	−535	−586	−701	−802	−942	−1,221	−1,328	−1,800
U.S. Government payments	31	−332	−278	−339	−401	−453	−489	−549	−598	−702
U.S. military grants of goods and services, net	32	**−1,695**	**−1,465**	**−1,537**	**−1,562**	**−1,340**	**−1,636**	**−1,892**	**−2,039**	**−2,547**
Unilateral transfers (excluding military grants of goods and services), net	33	**−2,308**	**−2,524**	**−2,638**	**−2,754**	**−2,781**	**−2,854**	**−2,932**	**−3,125**	**−2,952**
U.S. Government grants (excluding military grants of goods and services)	34	−1,672	−1,855	−1,916	−1,917	−1,888	−1,808	−1,910	−1,805	−1,709
U.S. Government pensions and other transfers	35	−214	−235	−245	−262	−279	−369	−367	−441	−407
Private remittances and other transfers	36	−423	−434	−477	−575	−614	−677	−655	−879	−836
U.S. assets abroad, net (increase/capital outflow (−))	37	**−4,099**	**−5,538**	**−4,174**	**−7,270**	**−9,560**	**−5,716**	**−7,321**	**−9,757**	**−10,977**
U.S. official reserve assets, net [4]	38	2,145	607	1,535	378	171	1,225	570	53	−870
Gold	39	1,703	857	890	461	125	1,665	571	1,170	1,173
Special drawing rights	40									
Reserve position in the International Monetary Fund	41	442	−135	626	29	266	−94	537	−94	−870
Foreign currencies	42		−115	19	−112	−220	−346	−538	−1,023	−1,173

Table 3-3 Continued

U.S. Government assets, other than official reserve assets, net	43	−1,100	−910	−1,085	−1,662	−1,680	−1,605	−1,543	−2,423	−2,274
U.S. loans and other long-term assets	44	−1,214	−1,928	−2,128	−2,204	−2,382	−2,463	−2,513	−3,638	−3,722
Repayments on U.S. loans [5]	45	642	1,279	1,288	988	720	874	1,235	1,005	1,386
U.S. foreign currency holdings and U.S. short-term assets, net	46	−528	−261	−245	−447	−19	−16	−265	209	62
U.S. private assets, net	47	−5,144	−5,235	−4,623	−5,986	−8,050	−5,336	−6,347	−7,386	−7,833
Direct investment	48	−2,940	−2,653	−2,851	−3,483	−3,760	−5,011	−5,418	−4,805	−5,295
Equity and intercompany accounts	49	−1,674	−1,598	−1,654	−1,976	−2,328	−3,468	−3,625	−3,049	−2,855
Reinvested earnings of incorporated affiliates	50	−1,266	−1,055	−1,197	−1,507	−1,432	−1,543	−1,793	−1,756	−2,440
Foreign securities	51	−663	−762	−969	−1,105	−677	−759	−720	−1,308	−1,569
U.S. claims on unaffiliated foreigners reported by U.S. nonbanking concerns:										
Long-term	52	−40	−127	−132	162	−485	−88	−112	−281	−220
Short-term	53	−354	−431	−222	−5	−623	429	−330	−498	−982
U.S. claims reported by U.S. banks, not included elsewhere:										
Long-term	54	−153	−136	−126	−775	−981	−232	317	235	338
Short-term	55	−995	−1,125	−324	−781	−1,524	325	−84	−730	−105
Foreign assets in the United States, net (increase/capital inflow (+))	56	**2,294**	**2,705**	**1,911**	**3,217**	**3,643**	**742**	**3,661**	**7,379**	**9,928**
Foreign official assets in the United States, net	57	1,473	765	1,270	1,986	1,660	134	−672	3,451	−774
U.S. Government securities	58	655	233	1,409	816	432	−141	−1,527	2,261	−769
U.S. Treasury securities [6]	59	655	233	1,410	803	434	−134	−1,548	2,222	−798
Other [7]	60			−1	12	−2	−7	21	39	29
Other U.S. Government liabilities [8]	61	215	25	152	429	298	65	113	83	−15
U.S. liabilities reported by U.S. banks, not included elsewhere	62	603	508	−291	742	930	210	742	1,106	10
Other foreign official assets [9]	63									
Other foreign assets in the United States, net	64	821	1,939	641	1,231	1,983	607	4,333	3,928	10,703
Direct investment	65	315	311	346	231	322	415	425	698	807
Equity and intercompany accounts	66	141	73	132	−5	−5	57	86	258	319
Reinvested earnings of incorporated affiliates	67	174	238	214	236	327	358	339	440	488
U.S. Treasury securities	68	−364	151	−66	−149	−146	−131	−356	−135	136
U.S. securities other than U.S. Treasury securities	69	282	324	134	287	−85	−358	906	1,016	4,414
U.S. liabilities to unaffiliated foreigners reported by U.S. nonbanking concerns:										
Long-term	70	1	50	3	−13	−38	29	180	85	715
Short-term	71	−91	176	−112	−23	113	149	296	499	759
U.S. liabilities reported by U.S. banks, not included elsewhere:										
Long-term [10]	72	6	−5	5	53	88	241	188	158	72
Short-term [10]	73	672	933	331	845	1,730	262	2,694	1,607	3,799
Allocations of special drawing rights	74									
Statistical discrepancy (sum of above items with sign reversed)	75	**−1,019**	**−989**	**−1,124**	**−360**	**−907**	**−458**	**629**	**−205**	**438**
Memoranda:										
Balance on merchandise trade (lines 2 and 18)	76	4,892	5,571	4,521	5,224	6,801	4,951	3,817	3,800	635
Balance on goods and services (lines 1 and 17) [11]	77	5,132	6,346	6,025	7,167	9,604	8,285	5,963	5,708	3,563
Balance on goods, services, and remittances (lines 77, 35, and 36)	78	4,496	5,677	5,303	6,331	8,711	7,239	4,941	4,388	2,320
Balance on current account (lines 77 and 33) [11]	79	2,824	3,822	3,387	4,414	6,823	5,432	3,031	2,583	611
Transactions in U.S. official reserve assets and in foreign official assets in the United States:										
Increase (−) in U.S. official reserve assets, net (line 38)	80	2,145	607	1,535	378	171	1,225	570	53	−870
Increase (+) in foreign official assets in the United States (line 57 less line 61)	81	1,258	741	1,118	1,558	1,362	69	−785	3,368	−759

1969	1970	1971	1972	1973	1974	1975	1976	1977	1978	1979	1980	1981	Line
57,522	**65,674**	**68,838**	**77,495**	**110,241**	**146,666**	**155,729**	**171,630**	**184,337**	**220,137**	**286,772**	**342,102**	**372,892**	1
36,414	42,469	43,319	49,381	71,410	98,306	107,088	114,745	120,816	142,054	184,473	224,237	235,254	2
1,528	1,501	1,926	1,364	2,559	3,379	4,049	5,454	7,351	7,973	6,549	8,306	9,747	3
2,043	2,331	2,534	2,817	3,412	4,032	4,697	5,742	6,150	7,183	8,441	10,058	12,168	4
450	544	615	699	975	1,104	1,039	1,229	1,366	1,603	2,156	2,582	2,991	5
2,652	3,125	3,299	3,579	4,465	5,697	5,840	6,747	7,264	8,399	10,028	11,497	12,168	6
1,533	1,758	1,927	2,115	2,513	3,070	3,543	3,531	3,883	4,705	4,980	5,780	5,867	7
486	573	618	655	712	751	757	822	923	1,059	1,100	1,185	1,386	8
1,160	1,294	1,546	1,764	1,985	2,321	2,920	3,584	3,848	4,296	4,396	5,412	5,940	9
343	332	347	357	401	419	446	489	557	620	520	362	426	10
7,649	8,169	9,160	10,949	16,542	19,157	16,595	18,999	19,673	25,458	38,183	37,150	31,873	11
4,819	4,992	5,983	6,416	8,384	11,379	8,547	11,303	13,277	14,115	19,219	20,133	18,894	12
2,830	3,177	3,177	4,532	8,158	7,777	8,048	7,696	6,396	11,343	18,965	17,017	12,978	13
2,338	2,671	2,641	2,949	4,330	7,356	7,644	8,955	10,881	14,944	23,654	32,987	50,407	14
925	907	906	866	936	1,074	1,112	1,332	1,625	1,843	2,292	2,549	3,665	15
2,610	**2,713**	**3,546**	**4,492**	**2,810**	**1,818**	**2,207**	**373**	**203**	**236**	**465**	**631**	**602**	16
−54,129	**−60,050**	**−66,569**	**−79,435**	**−99,219**	**−137,357**	**−132,836**	**−162,248**	**−193,788**	**−229,880**	**−281,677**	**−333,800**	**−361,813**	17
−35,807	−39,866	−45,579	−55,797	−70,499	−103,649	−98,041	−124,051	−151,689	−175,813	−211,819	−249,575	−264,143	18
−4,856	−4,855	−4,819	[12] −4,784	[12] −4,629	−5,032	−4,795	−4,895	−5,823	−7,352	−8,584	−10,777	−11,288	19
−3,373	−3,980	−4,373	−5,042	−5,526	−5,980	−6,417	−6,856	−7,451	−8,475	−9,413	−10,397	−11,460	20
−1,080	−1,215	−1,290	−1,596	−1,790	−2,095	−2,263	−2,568	−2,748	−2,896	−3,184	−3,607	−4,487	21
−2,455	−2,843	−3,130	−3,520	−4,694	−5,942	−5,688	−6,852	−7,874	−8,939	−10,457	−11,073	−11,611	22
−101	−111	−118	−155	−209	−160	−287	−293	−243	−393	−523	−514	−429	23
−120	−114	−123	−139	−176	−186	−186	−189	−196	−214	−241	−247	−264	24
−751	−827	−956	−1,043	−1,180	−1,262	−1,551	−2,006	−2,190	−2,573	−2,824	−3,065	−3,294	25
−717	−725	−746	−788	−862	−967	−1,044	−1,227	−1,358	−1,545	−1,718	−1,769	−1,930	26
−848	−875	−1,164	−1,284	−1,610	−1,331	−2,234	−3,110	−2,834	−4,211	−6,357	−9,470	−7,808	27
−417	−441	−621	−715	−699	−266	−1,046	−1,451	−1,248	−1,628	−2,402	−3,303	−3,708	28
−431	−434	−542	−569	−910	−1,065	−1,189	−1,659	−1,586	−2,583	−3,955	−6,167	−4,039	29
−3,244	−3,617	−2,428	−2,604	−4,209	−6,491	−5,788	−5,681	−5,841	−8,795	−15,481	−20,794	−28,352	30
−777	−1,024	−1,844	−2,684	−3,836	−4,262	−4,542	−4,520	−5,542	−8,674	−11.076	−12,512	−16,748	31
−2,610	**−2,713**	**−3,546**	**−4,492**	**−2,810**	**−1,818**	**−2,207**	**−373**	**−203**	**−236**	**−465**	**−631**	**−602**	32
−2,994	**−3,294**	**−3,701**	**−3,854**	**−3,881**	[13] **−7,186**	**−4,613**	**−4,998**	**−4,617**	**−5,030**	**−5,561**	**−6,783**	**−6,608**	33
−1,649	−1,736	−2,043	−2,173	−1,938	[13] −5,475	−2,894	−3,146	−2,787	−3,176	−3,550	−4,681	−4,504	34
−406	−462	−542	−572	−693	−694	−813	−934	−971	−1,086	−1,180	−1,303	−1,459	35
−939	−1,096	−1,117	−1,109	−1,250	−1,017	−906	−917	−859	−768	−832	−798	−645	36
−11,585	**−9,337**	**−12,475**	**−14,497**	**−22,874**	**−34,745**	**−39,703**	**−51,269**	**−34,785**	**−61,130**	**−64,344**	**−86,026**	**−109,294**	37
−1,179	2,481	2,349	−4	158	−1,467	−849	−2,558	−375	732	−1,133	−8,155	−5,175	38
−967	787	866	547					−118	−65	−65		(*)	39
	−851	−249	−703	9	−172	−66	−78	−121	1,249	−1,136	−16	−1,824	40
−1,034	389	1,350	153	−33	−1,265	−466	−2,212	−294	4,231	−189	−1,667	−2,491	41
822	2,156	382	−1	182	−30	−317	−268	158	−4,683	257	−6,472	−861	42

Table 3-3 Continued

−2,200	−1,589	−1,884	−1,568	−2,644	366	−3,474	−4,214	−3,693	−4,660	−3,743	−5,126	−5,137	43
−3,489	−3,293	−4,181	−3,819	−4,638	[13] −5,001	−5,941	−6.943	−6,445	−7,470	−7,676	−9,854	−9,710	44
1,200	1,721	2,115	2,086	2,596	[13] 4,826	2,475	2,596	2,719	2,941	3,908	4,459	4,370	45
89	−16	182	165	−602	[13] 541	−9	133	33	−131	25	269	204	46
−8,206	−10,229	−12,940	−12,925	−20,388	−33,643	−35,380	−44,498	−30,717	−57,202	−59,469	−72,746	−98,982	47
−5,960	−7,590	−7,618	−7,747	−11,353	−9,052	−14,244	−11,949	−11,890	−16,056	−25,222	−19,238	−8,691	48
−3,130	−4,413	−4,441	−3,214	−3,195	−1,275	−6,196	−4,253	−5,494	−4,713	−6,258	−2,221	4,287	49
−2,830	−3,177	−3,177	−4,532	−8,158	−7,777	−8,048	−7,696	−6,396	−11,343	−18,965	−17,017	−12,978	50
−1,549	−1,076	−1,113	−618	−671	−1,854	−6,247	−8,885	−5,460	−3,626	−4,726	−3,524	−5,429	51
−424	−586	−168	−243	−396	−474	−366	−42	−99	−53				52
298	−10	−1,061	−811	−1,987	−2,747	−991	−2,254	−1,841	−3,800	[14] −3,307	[14] −3,146	[14] −331	53
297	155	−612	−1,307	−933	−1,183	−2,357	−2,362	−751					54
−867	−1,122	−2,368	−2,199	−5,047	−18,333	−11,175	−19,006	−10,676	[15] −33,667	[15] −26,213	[15] −46,838	[15] −84,531	55
12,702	**6,359**	**22,970**	**21,461**	**18,388**	**34,241**	**15,670**	**36,518**	**51,319**	**64,036**	**38,460**	**54,484**	**77,921**	56
−1,301	6,908	26,879	10,475	6,026	10,546	7,027	17,693	36,816	33,678	−13,697	15,442	4,785	57
−2,343	9,439	26,570	8,470	641	4,172	5,563	9,892	32,538	24,221	−21,972	11,895	6,272	58
−2,269	9,411	26,578	8,213	59	3,270	4,658	9,319	30,230	23,555	−22,435	9,708	4,983	59
−74	28	−8	257	582	902	905	573	2,308	666	463	2,187	1,289	60
251	−456	−510	182	936	301	1,517	4,627	1,400	2,476	−73	561	−69	61
792	−2,075	819	1,638	4,126	5,818	−2,158	969	773	5,551	7,213	−159	−4,083	62
			185	323	254	2,104	2,205	2,105	1,430	1,135	3,145	2,665	63
14,002	−550	−3,909	10,986	12,362	23,696	8,643	18,826	14,503	30,358	52,157	39,042	73,136	64
1,263	1,464	367	949	2,800	4,760	2,603	4,347	3,728	7,897	11,877	13,666	21,301	65
832	1,030	−175	380	1,890	3,695	1,414	2,687	2,142	5,313	7,921	7,500	17,201	66
431	434	542	569	910	1,065	1,189	1,659	1,586	2,583	3,955	6,167	4,099	67
−68	81	−24	−39	−216	697	2,590	2,783	534	[16] 2,178	[16] 4,960	[16] 2,645	[16] 2,932	68
3,130	2,189	2,289	4,507	4,041	378	2,503	1,284	2,437	2,254	1,351	5,457	7,109	69
701	1,112	384	594	298	−90	406	−1,000	−347	−190				70
91	902	−15	221	737	1,934	−87	422	1,433	2,079	[14] 1,362	[14] 6,530	[14] 532	71
160	23	−250	149	227	9	−280	231	373					72
8,726	−6,321	−6,661	4,605	4,475	16,008	908	10,759	6,346	16,141	32,607	10,743	41,262	73
	867	717	710							1,139	1,152	1,093	74
−1,516	**−219**	**−9,779**	**−1,879**	**−2,654**	**−1,620**	**5,753**	**10,367**	**−2,465**	**11,866**	**25,212**	**28,870**	**25,809**	75
607	2,603	−2,260	−6,416	911	−5,343	9,047	−9,306	−30,873	−33,759	−27,346	−25,338	−27,889	76
3,393	5,625	2,269	−1,941	11,021	9,309	22,893	9,382	−9,451	−9,743	5,095	8,303	11,079	77
2,048	4,067	610	−3,622	9,078	7,599	21,175	7,531	−11,281	−11,597	3,083	6,202	8,975	78
399	2,331	−1,433	−5,795	7,140	2,124	18,280	4,384	−14,068	−14,773	−466	1,520	4,471	79
−1,179	2,481	2,349	−4	158	−1,467	−849	−2,558	−375	732	−1,133	−8,155	−5,175	80
−1,552	7,364	27,389	10,293	5,090	10,244	5,509	13,066	35,416	31,202	−13,624	14,881	4,854	81

Footnotes to Table 3-3.

[1] Credits, +; exports of goods and services, unilateral transfers to U.S.; capital inflows (increase in foreign assets [U.S. liabilities] or decrease in U.S. assets); decrease in U.S. official reserve assets. Debits, –; imports of goods and services; unilateral transfers to foreigners; capital outflows (decrease in foreign assets [U.S. liabilities] or increase in U.S. assets); increase in U.S. official reserve assets.

[2] Excludes transfers of goods and services under U.S. military grant programs (see line 16).

[3] Excludes exports of goods under U.S. Military agency sales contracts identified in Census export documents, excludes imports of goods under direct defense expenditures identified in Census import documents, and reflects various other adjustments (for valuation, coverage, and timing) of Census statistics to balance of payments basis.

[4] For all areas, amounts outstanding March 31, 1982 were as follows in millions of dollars: line 38, 29,944; line 39, 11,150; line 40, 4,306; line 41, 5,367; line 42, 9,121.

[5] Includes sales of foreign obligations to foreigners.

[6] Consists of bills, certificates, marketable bonds and notes, and nonmarketable convertible and nonconvertible bonds and notes.

[7] Consists of U.S. Treasury and Export-Import Bank obligations, not included elsewhere, and of debts securities of U.S. Government corporations and agencies.

[8] Includes, primarily, U.S. Government liabilities associated with military sales contracts and other transactions arranged with or through foreign official agencies.

[9] Consists of investments in U.S. corporate stocks and in debt securities of private corporations and State and local governments.

[10] Beginning with estimates for the second quarter of 1978, the distinction between short- and long-term liabilities is discontinued.

[11] Conceptually, the sum of lines 79 and 74 is equal to "net foreign investment" in the National Income and Product Accounts (NPA's). However, the foreign transactions account in the NIPA's (a) includes adjustments to the international transactions accounts for the treatment of gold, (b) excludes capital gains and losses of foreign affiliates of U.S. parent companies from the NIPA's measure of income and receipts from direct investment abroad, and from the corresponding income payments, and (c) beginning with 1973-IV, excludes shipments and financing of military orders placed by Israel under Public Law 93-199 and subsequent similar legislation. Line 77 differs from "net exports of goods and services" in the NIPA's for the same reasons with the exception of the military financing, which is excluded, and the additional exclusion of U.S. Government interest payments to foreigners. The latter payments, for NIPA's purposes, are excluded from "net exports of goods and services" but included with transfers in "net foreign investment." A reconciliation table of the international accounts and the NIPA's foreign transactions account appears in the "Business Situation" in this issue of the *Survey of Current Business*.

[12] Includes return import into the U.S., at a depreciated value of $21 million in 1972-IV and $22 million in 1973-II, of aircraft originally reported in 1970-III in line 3 as a long-term lease to Australia.

[13] Includes extraordinary U.S. Government transactions with India. See "Special U.S. Government Transactions," June 1974 *Survey*, p. 27.

[14,15] The maturity breakdown is available only on a limited basis.

[16] Includes foreign currency denominated notes sold to private residents abroad.

Source: U.S. Department of Commerce, *Survey of Current Business* (June 1982), pp. 42-43 and p. 61.

in surplus during the early 1960s. From the mid-1960s to the early 1970s, the U.S. merchandise trade moved gradually from surplus to deficit. This movement was interrupted during the 1974-1975 worldwide economic recession. During this period the United States suffered a more economic contraction than most of the major trading nations in the world. Thus, the U.S. merchandise trade balance swung into surplus in 1975, even though there was a sizable increase in U.S. outlays for imported oil. The surplus proved short-lived because the U.S. merchandise trade deficit rose sharply from 1976 through 1981. The causes most frequently cited for this change include more competition in export markets, reduced demand for U.S. goods in foreign countries as local sources of supply developed, and an overvalued dollar which persisted under the fixed exchange rate system.

However, U.S. exports of services (lines 3 through 15) have consistently exceeded its imports of services (lines 19 through 31) for

Figure 3-1 U.S. Balance of Trade from 1970 to 1981

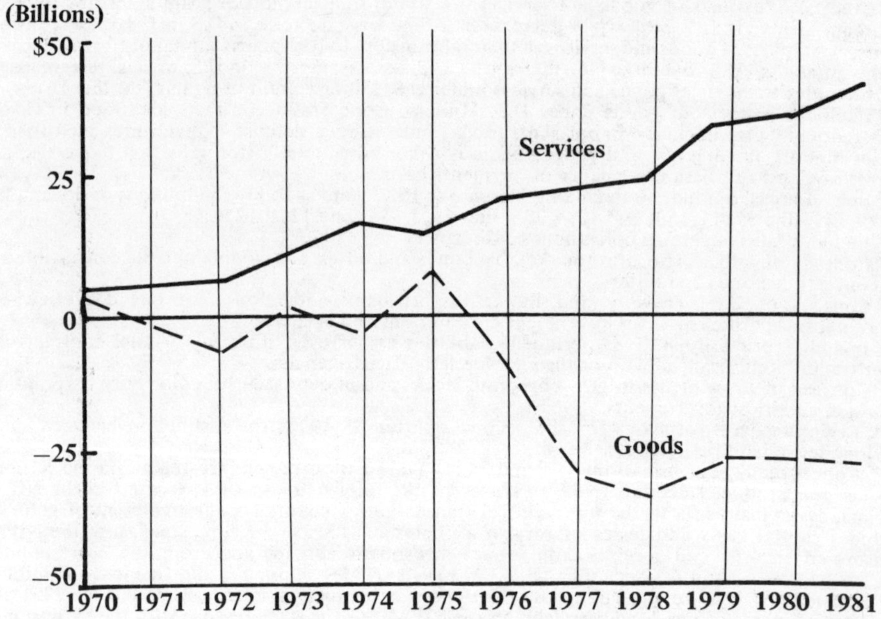

the last two decades. These service transactions have kept the U.S. balance of trade (line 77) in surplus despite the large deficit on goods over much of the past dozen years. This support can be seen in Figure 3-1, which traces the yawning dichotomy that has developed since 1970 within the U.S. overall trade position. In recent years, trade within each of the major service categories–travel, passenger fares, transportation, royalties and fees, and investment income–has risen. But as the expanding surplus in services indicates, the sharper gains have come on the export side of the ledger. In every instance, the export rise has exceeded the import increase by an appreciable margin.

Service transactions have played a crucial role in keeping the U.S. trade balance in surplus, but this role has tended to escape attention for several reasons. First, some service-trade categories reflect transactions that hardly come to mind when the topic is trade. Second, service items have remained a relatively minor part of overall trade volume. Third, international trade negotiations have tended to focus on barriers to merchandise trade.

The U.S. current account (line 79) was in surplus during the early 1960s, growing in magnitude to $6.8 billion in 1964. Since 1964 the surpluses fell drastically and ultimately led to substantial deficits. In fact, the U.S. current account deficit exceeded over $14 billion in

1977 as well as 1978. But the United States registered some surpluses in its balance of payments on the current account in 1980 and 1981. Many experts in the field expect the United States to experience substantial deficits for the next few years. First, U.S. exports and imports have become more competitive as the dollar has appreciated for the last few years. Second, both U.S. export sales and earnings on foreign investment are also expected to decrease because of slow business conditions abroad. Third, U.S. military expenditures and grants in foreign aids are expected to increase substantially.

"Statistical discrepancy" (line 75) was called "errors and omission" until 1976, when the label, with its somewhat embarrassing connotation, was officially dropped. This item has become uncomfortably large in recent years–it reached a record of $28.9 billion in 1980. A plus figure reflects an inflow of funds and a minus figure reflects an outflow of funds. U.S. exports of goods and services (line 1) increased from $65.7 billion in 1970 to $342.1 billion in 1980–a five-fold increase. But the 1980 discrepancy of plus $28.9 billion was more than 100 times the size of the 1970 discrepancy of minus $219 million. No one knows exactly what it represents, except that it may constitute a sort of barometer for such things as political unrest, crime, sloppy paper work, and deception among central bankers.

The discrepancy may be due to the unreported foreign funds coming into the United States for investment in some form of asset. Some analysts believe that many affluent foreigners–particularly those from politically unstable countries–move large sums of money into this country without government knowledge. This is because they perceive the United States as a safe political haven. Some observers fear that this may cause the Federal Reserve System of the United States to underestimate the amount of credit expansion.

Another important factor in the increasing payments discrepancy is the role of currency trading. Increased trading in foreign currencies in combination with the flexible exchange system undoubtedly introduces larger errors in payments figures. Some analysts believe that certain countries such as Japan or Germany may deliberately underestimate the number of dollars held by their central banks in order to avoid the U.S. government pressure to reduce their exports to the United States. On the other hand, some poor countries may deliberately underestimate the amount of their dollar holdings in order to obtain low-interest rate loans from such organizations as the International Monetary Fund.

Another factor is sloppy paper work. Most payments data depend on people in banks and other business offices who fill out federal forms. Unfortunately, these people sometimes make multi-million dollar mistakes.

HOW TO RESTORE INTERNATIONAL EQUILIBRIUM

Although some countries have had deficits for many years, their compensating transactions cannot be maintained indefinitely. Hence, some adjustments must ultimately be made to correct the balance-of-payments deficit. Three ways to restore international equilibrium are: price mechanism, income mechanism, and public controls.[8]

Price Mechanism

In international finance, price mechanism refers to exchange rates. Exports and imports between countries with different units of money introduce a new economic factor called the foreign exchange rate. The foreign exchange rate is the rate of exchange between our own currency and a foreign currency. The equilibrium exchange rate occurs at the point where demand for foreign exchange equals its supply. At the equilibrium exchange rate there would be no tendency for the exchange rate to rise or to fall. Debit and credit items in the balance of payments cause demand and supply for foreign exchange. Thus, equilibrium for a foreign exchange rate also implies some form of equilibrium in the balance of payments.

The exchange rate is a special price because it is the relationship between all domestic prices and all foreign prices. Consider the exchange rate between the U.S. dollar and the Italian lira. A change in the exchange rate would alter the prices of all American products to Italians and all Italian products to Americans. Such a change in the exchange rate could cause the relative attractiveness of American exports and imports to change in such a way that it restores equilibrium in the U.S. balance of payments.

The price mechanism restores international equilibrium through changes in interest rates and commodity prices. Assume that the United States is the deficit country and Italy is the surplus country. In this case money tends to move from the United States to Italy in order to finance the U.S. deficit. Unless the Federal Reserve System of the United States counteracts these flows, money supply in the United States will decrease. The decrease in the U.S. money supply will push U.S. interest rates up. In Italy the money supply will increase. Such an increase in money supply will push Italian interest rates down. The new relative yields will encourage capital flows from the surplus country (Italy) to the deficit country (the United States). Such a reverse movement of money will help to bring the U.S. payments into balance.

[8] For a collection of articles on the restoration of international equilibrium, see the *International Adjustment Mechanism* (Boston: Federal Reserve Bank of Boston, 1970).

If prices are flexible in both countries, commodity prices in the United States will fall because its deficit implies a decrease in demand for American products. In contrast, commodity prices in Italy will rise because its surplus means an increase in demand for Italian products. Such a change in relative prices will stimulate the demand for American products and curb the demand for Italian products, thereby restoring the balance in the United States.

The operation of freely fluctuating exchange rates as reflected by changes in interest rates and commodity prices is supposed to correct the U.S. balance-of-payments deficit automatically. However, it is also possible that the fluctuation of exchange rates may be insufficient to correct the original deficit. The ability of the price mechanism to correct the balance-of-payments deficit depends on the responsiveness of quantity demanded to changes in prices, i.e., the price elasticity of demand for imported goods. If price elasticities for imported products are high, the price mechanism will work to result in a large increase in the exports of the deficit country and in the imports of the surplus country. Such a change in exports and imports will restore international equilibrium. But if the price elasticities are low, the price adjustment may be insufficient to correct the balance-of-payments deficit.

Income Mechanism

The equilibrium level of income exists where the aggregate quantity demanded (spending) equals the aggregate quantity supplied (income). In an open economy, the equilibrium condition is:

$$C + I + G + Ex - Im = C + S + T \qquad (3\text{-}1)$$

where C = consumption, I = investment, G = government purchases of goods and services, Ex = exports, Im = imports, S = savings, and T = taxes.

It is important to recognize that the left-hand side of Equation 3-1 represents an aggregate spending and its right-hand side represents an aggregate income. If exports exceed imports, domestic spending is smaller than domestic income. If imports exceed exports, domestic spending is larger than domestic income. When the excess of imports over exports is extremely large or continues too long, the obvious remedies would be an increase in income or a reduction in spending.

Income changes in one country affect other countries. An increase in U.S. imports means more export sales for Italy. This has an expansionary effect in the Italian economy and thus Italy will increase its imports. If Italy buys more goods and services from the United States as a result of its increased income, the United States will find its exports increasing. The increase in U.S. exports will partly eliminate its original deficit caused by rising imports. At the same time increased exports by Italy mean more imports by the United States. An increase in U.S. imports means a reduction in U.S. income. As a result of its reduced income, the United States will reduce its consumption and imports after a time. Reduced imports by the United States will partly eliminate the original increase in Italian exports. When these two forces are combined, the increase in exports by the deficit country (the United States) and the decrease in exports by the surplus country (Italy) contribute to the restoration of international equilibrium.

Income changes also tend to restore international equilibrium through the impact of changes in interest rates on domestic investment in capital assets. Investment in capital assets, such as plant and equipment, tends to increase as interest rates fall. Because capital flows from the deficit country to the surplus country, interest rates in the United States start to increase. The increase in U.S. interest rates contributes to the reduction of U.S. investment in assets. As a result of its reduced investment in capital assets, the United States will find its national income and imports falling. The reverse is true in Italy where declining interest rates push investment in capital assets to rise. The increased investment in assets will push Italian income and its imports to rise. This mechanism continues to operate as long as there is a surplus or deficit. It could eventually eliminate international disequilibrium.

Public Controls

Pleas for liberal trade and automatic adjustments policies are applauded by most leading economists and by the leaders of practically all commercial nations. Nevertheless, free trade among nations and automatic adjustment mechanisms have recently faced their most serious challenge. Governments have two significant reasons for their balance-of-payments controls. First, they may find their international reserves inadequate to finance their deficits. Second, the free fluctuation of exchange rates may be insufficient to completely eliminate international disequilibrium. In general, there are two types of public controls: foreign exchange controls and trade controls. Think of a case in which increased U.S. imports create its foreign exchange shortage. Under exchange controls, the U.S. government would force its exporters and other recipients to sell their foreign exchange to the government or to designated banks. Then, the government would allocate this foreign exchange among the various users of foreign exchange. In this way the U.S. government restricts American imports to the amount of foreign exchange earned by American exports. Thus, imports under exchange controls are less than they would be under free market conditions.

When governments are faced with their serious payments deficit, they may manipulate exports and imports through tariffs, quotas, and subsidies. High tariffs on imported goods and import quotas by the United States would reduce American imports. On the other hand, the U.S. government may subsidize certain American exports to make them more competitive in world markets and to increase the volume of American exports. Special taxes on direct foreign investments by American firms tend to reduce U. S. capital outflows.

SUMMARY

The balance of payments summarizes all international transactions between residents of a country and those of all foreign countries during a specified period of time. The systematic record of these international transactions requires pre-established principles. These principles include rules or procedures such as the double-entry accounting rule and definitions of terminology such as the current account.

The balance of payments depends on the principle of double-entry accounting which records each transaction as both a debit and a credit of equal amount. Increases in assets and decreases in liabilities or net worth constitute debits (uses of funds). On the other hand, decreases in assets and increases in liabilities or net worth represent credits (sources of funds). Some international transactions such as exports or imports occur due to purely economic reasons. These transactions are called autonomous transactions. Such transactions as sales of gold or increases in foreign debts take place to account for differences between international payments and receipts. These transactions are often called compensating transactions.

Some countries have had deficits for many years. These deficits cannot indefinitely be financed by compensating transactions. The balance-of-payments deficit can be corrected by means of freely fluctuating exchange rates, changes in income, and government controls. The first two methods are supposed to correct international disequilibrium through changes in interest rates, commodity prices, and income. Government controls such as exchange and trade controls can be used to alleviate or correct the balance-of-payments deficit.

PROBLEMS

A series of transactions between the United States and the rest of the world are given below:

a. An American company exports goods to a British company for $2,000. The British company signs a bill of exchange for its imports.
b. An Italian-American ships $3,000 worth of goods to his relatives in Italy.
c. An American company imports $500 worth of goods from Canada. The American company pays for the merchandise with a loan in Canadian currency.
d. An American citizen goes on vacation to Mexico. He spends $5,000 before he returns to the United States.
e. An American auto company decides to build an assembly plant in Hong Kong. The American auto company ships $4,000 worth of materials for this purpose to Hong Kong.
f. The American auto company finds it necessary to increase its investment by $2,500 for the completion of the plant. It sells $2,500 worth of its bonds to the citizens of Hong Kong.
g. An American citizen buys Korean government bonds for $3,000 in cash.
h. A South African gold producer sells $1,200 worth of gold to the Federal Reserve System of the United States.

3-1 Record each transaction as debit and credit.

3-2 Enter these transactions in the appropriate T-accounts.

Exports	Imports
Services	Unilateral Transfers
Direct Investment	Long-Term Financial Assets
Short-Term Financial Assets	Long-Term Liabilities
Short-Term Liabilities	Gold

3-3 Prepare the balance of payments for the United States.

REFERENCES

3-1 Baldry, Jonathan C., "The Effects of a Minimum Wage on Foreign Factor Rewards," *Journal of International Economics* (August 1981), pp. 415-422.

3-2 Baldwin, Robert E., and J. David Richardson, eds., *International Trade and Finance* (Boston: Little, Brown and Company, 1981).

3-3 Brown, Kenneth M., "North American Trade Policies: Implications for U.S. Business Firms," *Business Economics* (January 1982), pp. 47-55.

3-4 Cline, William R., "Imports and Consumer Prices: A Survey Analysis," *Journal of Retailing* (Spring 1979), pp. 3-24.

3-5 Feiger, George, and Bertrand Jacquillat, *International Finance* (Boston: Allyn and Bacon, Inc., 1982), Chapters 3 and 4.

3-6 Finley, Murray H., "Foreign Trade and United States Employment," in William G. Dewald, *The Impact of International Trade and Employment,* (ed.) (Washington, D.C.: U.S. Department of Commerce, 1978), pp. 129-134.

3-7 Goldstein, Morris, and Mohsin S. Khan, "Large Versus Small Price Changes and the Demand for Imports," *IMF Staff Papers* (March 1976), pp. 200-225.

3-8 Green, Robert R., and James M. Lutz, "U.S. High Technology Import/Export Performances in Three Industries," *Journal of International Business Studies* (Fall 1980), pp. 112-117.

3-9 Hein, John, *Understanding the Balance of Payments* (New York: National Industrial Conference Board, 1970).

3-10 Hillman, Arye L., "Unilateral and Bilateral Trade Policies for a Minimum-Wage Economy," *Journal of International Economics* (August 1981), pp. 407-414.

3-11 *The International Adjustment Mechanism,* ed., (Boston: Federal Reserve Bank of Boston, 1970).

3-12 Kim, Suk H., and Henry J. Guithues, *Finance Principles: An Introduction* (Richmond: Robert F. Dame, Inc., 1982), Chapter 4.

3-13 Rabino, Samuel, "An Attitudinal Evaluation of an Export Incentive Program: The Case of DISC, " *Columbia Journal of World Business* (Spring 1980), pp. 61-65.

3-14 Reich, Robert B., "Why the U.S. Needs an Industrial Policy," *Harvard Business Review* (January-February 1982), pp. 58-73.

3-15 Robinson, Richard D., "Background Concepts and Philosophy of International Business from World War II to the Present," *Journal of International Business Studies* (Spring/Summer 1981), pp. 13-22.

3-16 Rodriguez, Rita M., and E. Eugene Carter, *International Financial Management* (Englewood Cliffs, N.J.: Prentice-Hall, Inc., 1979), Chapters 3 and 4.

3-17 Stobaugh, Robert B., "Energy Future and International Trade," *Journal of International Business Studies* (Spring/Summer 1981), pp. 23-29.

3-18 Whitman, Marina, "The Payments Adjustment Process and the Exchange Rate Regime: What Have We Learned?" *American Economic Review* (May 1975), pp. 133-146.

FOUR

THE INTERNATIONAL MONETARY SYSTEM

The international monetary system consists of such elements as laws, rules, institutions, instruments, and procedures which involve international money. These elements affect foreign exchange rates, international trade and capital flows, and balance-of-payments adjustments. Foreign exchange rates determine prices of goods and services across national boundaries. International loans and foreign investment are also influenced by foreign exchange rates. Hence, the international monetary system plays a critical role in the financial management of multinational business and economic policies of individual countries.

The access of a multinational company to international capital markets and its freedom to move funds across national boundaries are subject to a variety of national constraints. These constraints are frequently imposed to meet international monetary agreements on the determination of exchange rates. Constraints may also be imposed to correct the balance-of-payments deficit or to promote national economic goals.

A successful exchange system is necessary to stabilize the international payment system. Such an exchange system should meet three conditions: (1) Balance-of-payments deficits or surpluses by individual countries should not be too large or prolonged. (2) Such deficits or surpluses should be corrected in ways that do not cause unacceptable inflation or physical restrictions on trade and payments for either individual countries or the world. (3) The maximum sustainable expansion of trade and other international economic activities should be facilitated.[1]

Theoretically, continuous payments deficits and surpluses cannot exist around the world. Under a system of freely flexible exchange rates, a foreign exchange market clears itself in the same way a competitive market for goods does. Just like every commodity price, each exchange rate moves to a level where demand and supply are equal. Under a system of fixed exchange rates, central banks or other designated agencies buy and sell on the open market to absorb surpluses and to eliminate deficiencies of foreign currencies at the fixed exchange rates.

This chapter has three major sections. The first presents a history of the evolution of the international monetary system from the gold standard of the late nineteenth century to the dirty floating system that prevails today. The second section examines some new developments which have occurred since the breakdown of the Bretton Woods System. The third section discusses some proposals for further international monetary reform.

THE PRE-1914 GOLD STANDARD

In the pre-1914 era (before World War I), most of the major trading nations used gold as a medium of exchange and a store of value. These nations accepted and participated in an international monetary system called the *gold standard*, which was characterized by exchange rate stability. A nation's monetary unit was defined as a certain weight of gold.

If pure gold bars were used everywhere as a medium of exchange, there would be no foreign exchange rate problem. As long as there was a guarantee of its purity and weight, the shape of the gold metal would not matter. The purchase of an airplane in the United States would simply require payment in gold at a price expressed in ounces

[1] Sir Maurice Parsons, "Stabilizing the Present International Payment System," *The International Adjustment Mechanism* (Boston: Federal Reserve Bank of Boston, 1970), p. 41.

of gold. The purchase of a truck in the Soviet Union would involve the same kind of payment.

Gold bars are not only inconvenient to carry but also their purity and precise weight are difficult to determine. Thus, it became customary in earlier days for a state to stamp out in coin form with a specified number of ounces of gold. Such gold coins carried the seal of the state which guaranteed its purity and weight. With gold coins as the exchange medium, international trade would still be like domestic trade with two minor differences. First, if the United States used ounces and Great Britain used grams to measure weight, the conversion problem would arise. But a table of conversion would solve this problem. Second, the same problem would occur if the United States chose to make its one dollar coin 1/12 ounce of gold and Britain chose to make its one pound coin 1/3 ounce of gold. In this case, the pound would be four times as heavy as the dollar. Thus, these two currencies would have an exchange rate of $4 to £1.

Since gold coins were inconvenient to carry for spending purposes, governments issued paper certificates that could be converted into gold metal. The gold standard requires that each nation define its monetary unit in a certain quantity of gold. The rate stipulated in its definition of the monetary unit must then be used to convert certificates into gold and gold into certificates. Another condition for the gold standard is that each nation must allow gold to be freely exported and imported. The definition of the monetary unit in terms of gold by each nation would establish an exchange rate between the different countries, *i.e.*, $4 = £1. The free flow of gold between nations would result in fixed exchange rates for all practical purposes.

Gold Export and Import Points

In the pre-1914 era, the central banks redeemed legal tender (paper money) for bullion at fixed rates per ounce of gold. In this system, the exchange rate between any two different currencies was virtually fixed, fluctuating only between the gold export and import points.

The dollar price of pound sterling and the transportation cost of gold determined the range within which exchange rates could fluctuate. In terms of gold, a pound sterling was once $4. This amount was called the par value of the pound or the mint par of the pound. In earlier days, ocean transport was the only means of transportation to move gold from one nation to another. The transportation was slow and costly. Assume that it cost 5 cents to ship 1/3 ounce of gold either way across the Atlantic Ocean. No one in the United States would pay more than $4.05 for £1. Nor would an Englishman pay more than £1 for $3.95. Whenever the dollar price of sterling rose above $4.05 or fell below $3.95, the arbitrage transaction could take place. Arbitrage involves the purchase of something in one market and its sale in another market to take advantage of discrepancies between prices prevailing at the same time in different markets.[2]

Americans would pay up to $4.05 for £1 rather than buy and export 1/3 ounce of gold to obtain that pound. It would cost them $4 for the 1/3 ounce of gold and 5 cents to ship it to England for £1. When the dollar price of sterling rose above the $4.05, gold would begin to flow out of the United States. This $4.05 exchange rate is called the *gold export point*. On the other hand, Englishmen would accept as little as $3.95 in exchange for £1. They could buy 1/3 ounce of gold in England for £1 and resell it in the United States for $4. The exchange rate would fall to the $3.95 before gold would flow into the United States because it would cost Englishmen 5 cents to send gold to the United States to be exchanged for $4. This $3.95 exchange rate is called the *gold import point*.

As long as Americans could obtain pound sterling through the acquisition and export of gold for no more than $4.05 per pound, there was no reason for the exchange rate to increase beyond that point. By the same token, there was no reason for the exchange rate to fall below $3.95. Thus, it was possible for the exchange rate to fluctuate between only the gold export and import points. The spread between the mint par ($4 per £1) and each of the two gold points represented such costs as shipping, insurance, and interest. Some of these costs were matters of approximate estimates and some others changed from time to time. Hence, the spread was neither constant nor accurate. The limits to exchange rate fluctuation under the gold standard typically remained close to par value.

London's Dominance in International Finance

The gold standard as an international monetary system worked adequately in the period before World War I because of London's dominance in international finance. The keystone of the system was the confidence in the stability of the British financial system. It was

[2] Chapter 5 will discuss arbitrage in detail.

organized around sterling as the sole reserve currency and London as the financial center for almost 90 percent of world trade.[3] Such commercial transactions as factoring receivables and discounting bills from all corners of the world took place in London. Sterling was convenient because it was universally used and convertible into gold at the Bank of England. Trade and loans were denominated in sterling rather than gold.

The Bank of England backed sterling with an unbelievably small amount of gold reserve which was estimated at two or three percent of the total money supply. The Bank of England maintained this small gold reserve because it manipulated the bank rate to safeguard the gold stock. The bank rate was the rate at which the Bank of England rediscounted commercial paper. Gold outflows resulted in an increase in bank rate which attracted short-term deposits into London. Gold inflows were met by decreases in bank rate. Such a manipulation produced unmatched stability in the capital markets. "...from January 1876 to July 1914, bank rate moved rather narrowly around an average somewhat above three percent. Never in that period did it stand at or above five percent for longer than 26 consecutive weeks."[4]

The Gold Standard and International Adjustments

The flow of gold between nations would do more than fix exchange rate. To clarify this point, let us assume that the United States imports more from England than it exports to England. To settle the U. S. deficit, gold will flow from the United States to England and this will increase the dollar price of pounds up to the $4.05 export point. The loss of gold by the United States reduces its bank reserves, the amount of money in circulation, and credit availability. Everything else being equal, this contributes to a decline in aggregate demand, national income, and the price level in the United States. The opposite occurs in England. British gain in gold expands its bank reserves, national income, and money supply. Aggregate demand and the price level are thereby increased. Under these circumstances, American goods become cheaper, while British goods become more expensive. Thus, the United States will reduce its imports of expensive British goods and increase its exports of cheap home-made

[3] Albert C. Whitaker, *Foreign Exchange* (New York: Appleton, 1933), p. 157.

[4] Leland B. Yeager, *International Monetary Relations: Theory, History, and Policy* (New York: Harper and Row, 1976), p. 307.

goods. In contrast, England will find its expensive exports falling in physical amount and its imports of cheap American goods rising. The result of the price-level mechanism through the flow of gold is to reduce the U. S. deficit and to decrease the British surplus until equilibrium in international trade is established. Equilibrium should be at relative prices that keep exports and imports in balance. Income changes will produce the same result. As their incomes fall, Americans purchase less British goods. As their incomes increase, Englishmen buy more American goods.

MONETARY DISORDER: 1914-1945

The gold standard as an international monetary system worked well until World War I interrupted trade patterns and ended the stability of exchange rates for currencies of major industrial countries. Currencies fluctuated fairly widely in terms of gold during World War I and in the early 1920s. World War I also ended the period during which the United Kingdom was the world's major creditor nation. The United States began to assume the role of the leading creditor nation.

Several attempts were made to restore the gold standard during the 1920s. The United States returned to the gold standard in 1919, the United Kingdom in 1925, and France in 1928. However, these attempts failed mainly due to the Great Depression of 1929-1932 and the international financial crisis of 1931.

The international monetary chaos of the 1930s began with the insolvency of a branch banking institution in Austria called the Kredit-Anstalt in early 1931. Sterling was devalued in 1933 and then the U. S. dollar was devalued in January 1934 with the famous peg of $35 per ounce of gold. These actions by the United Kingdom and the United States left the currencies of the "gold bloc" countries (France, Switzerland, Netherlands, Belgium, Italy, and Poland) overvalued with respect to the pound and the dollar. Belgium abandoned the gold standard in March 1935 and the rest of the gold bloc countries in September 1936.

Fluctuating Exchange Rate and International Adjustments

World War I ended the stability of exchange rates for currencies of major trading nations. The international monetary system of the

1930s presented a mixture of widely fluctuating exchange rates and exchange rates maintained by exchange controls.

Fluctuating exchange rates are rates of foreign exchange that are determined in the markets by supply and demand without government intervention on the extent to which rates can move. Supply and demand for a nation's exports and imports cause mild changes in its exchange rate around a central equilibrium value. Thus, this system relies on automatic mechanisms to correct disequilibria in the balance of payments. Although governments do not attempt to prevent fundamental changes in the exchange rate between their own currency and other currency, they typically attempt to maintain orderly trading conditions in the market.

In the floating system, exchange rates are free to fluctuate in response to changes in the forces of supply and demand. Proponents of fluctuating exchange rates argue that this system would automatically and quickly correct balance-of-payments disequilibria. If a country experiences a balance-of-payments deficit, the external value of its currency will automatically fall and depreciate. This currency depreciation could encourage its exports and discourage its imports, thereby correcting the original deficit. Hence, it is not surprising to find that many countries have frequently permitted their currencies to depreciate in a large degree in order to stimulate their exports and to lower their imports.

Critics of fluctuating exchange rates argue that the exchange rates under a pure version of this system would be highly unstable and that such risks are likely to discourage the flow of world trade. Supporters of fluctuating exchange rates contend that there is no reason to believe that this would be the case, because changes in the exchange rate would reflect basic economic conditions. However, we cannot deny the fact that the fluctuating exchange rates would significantly complicate the pricing mechanism of goods and services in world trade. This complication would add to the risk of foreign trade and thus lead to the reduction in the volume of world trade.

THE BRETTON WOODS SYSTEM: 1945-1973

The international monetary disorder of the 1930s justified the relative rigidity of the postwar par value system designed at Bretton

Woods in 1944. The monetary system that prevailed from the end of World War II to 1973 was a system of fixed exchange rates on a modified gold standard called the *gold exchange standard*. Under this system, each currency was kept fixed within a narrow range of values relative to gold or some reference currency by governmental action. The U. S. dollar was the most frequently used reference currency to establish the relative prices of all other major currencies.

At the end of World War II, the leading nations of the free world recognized that the reconstruction of world economy would depend on the establishment of a viable international monetary system. These leading nations held an international finance conference at Bretton Woods, New Hampshire, in 1944. At this conference they agreed to establish a new monetary order which centered around the International Monetary Fund and the International Bank for Reconstruction and Development.

The basic purpose of this new monetary system was to facilitate the expansion of world trade and to use the U. S. dollar as a standard of value. The Bretton Woods Agreement produced three propositions. (1) The stable exchange rates under the gold standard before World War I were desirable, but there are certain conditions to make adjustments in exchange rates necessary. (2) Performance of fluctuating exchange rates had been unsatisfactory. (3) The complex network of government controls during 1931-1945 deterred the expansion of world trade and investment. However, there are certain conditions which require government controls over international trade and payments.

The Bretton Woods Agreement placed major emphasis on the stability of exchange rates by adopting the concept of fixed but adjustable rates. The keystones of the system were: (1) no provision was made for the United States to change the value of gold as $35 per ounce and (2) each country was obligated to define its monetary unit in terms of gold or dollars. While other currencies were not required to exchange their currencies for gold, U. S. dollars remained convertible into gold at $35 per ounce. Thus, each country established par rates of exchange between its currency and the currencies of all other countries. Each currency was permitted to fluctuate within plus or minus one percent of par value by buying or selling foreign exchange and gold as needed. However, if a currency became too weak to maintain its par value, it was allowed to devalue up to ten percent without formal approval by the International Monetary Fund (IMF).

Breakdown of the Bretton Woods System

Depreciation and appreciations occurred only rarely before 1971 thanks to the fixed exchange-rate system administered by the IMF. The key elements of the Bretton Woods system were the stable value of the U. S. dollar in terms of gold and its convertibility into gold at least for foreign central banks.[5] The late 1940s marked the beginning of large deficits in the U. S. balance of payments. By 1971, the U. S. payments deficit exploded. America's chronic payments deficits turned into a spectacular dilution of U. S. gold and other reserves during the 1960s and early 1970s. Hence, many people were not surprised to observe that the dollar had to be devalued in 1971, and again in 1973. Moreover, on August 15, 1971, the United States decided to suspend the conversion of dollars into gold and to permit the dollar to float in relation to other currencies.

The Smithsonian Agreement. From August to December 1971, most major currencies were permitted to fluctuate. U. S. dollars fell in value against a number of major currencies. Several countries imposed some trade and exchange controls, which caused major concern. It was feared that such protective measures might become sufficiently widespread to limit international commerce. In order to solve these problems, the world's leading trading countries, called the "Group of Ten," produced the Smithsonian Agreement on December 18, 1971. The Agreement established a new set of parity rates. These parity rates were called central rates because they lacked the approval of the IMF.

Although U. S. dollars were not convertible into gold, they were still defined in terms of gold. The other nine currencies were defined in terms of either gold or the dollar. The United States agreed to devalue the dollar from $35 per ounce of gold to $38 in return for promises from other members to upvalue their currencies relative to the dollar by specified amounts, as shown in Table 4-1.

In order to maintain market exchange rates relatively close to the central rates without constant government intervention, currencies were permitted to fluctuate over a wider band than in the past. Although a currency was allowed to fluctuate within a margin of 2.25 percent from the central rates without government intervention, it

[5] There could be some disagreement concerning when the Bretton Woods Agreement ended. If the stable value of the U. S. dollar in terms of gold and its convertibility into gold were essential for the Agreement, its breakdown came in 1971. However, if stable but adjustable exchange rates were essential for the system, its end came in 1973.

Table 4-1 Currency Value Changes Under the Smithsonian Agreement

Currency	Exchange Rate: Currency Units per $1 May 1, 1971	December 18, 1971	Percentage Upvaluation
Belgian franc	50.00	44.82	11.57
British pound	0.42	0.38	8.57
French franc	5.55	5.12	8.57
German mark	3.66	3.22	13.58
Italian lira	625.00	581.50	7.48
Japanese yen	360.00	308.00	16.88
Dutch guilder	3.62	3.25	11.57
Swedish krona	5.17	4.81	11.57
Swiss franc	4.37	3.84	13.86

Source: Federal Reserve Bank of New York, *Monthly Review* (March 1972), p. 44.

could fluctuate by as much as 9 percent against any currency except the dollar. Because a currency was permitted to fluctuate up to 2.25 percent on either side of the central rate, its total fluctuation against the dollar could be as much as 4.5 percent. Let us assume for purposes of illustration that Japanese yen upvalued by 4.5 percent against the dollar and that Italian lira devalued by 4.5 percent against the dollar. Under these circumstances, these two currencies would change by 9 percent against one another.

Proponents of the Smithsonian Agreement argued that a wider band would allow countries to retain: (1) discipline that they would expect from the fixed exchange-rate system and (2) greater freedom and a smoother adjustment process of flexible exchange rates. Although the Agreement was a historical event in international monetary affairs, it failed to reduce speculation. Government control on the foreign exchange, likewise, did not decrease. For all practical purposes, the Agreement came to an end in March 1973, because most "Group of Ten" countries allowed their currencies to float according to market forces.

THE POST-1973 DIRTY FLOATING SYSTEM

From the end of World War II to 1973, international business and multinational corporations operated under a fixed exchange system. Since 1973, most industrial countries and many developing countries have permitted their currencies to float with frequent governmental intervention in the exchange market. This monetary system is known as a *dirty* or *managed floating system*. Governments have frequently intervened to maintain orderly markets and to keep their average exchange rate at a level deemed desirable by their economic policy.

Since March 1973, exchange rate practices have varied from country to country. Table 4-2 shows that at the end of September 1981, 58 currencies were pegged to a single currency (39 to the U. S. dollar, 14 to the French franc, two to the South African rand, and one each to the British pound, the Spanish peseta, and the Indian rupee). Fifteen currencies were pegged to the SDR and another 21 to other currency composites. Four countries were adjusting their exchange rates according to a set of indicators, eight were maintaining cooperative exchange arrangements, while 39 were maintaining other, more flexible, exchange arrangements.

It was fortunate that the fixed exchange system collapsed in March 1973. This is because floating rates enabled the international monetary system to ride out the 1973-1974 Arab oil embargo and the subsequent inflation without any major currency crisis.[6] The IMF annual report for 1975 admitted that "on the whole, exchange rate flexibility appears to have enabled the world economy to surmount a succession of disturbing events, and to accommodate divergent trends in costs and prices in national economies with less disruption of trade and payments than a system of par values would have been able to do."

What Is Ahead in the 1980s?[7]

The evolution of international monetary relations in the 1980s is likely to occur along a number of fronts. The movement toward joint floating and other cooperative exchange arrangements can be expected to continue. Even some nations that do not belong to a currency group can be expected to cooperate in the determination of their economic objectives to a much greater extent than in the past. The United States is expected to continue taking a more active part in the management of its exchange rates, in contrast to the passive role it played in the Bretton Woods system.

[6] George Feiger and Bertrand Jacquillat, *International Finance* (Boston: Allyn and Bacon, Inc., 1982), p. 45.

[7] This section is adopted from Nicholas Carlozzi, "Pegs and Floats: The Changing Face of the Foreign Exchange Market," *Current Federal Reserve Readings in Economics for Teachers* (Federal Reserve Bank of New York, November 1980), p. 247.

Table 4-2 Exchange Rates and Exchange Arrangements, September 30, 1981

Member (currency)	Exchange Rate Maintained Against	Exchange Rate [1]	Exchange Rate Otherwise Determined [2,3]
Afghanistan (Afghani)			50.60
Algeria (dinar) [4]	bskt	4.3775	
Argentina (peso) [4]			7,645.0
Australia (dollar)			0.876117
Austria (schilling)	bskt	16.297	
Bahamas (dollar) [4]	$	1.00	
Bahrain (dinar)			0.377
Bangladesh (taka) [4]	bskt	19.2954	
Barbados (dollar) [4]	$	2.0113	
Belgium (franc) [4]			37.9475 [5]
Benin (franc)	F	50.00	
Bhutan (ngultrum)	Re	1.00	
Bolivia (peso)			24.51
Botswana (pula)	bskt	0.887154	
Brazil (cruzeiro)			108.1 [6]
Burma (kyat)	SDR	8.50847	7.43358 [2]
Burundi (franc)	$	90.00	
Cameroon (franc)	F	50.00	
Canada (dollar)			1.2068
Cape Verde (escudo)	bskt	50.6842	

Member (currency)	Exchange Rate Maintained Against	Exchange Rate [1]	Exchange Rate Otherwise Determined [2,3]
Iran (rial) [4]	SDR	92.30	80.6396
Iraq (dinar)	$	0.295314	
Ireland (pound)			0.638488 [5]
Israel (shekel)			13.4401
Italy (lira) [4]			1,177.50 [5]
Ivory Coast (franc)	F	50.00	
Jamaica (dollar) [4]	$	1.781423	
Japan (yen)			232.70
Jordan (dinar)	SDR	0.387	0.338110
Kampuchea, Democratic (riel) [7,8]			
Kenya (shilling) [4]	SDR	11.95	10.4403
Korea (won)			685.50
Kuwait (dinar)	bskt	0.28338	
Lao People's Dem. Rep. (kip) [4]	$	10.00	
Lebanon (pound) [7]			
Lesotho (maloti) [4]	R	1.00	
Liberia (dollar)	$	1.00	
Libya (dinar)	$	0.296053	
Luxembourg (franc) [4]			37.9475 [5]

Member (currency)	Exchange Rate Maintained Against	Exchange Rate [1]	Exchange Rate Otherwise Determined [2,3]
Solomon Islands (dollar)	bskt	0.876117	
Somalia (shilling) [4]	$	12.59	
South Africa (rand) [4]			0.954745
Spain (peseta)			96.475
Sri Lanka (rupee)			20.785
Sudan (pound) [4]	$	0.50	
Suriname (guilder)	$	1.785	
Swaziland (lilangeni) [4]	R	1.00	
Sweden (krona)	bskt	5.598	
Syrian Arab Rep. (pound) [4]	$	3.925	
Tanzania (shilling)	bskt	8.36939	
Thailand (baht)			23.00
Togo (franc)	F	50.00	
Trinidad and Tobago (dollar)	$		2.409
Tunisia (dinar)	bskt	0.51305	
Turkey (lira) [4]			122.21
Uganda (shilling) [7]			
United Arab Emirates (dirham)			3.671
United Kingdom (pound)			0.555401

Central African Republic (franc)	F	50.00	
Chad (franc)	F	50.00	
Chile (peso)	$	39.00	
China, People's Republic (renminbi)[4]	bskt	1.7675	
Colombia (peso)			56.39[6]
Comoros (franc)	F	50.00	
Congo (franc)	F	50.00	
Costa Rica (colón)[4]	$	18.95	
Cyprus (pound)	bskt	0.444148	
Denmark (krone)			7.3025[5]
Djibouti (franc)	$	177.721	
Dominica (East Caribbean dollar)	$	2.70	
Dominican Rep. (peso)[4]	$	1.00	
Ecuador (sucre)[4]	$	25.00	
Egypt (pound)[4]	$	0.70	
El Salvador (colón)	$	2.50	
Equatorial Guinea (ekwele)[4]	P	2.00	
Ethiopia (birr)[4]	$	2.07	
Fiji (dollar)	bskt	0.895335	
Finland (markka)	bskt	4.4820	
France (franc)			5.567[5]

Madagascar (franc)	F	50.00	
Malawi (kwacha)	SDR	1.05407	0.920907
Malaysia (ringgit)	bskt	2.3217	
Maldives (rufiyaa)[4]			7.50
Mali (franc)	F	100.00	
Malta (pound)	bskt	0.399728	
Mauritania (ouguiya)	bskt	48.35	
Mauritius (rupee)[4]	SDR	12.00	10.4840
Mexico (peso)			25.2022
Morocco (dirham)			5.32315
Nepal (rupee)[4]	$	12.00	
Netherlands (guilder)			2.582[5]
New Zealand (dollar)			1.22160
Nicaragua (córdoba)[4]	$	10.05	
Niger (franc)	F	50.00	
Nigeria (naira)			0.662603
Norway (krone)	bskt	5.9560	
Oman (rial Omani)	$	0.3454	
Pakistan (rupee)	$	9.90	
Panama (balboa)	$	1.00	
Papua New Guinea (kina)	bskt	0.687711	

United States (dollar)			1.00
Upper Volta (franc)	F	50.00	
Uruguay (new peso)			11.1950
Vanuatu (vatu)	SDR	106.2	92.7835
Venezuela (bolívar)[4]	$	4.2925	
Viet Nam (dong)[4]	SDR	10.37883	9.06765
Western Samoa (tala)			0.915416
Yemen Arab Rep. (rial)	$	4.5625	
Yemen, People's Dem. Rep. (dinar)	$	0.345399	
Yugoslavia (dinar)			38.333
Zaïre (zaïre)	SDR	6.34921	5.54710
Zambia (kwacha)	SDR	1.02426	0.894863
Zimbabwe (dollar)	bskt		0.723014

$ U.S. dollar
£ pound sterling
F French franc
P Spanish peseta
R South African rand
SDR special drawing right
bskt currency basket other than SDR
Re Indian rupee

[1] Rates as notified to the Fund and in terms of currency units per unit listed; rates determined by baskets of currencies are in currency units per U.S. dollar.
[2] Market rates in currency units per U.S. dollar.
[3] Under this heading are listed those members that describe their exchange rate arrangements as floating independently or as adjusting according to a set of indicators (see footnote 6) and certain other members whose exchange arrangements are not otherwise described in this table. In addition, U.S. dollar quotations are given for the currencies that are pegged to the SDR and for those that participate in the European Monetary System (see footnote 5).

Table 4-2 continued

Member (currency)	Exchange Rate Maintained Against	Exchange Rate[1]	Exchange Rate Otherwise Determined[2,3]
Gabon (franc)	F	50.00	
Gambia, The (dalasi)	£	4.00	
Germany, Fed. Rep. (deutsche mark)			2.3225[5]
Ghana (cedi)[4]			2.75
Greece (drachma)[4]			57.835
Grenada (East Caribbean dollar)[4]	$	2.70	
Guatemala (quetzal)	$	1.00	
Guinea (syli)	SDR	24.6853	21.5668
Guinea-Bissau (peso)	SDR	44.00	38.4414
Guyana (dollar)			3.00
Haiti (gourde)	$	5.00	
Honduras (lempira)	$	2.00	
Iceland (króna)[4]			7.783
India (rupee)			9.10858
Indonesia (rupiah)			633.75

Member (currency)	Exchange Rate Maintained Against	Exchange Rate[1]	Exchange Rate Otherwise Determined[2,3]
Paraguay (guaraní)[4]	$	126.00	
Peru (sol)			453.958[6]
Philippines (peso)			8.022
Portugal (escudo)			65.039[6]
Qatar (riyal)			3.64
Romania (leu)[4]	$	15.00	
Rwanda (franc)	$	92.84	
St. Lucia (East Caribbean dollar)	$	2.70	
St. Vincent (East Caribbean dollar)	$	2.70	
São Tomé and Principe (dobra)	SDR	45.25	39.5335
Saudi Arabia (riyal)			3.415
Senegal (franc)	F	50.00	
Seychelles (rupee)	SDR	7.2345	6.32055
Sierra Leone (leone)	SDR	1.36693	1.19424
Singapore (dollar)	bskt	2.1147	

[4] Member maintains multiple currency practices and/or dual exchange market. A description of the member's exchange system as of December 31, 1980 is given in the *Annual Report on Exchange Arrangements and Exchange Restrictions, 1981*.

[5] Belgium, Denmark, France, Germany, Ireland, Italy, Luxembourg, and the Netherlands are participating in the exchange rate and intervention mechanism of the European Monetary System and maintain maximum margins of 2.25 per cent (in the case of the Italian lira, 6 per cent) for exchange rates in transactions in the official markets between their currencies and those of the other countries in this group. No announced margins are observed for other currencies.

[6] Exchange rates adjusted according to a set of indicators.

[7] Exchange rate data not available.

[8] Information on exchange arrangements not available.

Source: IMF Survey (October 26, 1981), p. 337.

There may be further reforms to control the stock of international reserves available to IMF members. Those reforms could include the increased use of the SDR as a means of payment among member governments, the possibility of a substitution account to promote the diversification of international reserve holdings, and the introduction of government regulation in the Eurocurrency financial markets.

As innovations in communications and transportation continue to bring nations closer together, it will be necessary for the international monetary system to maintain both its flexibility and diversity. Hopefully, enough of both will be present in order to stabilize and promote the growth of the world economy as effectively as the Bretton Woods system did in the past.

THE INTERNATIONAL MONETARY FUND

The IMF was created as a weak kind of central banks' central bank at the Bretton Woods conference to make the new monetary system feasible and workable. Its major purpose was to assist its members that would have structural trade problems or highly unstable currencies in value. The IMF permitted its deficit members to buy with their local currencies some of its own holdings of convertible currencies. After these deficit countries had improved their balances of payments, they were expected to buy back with gold or other convertible currencies the local currencies they had sold to the IMF. Hence, the IMF's major weapon was the power to declare its members ineligible to utilize its holdings of international reserves.

The IMF established rules and procedures to keep participating countries from going too deeply into balance-of-payments deficits. Those countries with short-term payments difficulties could draw upon their reserves. The amount of such reserves was defined in relation to each member's quota. This quota was determined on the basis of such factors as trade, national income, and international payments. Up to 1976, each member was required to subscribe 75 percent of its quota in its own currency and 25 percent in gold. The 25 percent share was known as *gold tranche*. However, since 1976 each member has been required to contribute 75 percent of its quota in its own currency and 25 percent in SDRs or convertible currencies.

In its Seventh General Review of Quotas, the IMF proposed a 50 percent increase in quotas. On November 1, 1978, more than the required 75 percent of its members approved the proposal. However, an individual member's increase in quota does not become effective unless the member has consented to the increase and has paid the increase in full. On December 1, 1980, the IMF announced that members had met the minimum participation requirements for implementation of the increase. As of March 1, 1981, Iran's consent had not been received, and Oman had consented to a quota of SDR30 million, against a proposed SDR35.1 million. All other members had consented to the full increase proposed for them. Thus, the aggregate of IMF quotas increased to SDR59,605.5 million from SDR39,766.5 prior to the increase. Both old and current quotas (valued in SDRs) are given in Table 4-3. Members are required to pay 25 percent of the increase in SDRs and 75 percent in their own currencies.

IMF members borrow by exchanging their own currencies for convertible currencies of other member countries. A member country is free to draw 100 percent of its quota from the IMF at any time (virtually at will). Beyond this amount a country could borrow up to an additional 100 percent of its quota. This 100 percent is called the *credit tranche*. Thus, a member country could conceivably borrow 200 percent of its quotas in convertible currencies. But in order to borrow more than 100 percent of its quota, any member must accept restrictions imposed by the IMF to ensure that steps are being taken to correct the borrower's currency problems. The IMF adopted its new guidelines on the scale of its assistance in January 1981. These new guidelines provide for members to have an annual access to IMF resources of up to 150 percent of their new quotas or up to 450 percent over a three-year period. The IMF is expected to continue its policy of this enlarged access to its resources until more loanable funds can be found.

Under the previous fixed exchange system, member countries were not allowed to change the par values of their currencies, except where they had a fundamental disequilibrium. Since the term "fundamental disequilibrium" was not defined, a considerable controversy arose about its interpretation. The IMF permitted any member with a fundamental disequilibrium to depreciate or appreciate its currency up to ten percent without approval from the IMF. The IMF could object to larger changes but required its members to state their position within 72 hours if changes were less than 20 percent. This soft rule was necessary because changes in the exchange rate had to be made quickly to eliminate a chance for speculators to make large profits.

A series of negotiations among important IMF member countries during 1973-1976 produced an agreement to change some of the

Table 4-3

Old and New Quotas of IMF Members on March 1, 1981
(million SDRs)

	Quota Prior to Increase	New Quota		Quota Prior to Increase	New Quota		Quota Prior to Increase	New Quota
Afghanistan	45.0	67.5	Haiti	23.0	34.5	Romania	245.0	367.5
Algeria	285.0	427.5	Honduras	34.0	51.0	Rwanda	23.0	34.5
Argentina	535.0	802.5	Iceland	29.0	43.5	St. Lucia	3.6	5.4
Australia	790.0	1,185.0	India	1,145.0	1,717.5	St. Vincent	1.7	2.6
Austria	330.0	495.0	Indonesia	480.0	720.0	São Tomé & Principe	2.0	3.0
Bahamas	33.0	49.5	Iran[1]	660.0	1,075.0	Saudi Arabia	600.0	1,040.1
Bahrain	20.0	30.0	Iraq	141.0	234.1	Senegal	42.0	63.0
Bangladesh	152.0	228.0	Ireland	155.0	232.5	Seychelles	1.3	2.0
Barbados	17.0	25.5	Israel	205.0	307.5	Sierra Leone	31.0	46.5
Belgium	890.0	1,335.0	Italy	1,240.0	1,860.0	Singapore	49.0	92.4
Benin	16.0	24.0	Ivory Coast	76.0	114.0	Solomon Islands	2.1	3.2
Bolivia	45.0	67.5	Jamaica	74.0	111.0	Somalia	23.0	34.5
Botswana	9.0	13.5	Japan	1,659.0	2,488.5	South Africa	424.0	636.0
Brazil	665.0	997.5	Jordan	30.0	45.0	Spain	557.0	835.5
Burma	73.0	109.5	Kampuchea, Democratic	25.0	25.0	Sri Lanka	119.0	178.5
Burundi	23.0	34.5						
Cameroon	45.0	67.5	Kenya	69.0	103.5	Sudan	88.0	132.0
Canada	1,357.0	2,035.5	Korea	160.0	255.9	Suriname	25.0	37.5
Cape Verde	2.0	3.0	Kuwait	235.0	393.3	Swaziland	12.0	18.0
Central African Republic	16.0	24.0	Lao, People's Democratic Rep. of	16.0	24.0	Sweden	450.0	675.0
						Syrian Arab Republic	63.0	94.5
Chad	16.0	24.0	Lebanon	12.0	27.9	Tanzania	55.0	82.5
Chile	217.0	325.5	Lesotho	7.0	10.5	Thailand	181.0	271.5
China	1,200.0	1,800.0	Liberia	37.0	55.5	Togo	19.0	28.5
Colombia	193.0	289.5	Libya	185.0	298.4	Trinidad and Tobago	82.0	123.0

Table 4-3 continued

	Quota Prior to Increase	New Quota
Comoros	2.3	3.5
Congo	17.0	25.5
Costa Rica	41.0	61.5
Cyprus	34.0	51.0
Denmark	310.0	465.0
Dominica	1.9	2.9
Dominican Republic	55.0	82.5
Djibouti	3.8	5.7
Ecuador	70.0	105.0
Egypt	228.0	342.0
El Salvador	43.0	64.5
Equatorial Guinea	10.0	15.0
Ethiopia	36.0	54.0
Fiji	18.0	27.0
Finland	262.0	393.0
France	1,919.0	2,878.5
Gabon	30.0	45.0
Gambia, The	9.0	13.5
Germany, Fed. Rep. of	2,156.0	3,234.0
Ghana	106.0	159.0
Greece	185.0	277.5
Grenada	3.0	4.5
Guatemala	51.0	76.5
Guinea	30.0	45.0
Guinea-Bissau	3.9	5.9
Guyana	25.0	37.5
Luxembourg	31.0	46.5
Madagascar	34.0	51.0
Malawi	19.0	28.5
Malaysia	253.0	379.5
Maldives	0.9	1.4
Mali	27.0	40.5
Malta	20.0	30.0
Mauritania	17.0	25.5
Mauritius	27.0	40.5
Mexico	535.0	802.5
Morocco	150.0	225.0
Nepal	19.0	28.5
Netherlands	948.0	1,422.0
New Zealand	232.0	348.0
Nicaragua	34.0	51.0
Niger	16.0	24.0
Nigeria	360.0	540.0
Norway	295.0	442.5
Oman	20.0	30.0
Pakistan	285.0	427.5
Panama	45.0	67.5
Papua New Guinea	30.0	45.0
Paraguay	23.0	34.5
Peru	164.0	246.0
Philippines	210.0	315.0
Portugal	172.0	258.0
Qatar	40.0	66.2
Tunisia	63.0	94.5
Turkey	200.0	300.0
Uganda	50.0	75.0
United Arab Emirates	120.0	202.6
United Kingdom	2,925.0	4,387.5
United States[1]	8,405.0	12,607.5
Upper Volta	16.0	24.0
Uruguay	84.0	126.0
Venezuela	660.0	990.0
Viet Nam	90.0	135.0
Western Samoa	3.0	4.5
Yemen Arab Republic	13.0	19.5
Yemen, People's Democratic Rep. of	41.0	61.5
Yugoslavia	277.0	415.5
Zaïre	152.0	228.0
Zambia	141.0	211.5
Zimbabwe	100.0	150.0

[1] Members from which notification of consent to an increase in quota had not been received by the Fund as of March 1, 1981.

Source: IMF Survey (December 15, 1980), p. 387.

Bretton Woods Agreement. The Board of Governors of the IMF approved these changes in April 1976 and the proposed changes went into effect two years later in April 1978. This amendment legalized the existing system of floating exchange rates and freedom for each member to peg or to float the value of its currency. The amendment also terminated the par value system based on gold. Thus, the fixed exchange system based on the Bretton Woods Agreement officially ended in 1976, even if it ended in 1973 for all practical purposes.

SPECIAL DRAWING RIGHTS

The viability of the Bretton Woods system assumed adequate reserves. These reserves consisted of gold and key currencies such as dollars and pounds. Various developments such as GATT, EEC, and the Marshall Plan[8] caused a rapid increase in trade and foreign investment in the postwar period. But monetary gold stocks had remained virtually constant since the end of World War II. Some key reserve currency countries, such as the United States, England, and France, ran large deficits. Although these large deficits increased the world's monetary reserves, these additional reserves were not enough to sustain the continued expansion of world trade. Furthermore, such huge deficits by these key reserve-currency countries raised a credibility gap. Speculators and central bankers began to doubt whether the reserve-currency countries could continue to convert their currencies into gold (in the case of dollars) and dollars (in the case of non-dollar reserve currencies). Another problem was that the reserve-currency countries could not continue to incur large deficits forever. The correction of these deficits would mean the contraction of the world's monetary reserves and the eventual reduction of world trade.

The IMF had been concerned about the lack of growth in gold holdings and the consequent slower growth in international reserves than world trade. To solve these problems, an agreement was reached at the 1967 Rio de Janeiro meeting for the IMF to create SDRs as another reserve asset. These SDRs became an international reserve

[8] The Marshall Plan was the European Economic Recovery Program established by the United States in 1948. The overriding objective of the Plan was to restore the productive capacity of European industry and agriculture destroyed during World War II. The Marshall Plan existed slightly less than four years and channeled more than $10 billion in American aid to Europe. Most of this aid was in the form of outright grants.

asset on July 28, 1969, when more than the required 85 percent of IMF members approved the plan. The basic idea was to manage the stock of SDRs in such a way that world monetary reserves would grow in line with world trade.

SDRs were created in a world of fixed exchange rates that reflected fixed par values of currencies in terms of gold or the dollar. The SDRs were initially given a par value of $1 = one SDR or equivalently 35 SDR = one ounce of gold, when the official gold price was $35 per ounce. The values of all other currencies in terms of SDRs were determined through their value in terms of gold. Two subsequent devaluations of the dollar raised the gold price to $42.22 per ounce and the dollar value of one SDR to $1.20635.

The dollar devaluation and the advent of floating exchange rates caused the SDR's value, relative to other currencies, to fluctuate along with the dollar. On June 28, 1974, the IMF introduced a system under which the value of an SDR was based on a weighted value of a "basket" of 16 major currencies.[9] These 16 currencies were the currencies of those nations that each represented at least one percent of world trade during the 1968-1972 period. The countries' weights in the basket reflected their shares in world trade. But the trade weights of the other 15 countries were scaled down to raise the dollar's weight to 33 percent.[10] This was due to the dollar's importance in world finance.

In a step to further enhance the attractiveness of the SDR, the IMF began on January 1, 1981 to use a simplified basket of five currencies for determining its daily valuation. The decision established percentage weights to be used for the five currencies of 42 for the U. S. dollar, 19 for the Deutsche mark, and 13 each for the Japanese yen, the French franc, and the pound sterling.[11] These weights were applied using market exchange rates on December 31, 1980 to calculate the amount of each currency that determines the value of the SDR. These currency amounts (see column 1 in Table 4-4) remain the same from day to day.

[9] These 16 currencies with their weights in parenthesis were: U. S. dollar (33.0%), German mark (12.5%), pound sterling (9.0%), French franc (7.5%), Japanese yen (7.5%), Canadian dollar (6.0%), Italian lira (6.0%), Dutch guilder (4.5%), Belgian franc (3.5%), Swedish Krona (2.5%), Australian dollar (1.5%), Danish krone (1.5%), Norwegian krone (1.5%), Spanish peseta (1.5%), Austrian schilling (1.0%), and South African rand (1.0%).

[10] The United States accounted for only 21 percent of the world trade during the 1968-1972 period.

[11] These five currencies were those currencies of the nations that had largest exports of goods and services during the 1975-1979 period. They were already used for determining the interest rate on the SDR. The currency baskets that determine the value of and the interest rate on the SDR were therefore united as of January 1, 1981.

Table 4-4 SDR Valuation on January 2, 1981

Currency	Currency Amount (1)	Exchange Rate on January 2, 1981 (2)	U. S. Dollar Equivalent (3)
U. S. dollar	0.5400	1.00000	0.540000
Deutsche mark	0.4600	1.97400	0.233029
French franc	0.7400	4.56000	0.162281
Japanese yen	34.0000	202.87000	0.167595
Pound sterling	0.0710	2.37800	0.168838
		Total	1.271743
		SDR value of US$1.00 =	0.786322
		U. S. dollar value of SDR =	1.27174

Column 1: The currency components of the basket.

Column 2: Exchange rates in terms of currency units per U. S. dollar, except for the pound sterling, which is expressed as U. S. dollars per pound sterling. All rates are at noon in the London foreign exchange market.

Column 3: The U. S. dollar equivalents of the currency amounts in Column 1 at the exchange rates in Column 2; that is, Column 1 divided by Column 2 except for the pound sterling, for which the amounts in the two columns are multiplied.

Source: IMF Survey (January 12, 1981), p. 5.

Although the number of currencies in the SDR basket has been reduced from 16 to five currencies effective January 1, 1981, the method of calculating the U. S. dollar/SDR exchange rate remains the same. The currency amounts making up the SDR basket are converted into U. S. dollar equivalents using market exchange rates. These U. S. dollar equivalents (carried to six decimal places) are then added together and the reciprocal of this total is rounded to six significant figures to establish the SDR value of the U. S. dollar. The same total is rounded (also to six significant figures) to determine the U. S. dollar value of the SDR. Table 4-4 shows the computation process of these two values using exchange rates on January 2, 1981.

The market rates used in this calculation are the midpoints between buying and selling rates at noon in the London foreign exchange market, including the rate for the Japanese yen previously obtained from the Tokyo market. When the London market is closed, the rates used would be from New York at noon. If both the London and New York markets are closed, fixing rates from the Frankfurt market would be used.

As in the past, once the U. S. dollar/SDR exchange rate has been determined, the rate for any other currency in terms of the SDR is calculated using the U. S. dollar/SDR exchange rate and the market rate for the currency in terms of the U. S. dollar. The market rates used in the calculation of these rates are so-called "representative" rates, which are defined by the IMF.

For example, for the Deutsche mark it is the fixing rate against the U. S. dollar in the Frankfurt market. The representative for the Deutsche mark was DM1.9768 per U. S. dollar on January 2, 1981. Thus, the SDR/the Deutsche mark rate for January 2, 1981 was calculated by dividing 0.786322 (that is, the SDR value of US$1 shown in Table 4-4) by 1.9768 to yield SDRO.397775 = DM1. The reciprocal rate of the SDR/the Deutsch mark rate would be calculated by multiplying 1.27174 (that is, the U. S. dollar value of the SDR shown in Table 4-4) by 1.9768 to yield DM2.51398 = SDR1.

SDR rates for more than 40 currencies are made available to the public each day. These rates are carried by several wire services on a daily basis and are published twice monthly in the IMF Survey. Some daily newspapers and financial periodicals also publish the SDR rates for major currencies. Table 4-5 shows the currency units per SDR from January 2 to January 14, 1981.

In December 1980, the IMF prescribed the International Bank for Reconstruction and Development and its affiliate the International Development Association as "other holders" of SDRs.[12] This action brought the number of official institutions to nine, in addition to the IMF and its 141 member countries, authorized to deal in SDRs. The Andean Reserve Fund, Bogota; the Arab Monetary Fund, Abu Dhabi; the Bank for International Settlements, Basle; the East Caribbean Currency Authority, St. Kitts; the International Fund for Agricultural Development, Rome; the Nordic Investment Bank, Helsinki; and the Swiss National Bank, Zurich, have already been prescribed by the IMF as "other holders."

Each of these institutions can acquire and use SDRs in transactions and operations with any other prescribed holder and with any of the IMF members. "Other holders" have the same degree of freedom as IMF members to buy and sell SDRs both spot and forward, and to receive or use SDRs in loans, pledges, swaps, or donations.

THE EUROPEAN MONETARY SYSTEM

In May 1972, the European Economic Community (EEC) agreed to allow their currencies to fluctuate a maximum of 2.25 percent

[12] SDRs are directly useable only among the central banks of IMF member countries and official institutions authorized by the IMF. They are convertible into any currency except gold.

Table 4-5

Currency Units Per SDR

Currency	December[1] 31	Currency	January[2] 2	5	6	7	8	9	12	13	14
Australian dollar	1.08022	Deutsche mark	2.51398	2.50310	2.48406	2.49055	2.50569	2.50945	2.51287	2.53221	2.52794
Austrian schilling	...	French franc	5.82521	5.79090	5.75096	5.76583	5.79548	5.80111	5.82380	5.85871	5.85075
Belgian franc	40.2041	Japanese yen	...	257.601	255.970	256.359	256.087	257.232	255.921	258.981	257.806
Canadian dollar	1.52373	Pound sterling	0.534794	0.532494	0.530315	0.530353	0.531453	0.531007	0.529744	0.530352	0.529962
Deutsche mark	2.49853	U.S. dollar	1.27174	1.27905	1.28628	1.28372	1.27724	1.27532	1.27324	1.26579	1.26873
French franc	...	Argentine peso	2535.85	2552.34	2568.70	2565.51	2554.48	2552.55	...	2537.28	...
Iranian rial	92.3000	Australian dollar	1.07747	1.08394	1.08245	1.08048	1.07693	1.07695	1.07765	1.07298	1.07547
Italian lira	1186.77	Austrian schilling	17.7904	17.7443	...	17.6370	17.7587	17.7792	17.7783	17.9097	17.8942
Japanese yen	258.908	Bahrain dinar	0.479446	0.482202	0.484928	0.483962	0.481519	0.480796	0.480011	0.477203	0.478311
Netherlands guilder	2.71599	Belgian franc	40.4477	40.2869	40.0001	40.1227	40.3352	40.3671	40.4190	40.7331	40.7009
Norwegian krone	6.60662	Brazilian cruzeiro	82.8793	83.3557	83.8269	85.7525	85.3196	85.1914	85.0524	84.5548	84.7512
Pound sterling	0.534763	Canadian dollar	1.51973	1.52066	1.52797	1.52493	1.51672	1.51521	1.51426	1.50692	1.51080
Saudi Arabian riyal	4.24074	Colombian peso	64.7570	65.1292	...	65.3670	65.0371	64.9393	64.8334	64.4540	64.6037
Spanish peseta	...	Danish krone	7.69403	7.68837	7.65722	7.66060	7.71453	7.73290	7.72220	7.77512	7.78683
Swedish krona	...	Ecuadoran sucre	31.7935	31.9763	32.1570	32.0930	31.9310	31.8830	31.8310	31.6448	31.7183
U.S. dollar	1.27541	Finnish markka	4.89493	4.90644	4.89172	4.89226	4.90332	4.89595	4.88542	4.89987	4.90110
Argentine peso	...	Guatemalan quetzal	1.27174	1.27905	1.28628	1.28372	1.27724	1.27532	1.27324	1.26579	1.26873
Bahrain dinar	0.480830	Indian rupee	10.0809	10.0375	10.1290	10.1297	10.1507	10.1422	10.1181	10.1297	10.1223
Brazilian cruzeiro	...	Indonesian rupiah	797.063	801.645	805.854	804.572	800.829	799.626	798.321	793.650	795.494
Colombian peso	...	Iranian rial	92.3000	92.3000	92.3000	...	92.3000	92.3000	92.3000	92.3000	92.3000
Danish krone	7.67159	Iraqi dinar	0.375562	0.377721	0.379856	0.379100	0.377187	0.376620	0.376005	0.373805	0.374674
Ecuadoran sucre	...	Irish pound	0.676998	0.672123	0.667504	0.670525	0.674717	0.674166	0.673494	0.677618	0.677017
Finnish markka	4.89757	Italian lira	1190.98	1187.92	1182.09	1185.19	1190.71	1192.11	1194.30	1202.50	1202.12
Guatemalan quetzal	1.27541	Kuwaiti dinar	0.345023	0.347006	0.347952	0.347375	0.345774	...	0.345099	0.344016	0.344080

Table 4-5 continued

Currency	December[1] 31		January[2] 2	5	6	7	8	9	12	13	14
Indian rupee	10.0803	Libyan dinar	0.376499	0.378663	0.380803	0.380045	0.378127	0.377558	0.376943	0.374737	0.375608
Indonesian rupiah	799.363	Malaysian ringgit	2.82085	2.83501	2.83818	2.83843	2.82845	. . .	2.82277	2.82841	2.83257
Iraqi dinar	0.376646	Malta pound	0.451949	0.452697	0.449717	0.450428	0.451385	0.451697	0.449590	0.450908	0.452778
Irish pound	0.672153	Mexican peso	29.5864	29.7737	29.9532	29.8975	29.7760	29.7621	29.7327	29.5714	29.6488
Kuwaiti dinar	0.346019	Netherlands guilder	2.72725	2.71798	2.70247	2.71186	2.72308	2.72855	2.73365	2.75056	2.75061
Libyan dinar	0.377585	Nigerian naira	0.671847	0.675709	0.679529	0.678176	0.674824	0.673739	0.672640	0.668704	0.670257
Malaysian ringgit	2.82822	Norwegian krone	6.60923	6.59990	6.59347	6.56559	6.56821	6.55770	6.55655	. . .	6.57583
Malta pound	0.451680	Omani rial	0.439259	0.441784	0.444281	0.443397	0.441159	0.440496	0.439777	0.437204	0.438219
Mexican peso	. . .	Portuguese escudo	67.6807	67.7884	67.6596	67.6623	67.7576	67.8075	67.7402	67.9020	67.9671
Nigerian naira	0.673786	Qatar riyal	4.62913	4.65574	4.68206	4.67274	4.64915	. . .	4.63459	4.60748	. . .
Omani rial	. . .	Saudi Arabian riyal	4.22854	4.25284	4.27688	4.26837	4.24682	4.24044	4.23352	4.20875	4.21853
Portuguese escudo	67.6477	Singapore dollar	2.65857	2.67130	2.67032	2.67014	2.66177	2.65777	2.64770	2.65120	2.65101
Qatar riyal	4.64249	South African rand	0.949343	0.951533	0.952095	0.952315	0.949621	0.949747	0.949117	0.948655	0.949222
Singapore dollar	2.67007	Spanish peseta	101.520	101.441	. . .	101.284	101.767	101.708	101.575	102.033	102.079
South African rand	. . .	Swedish krona	5.58421	5.60352	. . .	5.57841	5.58537	5.59929	5.58125	5.62011	5.61515
Swiss franc	2.24919	Swiss franc	. . .	2.26302	2.25060	2.25254	2.26966	2.26918	2.28394	2.29766	2.29006
Trinidad and Tobago dollar	3.06098	Trinidad and Tobago dollar	3.05218	3.06972	3.08707	3.08093	3.06538	3.06077	3.05578	3.03790	3.04495
U.A.E. dirham	4.68203	U.A.E. dirham	4.66856	4.69539	4.72193	4.71254	4.68875	4.68170	4.67406	4.64672	4.65751
Venezuelan bolívar	5.47470	Venezuelan bolívar	5.45894	. . .	5.52136	5.51037	5.48255	5.47431	5.46538	5.43340	5.44602

[1] Until December 31, 1980, the value of the SDR in terms of the U.S. dollar was determined as the sum of the dollar values, based on market exchange rates, of specified quantities of the first 16 currencies shown.

[2] Beginning January 1, 1981, the value of the SDR in terms of the U.S. dollar is determined as the sum of the dollar values, based on market exchange rates, of specified quantities of the first 5 currencies shown.

Source: IMF Survey (February 9, 1981), p. 38.

against one another, while permitting a 4.5 percent against other countries. This system became known as "a snake within a tunnel." The snake was the narrower band of 2.25 percent permitted among the EEC countries and the tunnel was the wider band of 4.5 percent allowed by the Smithsonian Agreement.

England, Ireland, and Denmark joined the EEC in 1973. This was followed by a series of international monetary crises such as a devaluation of the U. S. dollar in February. In mid-March, the values of all major currencies were permitted to fluctuate according to market forces. Thus, the tunnel was gone in March 1973, but the EEC countries had tried to maintain the snake. Some of these attempts had been short-lived. For instance, such countries as France had withdrawn from the snake and rejoined it several times. Finally, France abandoned the snake in March 1976. Many causes of conflict between domestic economic goals and exchange stability had intensified domestic pressures of many participating countries to abandon the snake. The number of participating countries in the snake fell to six by late 1978: the German mark, the Dutch guilder, the Norwegian krone, the Belgian franc, the Danish krone, and the Luxembourg franc. The three main initial members of the snake–England, France, and Italy–had abandoned it some years earlier.

Many problems had raised serious questions about the snake's viability. The sharp decline in the exchange rate of the U. S. dollar during the second half of 1978 further bolstered the desire of European countries for exchange stability. On December 5, 1978, the European Council[13] adopted a resolution to establish the European Monetary System (EMS), which went into effect on March 13, 1979. The EMS is a complex exchange rate and intervention system combined with large credit facilities. All EEC members except England had subsequently declared that they would participate in the EMS. The EMS officially replaced the snake.

The European Currency Unit (ECU) is the cornerstone of the EMS. The ECU is used as the denominator for the exchange rate mechanism, as the basis for a "divergence indicator" to show when one currency diverges from the average of the other participating currencies, and as the denominator for operations under both the intervention and credit mechanisms. The value of an ECU is a weighted average value of a basket of the nine currencies of the EEC countries. The value of the basket was equal to one SDR on June 28, 1974, but

[13]The European Council consists of the Heads of State and Governments of the EEC countries.

these two values have developed differently since then. For example, on March 1, 1979, the value of an SDR was $1.28800, while the value of an ECU was $1.35219. The difference between the two values reflects differences in their composition. Table 4-6 shows the units of each currency in the ECU and its percentage weight.

Each participating currency has a central rate in terms of ECUs. These central rates determine a grid of bilateral central rates. Each currency is allowed to fluctuate within a margin of plus or minus 2.25 percent from the bilateral central rate. Those EEC countries that did not participate in the snake may temporarily set their fluctuation margins of up to plus or minus six percent. Of course, they should gradually reduce these margins as soon as their economic conditions allow. Table 4-7 shows ECU central rates and intervention limits as of March 23, 1981.

PROPOSALS FOR FURTHER INTERNATIONAL MONETARY REFORM

The reader would suspect by now that the Bretton Woods system had three basic defects: (1) pegged parities, (2) dollar disequilibrium, and (3) inadequate international reserves. Some important reforms introduced to solve these problems include SDRs, the Smithsonian Agreement, the snake within the tunnel, and the European Monetary System. These reforms are inadequate to maintain orderly markets

Table 4-6 Currency Weights of the ECU

Currency	Absolute Amounts of Currency	Percentage Shares on the Basis of Market Rates on March 1, 1979
German mark	0.82800	33.02
French franc	1.15000	19.89
Pound sterling	0.08850	13.25
Dutch guilder	0.28600	10.56
Italian lira	109.00000	9.58
Belgian franc	3.66000	9.23
Danish krone	0.21700	3.10
Irish pound	0.00759	1.11
Luxembourg franc	0.1400	0.35

Source: IMF Survey (March 19, 1979), p. 1.

Table 4-7

European Monetary System:
ECU-Related Central Rates and Intervention Limits (as of March 23, 1981)

Currency Units		100 Belgian/ Luxembourg francs	100 Danish kroner	100 Deutsche mark	100 French francs	100 Italian lire	100 Irish pounds	100 Netherlands guilders	1 ECU
Belgian/ Luxembourg franc	U	...	526.9	1,639.55	696.0	3.430	6,090.2	1,483.25	
	C	...	515.186	1,603.07	680.512	3.23048	5,954.71	1,450.26	40.7985
	L	...	503.75	1,567.4	665.375	3.0425	5,822.25	1,418.0	
Danish krone	U	19.8520	...	318.26	135.095	0.6658	1,182.14	287.90	
	C	19.4105	...	311.165	132.091	0.627052	1,155.84	281.503	7.91917
	L	18.9785	...	304.23	129.15	0.59056	1,130.13	275.245	
Deutsche mark	U	6.38	32.87	...	43.415	0.2140	379.9	92.525	
	C	6.238	32.1373	...	42.4505	0.201518	371.457	90.4673	2.54502
	L	6.099	31.42	...	41.505	0.1898	363.2	88.455	
French franc	U	15.029	77.43	240.93	...	0.50405	894.95	217.96	
	C	14.6948	75.7054	235.568	...	0.474714	875.034	213.113	5.99526
	L	14.368	74.02	230.33	...	0.4471	855.55	208.38	
Italian lira	U	3,286.80	16,933.0	52,690.0	22,367.0	...	195,721.0	47,668.0	
	C	3,095.51	15,947.6	49,623.2	21,065.3	...	184,329.0	44,893.0	1,262.92
	L	2,915.30	15,019.0	46,735.0	19,839.5	...	173,600.0	42,280.0	
Irish pound	U	1.71755	8.84854	27.533	11.6881	0.0576034	...	24.9089	
	C	1.67934	8.65169	26.921	11.4281	0.0542508	...	24.3548	0.685145
	L	1.64198	8.45922	26.323	11.1739	0.0510933	...	23.813	
Netherlands guilder	U	7.052	36.33	113.05	47.99	0.236525	419.95	...	
	C	6.89531	35.5237	110.537	46.9235	0.222752	410.597	...	2.81318
	L	6.742	34.735	108.0775	45.88	0.2098	401.45	...	

Legend: U = Upper limit.
C = Bilateral central rate.
L = Lower limit.

Source: IMF Survey (April 6, 1981), p. 111.

for many reasons. Some of these reasons include: (1) continuous huge trade surpluses of Germany and Japan; (2) the build-up of funds in the hands of oil exporting countries; (3) increasing economic difficulties of some industrial countries such as England and Italy; (4) huge U. S. balance of merchandise trade deficits, and (5) the recent collapse of a pro-Western government in Iran. These and other problems have recently increased the need for further international monetary reform. Proposals for further international monetary reform may be divided into two broad categories: proposals for greater flexibility and other proposals.

Proposals for Greater Flexibility

The concept of additional flexibility or even a system of freely flexible exchange rates has been suggested to restructure the current international monetary system so that deficit countries might solve their payments problems. It appears reasonable to assume that fixed exchange rates, which existed under the gold standard before World War I, are now practically impossible. A quarter of a century after the Bretton Woods Agreement, fixed but adjustable exchange rates could not accommodate highly diversified modern economies. Countries differ too much in price levels, wage costs, monetary policies, and extent of international capital flows to keep fixed exchange rates.

A wider band has been frequently suggested as an alternative to the present international monetary system. The Bretton Woods Agreement allowed a band of two percent. The Smithsonian Agreement approved a band of 4.5 percent. Proponents of this wider band would like to see the band expanded further. They argue that the wider band would allow central banks to enjoy greater freedom for independent monetary policies.

The crawling peg is another proposal made by some people. This proposal would provide for regular modification of par value according to an agreed formula. Under this system, a country would permit its currency to appreciate or depreciate slowly rather than fight to maintain a band of certain percentages around par value. This proposal would provide relatively stable exchange rates for those nations which consider this stability essential for international transactions. Balance of payments problems would also be self-adjusted through international price mechanisms rather than through exchange controls, restrictions on growth of national income and employment, price controls, or other unpopular internal policies.

Finally, the crawling or gliding band combines the wider band and the crawling peg. In other words, this proposal represents a compromise between the inflexible exchange rates of the gold standard and a system of indefinitely fluctuating exchange rates. Each parity level would be adjusted upward or downward as a moving average of the actual exchange rates that could fluctuate within a wider band. (1) Within one year the exchange rate parity would be allowed to move a predetermined maximum, say, two percent. This two percent is called an annual crawling. (2) This slowly crawling peg would be surrounded by a wider band within which the actual exchange rate can fluctuate.

> ***Example 4-1*** Assume: (1) the dollar-pound parity begins at \$4.00 in 1980; (2) the parity can move up to two percent each year; (3) the actual exchange rate is permitted to float within 2.5 percent on either side of the parity; and (4) British costs rise faster than American.

Figure 4-1 shows how the crawling band might work. Even if the IMF permits a wider band of five or six percent, pegging the dollar-pound parity at \$4.00 per pound would eventually lead to huge English deficits and American surpluses. This is because England's costs

Figure 4-1 Hypothetical Crawling Band.

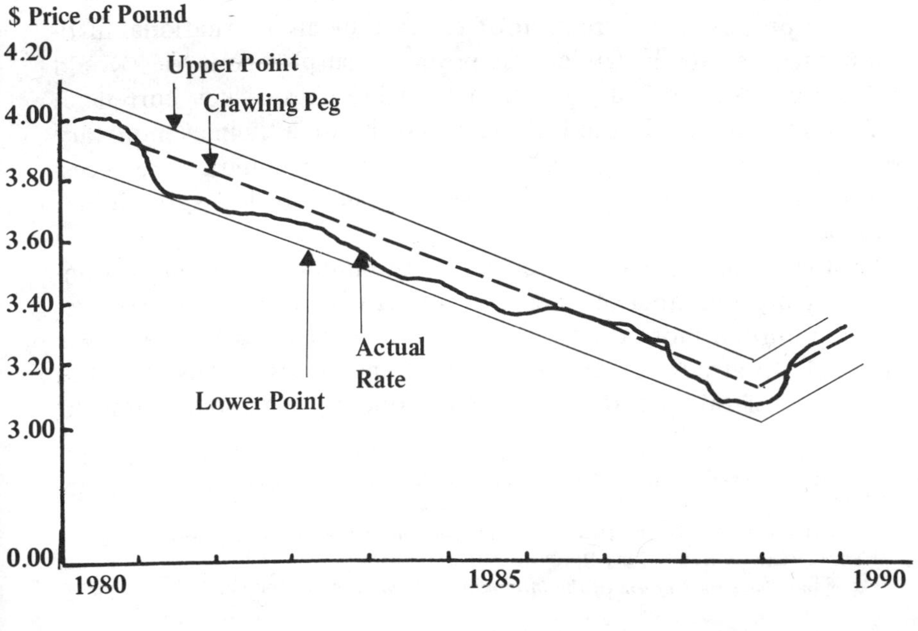

rise faster than America's. However, under the crawling band, the exchange rate is not held within the band as formerly set by the gold points or IMF system. The exchange rates can vary between a lower point of \$3.90 (\$4.00 – \$4.00 × 0.025) and an upper point of \$4.10 (\$4.00 + \$4.00 × 0.025) in 1980. In 1981, with parity moved to \$3.92 (\$4.00 – \$4.00 × 0.02) by the British deficit, the range would be from \$3.822 (\$3.92 – \$3.92 × 0.025) to \$4.018 (\$3.92 + \$3.92 × 0.025). Thus, if the parity is allowed to move by two percent per year, it would produce enough flexibility to permit a 20 percent adjustment of exchange rates over a period of ten years. This 20 percent adjustment and a wider ban of five percent should be sufficient to adjust for the normal differences between England and America in their trends of cost-push inflations.

Other Proposals

A number of proposals over the years have suggested the creation of a supercentral institution which would perform the same functions for an international economy as the commercial banking system performs for a domestic economy.

Keynes proposed the establishment of an International Clearing Union that would create an international money called bancors.[14] Under this system, deficit countries could borrow bancors to finance their deficits.

Triffin proposed the creation of reserves by an international institution such as IMF.[15] Under this proposal, surplus countries would be required to deposit a portion of their holdings of key currencies (dollars and pounds) in the IMF instead of holding them as monetary reserves. On the basis of these deposits, the IMF could create necessary international monetary reserves through its loans to deficit countries.

Another proposal calls for enlarging the number of reserve countries.[16] A larger number of reserve countries would spread the reserve-currency burden more evenly and provide the monetary system less vulnerable to attack. Freely flexible exchange rates, discussed in the earlier part of this chapter, have been frequently suggested to reform

[14] Fritz Machlup, *Plans for Reform of the International Monetary System*, Special Papers in International Economics, No. 3 (Princeton, N. J.: Princeton University Press, 1964), pp. 39-45.

[15] Robert Triffin, *Our International Monetary System: Yesterday, Today, and Tomorrow* (New York: Random House, Inc., 1968).

[16] Machlup, *Plans for Reform of the International Monetary System*, pp. 24-30.

the international monetary system. Completely flexible exchange rates have never been tried. It seems unlikely they ever will be.

SUMMARY

The efficient management of multinational business requires the financial manager to understand the international monetary system. Foreign exchange rates determine prices of goods and services which multinational companies buy and sell across national boundaries. The exchange rates also have an important impact on foreign investments.

This chapter has discussed the evolution of the international monetary system of the late nineteenth century to the current dirty floating system. The pre-1914 gold standard represents one extreme of the international monetary system. Under this system, the exchange rate for each currency was fixed in terms of gold. The flow of gold restored the balance-of-payments equilibrium. In the case of the deficit, a gold outflow would take place to finance the external deficit. In the case of the surplus, a gold inflow would occur to eliminate the external surplus.

The world had experienced the international monetary disorder from 1914 to 1945. World War I ended the stability of exchange rates for currencies of major trading nations. The Great Depression of 1929-1932 and the subsequent international financial crisis resulted in the international monetary chaos. Thus, the international monetary system from 1914 to 1945 presented a mixture of widely fluctuating exchange rates and exchange rates maintained by exchange controls.

The Bretton Woods Agreement of 1945 marked a new era for the operation of the international monetary system. This monetary system was a system of fixed exchange rates based on a revised gold standard called the gold exchange standard. Each currency was kept fixed within a narrow range of values in relation to gold or the U. S. dollar. The complexity of the provisions and a conflict of interests among countries led to some disputes and unwillingness to abide by the Agreement. However, the Bretton Woods Agreement and the activity of the IMF were the main features of the international monetary system from 1945 to 1973.

Two problems raised serious questions about the viability of the Bretton Woods Agreement as the international monetary system. The first problem had to do with the possibility of inadequate growth of monetary reserves. The second problem was the question of whether effective balance-of-payments adjustments could be achieved under the Agreement. Attempts to save the Bretton Woods Agreement through the introduction of SDRs and the Smithsonian Agreement failed. The various stresses eventually brought down the whole system in 1973. Since 1973, the international monetary system has been characterized by a confusing mixture of freely floating, managed floating, joint floating, and fixed rates.

REFERENCES

4-1 Baldwin, Robert E., and J. David Richardson, eds., *International Trade and Finance* (Boston: Little, Brown and Company, 1981), Part V.

4-2 Bodner, David E., "Official Intervention in the Foreign Exchange Market: The System in Transition," *Columbia Journal of World Business* (Fall 1976), pp. 16-22.

4-3 Carlozzi, Nicholas, "Pegs and Floats: The Changing Face of the Foreign Exchange Market," *Current Federal Reserve Readings in Economics for Teachers* (Federal Reserve Bank of New York, 1980), pp. 239-249.

4-4 Cline, William R., *International Monetary Reform and the Developing Countries* (Washington, D. C.: The Brookings Institute, 1976).

4-5 Driskill, Robert. "Exchange Rate Overshooting, the Trade Balance, and Rational Expectations," *Journal of International Economics* (August 1981), pp. 361-378.

4-6 Eitman, David K., and Arthur I. Stonehill, *Multinational Business Finance* (Readings, Mass.: Addison-Wesley Publishing Co., 1979), 26-38.

4-7 Feiger, George, and Bertrand Jacquillat, *International Finance* (Boston: Little, Brown and Company, 1982), Chapter 2.

4-8 Friedman, Milton, and Robert V. Roosa, "Free Versus Fixed Exchange Rates: A Debate," *Journal of Portfolio Management* (Spring 1977), pp. 68-73.

4-9 Henning, Charles N., William Piggot, and Robert H. Scott, *International Financial Management* (New York: McGraw-Hill Book Co., 1978), pp. 85-96.

4-10 Johnson, Harry G., *The Problem of International Monetary Reform* (London: Athlone Press, 1974).

4-11 Machlup, Fritz, *Plans for Reform of the International Monetary System* (Princeton, N. J.: Princeton University Press, 1964).

4-12 Solomon, Robert, "On the Past and Future of the International Monetary System," *Columbia Journal of World Business* (Fall 1976), pp. 23-27.

4-13 Triffin, Robert, *Our International Monetary System: Yesterday, Today and Tomorrow* (New York: Random House, Inc., 1968).

4-14 Whitman, Marina N., "Global Monetarism: Theory, Policy and Critique," *Journal of Portfolio Management* (Spring 1977), pp. 7-18.

4-15 Wilby, William L., "Interest Rates and Exchange Rates under the Fed's New Operating Procedures: The Uneasy Marriage," *Economic Perspectives* (Federal Reserve Bank of Chicago, 1980), 3-13.

4-16 Yeager, Leland B., *International Monetary Relations: Theory, History, and Policy* (New York: Harper and Row, 1976).

APPENDIX 4A
AMENDED ARTICLES OF AGREEMENT OF THE IMF[1]

Reform of the international monetary system that began in 1971 following the collapse of the postwar Bretton Woods system was formally completed April 1, 1978, when the Second Amendment to the International Monetary Fund's Articles of Agreement went into force with ratification by the required majority of the 133 member nations.

The Second Amendment contains several major provisions, some of which have been already informally adopted by member nations. Provisions on exchange rate arrangements are based on recognition that the essential purpose of the international monetary system is to provide a framework that both facilitates the exchange of goods, services, and capital among countries and sustains sound economic growth for all nations. In ratifying the amendment, members undertake a general obligation to collaborate with the IMF and with other members to ensure orderly exchange arrangements and promote a stable system of exchange rates. Members are required to seek to promote stability by fostering orderly underlying economic and financial conditions and a monetary system that does not tend to produce erratic disruptions. They must avoid manipulating exchange rates or the international monetary system in order to prevent effective balance of payments adjustment or to gain an unfair competitive advantage over other members. Members are free to apply the exchange arrangements of their choice, except that they are not to maintain a value for their currencies in terms of gold. They are required to notify the IMF of the exchange arrangements they intend to apply and of any subsequent changes in these arrangements. The IMF will oversee the international monetary system to ensure its effective operation.

The most important changes with respect to the role of gold in the international monetary system are as follows: (1) gold has been eliminated as the unit of value of the SDR and cannot be used as a common denominator for par values of currencies, even if some future time par values were introduced; (2) the official price of gold has been abolished and members are free to deal in gold in the market and among themselves without reference to any official price; (3) obligatory payments in gold by members between the IMF and its members have been abrogated; and the IMF can accept gold only under decisions taken with an 85 percent majority of the total voting power; (4) the IMF will be required to complete the announced

[1] Federal Reserve Bank of Chicago, *International Letter* (April 28, 1978).

program of disposing of a total of 50 million ounces of gold and will have powers to make further gold sales both on the basis of prices in the market and at the official price in effect before the Second Amendment (SDR 35 per ounce); (5) profits beyond the former official price on any such further sales will be placed in a Special Disbursement Account for use in the ordinary operations and transactions of the IMF or for other uses, including balance-of-payments assistance for the benefit of developing members in difficult circumstances.

The modifications in the provisions relating to the Special Drawing Rights (SDR) are intended to help make the SDR the principal reserve asset in the international monetary system. Under the amended Articles: (1) the method of valuing the SDR can be determined by the IMF by a 70 percent majority; (2) participants can enter into transactions by agreement without general or special decisions by the IMF, and transfers of SDRs in such transactions are not subject to the requirement of need to use reserve assets; (3) the SDR replaces gold in certain payments between the IMF and its members, and its possible use in operations and transactions conducted through the IMF's General Department (formerly the General Account) are to be expanded.

$£¢

FIVE

THE FOREIGN EXCHANGE MARKET

The efficient operation of the international monetary system has necessitated the creation of an institutional structure. This structure is usually called the *foreign exchange market*. It is a market where one country's currency can be exchanged for another country's. Unlike the term might suggest, the foreign exchange market is not a geographic location. It is an informal network of telephone and telex communications between banks, foreign exchange brokers, and foreign exchange dealers. The market operates simultaneously at three tiers. (1) Individuals buy and sell foreign exchange through their banks. (2) Commercial banks trade in foreign exchange with other commercial banks in the same financial center. (3) Commercial banks trade in foreign exchange with commercial banks in other financial centers.

In order to understand the complex functions of the international financial management, one must first understand the organization and dynamics of the foreign exchange market. This chapter explains the roles of the major participants in the exchange market, describes the spot and forward markets, discusses the theories of exchange rate determination, and examines the roles of arbitrageurs.

THE MAJOR PARTICIPANTS IN THE EXCHANGE MARKET

The foreign exchange market consists of a spot market and a forward market. In the spot market, foreign currencies are sold and bought for delivery within two business days after the day of the trade. In the forward market, foreign currencies are currently sold or bought for future delivery.

There are many types of participants in the foreign exchange market: arbitrageurs, importers, exporters, multinational firms, tourists, governments, commercial banks, and central banks. But large commercial banks and central banks are the two major participants in the foreign exchange market.

Commercial Banks

Commercial banks participate in the foreign exchange market as an intermediary for customers such as multinational companies and exporters. These commercial banks also maintain an interbank market. In other words, they accept deposits of foreign banks and maintain deposits in banks abroad. Commercial banks play three roles in international transactions. (1) They operate the payment mechanism. (2) They extend credit. (3) They help to reduce risk.

The commercial banking system provides the mechanism by which international payments can be most quickly and efficiently made. This mechanism is a collection system through which drafts, notes, and money transfers by other means are made internationally. In order to operate an international payments mechanism, banks maintain deposits in banks abroad and accept deposits of foreign banks. These accounts are debited and credited when payments are made. They can make international money transfers very quickly and efficiently by using telegraph and telephone services.

Commercial banks also provide credit for international transactions and for business activity within foreign countries. They make loans to those engaged in international business on either an unsecured or a secured basis. U. S. banks cannot have branches outside their home state. They also cannot own shares of foreign banking subsidiaries. However, the Edge Act of 1919 allowed American banks to act as holding companies and to own stock in foreign banks. Thus, American banks can provide loans and other banking services for American-owned companies in most countries around the world.

The letter of credit is used as a major means to reduce risks in international transactions. It is a document issued by a bank at the request of the importer. In the document, the bank agrees to honor a draft drawn on the importer if the draft accompanies specified documents. The letter of credit is advantageous to exporters. Exporters sell their goods abroad against the promise of a bank rather than a commercial firm. Banks are usually larger, better known, and better credit risks than most business firms. Thus, exporters are almost completely assured of payment if they meet specific conditions under letters of credit.

Central Banks

Central banks, such as the Federal Reserve System of the United States and the Bank of England, attempt to control the growth of the money supply within their jurisdictions. They also strive to maintain the value of their own currency against any foreign currency.

In a system of fixed exchange rates, central banks usually absorb the difference between supply and demand for foreign exchange in order to maintain the par value system. Under this system, the central banks agree to maintain the value of their currencies within a narrow band of fluctuations. If such pressures as huge trade deficits and high inflation develop, the price of a domestic currency approaches the lower limit of the band. Then, the central bank is obliged to intervene in the foreign exchange market. This intervention is designed to counteract the forces prevailing in the market. In a system of flexible exchange rates, central banks do not attempt to prevent fundamental changes in the rate of exchange between their own currency and any other currency. However, even within the flexible exchange-rate system, they intervene in the foreign exchange market at least in order to maintain orderly trading conditions.

SPOT AND FORWARD EXCHANGE RATES

The foreign exchange market encompasses both spot and forward exchange rates. The spot rate is the rate paid for delivery within two business days after the day of the trade. Most currency transactions take place in the spot market. The forward rate is the rate to be paid for delivery of a currency at some future date. The exchange rate is established at the time the contract is made, but payment and delivery are not required until maturity. Forward rates are usually quoted for fixed periods of 30, 90, or 180 days from the day of the contract. In some instances, actual contracts in major currencies can be arranged for delivery at any specified date up to one year.

Foreign Exchange Quotation

Most foreign exchange quotations are made in the number of units of local currency required to buy one unit of foreign currency. Hence, the United States quotes its exchange rates in the amount of dollars that can be exchanged for one unit of foreign exchange, *i.e.*, \$0.4285/GM.[1] The quotation "\$0.4285/GM" means that one can buy one German mark for \$0.4285. The major exception to this practice is England. This nation quotes its foreign exchange rates in terms of foreign monetary units required to purchase one pound sterling. The exchange rates for the leading partners of the United States appear in the *Wall Street Journal* each day. Table 5-1 shows the spot rates for a selected number of currencies on May 27, 1982.

Column 2 in Table 5-1 shows the amount of U. S. dollars required to buy one unit of foreign currency. Given this amount, one can determine the number of foreign monetary units required to buy one U. S. dollar. This conversion can be achieved by simply taking the reciprocal of the given quotation. For example:

$$\$0.4285/\text{GM is identical with } \$1 = \frac{\text{GM}1}{\$0.4285}$$

$$= \text{GM}2.334$$

In other words, the relationship between U. S. dollars and German marks can be expressed in the two different ways which have the same meaning: (1) one can buy one German mark for \$0.4285 or (2) one can buy 2.334 German marks for \$1.00. Column 3 presents the reciprocals of the exchange rates in Column 2. Column 3 equals 1.0 divided by Column 2.

Once we understand how the two currencies in an exchange quote can be converted into each other, we can go on to see how the relationships among three or more currencies are reflected in exchange quotes. Column 2 in Table 5-2 shows that the dollar price of the British pound is \$1.7980 per pound and that the dollar price of the Canadian dollar is \$0.8089 per Can\$. To determine the price of pounds in terms of Canadian dollars or the price of Canadian dollars in terms of pounds, one must convert both quotations to a common denominator, *i.e.*, the U. S. dollar:

$$\$1.7980/£\text{: } £1/\$1.7980 = £0.5562/\$$$

$$\$0.8089/\text{Can}\$\text{: Can}\$1/\$0.8089 = \text{Can}\$1.2362/\$$$

[1] A foreign exchange trader generally quotes two numbers: the buying rate and the selling rate. The buying rate is called the bid price and the selling price is called the offer or ask price. But this chapter ignores the existence of bid and ask prices. It is assumed that there is just one rate; this rate may be treated as the mid-point between bid and ask prices. The foreign exchange rates that appear on the *Wall Street Journal* each day are quoted in terms of the selling price.

Table 5-1 Spot Rates for A Number of Currencies

Currency (1)	U. S. $ Equivalent (2)	Currency per U. S. $ (3)
Brazil (cruzeiro)	0.00612	163.35
Britain (pound)	1.7980	0.5562
Canada (dollar)	0.8089	1.2362
France (franc)	0.1658	6.0300
Hong Kong (dollar)	0.1749	5.7160
Italy (lira)	0.000779	1284.00
Japan (yen)	0.004157	240.55
Mexico (peso)	0.0213	47.07
Norway (krone)	0.1672	5.9820
Saudi Arabia (riyal)	0.2915	3.4305
South Korea (won)	0.00137	728.80
Sweden (krona)	0.1722	5.8065
Switzerland (franc)	0.5074	1.9710
Venezuela (bolivar)	0.2326	4.2987
West Germany (mark)	0.4285	2.334
SDR	1.13210	0.883312

Source: Wall Street Journal (May 27, 1982), p. 38.

Note: Because there is one-day time lag between the transactions of foreign exchange and the report of these transactions, we obtained the May 26, 1982 quotations from the May 27 *Wall Street Journal.*

If the prices of dollars are quoted in terms of both pounds and Canadian dollars, one can obtain the price of pounds in terms of Canadian dollars:

$$\text{Can\$/£} = \frac{1.2362}{0.5562} = \text{Can\$2.2226/£}$$

Similarly, one can determine the price of Canadian dollars in terms of pounds:

$$\text{£/Can\$} = \frac{0.5562}{1.2362} = \text{£0.4499/Can\$}$$

The exchange rate between two currencies is called the cross rate if it is obtained from the rates of these two currencies in terms of a third currency.

Foreign Exchange Quotation: Forward Rate

Table 5-2 shows the forward rates for Canadian dollars and German marks along with the spot rates from Table 5-1. During a period of foreign exchange stability, the current spot rate and the forward rate may be the same. However, there is usually a difference between the spot rate and the forward rate, which is known as the *spread.*

Forward quotations are made either "outright" or in terms of the spread on the spot rate. Table 5-2 shows that the 90-day outright forward quotation for Canadian dollars is $0.8059 per Can$. The spread

Table 5-2 Spot and Forward Rates

Spot or Forward Rate	Canadian Dollars	German Marks
Spot rate	$0.8089	$0.4285
30-day forward rate	0.8078	0.4308
90-day forward rate	0.8059	0.4349
180-day forward rate	0.8048	0.4407

Source: Wall Street Journal (May 27, 1982), p. 38.

is stated in terms of points; one point equals 0.01 percent or $0.0001. Point quotations for the two 90-day forward rates are determined as follows:

Spot or Forward Rate	Canadian Dollars	German Marks
90-day forward rate	$0.8059	$0.4349
less spot rate	0.8089	0.4285
90-day forward quote in points	−30	+64

In giving a forward quote for the Canadian dollar, the trader might say "minus 30" or "a discount of 30." For the German mark, the trader would say "plus 64" or "a premium of 64." Thus, when the forward rate is less than the spot rate, it is said to be at a *discount*. When the forward rate is greater than the spot rate, it is said to be at a *premium*. Outright quotations are normally used for retail customers of the bank, while point quotations are usually employed for traders.

Forward premium or discount is sometimes expressed in terms of the annualized percentage deviation from the spot rate. The premium or discount is computed by the following formula:

$$\text{Premium (discount)} = \frac{\text{n-day forward rate} - \text{spot rate}}{\text{spot rate}} \times \frac{360}{n} \qquad (5\text{-}1)$$

Applying Equation 5-1 to the 90-day forward quote for Canadian dollars, we obtain:

$$\text{Forward discount} = \frac{\$0.8059 - \$0.8089}{\$0.8089} \times \frac{360}{90}$$

$$= -0.0148 \text{ or } -1.48\%$$

Applying Equation 5-1 to the 90-day forward quote for German marks, we obtain:

$$\text{Forward premium} = \frac{\$0.4349 - \$0.4285}{\$0.4285} \times \frac{360}{90}$$

$$= +0.0597 \text{ or } +5.97\%$$

The Major Reason for Forward Exchange Transactions

Individuals and corporations buy and sell forward currencies to provide protection against future changes in exchange rates. So long as we do not have a single world currency, some degree of exchange risk exists in any system. In either the fixed exchange-rate system or the flexible exchange-rate system, we cannot eliminate some possibility of foreign exchange losses.

> ***Example 5-1*** Assume that an American firm purchased machinery through its U. K. branch for 10,000 pounds with terms of 90 days. Let us also assume that the spot rate for pounds is $1.70 and the 90-day forward rate for pounds is $1.80. Payment should be made in British pounds 90 days from the day of the shipment.

Actually, there are two alternative ways of payment available to the American firm. (1) It could buy pounds in the spot market 90 days from the day of the shipment to pay the credit. If the spot rate for pounds rises to $2.00 during this time, the American firm should spend $20,000 to buy the sum of 10,000 pounds. (2) It could also buy 10,000 pounds in the forward market for $18,000 to pay the credit on the due date. By so doing, the American firm would avoid the risk of a $2,000 loss ($20,000 – $18,000). However, if the spot rate for pounds declines to $1.50 during this period, it would incur a loss of $3,000 ($15,000 – $18,000) under the forward contract.

THEORIES OF FOREIGN EXCHANGE-RATE DETERMINATION

In this section, specific attention is given to the theory of exchange rate determination. This theory is based on the relationship between the money market and the foreign exchange market. The relationship discussed here prevails without restrictions imposed by governmental policy on the extent to which rates can move. Such a free market situation will establish the nature of interrelationships among the money markets and the foreign exchange markets.

There are five major theories of exchange-rate determination: (1) the purchasing power parity theory, (2) the interest parity theory, (3) the balance of payments theory, (4) the monetary approach, and (5) the asset markets or portfolio balance approach. When considered in isolation, each may project a different course for exchange rates, but the actual exchange rate depends on a number of variables. This is because these variables are highly interrelated with each other. For example, relative inflation rates affect both interest and exchange rates. If foreign countries have higher rates of inflation than the United States, they tend to have higher interest rates. Of course, foreign countries are likely to have lower interest rates.

Efficient Exchange Markets

Investors make risk-return decisions in the framework of available exchange markets. Our discussion for the theories of exchange rate determination is based on the assumption of efficient exchange markets. Efficient exchange markets exist when exchange rates reflect all available information and adjust quickly to new information. Because exchange markets are highly competitive in such a situation, the market participants buy and sell foreign exchange in a way that eliminates all profits in excess of the minimum required to sustain their continued participation.

In other words, the concept of efficient exchange markets depends on two hypotheses. (1) Market prices such as spot rates, forward rates, and interest rates should reflect the market's consensus estimate of the future spot rate. (2) Investors should not earn unusually large profits in forward speculation. Because exchange-rate forecasts based on market prices are accurate, publicly available forecasts of the future spot rate do not lead to unusual profits in forward speculation.

Certainly these conditions are not completely met in practice. Thus, exchange markets are assumed to be efficient if the conditions are only reasonably met. There are many indications that support the efficient market assumption for international money and exchange markets. First, foreign currencies and other financial assets are traded by companies and individuals who have broad market contacts, sophisticated analytical capabilities, and modern communications. Because new information is widely, quickly, and cheaply disseminated to investors, market prices are rapidly adjusted to reflect significant developments. Second, since 1973 the major trading countries of the world have adopted the system of freely floating rates and their governmental interference in exchange markets has been minimal.

Market Equilibrium

Exchange rates represent prices of one currency in terms of another currency. In a free market, they are determined by the forces of supply and demand, just like other free market prices.

Demand for foreign exchange comes from debit items in the balance of payments such as imports. As the foreign exchange rate falls, the corresponding quantity of the foreign exchange demanded rises. Alternatively, as the exchange rate increases, the corresponding quantity demanded falls. In short, there is an inverse relationship between exchange rate and quantity demanded. This inverse relationship explains why the demand curve for foreign exchange is down-sloping. The supply of foreign exchange comes from credit items in the balance of payments such as exports. As the foreign exchange rate falls, the corresponding quantity of the foreign exchange supplied falls. As the exchange rate increases, the corresponding quantity supplied also increases. This direct relationship between exchange rate and quantity supplied explains why the supply curve for foreign exchange is upsloping.

Figure 5-1 shows the downsloping demand curve D and the upsloping supply curve S. The intersection of these two curves indicates the equilibrium exchange rate (E1) and quantity (Q1). If the actual exchange rate is below the equilibrium point E1, it will rise because demand exceeds supply. If the actual exchange rate is above point E1, it will fall because supply exceeds demand.

Figure 5-1 Market Determination of Exchange Rates.

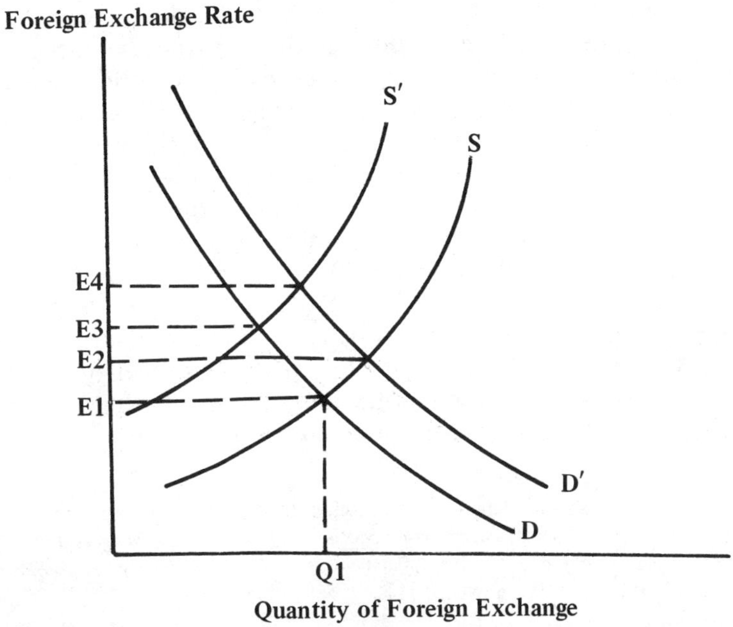

Demand for foreign exchange and its supply could change over time. These changes cause demand and supply schedules to shift upward or downward. For example, an increase in imports of goods priced in foreign currencies and a rise in prices of such goods may cause a shift of the demand curve for foreign exchange to the right. If the demand curve shifts from D to D′, the equilibrium exchange rate rises to E2. In contrast, a decrease in exports of goods priced in foreign currencies and a reduction in prices of such goods may shift the supply curve to the left. If the supply curve shifts from S to S′, the equilibrium exchange rate rises to E3. What happens to the equilibrium exchange rate if the demand curve D and the supply curve S shift to D′ and S′ simultaneously? The equilibrium exchange rate would rise still further, to E4.

The Purchasing Power Parity Theory

The theory of purchasing power parity (PPP) in its simplest form says that the exchange rate must change so as to equate the prices of goods in both countries in terms of a single currency.[2] For example, if the prices of Japanese goods rose relative to the prices of U. S. goods, the Japanese yen should depreciate to keep the dollar prices of goods in Japan the same as the dollar prices of identical goods in the United States. Otherwise, arbitrageurs would have an incentive to purchase goods in the United States and sell them in Japan until these prices were again equalized.

There are two versions of the PPP theory: absolute version and relative version. The absolute version of the PPP theory states that the equilibrium exchange rate between domestic and foreign currencies equals the rate between domestic and foreign prices. To illustrate, assume that one American dollar can buy two bushels of wheat and one Dutch guilder can buy one bushel of wheat. In the United States, exchange rates are quoted in terms of dollars required to buy one unit of foreign currency. Thus, the number of dollars required to purchase one unit of Dutch guilder or the exchange rate is $0.50 per guilder.

The relative version of the PPP doctrine indicates that in the long run, exchange rates reflect the relative purchasing power of currencies. In other words, it relates equilibrium changes in the exchange rate to changes in the ratio of domestic and foreign prices.

[2] The PPP theory was advanced by Gustav Cassel, even though it can be found in economic theory much earlier. See Gustav Cassel, *Money and Foreign Exchange after 1914* (New York: Macmillan Company, 1927); and Gustav Cassel, *The Theory of Social Economy* (New York: Harcourt, Brace & Javanovich, 1934).

Example 5-2 This time let us assume that the exchange rate between U. S. dollars and British pounds is $2 per pound. Let us further accept the fact that the United States will have an inflation rate of 10 percent for the coming year and England will have an inflation rate of 20 percent over the same period.

The PPP theory suggests that the U. S. dollar should increase in value by 10 percent relative to the British pound. The new exchange rate of $1.83 per pound is obtained in this way:[3]

$$\text{New exchange rate} = \frac{\$2(1 + 0.10)}{£1(1 + 0.20)} = \$1.83/£$$

If a country experiences higher inflation rates than its major trading partners, its exports will become more expensive and its imports will become relatively less costly. This combination will lead the country with higher inflation rates to develop a deficit in its balance of payments. This deficit will put downward pressure on the country's spot rate because its demand for foreign currency to settle its imports will be greater than other countries' demand for the country's currency for the same purpose. Simultaneously, the additional supply of imports in the country has a depressing effect on the country's overall price level. Normally, an increased supply of relatively inexpensive imports should reduce the price inflation in the country. Thus, the PPP theory works on both the exchange rate and the relative price levels to restore equilibrium in the balance of payments between countries.

Empirical Evidence. As mentioned earlier, the PPP theory of exchange rate determination explains exchange rate movements by differences in inflation rates between countries. In other words, currencies of countries with higher inflation rates than the United States tend to depreciate in value against the dollar. By the same token, currencies of countries with lower inflation rates than the United States tend to appreciate in value against the dollar.

Figure 5-2 illustrates how currencies of U. S. major trading partners have moved in comparison to the U. S. dollar during the 1975-1981 period. Figure 5-3 shows the relative rates of inflation between the United States and each of its major trading partners during the 1975-1981 period.

The casual empiricism confirms the general legitimacy of the pur-

[3] Typically, a decrease in the price of an item accompanies a lower number while an increase in the price of an item accompanies a higher number. This may not be true in a foreign exchange quotation. In our example, the price of British pounds in terms of U. S. dollars has decreased from $2.00 per pound to $1.83 per pound. In this case, one can say that the dollar has appreciated by $0.17. Alternatively, one can say that the pound has depreciated by $0.17.

Figure 5-2 Movements in Exchange Rates.

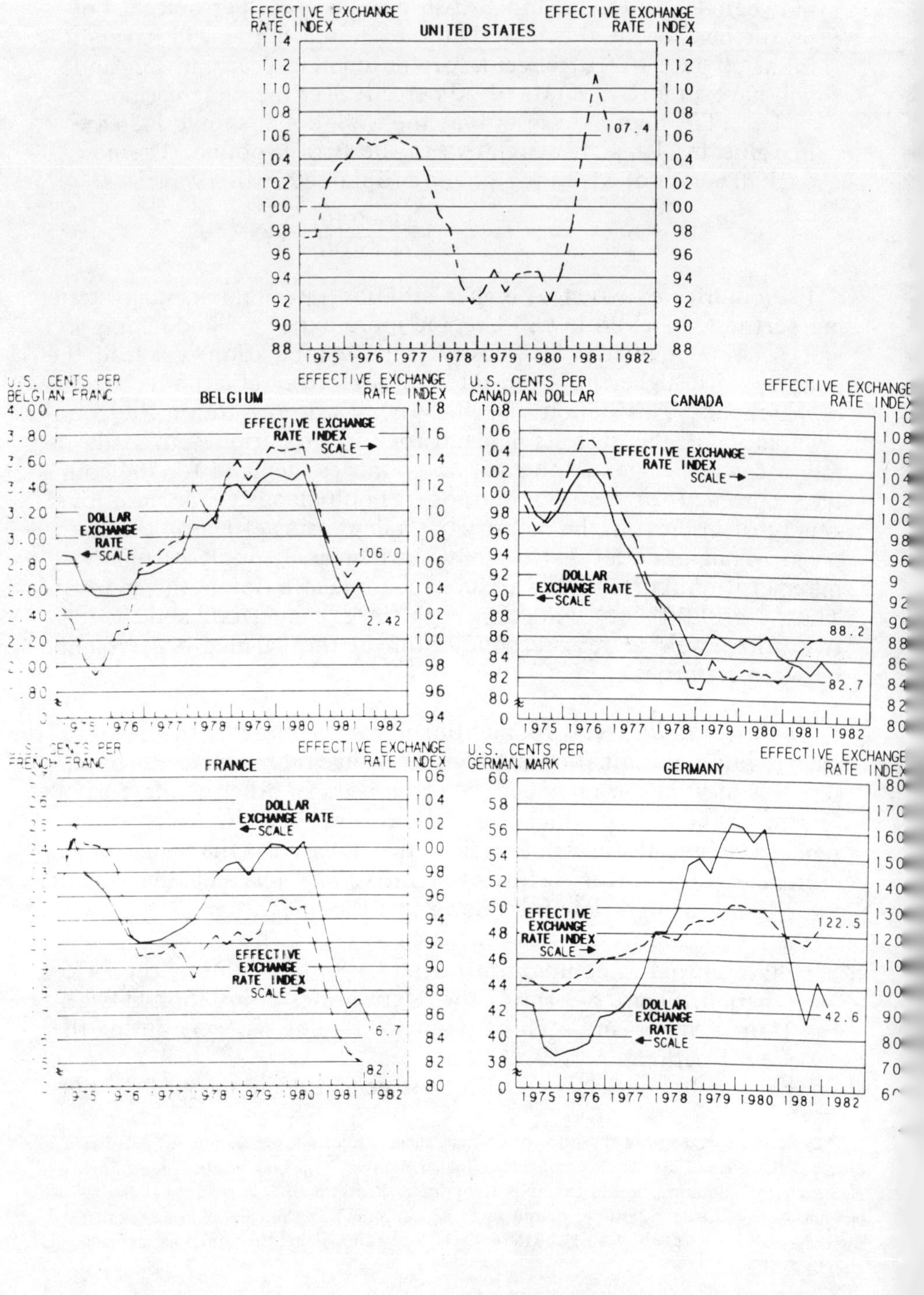

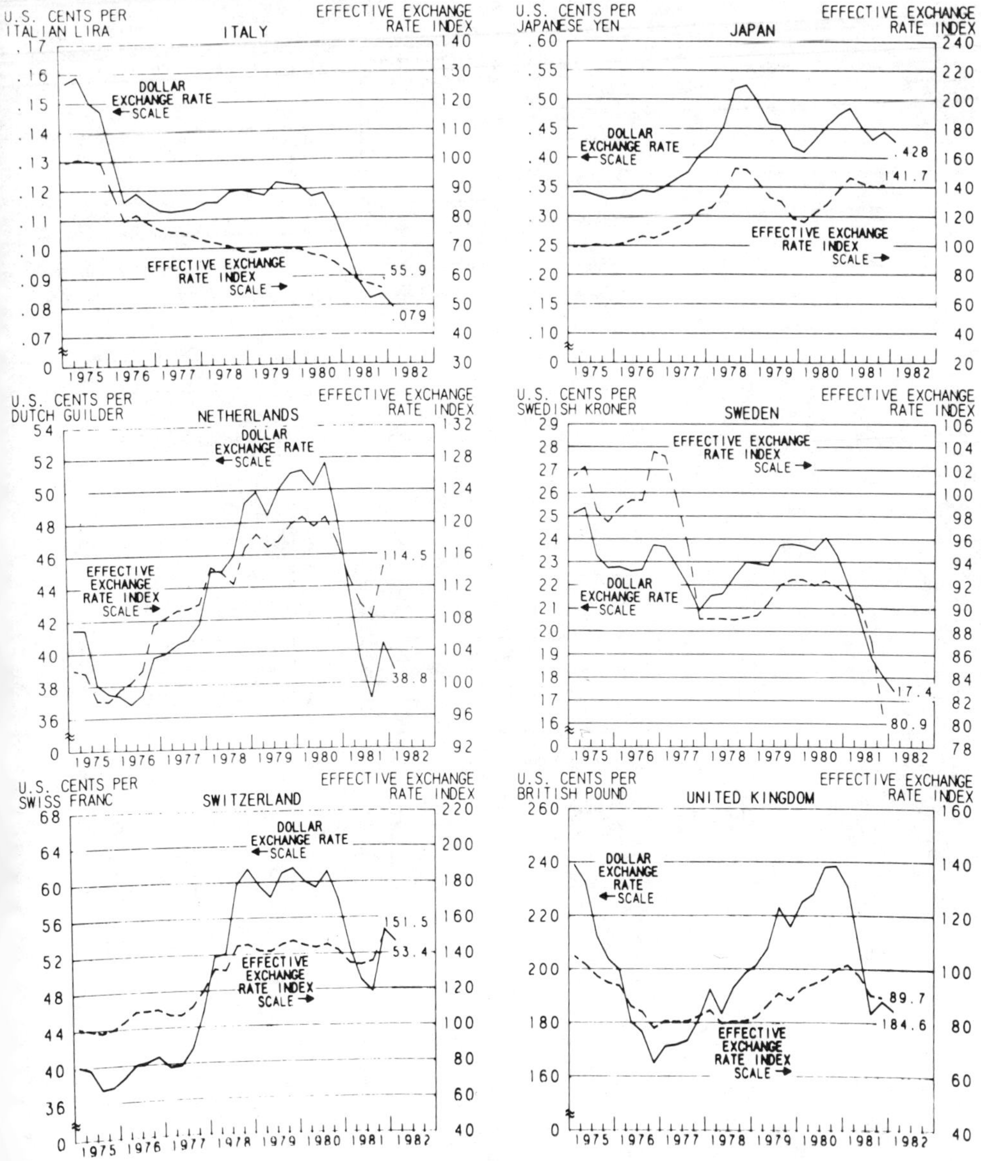
ITALY
U.S. CENTS PER ITALIAN LIRA
EFFECTIVE EXCHANGE RATE INDEX
DOLLAR EXCHANGE RATE ←SCALE
EFFECTIVE EXCHANGE RATE INDEX SCALE →
55.9
.079
JAPAN
U.S. CENTS PER JAPANESE YEN
DOLLAR EXCHANGE RATE ←SCALE
EFFECTIVE EXCHANGE RATE INDEX SCALE →
.428
141.7
NETHERLANDS
U.S. CENTS PER DUTCH GUILDER
DOLLAR EXCHANGE RATE ←SCALE
EFFECTIVE EXCHANGE RATE INDEX SCALE →
114.5
38.8
SWEDEN
U.S. CENTS PER SWEDISH KRONER
EFFECTIVE EXCHANGE RATE INDEX SCALE →
DOLLAR EXCHANGE RATE ←SCALE
17.4
80.9
SWITZERLAND
U.S. CENTS PER SWISS FRANC
DOLLAR EXCHANGE RATE ←SCALE
EFFECTIVE EXCHANGE RATE INDEX SCALE →
151.5
53.4
UNITED KINGDOM
U.S. CENTS PER BRITISH POUND
DOLLAR EXCHANGE RATE ←SCALE
EFFECTIVE EXCHANGE RATE INDEX SCALE →
89.7
184.6
1975 1976 1977 1978 1979 1980 1981 1982

Figure 5-3 Relative Rates of Inflation.

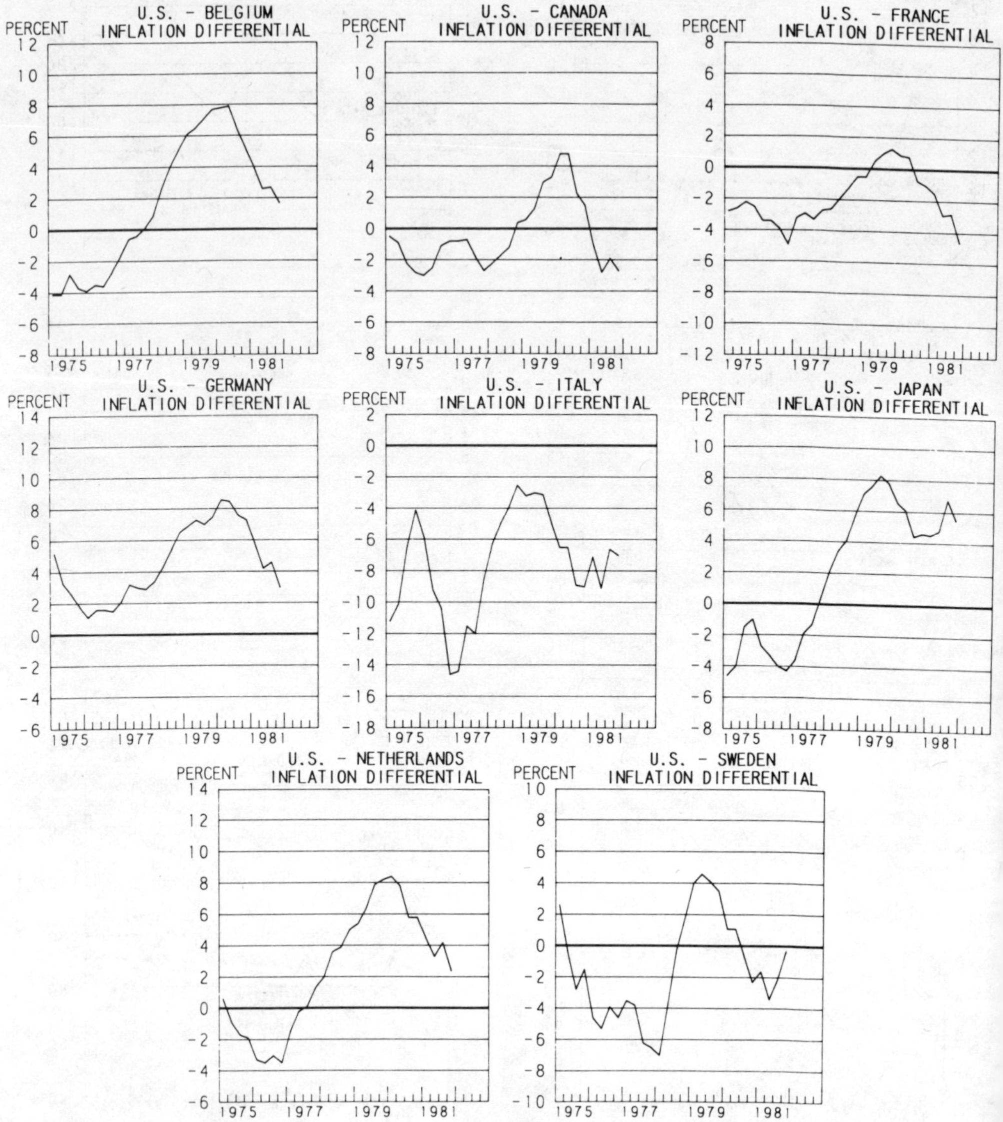

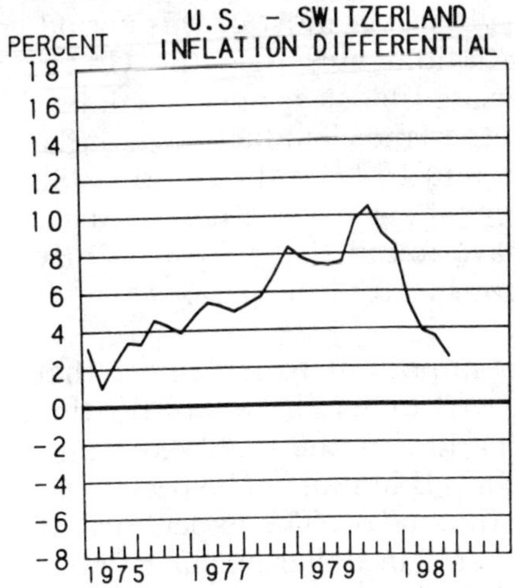

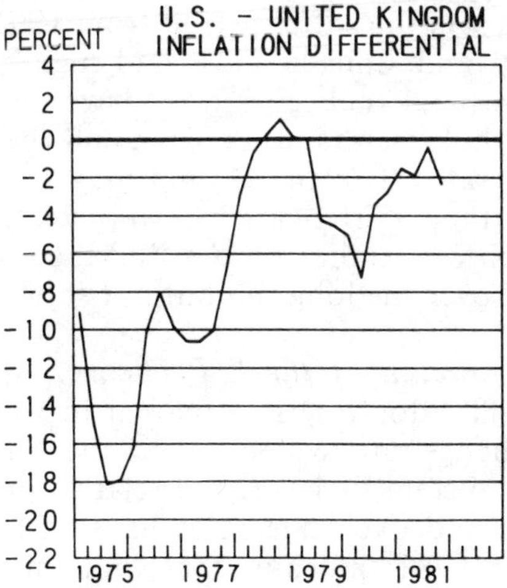

Note: Effective exchange rate changes are an indicator to which the external value of a country's currency has moved relative to other currencies. Effective exchange rate changes are computed as an index, combining the exchange rates between the currency in question and seventeen other major currencies with weights derived from the International Monetary Fund's "Multilateral Exchange Rate Model."* Each weight represents the model's estimate of the effect on the trade balance of the country in question of a change of one percent in the domestic currency price of one of the other currencies. The weights, therefore, take account of the size of trade flows as well as of the relevant price elasticities and the feedback effects of exchange rate changes on domestic costs and prices. The measure is expressed as an index based on average exchange rates during 1975.

Relative rates of inflation are the comparison of rates of changes in consumer price index over corresponding four-quarter periods. For example, the U. S.-Belgium inflation differential for 1/77 is computed by subtracting the percentage change in the Belgian CPI over the 1/76-1/77 period from the percentage change in the U. S. CPI over the same four-quarter period. Data are *seasonally adjusted*.

*Jacques R. Artus and Rudolf R. Rhomberg, "A Multilateral Exchange Rate Model," *International Monetary Fund Staff Papers* (November 1973), pp. 591-611.

Source: International Economic Conditions (Federal Reserve Bank of St. Louis, April 20, 1982), pp. 3-5.

chasing power parity doctrine. Although the year-to-year changes in the inflation rates and exchange rates frequently diverge, there is a rough correspondence between these two changes for some countries over the entire period from 1975-1981. Over most of this period, Italy and Canada have had higher inflation rates than the United States and their currencies have depreciated most against the dollar. On the other hand, Belgium and the Netherlands had had lower inflation rates than the United States from mid-1977 to the end of 1980 and their currencies had appreciated most against the dollar. Many empirical studies of the PPP theory have found that it works fairly well over the long run but not so well for shorter time periods.[4]

Appraisal of the PPP Theory. It is important to remember that the PPP doctrine is supposed to work well under the freely floating exchange-rate system. With the termination of the fixed exchange-rate system in 1973, the relative price levels in most industrial countries and exchange rates have widely fluctuated. The experience of 1975-1981 indicates that while movements in dollar exchange rates for some major currencies reflected differences in inflation rates, it was not the case for sharp short-period fluctuations in these rates. In addition, the PPP theory did not work that well for some other currencies.

There are some obvious weaknesses of the PPP theory. First, the theory assumes that goods are identical across countries and are readily transported for arbitrage purposes. This is not the case for such goods as housing and medical services. The PPP theory relies on an index of prices such as the consumer price index. This may be misleading because only traded goods directly affect the balance on goods and services. However, even nontraded goods indirectly affect the price of traded goods through their impact on the overall cost of living and on wage demands.

Second, the tests of the PPP theory require us to compare a similar basket of goods in each country with its trading partners. In order to compare the prices of dissimilar goods, we have to rely on price indices. It then becomes a question of which index is most reflective of goods traded between countries.

[4] For example, see Edward M. Bernstein, "The Dollar Under the Regime of Floating Exchange Rates," in Mark B. Winchester, *The International Essays for Business Decision Makers* (edited), (Houston: The Center for International Business, 1980), pp. 244-249; Richard J. Rogalski and Joseph D. Vinso, "Price Level Variations as Predictors of Flexible Exchange Rates," *Journal of International Business Studies* (Spring/Summer 1977), pp. 71-81; Lawrence H. Officer, "The Purchasing-Power-Parity Theory of Exchange Rates," *IMF Staff Papers* (March 1976), pp. 1-60; and Henry J. Gailliot, "Purchasing Power Parity as Explanation of Long-Term Changes in Exchange Rates," *Journal of Money, Credit, and Banking* (August 1970), pp. 348-357.

Third, many other factors influence exchange rates besides relative prices. They include relative interest rates, government interference in the foreign exchange market, and multiple currency practices such as the joint floating system of the EEC. Thus, it is difficult to measure the precise magnitude of exchange rate movements attributable to differences in inflation rates.

Despite all these limitations, the main implication of the PPP theory is quite useful and remains at least approximately valid over the long run. If a country's inflation rate remains higher than that of its trading partners for a long period of time, that country's currency will tend to depreciate so that it does not price itself out of the export market. According to many empirical studies, this fact exists regardless of whether it is caused by the PPP doctrine alone or by a combination of many factors.

The Interest Parity Theory

The interest parity theory depends on the Fisher Effect.[5] The Fisher Effect assumes that nominal interest rates in each country consist of the real interest rate (the required rate of return to the investor) and the expected rate of inflation. In a free market where investors can buy any interest-bearing securities, real interest rates are identical everywhere, but nominal interest rates will vary by the difference in expected rates of inflation. The international Fisher Effect holds that the exchange rate should move in response to interest rate differentials.

The interest parity theory states that the differences between the spot rate and the forward rate equals the difference between the domestic interest rate and the foreign interest rate:

$$\frac{\text{n-day F} - \text{S}}{\text{S}} \times \frac{360}{\text{n}} = i_d - i_f \qquad (5\text{-}2)$$

where n-day F = n-day forward rate, S = spot rate, i_d = domestic interest rate, and i_f = foreign interest rate.

Example 5-3 Let us assume four things: (1) the German interest rate = 9%; (2) the U. S. interest rate = 7%; the spot rate for the German mark = \$0.4000; and (4) the 180-day forward rate for the German mark = \$0.3960.

In this case, the percentage discount on the 180-day forward rate is equal to the interest rate differential:

[5] David K. Eiteman and Arthur I. Stonehill, *Multinational Business Finance* (Reading, Mass.: Addison-Wesley Publishing Co., 1979), pp. 54-56.

$$\frac{\$0.3960 - \$0.4000}{\$0.4000} \times \frac{360}{180} = 0.07 - 0.09$$

$$-0.02 = -0.02$$

German securities would earn 2 percent more than the American securities, but German marks sell in the forward market at a 2 percent discount.

Empirical Evidence. The interest parity theory of exchange rate determination explains exchange rate movements by differences in interest rates between countries. In other words, currencies of countries with higher interest rates than the United States tend to appreciate in value against the dollar. Higher interest rates in a given country would cause the value of its currency to rise because higher interest rates could attract capital from investors in other countries. By the same token, currencies of countries with lower interest rates than the United States tend to depreciate in value against the dollar. Thus, the exchange rate moves in the same direction to the difference in interest rates between two countries.

In recent years, participants in foreign exchange markets have watched closely the difference between short-term U. S. and short-term foreign market interest rates as a primary determinant of short-run exchange rate movements. In particular, with a change in interest rate differentials, investors seek to change the currency denomination of their portfolios, thereby motivating short-run international capital flows which in turn lead to corresponding movements in exchange rates.

In such an environment, monetary authorities may attempt to offset partially or even completely the impact of changing interest rate differentials on the value of their currency. Specifically, a monetary authority faced with the situation in which domestic market interest rates are below those of another country has essentially three policy choices. First, it could not react at all and allow its currency to depreciate until the exchange differential offsets the interest differential. Second, it could adopt a tighter domestic monetary policy in order to raise short-term domestic interest rates, thereby reducing the differential and mitigating the downward pressure on its exchange rate. Third, it could intervene in foreign currency markets, buying its own currency with foreign currency. This would result in an increased demand for its currency relative to the foreign currency and a subsequent reduction in the downward pressure on its exchange rate. This alternative, however, is tantamount to choosing a tighter monetary stance and conducting it within foreign exchange markets instead of domestic securities markets.

As shown in Figure 5-2, the value of the U. S. dollar had increased dramatically against most major foreign currencies from the first quarter of 1980 to the second quarter of 1981 mainly due to higher U. S. interest rates. European central banks had responded to the rising dollar at the beginning of 1981 by adopting the tighter monetary policy. This tighter monetary policy caused their domestic interest rates to rise and stopped the appreciation of the U. S. dollar. The reemergence of a strong U. S. dollar at the end of 1981 and the beginning of 1982 did not produce a similar response, thereby allowing their currencies to depreciate again.

Figure 5-4 illustrates movements in the value of the trade-weighted dollar and U. S.-foreign interest differentials.[6] The trade-weighted value of the dollar declined from mid-1976 to late 1978 even though the interest differential favoring the United States increased continuously throughout this period. Movements in U. S. interest rates and the trade-weighted dollar showed a somewhat different pattern in the period between November 1978 and October 6, 1979. In the first half of this period, both the interest rate differential and the dollar remained relatively flat. In the second half of the period, the interest differential rose while the dollar fell slightly. Since October, 1979, the interest differential and the trade-weighted dollar rose and fell together.

In recent years, movements in the value of the dollar has shown an increased sensitivity to movements in U. S. short-term interest rates. Empirical studies also support the basic idea of the interest parity theory.

Figure 5-4 The Trade-Weighted Dollar Versus the U.S.-Foreign Interest Differential, 1976-80.

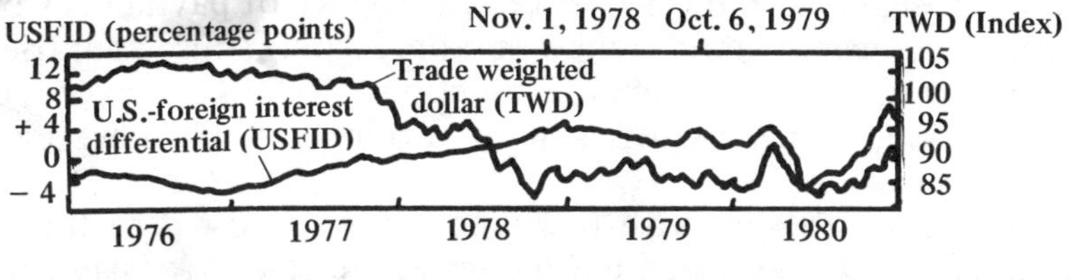

Source: William L. Wilby, "Interest Rates and Exchange Rates under the Fed's New Operating Procedure." *Economic Perspective* (Federal Reserve Bank of Chicago, September/October 1981), p. 4.

[6] The value of the trade-weighted dollar is the weighted average exchange value of the U.S. dollar against currencies of Germany, Japan, France, United Kingdom, Canada, Italy, Netherlands, Belgium, Sweden, and Switzerland. The interest differential is the difference between the U.S. rate on 90-day certificates of deposit and a weighted average of foreign interest rate on similar 90-day money market instruments. The countries entering into the weighted average are the same as those used in computing the trade-weighted value of the dollar.

However, the interest parity theory of exchange rate determination has a number of limitations. First, movements of interest differentials and exchange rates have not always displayed such consistency. The active policy stance of the Federal Reserve System since October 6, 1979 is responsible at least partially for the consistent relationship between these two variables. Thus, if the Federal Reserve System modifies its monetary policy operating procedure, this consistent relationship might be distorted. In addition, if other central banks modify their interest rate policies, the consistent relationship between interest differentials and exchange rates might be also upset.

Second, the relationship between interest rates and exchange rates is a complex one which incorporates many parameters. Relative rates of inflation, rates of monetary growth, and international monetary flows all affect interest rates as well as the exchange rate. Hence, it is difficult to measure the precise magnitude of exchange rate movements attributable to interest differentials.

Other Theories of Exchange Rate Determination

In addition to the PPP doctrine and the interest parity theory, it is possible to identify three other major theories of exchange rate determination: (1) the balance-of-payments approach, (2) the monetary approach, and (3) the asset markets approach.

The Balance-of-Payments Approach. The balance-of-payments approach to exchange rate determination is quite straightforward. A deterioration in a country's balance of payments would be expected to cause the foreign exchange value of its currency to depreciate. On the other hand, an improvement in its balance of payments would be expected to cause its currency to appreciate. Thus, countries with deficits in their international transactions would have exchange rate depreciation, while countries with surpluses would have exchange rate appreciation.

The major problem with this theory is how to define the balance of payments. As discussed in Chapter 3, the balance of payments can be defined as the trade account, the current account, or various arbitrary breakdowns of the capital account. None of these accounts by itself can explain movements in the exchange rate, but the current account balance will influence the exchange rate directly over the long run.

The Monetary Approach. The monetary approach emphasizes the demand for and supply of money. If there is an excessive supply of money in a country, part of that excess would cause residents of the country to rid themselves of their unwanted money holdings. This will cause a depreciation in the country's currency. In practice, the demand for money is an unobservable quantity strongly influenced by expectations, even though the growth rate of money supply is not that difficult to predict. Under this condition, it is difficult to determine the precise amount of the excess money supply, which in turn would make it difficult to predict accurately the direction of exchange rate changes.

The Asset Markets Approach. The asset markets or portfolio balance approach emphasizes the fact that national currencies are one among an entire spectrum of real and financial assets desired by investors. Each asset, including national currencies, offers a combination of risk and expected return. Both risk and return are based partly on anticipations about the future as well as on current economic conditions. Shifts in these perceived risks and returns induce investors to reallocate their portfolios between assets denominated in different currencies, thereby bringing about changes in the exchange rate.

ARBITRAGES

Arbitrage is the purchase of something in one market and its sale in another market to take advantage of price differential. Professional arbitrageurs quickly transfer funds from one currency to another in order to profit from discrepancies between exchange rates in different markets. The process of arbitrage also works through the foreign exchange market to bring interest rates in national markets closer together. Even small discrepancies between the exchange rates and interest rates in different markets would motivate enough arbitrage to wipe these discrepancies out quickly.

Geographic Arbitrage

In principle, the exchange rate for a given currency should be the same in every geographic market. But local demand-and-supply conditions might create temporary discrepancies among various markets. Arbitrage specialists would buy the currency in the market where its price is lower and then sell the currency where its price is higher. If the exchange rate differential is larger than the transaction cost, an arbitrage profit would be made.

Suppose, for example, that the quotes of the French franc against the U. S. dollar are $0.20 in New York and $0.25 in Paris. The price of francs in terms of dollars is higher in Paris than in New York. An arbitrageur could benefit by buying francs with dollars in New York and then selling the francs in exchange for dollars in Paris. Arbitrage tends to wipe out the exchange rate differential that originally triggered it. The purchase of francs in New York would drive the price of francs against the dollar up toward the Paris rate. The sale of francs in Paris would drive the price of francs against the dollar down toward the New York rate. This arbitrage process would continue until the price of francs in terms of the dollar is the same in both markets.

The basic economic principle of "buy low-sell high" dominates the arbitrage transaction of buying and selling currencies in two national money markets. Exchange rates in two different locations must be stated in a given currency if this principle to foreign exchange is to be applied. Thus, the arbitrage process becomes slightly more difficult to understand if exchange rates are quoted in different currencies. Let us restate our previous example in a slightly different way. The price of francs against the dollar is $0.20 in New York. The price of dollars against the franc is FF4 in Paris. The quotes in both locations in terms of $/FF are as follows:

New York	Paris
$0.20/FF (as initially given)	$0.25/FF (1 ÷ 4)

The franc enjoys a higher price against the dollar in Paris than in New York. This price differential leads to the following transactions in each market.

1. In New York, investors would buy francs and sell dollars.
2. In Paris, investors would sell francs and buy dollars.

The arbitrage transaction between two currencies is sometimes called a two-point arbitrage. A three-point arbitrage can occur if any of the three cross rates were out of line. Consider the possibility that the cross rates of exchange are BF60/$, BF10/SK, and SK3/$. An arbitrageur could make a profit of $1. He would buy 60 Belgian francs for $1, then purchase six Swedish kronas for 60 Belgian francs, and finally buy $2 for the six kronas. Such large transactions would strengthen the franc against the dollar, strengthen the krona against the franc, and strengthen the dollar against the krona. This arbitrage process causes some consistent patterns of rates to emerge at which no further arbitrage would be profitable.

Covered-Interest Arbitrage

When investors purchase the currency of a foreign country to take advantage of higher interest rates abroad, they must also consider any losses or gains. Such losses and gains might incur due to fluctuations in the value of the foreign currency prior to the maturity of their investment. Generally, they cover against such potential losses by contracting for the future sale or purchase of a foreign currency in the forward market.

Their actions in trying to profit from interest rate differentials between countries lead, in equilibrium, to the condition of so-called interest parity. The interest parity theory says that any exchange gains or losses incurred by a simultaneous purchase and sale in the spot and forward markets are just offset by the interest rate differential on similar assets. Under these conditions, there is no incentive for capital to move in either direction because the effective returns on foreign and domestic assets have been equalized.

Figure 5-5 represents a graphic presentation of the theoretical relationship between the forward premium or discount and the interest rate differential. The vertical axis represents the interest differential in favor of the foreign currency and the horizontal axis shows the forward premium or discount on that currency. The interest parity line shows the equilibrium state. This chapter ignores transaction costs for simplicity purposes. However, it is important to recognize the fact that transaction costs cause the interest parity line to be a band rather than a thin line.[7] Transaction costs include the foreign exchange brokerage costs on spot and forward contracts as well as the investment brokerage cost on buying and selling securities.

Point A of Figure 5-5 shows that the forward discount for foreign exchange is one percent and the foreign interest rate is two percent higher than the domestic interest rate. In this case, an arbitrageur could employ the so-called covered-interest arbitrage to make a profit. If the arbitrageur buys spot foreign currency with domestic currency and invests the foreign currency in foreign securities, he would earn two percent more than if he invested in home-country securities. Because the purchase of foreign currency with domestic currency means a flow of funds out of the country, the arbitrage transaction tends to reduce the money supply.

The arbitrageur would have to convert the foreign currency in

[7] For a detailed discussion of transaction costs and interest arbitrage, Jacob A. Frenkel and Richard M. Levich, "Transaction Costs and Interest Arbitrage: Tranquil Versus Turbulent Periods," *Journal of Political Economy* (November/December 1977), pp. 1209-1226.

Figure 5-5 Covered-Interest Arbitrage.

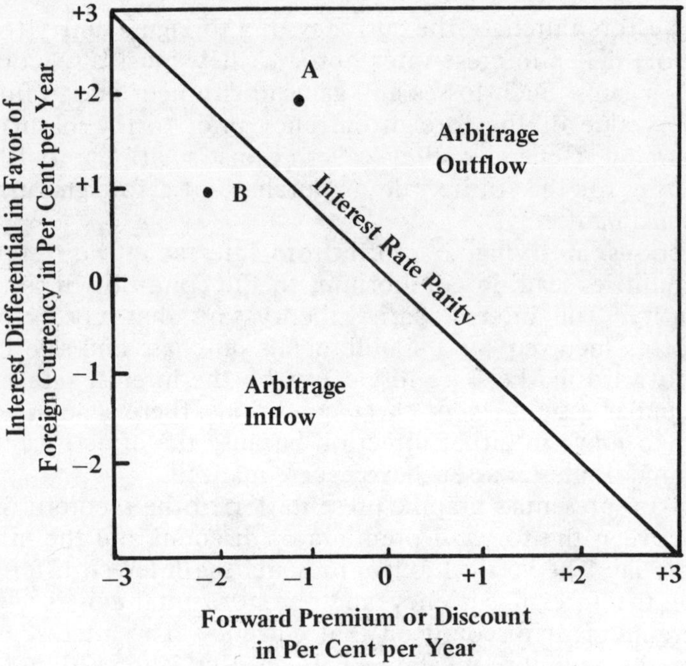

domestic currency at the end of maturity. The exchange rate may fall before the arbitrageur has returned his funds to his home country. For that reason, the arbitrage transaction involves foreign exchange risks. To avoid these risks, he will cover the transaction by selling forward the same amount of the foreign currency at one percent discount. The investment protected by forward sales is called covered-interest arbitrage.

Net gain is usually the interest rate differential minus the discount on the sale of forward foreign currency. Thus, this type of capital outflow occurs when the interest rate differential exceeds the forward discount. At Point A, the arbitrageur would earn two percent more on his investment in foreign securities and lose one percent on the repurchase of the domestic currency. The net result is that the arbitrageur would make a profit of one percent from this covered-interest arbitrage transaction.

Example 5-4 Suppose: (1) the Dutch interest rate = 10%; (2) the U. S. interest rate = 8%; (3) the spot rate for Dutch guilders = \$0.3000; and (4) the 180-day forward rate for Dutch guilders = \$0.2985.

The forward discount for the guilder is obtained by using Equation 5-1:

$$\text{Forward discount} = \frac{\$0.2985 - \$0.30000}{\$0.3000} \times \frac{360}{180} = -0.01 \text{ or } -1\%$$

The interest differential is two percent (10% – 8%) in favor of the Dutch guilder. The covered-interest arbitrage would work as follows:

1.	Borrow dollars in the United States Buy guilders spot with the dollars	–8%
2.	Invest the guilders in Dutch securities	+10%
3.	Sell guilders forward against dollars at a discount	–1%
	Net profit	+1%

These transactions would cause four tendencies in foreign exchange markets and money markets:

1. The spot rate of the guilder against the dollar will tend to appreciate as investors buy guilders against dollars.
2. The forward rate of the guilder against the dollar will tend to depreciate as investors sell guilders against dollars.
3. The U. S. interest rate will tend to rise as investors borrow dollars.
4. The Dutch interest rate will tend to fall as investors lend guilders.

The first two tendencies would increase the original forward discount of one percent toward the initial interest differential of two percent. The last two tendencies would reduce the initial interest differential of two percent toward the original forward discount of one percent. These four tendencies would continue until the forward discount for the guilder equals the interest rate differential in favor of the guilder.

At Point B of Figure 5-5, the foreign interest rate is one percent higher than the domestic interest rate. The cost of forward cover (forward discount) is two percent. In this case, the arbitrageur would sell the foreign currency for the domestic currency, invest this domestic currency in home-country securities, and repurchase the foreign currency in the forward market at a discount. He would lose one percent on his investment in home-country securities but earn two percent on the repurchase of the foreign currency. Hence, the arbitrageur would make a profit of one percent. This covered-interest arbitrage will tend to increase the initial interest differential of one percent between the foreign currency and the domestic currency. It will tend to decrease the original two percent forward discount of the foreign currency against the domestic currency. These two forces will work until the interest rate differential equals the forward discount.

The interest parity line of Figure 5-5 describes the equilibrium position for the relationship between interest rate differentials and forward premiums or discounts. Every point on this line represents a situation in which the interest rate differential equals the forward premium or discount. In this case, arbitrageurs would have no incentives to transfer funds from one country to the other. However, at any point off the line, there should be an incentive to move funds from one country to another. Such transfer of funds would cause interest differentials or forward premiums (discounts) to move toward the interest parity line.

The theoretical equilibrium position exists only under a free market system. Because there are a variety of artificial barriers and intervention by government authorities in both foreign exchange and money markets, this equilibrium condition hardly exists in practice.

SUMMARY

The major problem of multinational corporations is the fact that cash flows must cross national boundaries. These flows are subject to various constraints imposed by government authorities and exchange rate fluctuations. Trades in currencies take place in the foreign exchange market for immediate delivery (spot market) and future delivery (forward market). The foreign exchange market is a worldwide network of telephone and telex communications between banks.

Exchange rates represent prices of one currency in terms of another currency. They are determined by the forces of supply and demand under a free market system. The spot rate is the rate paid for delivery of a currency within two business days after the day of the trade. The forward rate is the rate at which two currencies are to be exchanged at some future date. The forward exchange rate is fixed at the time a contract is made. But payment and delivery are not required until maturity.

The PPP doctrine and the interest parity theory explain why exchange rates, in the long run, move toward equilibrium positions in which prices in different countries and their interest rates are the same. This is becuase arbitrageurs buy goods or currencies in one market and sell them in another market in order to take advantage of price or interest differentials prevailing at different national markets. Thus, the process of arbitrage works through the foreign exchange market to bring inflation and interest rates in different markets closer together.

PROBLEMS

5-1 Assume the following exchange rates for a selected number of currencies:

Currency	U. S. $ Equivalent
Brazil (cruzeiro)	0.00900
Britain (pound)	1.9000
Canada (dollar)	0.8500
France (franc)	0.1500
Hong Kong (dollar)	0.200
Italy (lira)	0.001000
Japan (yen)	0.005000
Mexico (peso)	0.0400

a. Determine the amount of each foreign currency required to buy one unit of the U. S. dollar.
b. Determine £/FF, FF/¥, and ¥/£.

5-2 Assume the following exchange rates for a selected number of currencies:

Currency	Currency per U. S. $
Norway (krone)	5.9000
Saudi Arabia (riyal)	3.5000
South Korea (won)	700.00
Sweden (krona)	5.0000
Switzerland (franc)	2.0000
Venezuela (bolivar)	4.50
West Germany (mark)	2.500

a. Determine the amount of U. S. dollars required to buy one unit of each foreign currency.
b. Determine W/SK, SK/GM, and GM/SK.

5-3 Using the data in Table 5-2, determine the 180-day forward discount or premium on both the Canadian dollar and the German mark.

5-4 Fill in the following blank spaces:

Direct (Outright)	British pounds	Swiss francs	French francs
Spot	\$2.0787	\$0.4108	\$0.2008
30-day forward		0.4120	
90-day forward		0.4144	
Points (Spread)			
30-day forward	−13		
90-day forward	−60		
Percentage Discount or Premium a Year			
30-day forward			−8.96%
90-day forward			−8.37%

5-5 The following quotations and expectations exist for the German mark:

Present spot rate	\$0.5000
90-day forward rate	0.5200
Your expectation of the spot rate 90 days hence	0.5500

a. What is the premium or discount on the forward German mark?
b. If your expectation proves correct, what would be your dollar profit or loss from investing \$4,000 in the spot market? How much capital do you need now to carry out this operation? What are the major risks associated with this speculation?
c. If your expectation proves correct, what would be your dollar profit or loss from investing \$4,000 in the forward market? How much capital do you need now to speculate in the forward market? What are the major risks associated with the speculation?

5-6 An American firm purchases \$4,000 worth of perfume (FF20,000) from a French firm. The American distributor must make the payment in 90 days in French francs. The following quotations and expectations exist for the French franc:

Present spot rate	\$0.2000
90-day forward rate	0.2200
Your expectation of the spot rate 90 days hence	0.2500
U. S. interest rate	15%
French interest rate	10%

a. What is the premium or discount on the forward French franc? What is the interest differential between the United States and France? Is there an incentive for covered interest arbitrage?
b. If there is an incentive for covered interest arbitrage, how can an arbitrageur take advantage of the situation? Assume: (1) the arbitrageur is willing to borrow \$4,000 or FF20,000 and (2) there are no transaction costs.

c. If transaction costs are $100, would an opportunity still exist for covered interest arbitrage?
d. What alternatives are open to the importer if he wants to cover his transaction against the foreign exchange risk?
e. Assume that your expectation proves correct and that the importer decides to cover his transaction. What would be the opportunity cost of each alternative? Which alternative is more attractive and why?
f. Would you advise the American firm to cover its foreign transaction? Why or why not?

REFERENCES

See references at the end of Chapter 12.

PART THREE

Financing International Transactions

$£¢

SIX

FINANCING FOREIGN TRADE

This book places its major emphasis on financial problems which arise in managing multinational operations. However, the financial manager of a multinational firm must be familiar with certain mechanics of financing foreign trade. This is because most multinational companies are frequently engaged in foreign trade activities. This chapter discusses a number of basic documents involved in foreign trade, the terms of foreign trade, and the sources of financing foreign trade.

Foreign trade differs from domestic trade in terms of the instruments and documents used. Most domestic sales are an open-account credit. Under this credit, the buyer does not need to sign a formal debt instrument because credit sales are made on the basis of the seller's credit investigation of the buyer. Buyers and sellers are typically farther apart in foreign trade than in domestic trade. Thus, the sellers are seldom able to ascertain the credit standing of their overseas customers. The buyers may also find it difficult to determine the integrity and reputation of the foreign sellers from which they wish to buy. The three important documents involved in foreign trade are: (1) a draft, which is an order to pay; (2) a bill of lading, which is a document involved in the physical movement of the merchandise by a common carrier; and (3) a letter of credit, which is a third party guarantee of the importer's credit worthiness.

Because trade competition has become increasingly severe, it is essential for multinational companies to know how best to finance their foreign trade. The terms and conditions under which foreign trade takes place vary significantly. They range from cash before delivery at one extreme to sales in a foreign currency with credit terms over one year. Supply and demand conditions at the time of sales determine the actual terms and conditions of any particular transaction. But most foreign transactions involve much longer credit terms than domestic transactions.

Banks, governments, and private nonbank financial institutions pool their resources to finance foreign trade. Banks finance foreign trade through trust receipts, bankers' acceptances, and a number of other means. The U. S. Export-Import Bank and the Foreign Credit Insurance Association are major forces for helping American exporters sell their goods and services to foreign importers. Certain financial institutions act as a factor that buys short-term receivables at their own risk.

BASIC DOCUMENTS IN FOREIGN TRADE

Drafts

A draft or a bill of exchange is an order written by an exporter that requires an importer to pay a specified amount of money at a specified time. Through the use of drafts, the exporter may use its bank as the collection agent on accounts that the exporter finances. The bank forwards the exporter's drafts to the importer directly or indirectly (through a branch or a correspondent bank) and then remits the proceeds of the collection back to the exporter.

A draft involves three parties: the drawer or maker, the drawee, and the payee. The drawer is the person or business who issues the draft. This person is ordinarily the exporter who sells and ships the merchandise. The drawee is the person or business against whom the draft is drawn. This person is usually the importer who must pay the draft at maturity. The payee is the person or business to whom the drawee will eventually pay the funds. If the draft is not a negotiable instrument, it designates a person or bank to whom payment is to be made. Such a person, known as the payee, may be the drawer himself or a third party such as the drawer's bank. However, this is generally not the case because most drafts are a bearer instrument. Drafts are negotiable if they meet a number of conditions. (1) They must be in writing and signed by the drawer-exporter. (2) They must contain an unconditional promise or order to pay an exact amount of money. (3) They must be payable on sight or at a specified time. (4) They must be made out to order or to bearer. If a draft is made out to order, the funds involved should be paid to the person specified. If it is made out to bearer, the funds should be paid to the person who presents it for payment.

There are two types of drafts: *sight drafts* and *time drafts.*[1] A sight draft is payable on demand to the drawee-importer. A time draft is payable a specified number of days after presentation to the drawee. When a time draft is presented to the drawee, the drawee or his bank accepts it. This acceptance acknowledges in writing the drawee's obligation to pay the sum indicated on the face of the draft. When drafts are accepted by the importer, they become trade acceptances. When drafts are accepted by the bank, they become bankers' acceptances.

Because bankers' acceptances are highly marketable, the exporter can sell them in the market or discount them at his bank. Whenever they are sold or discounted, the seller adds his endorsement on the back of the draft. In the event of the importer's failure to pay at maturity, the holder of the draft will have recourse for the full amount of the draft from the last endorser.

There are a number of reasons why drafts are used in foreign trade. (1) They provide written evidence of obligations in a comprehensive form. (2) They allow both the exporter and the importer to reduce the cost of financing and to divide the remaining costs equitably. (3) They are negotiable and unconditional. That is, drafts are not subject to disputes which may occur between the parties involved.

Bills of Lading

A bill of lading is a shipping document issued to the exporting firm or its bank by a common carrier that transports the goods. It is simultaneously a receipt, a contract, and a document of title. As a receipt, the bill of lading indicates that specified goods have been received by the carrier. As a contract, it evidences the obligation of the carrier to deliver the goods to the importer in exchange for certain charges. As a document of title, it establishes the ownership of the

[1] Drafts are also classified as clear or documentary. Unlike a documentary draft, a clean draft does not require any other document. When a clean draft is used in trade, the exporter usually sends the shipping documents directly to the buyer. Clean drafts are sometimes used when multinational companies ship the goods to their own subsidiaries, because matters of trust and credit are not important. However, most international trade transactions involve documentary drafts which require various shipping documents.

goods. Thus, the bill of lading can be used to insure payment before the goods are delivered. For example, the importer cannot take title to the goods until he obtains the bill of lading from the carrier.

Bills of lading may be either straight bills of lading or order bills of lading. A straight bill of lading requires that the carrier deliver the goods to the designated party, usually the importer. It is used when the goods have been paid for in advance; thus, it is not title to the goods. An order bill of lading provides that the carrier deliver the goods to the order of a designated party, usually the exporter. The exporting firm retains title to the goods until it receives payment. Once payment has been made, the exporting firm endorses the order bill of lading in blank or to its bank. The endorsed document can be used as collateral against loans. It accompanies a documentary draft, which requires such other documents as the bill of lading, commercial invoices, and insurance certificates. The procedures to handle these two types of bills of lading are well established. There are commercial banks and other financial institutions in almost every country which handle these documents efficiently.

Letters of Credit

A letter of credit is a document issued by a bank at the request of the importer. In the document, the bank agrees to honor a draft drawn on the importer if the draft accompanies specified documents such as the bill of lading. In a typical use, the importer asks that his local bank write a letter of credit. In exchange for the bank's agreement to honor the demand for payment that results from the import transaction, the importer promises to pay the bank the amount of the transaction and a specified fee.

A letter of credit may be either irrevocable or revocable. An irrevocable letter of credit can be neither revoked nor modified without the consent of all parties. A revocable letter of credit can be revoked or modified at any time before payment. A letter of credit may also be either confirmed or unconfirmed. A confirmed letter of credit is the letter of credit confirmed by a bank other than the opening bank. In this case, both banks are obligated to honor drafts drawn in accordance with the letter of credit. An unconfirmed letter of credit is the guarantee of only the opening bank. Thus, the strongest letter of credit is a confirmed, irrevocable letter of credit. Such a letter of credit cannot be cancelled by the opening bank and it requires both the opening and confirming banks to guarantee the payment on drafts issued in connection with the export transaction.

The letter of credit is of advantage to both exporters and importers because it facilitates international trade. It gives a number of benefits to exporters. First, they sell their goods abroad against the promise of a bank rather than a commercial firm. Because banks are usually larger and better credit risks than most business firms, exporters are almost completely assured of payment if they meet specific conditions. Second, they can obtain funds as soon as they have such necessary documents as the letter of credit and the bill of lading. When shipment is made, the exporter prepares a draft on the importer in accordance with the letter of credit and presents it to his local bank. If the bank finds that all papers are in order, it advances the funds, the face value of the draft less fees and interest.

Although its major beneficiaries are exporters, the letter of credit also gives a number of benefits to importers. First, it assures them that the exporter will be paid only if he provides certain documents, all of which are carefully examined by a bank. If the exporter is unable or unwilling to make proper shipment, recovery of the deposit is much easier from the bank than from the exporter. Second, the letter of credit enables the importer to remove the commercial risk for the exporter in exchange for other considerations. Thus, the importer can bargain for better terms such as a lower price. Moreover, it is comparatively cheaper to finance the goods under a letter of credit than by borrowing.

A Typical International Transaction

There are many steps and documents in the entire process of completing an international transaction. Each step or document is a subsystem of the entire transaction process which is closely connected by a variety of other subsystems. Thus, a successful completion of an international transaction may be viewed as an integral unit of many parts which are directly or indirectly interrelated. A typical international transaction might require the following 12 steps.[2]

1. A Chicago firm desires to import a $1 million shipment of machines from a London firm, thereby inquiring if the London firm is willing to ship under a letter of credit.
2. The London firm indicates its willingness to ship under a letter of credit. Simultaneously, it provides the Chicago firm with such information as prices, credit terms, and so on.

[2] Federal Reserve Bank of Chicago, *Business Conditions* (May 1976), p. 5; and David K. Eiteman and Arthur I. Stonehill, *Multinational Business Finance* (Reading, Mass.: Addison-Wesley Publishing Co., 1979), pp. 510-511.

3. The Chicago firm arranges to have its Chicago bank open a letter of credit in favor of the London firm.
4. The Chicago bank issues the letter of credit in favor of the London firm and sends it to a London bank, the London firm's bank.
5. The London firm ships the machines to the Chicago firm through a common carrier that issues an order bill of lading.
6. The London firm prepares a 60-day draft on the Chicago firm in accordance with the letter of credit and presents it to the London bank along with such other documents as the bill of lading. At the same time, the London firm endorses the order bill of lading so that title to the machines goes with the holder of the documents.
7. The London bank forwards the draft and other documents to the Chicago bank for acceptance. When the draft is accepted by the Chicago bank, it becomes a banker's acceptance. This means that the Chicago bank has promised to pay the draft in 60 days. Alternatively, if the London bank has asked the Chicago bank to accept and discount the draft, the Chicago bank returns cash less a discount fee rather than the banker's acceptance to the London bank.
8. When the London bank receives the banker's acceptance, it may sell the acceptance to an investor at a discount or hold the acceptance in its own portfolio.
9. If the London bank has discounted the acceptance with the Chicago bank or has sold it in the local money market, it transfers the proceeds less any fees and discount to the London firm. Another alternative is that the London firm may hold the acceptance for 60 days and presents it to the Chicago bank for payment.
10. The Chicago bank notifies the arrival of the documents to the Chicago firm. The Chicago firm signs a promissory note or some other arrangement to pay the Chicago bank for the machines in 60 days. Then the Chicago bank releases the documents so that the Chicago firm can claim the shipment.
11. In 60 days, the Chicago bank receives the funds from the Chicago firm to cover the maturing acceptance.
12. On the same day, the holder of the acceptance presents it to the Chicago bank for payment. Alternatively, the holder of the acceptance may return it to the London bank for collection through normal banking channels.

THE PAYMENT TERMS OF EXPORT TRANSACTIONS

Barter

Foreign trade is conducted in terms of money just as domestic trade is conducted in terms of money. However, foreign trade is possible without money through a barter system. Barter is an exchange of goods between two countries without the involvement of finance. Barter terms are usually arranged between two countries on a bilateral trading agreement. An exporter of one country ships certain goods to an importer of another country and receives goods from the importer in exchange for his shipment.

By far the largest volume of barter deals in the world today is made between the Soviet Union and its communist allies. Of course, individual transactions are made within the framework of intergovernmental trade agreements. Such barter deals are also popular among nonmarket countries and between Eastern and Western countries.

Barter deals allow countries with a shortage of foreign exchange to obtain their deficit goods in return for their surplus goods. They also permit companies in the foreign-currency-short country to obtain goods which they would not otherwise be able to obtain.

Switch Trading

Payments for exports to the East Bloc and nonmarket countries are often made through clearing units whereby sales are balanced with purchases from other countries. This clearing unit has led to many bilateral trading agreements under which attempts are made to identify the goods each country will trade and to set overall trade limits. The agreement also requires each country to deposit a certain amount of its own currency in a bilateral clearing account. Sales to each other are then paid out of this clearing account.

The basic purpose of switch trading is to eliminate the imbalance in barter trade between two countries. Unfortunately, one of the countries frequently fails to sell sufficient goods to its trading partner. At other times, one country fails to buy sufficient goods from its trading partner. In either case, a shortage in clearing funds will develop for the deficit country. Hence, one of the countries becomes a creditor and the other becomes a debtor. When this occurs, the bilateral trading agreement tends to break down.

A breakdown is harmful to both countries. There are two practical methods to avoid this breakdown. First, the bilateral trading agreement may specify that the debtor country pay amounts in excess of allowable variations in gold or convertible currency to the creditor country. Second, to reconcile the imbalance in barter transactions between them, two countries may agree to utilize a switch trade broker.[3]

Example 6-1 Assume that the Soviet Union has agreed to trade its machinery for Cuban sugar. Russian machinery and Cuban sugar are then given arbitrary unit prices in clearing dollars. The agreement specifies that $1 million in commodities would be exchanged during the following year. By the end of the year, Russia found that it had accumulated $400,000 in unneeded sugar.

To meet its obligations as well as to dispose of the unwanted goods, Russia may seek the services of a switch trader. It calls one of the switch trade brokers and offers him $400,000 worth of sugar in the clearing account at a discount of 30 percent. Once the actual value of the sugar has been ascertained by him, the broker calls sugar dealers who might pick up the credit. Eventually, he finds a buyer who offers 75 percent of the credit. Russia receives 70 percent of its $400,000 credit in hard currency for the unneeded sugar, the broker takes five percent on the deal, and the buyer purchases the sugar for $400,000 minus a 25 percent discount. Russia, the broker, and the buyer benefit from the deal, but Cuba may find that it undersold its sugar in world sugar markets by the unexpected dumping of its own goods.

Cash Terms

Cash terms may be either COD or CBD. COD terms mean cash on delivery of the goods and CBD terms mean cash before delivery of the goods. Under either COD or CBD terms, the exporter does not extend credit. Although credit risk does not exist under either terms, COD terms are accompanied by the risk that the importer may refuse the shipment while CBD terms avoid all risk. Under CBD terms, the exporter may insist on cash at the time of order or he may specify the time of cash payment prior to shipment. Another possible arrangement is that a part of the payment is made at the time of

[3] For a good outline of procedures on switch trading, see "How Switch Trading Works," *The Economist* (January 14, 1967); and "East-West Trade Pull a Switch," *Business Week* (March 11, 1967).

order, that progress payments are made between the time of order and the time of shipment, and that the final payment is made just before the release of the goods to a common carrier.

Cash terms are exceptional in these days of severe international competition. While cash-type transactions are ideal from the exporter's point of view, the importer does not like such transactions. This is because the importer is forced to accept all risks in transit, in exchange fluctuations, and in the quality of the goods received. Consequently, the exporter will insist on cash terms only in instances of the importer's poor credit standing or extreme political risks in the importing country. If the sale involves products specially manufactured for the importer, the exporter may demand some kind of advance-payment arrangement.

Consignments

Goods for export may be consigned to the exporter's own agent (subsidiary), an independent agent, or an import house. Assume that an exporter in New York ships to an importer in London, 100 cases of quart bottles on a consignment basis. Because the exporter pays all the expenses connected with the shipment, the importer incurs no expenses at the time this shipment is delivered to his warehouse. Actually, the 100 cases of bottles are still the exporter's inventory. Thus, if the importer should fail, the exporter can demand that all the unsold bottles be returned to him.

Let us further assume that this consignment arrangement involves a ten percent commission on all bottles sold. If the importer sold all the 100 cases at \$50 per case, he would deduct his commission of \$500 ($100 \times \$50 \times .10$) and remit to the exporter a dollar draft for \$4,500 on a New York bank.

Consignment to the independent agent or the import house raises most of the same problems encountered in open account transactions. Hence, this type of operation is usually confined to companies working very closely together and between companies that completely trust each other.

Credit Terms

Most importers are not required to pay for goods before or on delivery but are allowed a short deferment period before payment is made. During this period, the exporter extends credit to the importer. There are three types of trade credit: open account, notes payable, and trade or bankers' acceptances.

Open account credit does not require the importer to sign a formal debt instrument to evidence the amount that he owes the exporter. The importer simply charges his purchases, much in the same fashion that domestic retail stores extend credit to their customers. Then the importer's account is carried on the books of the exporter like any other receivables. This arrangement places the entire financial burden upon the exporter. Because banks usually refuse to advance against accounts receivable, it ties up large amounts of the exporter's capital. In addition, with this arrangement the exporter assumes the risks of foreign exchange blockage and buyer default. Therefore, open account terms are extended only to trusted customers in countries that have no foreign exchange or political problems.

In some export transactions, promissory notes are employed instead of open account credit. In this case, the importer is requested to sign a note that evidences his debt to the exporter. Thus, this arrangement makes the importer recognize his debt formally. The note calls for the payment of the obligation at some future date.

A trade acceptance is a form of short-term financing common in almost all foreign trade activities. In fact, it is the largest source of short-term funds for importers. Under this method of financing, the exporter draws a draft on the importer ordering him to pay the draft at some specified future date. The exporter will not release the goods until the importer accepts the draft. When the importer accepts the draft, it becomes a trade acceptance.

An exporter can specify the credit terms under which he is willing to extend with a foreign export sale. The degree of competition has a strong impact on the actual terms. The exporter may be compelled to grant 60 or 90 day credit even if he would like to be paid immediately after shipment. The shortest credit term is extended when the exporter draws a sight draft on a correspondent bank of the importer's bank. Payment is made to the exporter on demand when the draft arrives at the importer or his bank. Longer credit terms are achieved when the exporter draws a time draft, which specifies the time period after presentation when the funds must be paid.

When a time draft is employed in foreign trade, the exporter may carry the credit for his own account or refinance it through a local bank. Under the latter arrangement, the letter of credit ordinarily specifies who will pay the expenses of financing. Although these expenses may be paid by the exporter or the importer, the ultimate choice depends largely upon the conditions of competition at the time of the transaction.

SOURCES OF FINANCING FOREIGN TRADE

Bank Financing

Banks are important lenders to those engaged in international trade. They provide several forms of credit convenient to exporters and importers. These include trust receipts, bankers' acceptances, loans to exporters, and loans to importers.

Trust Receipts. A trust receipt establishes that borrowers hold certain goods in trust for the lender. When goods are shipped under a time draft, the importer generally signs a trust receipt that collateralizes the draft by the goods. The document provides that the importer will be the agent of his bank in the sale of the goods. The bank retains title to the goods until the importer has made full settlement. The importer is allowed to sell the goods but must turn the proceeds of the sale over to the bank in payment of the loan. The bank assumes any losses that occur under a trust receipt.

Bankers' Acceptances. Assume that a Detroit firm desires to import a $10,000 shipment of perfumes from a Mexican firm. The Mexican firm is willing to grant a 60-day credit. The Detroit firm may arrange to have his Detroit bank open a letter of credit in favor of the Mexican firm. The letter of credit states that the Detroit bank will honor drafts drawn on the Detroit firm if they are drawn in accordance with detailed terms in the letter of credit. When shipment is made, the Mexican firm prepares a 60-day draft on the Detroit firm and presents it to its Mexican bank. The Mexican bank will advance the peso equivalent of $10,000 less interest and fees to the Mexican firm. Then the Mexican bank will forward the draft along with such shipping documents as the bill of lading to its Detroit correspondent bank, which in turn will present it to the Detroit firm's bank for acceptance. If all papers are found to be in order, the Detroit bank accepts the draft and it becomes a bankers' acceptance.

Because bankers' acceptances are of very high quality, the Mexican bank can easily arrange its sale and thus recover the funds it had advanced. If the Mexican firm did not discount the draft at his Mexican bank, he could sell it to an investor at a discount by himself. The Detroit firm obtains the credit he wants and the risks with an exception of the accepting bank are minimal. The credit transaction is completed when in 60 days the bankers' acceptance is paid by the Detroit bank, which looks for repayment by the Detroit firm.

Loans to Exporters and Importers. The bankers' acceptance is a form of bank loan to exporters. In addition, banks can make loans to exporters by cashing, purchasing, discounting, and collecting drafts. Banks cash drafts if the drafts are denominated in local currency and are drawn on them. They purchase drafts if the drafts are denominated in foreign currencies. In this case, drafts are generally exchanged for local currency at an appropriate exchange rate. They discount drafts if the drafts are denominated in local currency and the terms of the sales involve time drafts. When banks collect drafts, they simply act as agents for exporters. However, they may lend against either a total or a percentage of the drafts outstanding.

In some situations the importer finances its imports through a local bank and notifies the exporter. Banks make loans to importers against import drafts in conjunction with trust receipt arrangements. Hence, bank loans support the import drafts which are collateralized by the goods themselves. While import drafts are the reverses of export drafts in terms of who creates them, the purpose is the same.

Export Credit Insurance in the United States

Most exporters sell under letters of credit as described in the earlier part of this chapter. In this case, all risks involved in export transactions are assumed by banks with some exceptions such as the use of revocable letters of credit. However, importers frequently do not want to open letters of credit because of cost, difficulty of securing letters of credit, etc. At other times, severe competition compels exporters to sell on open account or on draft terms without letters of credit. Under these circumstances, an exporter could suffer heavy losses even with the most critical examination of an importer's credit worthiness. These losses may develop from such situations as expropriation and riots beyond the control of the exporter or the importer.

The governments of most industrial countries have helped their exporters in many ways over the years. Although the U. S. Export-Import Bank had helped U. S. exporters reduce their risks since 1934, they still lacked the protective umbrella which many of their competitors were enjoying.[4] In the Fall of 1961, the Secretary of the

[4] The following indicates the chronology for foreign credit insurance programs established by the major trading partners of the United States:

United Kingdom (1919)	Italy (1927)	West Germany (1926)
Belgium (1921)	France (1929)	Canada (1944)
Norway (1922)	Spain (1929)	Switzerland (1934)
Denmark (1922)	Japan (1930)	
Netherlands (1925)	Sweden (1933)	

Treasury, the Export-Import Bank, and a number of leading insurance companies organized the Foreign Credit Insurance Association (FCIA).

The FCIA provides credit protection for U. S. exporters. It insures exporters for an agreed percentage of losses from credit risks. Credit risks may be commercial, political, or both. Commercial risks include such risks as the failure of the importer before payment and its protracted payment default. Political risks include currency inconvertibility, cancellation of import licenses, expropriation, and war or revolution.

The FCIA credit protection program for exporters covers short-term (up to 180 days) and medium-term (181 days to five years) cases. For these two cases there are five standard FCIA policies. (1) A short-term comprehensive policy covers 90 percent of the commercial credit losses and 100 percent of the political losses. (2) A short-term political risk policy covers 100 percent of the political losses only. (3) A medium-term comprehensive policy covers 90 percent of the credit losses and 100 percent of the political losses. (4) A medium-term political risk policy covers 100 percent of the political losses only. (5) A combined short-term/medium-term policy covers both short-term and medium-term risks.

The Export-Import Bank offers medium-term guarantees for exporters who seek financing from their commercial banks.[5] These guarantees require that the importer pay ten percent in cash, the exporter carry ten percent in his account, and the bank agree to finance the remaining portion without recourse to the exporter. The Export-Import Bank also has a guarantee program designed to protect foreign financial institutions which extend credits for the purchase of U. S. goods and services.

Under these five standard FCIA policies, 90-100 percent of losses are recoverable if:

1. All disputes on the loss between the exporter and the importer have been settled;
2. The loss is properly reported within eight months;
3. The exporter was unable to insure the loss under another policy;
4. U. S. labor and materials account for more than half of the value of the shipment;
5. The exporter is not negligent; or
6. Payment for the export was supposed to be made in the U. S. dollar.

[5] Chapter 7 will discuss the Export-Import Bank in detail.

Factoring

Factors buy a company's accounts receivable on a nonrecourse basis and thus accelerate the conversion of the company's claims against its customers. They also perform a number of additional functions such as credit checking, bookkeeping, the collection of accounts, and risk bearing. The factor reviews the credit of the borrower's customers and establishes credit limits in advance. The maximum amount of advance against uncollected accounts receivable is established as a percentage of the invoice value. The factor receives an interest charge on the daily balance of advances plus a commission for credit analysis, bookkeeping, the collection of accounts, and risk taking.

Exporters may turn to a factor when they have difficulty collecting on open account sales or when their bank is unwilling to collect notes receivable. Factors' rates on foreign accounts are usually much higher than those of banks. Thus, factors are frequently used as a last resort by exporters who need funds badly and/or who have almost no hope for collecting.

The factor's credit investigation of the exporter's customers is relatively quick and inexpensive. For this reason, even if the exporter does not discount his accounts receivable, he can still use the factor's facilities to estimate his prospective accounts' credit worthiness. If the exporter discounts his accounts receivable on a nonrecourse basis, the factor will assume all commercial and political risks of nonpayment. For these services, factors charge a commitment fee of one to two percent and a rate of interest in excess of the prime rate.

The utilization of factors by exporters depends upon two considerations. The first consideration is whether the exporter can perform credit evaluation functions as well as the factor. Because large international factors evaluate the same customer for many companies, they build up credit files and expertise which allow them to evaluate credit at a lower cost than the exporter. The second consideration is whether the availability of funds and the interest charged by alternative sources are more attractive than those offered by the factor.

SUMMARY

This chapter has discussed various documents and operations essential to finance foreign trade. The extension of credit on foreign trade is of critical importance to both parties in a transaction. For exporters, crucial determinants of sales volume across national boundaries are their willingness and ability to extend credit. For importers, their ability to continue operations relies on the lag between payments by their customers and remittances to their foreign suppliers.

The three basic documents used in normal export-import transactions are the draft, the bill of lading, and the letter of credit. A draft is an order written by an exporter that requires the importer to pay a specified amount at a specified time. It involves three parties: the drawer, the drawee, and the payee. The drawer is the person who issues the draft. The drawee is the person against whom the draft is drawn. The payee is the person or business to whom the drawee will eventually pay the funds. Drafts may be either sight or time drafts. A sight draft is payable upon presentation, while a time draft is payable at a specified future date.

A bill of lading is a shipping document issued to the exporting firm by a common carrier that transports the goods. It is simultaneously a receipt, a contract, and a document. Bills of lading may be straight or order bills of lading. A straight bill of lading requires that the carrier deliver the goods to the designated party. An order bill of lading provides that the carrier deliver the goods to the order of a designated party.

A letter of credit is a document issued by a bank at the request of the importer. In the document, the bank agrees to honor a draft which results from an import transaction by a foreign buyer. The letter of credit assures that there will be payments for goods shipped to the importer. Letters of credit may be irrevocable or revocable. They may also be confirmed or unconfirmed.

Barter and switch trading make international transactions possible without money. However, most transactions across national boundaries are conducted in terms of money. The payment terms of foreign trade include cash terms, consignments, and credit terms, all of which require money. The actual payment terms of exports depend largely upon competitive conditions prevailing at the time of initiating the transaction.

Finally, this chapter has examined a number of sources to finance foreign trade. Banks are important lenders to those engaged in foreign trade. Bank-financing operations include trust receipts, bankers' acceptances, and several other forms of loans. The use of foreign credit insurance reduces both commercial and political risks involved in foreign transactions. The U. S. Foreign Credit Insurance Association is a major force for helping U. S. exporters reduce their export risks. International factors buy accounts receivables from exporters and then collect them as they become due. Factors also perform such functions as credit analysis, bookkeeping, the collection of accounts receivable, and risk taking.

REFERENCES

6-1 Bayalis, Arthur E., "The Documentation Dilemma in International Trade," *Columbia Journal of World Business* (Spring 1976), pp. 15-22.

6-2 Bloch, Henry Simon, "Export Financing Emerging as a Major Policy Problem," *Columbia Journal of World Business* (Fall 1976), pp. 85-95.

6-3 Eiteman, David K., and Arthur I. Stonehill, *Multinational Business Finance* (Reading, Mass: Addison-Wesley Publishing Co., 1979), Chapter 14.

6-4 Federal Reserve Bank of Chicago, *Business Conditions* (May 1976).

6-5 Harrington, J. A., *Specifics on Commercial Letters of Credit and Bankers' Acceptances* (Jersey City, N.J.: Scott Printing Corporation, 1974).

6-6 Hollis, Stanley E., *Guide to Export Credit Insurance* (New York: Foreign Credit Insurance Association, 1971).

6-7 Kim, Suk H., and Henry J. Guithues, *Finance Principles: An Introduction* (Richmond: Robert F. Dame, Inc., 1982), pp. 424-426.

6-8 Root, Franklin R., *International Trade and Investment* (Cincinnati: South-Western Publishing Co., 1978), Chapter 9.

6-9 Rodriguez, Rita M., and E. Eugene Carter, *International Financial Management* (Englewood Cliffs, N.J.: Prentice-Hall, Inc., 1979), Chapter 6.

6-10 Zenoff, David B., and Jack Zwick, *International Financial Management* (Englewood Cliffs, N.J.: Prentice-Hall, Inc., 1969), Chapter 10.

APPENDIX 6A
COMMERCIAL ABBREVIATIONS[1]

A.A.R.	Against all risks
A.B.	Aktiebolag. Swedish; stock company
A.G.	Aktiengesellschaft. German; incorporated (stock company)
A/P	Authority to purchase, or authority to pay
B/E	Bill of exchange
B/L	Bill of lading
B.M.	Board measure
C.A.D.	Cash against documents
C. & D.	Collection and delivery
C. & F.	Cost and freight
C.F. & I.	Cost, freight, and insurance

[1] *International Trade Information* (San Francisco: Bank of America).

Cia.	Compania. Spanish; company
C.I.F.	Cost, insurance, freight
C.I.F. & C.	Cost, insurance, freight, and commission (or charges)
C.I.F. & E.	Cost, insurance, freight, and exchange
C.I.F. & I.	Cost, insurance, freight, commission (or charges), and interest
C. & I.	Cost and insurance
cwt	Hundredweight
D/A	Documents against acceptance
D/D	Days after date
D.F.	Dead freight
D.N.	Debit note
D/P	Documents against payment
D/S	Days after sight
D/TR	Documents against trust receipt
E. & O.E.	Errors and omissions excepted
E.O.M.	End of month
F.A.F.	Fly away free
F.A.Q.	Free at quay
F.A.S.	Free alongside
F.C. & S.	Free from capture and seizure
F.I.	Free in (all expenses for loading into the hold of the vessel are for the account of the consignee)
F.O.B.	Free on board
F.O.	Free out (all expenses covering unloading from the hold of the vessel are for the account of the consignee)
F.O.R.	Free on rails
F.P.A.	Free of particular average
F.P.A.A.C.	Free of particular average American conditions
F.P.A.E.C.	Free of particular average English conditions
G.A.	General average
Gebr.	German; Brothers
G.m.b.H.	Gesellschaft mit beschraenkter Haftung. German for limited liability company
G.T.	Gross ton
Hijo(s)	Spanish; Son(s)
Hnos	Spanish; Brothers
Inc.	Incorporated

Kd	Knocked-down
K.K.	Kabushiki-Kaisha, Japanese; stock company
L/C	Letter of credit
Ltd.	Limited. British; limited liability company
M.E.C.	Marine extension clause
m.n.	moneda nacional. Spanish; any local currency
M/R	Mate's receipt
M/V	Motor vessel
N.O.E.	Not otherwise enumerated
n.s.f.	not sufficient funds
N.V.	Naamloze vennootschap. Dutch; stock company (corporation)
O/A	Open account
O.C.P.	Overland common points
O.R.L.	Owner's risk of leakage
P/N	Promissory note
Pty. Ltd.	Proprietary Limited. Australian; privately owned corporation
R.R.	Railroad
S.A.C.I. or S.A.I.C.	Sociedad de Capital e Industria. Spanish; company of capital and industry
SA	Sociedad Anonima or Societe Anonyme, Spanish and French; corporation
SARL	Societe a Responsabilita Limitada or Societe a Responsabilitie Limitee. Italian or French; company with limited liability
S/D	Sight draft
S/D-B/L	Sight draft, bill of lading attached
S/D-D/P	Sight draft, documents against payment
S. de R.L.	Sociedad de Responsabilidad Limitada. Spanish; limited partnership
S. en C.	Sociedad en Camandita. Spanish; silent partnership
S.L. & C.	Shipper's load and count
S.P.A.	Societa per Azioni. Italian; corporation
S.P.R.L.	Societe de Personnes a Responsabilite Limitee. Belgian; company of persons with limited liability
S.R. & C.C.	Strikes, riots and civil commotion
S.S.	Steamship

T/A	Trade acceptance
T.T.	Telegraphic transfer
Vda de	Spanish; widow of
W.A.	With average
W.R.	War risk
W/R	Warehouse receipt
Wwe	German; Widow
Y.K.	Yugen-Kaisha. Japanese; limited liability company
Zoonen	Dutch; Sons

SEVEN

FINANCING FOREIGN INVESTMENTS

Multinational companies first decide on the nature of their needs for funds. The next step is to seek the funds. There are many sources of funds available. This chapter considers major sources of funds multinational companies invest overseas and the decision variables that affect the selection of particular sources.

Multinational companies may use internally generated funds, they may obtain their capital from sources within their home country, or they may seek funds overseas. While there are numerous parent-subsidiary financing methods, basically only two are used by parent companies to finance their foreign subsidiaries. These two methods are loans and equity financing.

If internal sources of funds are insufficient, multinational companies may seek outside sources of funds. Three major sources of external funds are joint ventures, borrowings from financial institutions in the parent country, and locally borrowed funds. Most countries allow foreign companies to issue stock or bonds for local sales. Although many host countries simply do not have large capital markets sufficient to meet the subsidiary's needs, they are actively encouraging foreign companies to enter their capital markets.

In addition to these internal and external sources of funds, development banks provide multinational companies with a variety of financing sources. They are worldwide, regional, or national. We shall describe the World Bank Group, leading regional lending agencies, and leading U.S. development banks. The World Bank Group consists of the International Bank for Reconstruction and Development, the International Development Association, and the International Finance Corporation. Leading regional lending agencies are the Inter-American Development Bank, the European Investment Bank, the Asian Development Bank, and the African Development Bank. Leading U.S. development banks are the Export-Import Bank, the Agency for International Development, and the Overseas Private Investment Corporation.

INTERNAL SOURCES OF FUNDS

Internal sources of funds are those funds generated within the parent-affiliate network. They include capital contributions from the parent, loans with parent company guarantees, funds provided by operations (retained earnings and depreciation), and intersubsidiary funds transfers. According to a Department of Commerce study of the 313 largest U.S. direct foreign investors in manufacturing, these internal sources of funds accounted for approximately 60 percent of the total required funds. Most of these internal funds were obtained from retained earnings (19 percent) and depreciation (29 percent).[1]

Funds from the Parent

The three major types of funds supplied by the parent are equity contributions, direct loans, and indirect loans under parent company guarantees.[2]

Equity contributions of cash are used to acquire going concerns from their previous owners, to buy out local minority interests, to set up new foreign subsidiaries, or to expand existing subsidiaries. Although they are a normal way of direct investments, in some develop-

[1] U.S. Department of Commerce, *Office of Foreign Direct Investments, Foreign Affiliate Financial Survey* (July 1971), p. 34.

[2] Sidney M. Robbins and Robert B. Stobaugh, "Financing Foreign Affiliates," *Financial Management* (Winter 1973), p. 57.

ing countries direct equity investments take the form of machinery or technology in lieu of cash. Some multinational enterprises have acquired a certain percentage of the common stock equity of foreign businesses in exchange for supplying machinery, equipment, tools, and intangibles (patents, engineering, etc.) necessary for manufacturing certain products.

Instead of increasing their equity contributions, multinational companies may lend money to their foreign subsidiaries. However, the parent lends money to its subsidiaries as an owner. Parent loans to foreign subsidiaries are usually more popular than equity contributions for a number of good reasons. First, parent loans provide greater flexibility in repatriating funds from foreign subsidiaries to the parent. In nearly every part of the world, it is legally more difficult to return funds to the parent through dividend payments or equity reductions than through interest and principal payments. Moreover, a reduction in equity is often construed as indicating plans to leave the country.

Second, tax considerations are another reason which favors parent loans over equity contributions. In most cases, interest payments on internal loans are tax deductible in the host country, while dividends are not. Moreover, principal payments, unlike dividend payments, do not generally constitute taxable income. Thus, it is possible that both the parent and its subsidiaries will save taxes by using loans instead of equity contributions.

Multinational companies can also provide credit to their subsidiaries not only by making loans but also by delaying the collection of accounts receivable. The amount of credit available through these intercompany accounts is limited to the amount of goods exchanged. Moreover, the length of the credit terms is frequently limited by governments. However, because intercompany accounts involve no formal documents, they are much easier to use. In addition, most governments interfere less with payments on intercompany accounts than loans.

When foreign subsidiaries have difficulties borrowing money, the parent may affix its own guarantees. While multinational companies have been traditionally reluctant to guarantee the debts of their subsidiaries, there are indications for an increased use of such guarantees. There are a variety of parent guarantees. (1) The parent may sign a purchase agreement under which it commits itself to buy its subsidiary's note from the lender in the event of the subsidiary's default. (2) The lender may be protected on only a part of the specific loan agreement. (3) Another type of guarantee is limited to a single loan agreement between a lender and a subsidiary. (4) The strongest type requires that the lender be protected on all loans to the subsidiary without amount or time limit. The types of loans with parent guarantees and the availability of such loans depend largely upon the parent's prestige and credit standing.

Funds Provided by Operations

Once a newly formed subsidiary gets on its feet, retained earnings and depreciation are the dominant sources of funds. These internal fund flows coupled with local credits leave relatively little need for fresh funds from the parent. As mentioned earlier, these two types of internal funds account for almost 50 percent of the total required funds.

Foreign subsidiaries are not always free to remit their earnings in hard currency elsewhere. Many developing countries have serious balance of payment problems and do not have sufficient international reserves. Thus, they restrict repatriation of funds for a specified number of years or to a certain percentage of the net income. These factors frequently force foreign subsidiaries to reinvest their internally generated funds in the host country. To use these internal fund flows for the expansion of an initial project in later years, the initial project may have to be smaller than actual demand requirements. If the anticipated expansion is necessary to meet current demand and the normal demand growth, multinational companies would have no difficulty in profitably using the internal fund flows in the host country.

Loans from Sister Subsidiaries

The availability of intersubsidiary credit in addition to funds from the parent vastly expands the number of possibilities for internal financing. If a subsidiary in Japan has some excess funds which it does not need immediately, it may lend these funds to a sister subsidiary in Canada, and vice versa. However, exchange controls and restrictions on capital movements imposed by many countries limit the range of possibilities for intersubsidiary loans. Moreover, the extensive use of intersubsidiary financial links makes it extremely difficult for the parent company to control its subsidiaries effectively.[3]

Nevertheless, many subsidiaries borrow cash from their sister subsidiaries. When there are only a few subsidiaries within the company family, it is fairly straightforward to arrange intersubsidiary loans.

[3] For example, an enterprise with a parent and 24 subsidiaries would have 3,000 intercompany financial links if there are 10 financial links between each company in the enterprise. For details, see Robbins and Stobaugh, "Financing Foreign Affiliates," *Financial Management*, pp. 56-65.

One subsidiary treasurer may negotiate directly with another sister subsidiary treasurer to obtain or give credit. However, a multinational company with many subsidiaries in many countries may prefer to have its central staff handle all excess funds or to establish a central pool of these funds on a worldwide basis for two reasons: (1) The number of financial relationships may exceed the capability of the main office to manage them effectively; and (2) the parent company does not want to lose control over its subsidiaries.

EXTERNAL SOURCES OF FUNDS

If a multinational company needs more funds than the amount that can be reasonably generated within the corporate family, the parent or its foreign subsidiaries may seek outside sources of funds. Such external sources of funds include joint business ventures with local owners and/or borrowings from financial institutions in the parent country or abroad.

Although subsidiaries can borrow directly outside the host country, most of them borrow locally for a number of reasons. (1) Local debts represent automatic protection against losses due to the devaluation of the local currency. (2) Subsidiary debts frequently do not appear on the consolidated financial statement issued by the parent as part of its annual report. (3) Some host countries such as Japan limit the amount of funds that foreign companies can import from outside the host country. (4) Foreign subsidiaries often borrow locally to maintain good relations with local banks.

Commercial Banks

As noted in Chapter 6, commercial banks are a major financial intermediary in trade credit. They are also the most important external source of financing nontrade international operations. The types of loans and services provided by banks vary from country to country, but all countries have some funds available at local banks.

Most of the local loans obtained by subsidiaries are short-term credits from commercial banks. These short-term credits are used largely to finance inventory and accounts receivable. They are self-liquidating loans to the extent that sufficient cash flows are produced to repay the credits as inventories are sold on credit and receivables are collected over the business cycle. The principal instruments used by banks to accommodate multinational firms' borrowing request are overdrafts, unsecured short-term loans, arbi loans, and link financing.

Overdrafts are one of the major short-term credits in Europe. An overdraft is a line of credit which permits the customer to write checks beyond deposits. The bank establishes the maximum amount of such credit based on its analysis of the customer's request, needs, and prospective cash flows. The borrower agrees to pay the amount overdrawn and interest on the credit. Although many banks waive service charges for their credit-worthy customers, some banks frequently require service charges and other fees.

Most short-term bank loans are made on an unsecured basis for multinational companies to cover seasonal increases in current assets. The percentages of such loans vary from country to country and reflect variations in individual bank policy and central government regulations. Most multinational firms prefer to borrow on an unsecured basis because the bookkeeping costs of the secured loans are high and they also have a number of highly restrictive provisions. However, some foreign subsidiaries cannot obtain loans on an unsecured basis because they are either financially weak or have not established a satisfactory performance record.

When foreign subsidiaries need short-term funds for only one purpose, they can obtain the funds by signing promissory notes. When they are in the process of obtaining long-term funds, these short-term loans may be made on a renewal basis. Such renewal short-term loans are frequently called bridge loans and repaid when the permanent financing arrangement is completed.

Currency swaps are agreements made between parties to exchange one currency with another for a specified period of time and then exchange the latter currency with the former currency. Arbi loans are the best known example of such swaps. An arbi loan is arranged in a country where money is readily available at reasonable rates. It is converted to the desired local currency, but the borrower arranges a forward exchange contract to insure conversion of the local currency into the foreign currency of original denomination at a specified future date. Thus, arbi loans allow multinational companies to borrow in one market for use in another market and to avoid foreign exchange risks. The cost of arbi loans include the interest on the loans and the charges associated with the forward exchange contract.

Link financing permits multinational companies in weak-currency countries to indirectly tap external sources of funds. Commercial banks in strong-currency countries help subsidiaries in weak-currency countries obtain loans by guaranteeing repayment on the loans. These subsidiaries borrow money from local banks or firms with excess weak money. Certainly, the banks in strong-currency countries require some sort of deposits from the borrower's parent company and the borrower must pay local interest rates. To protect the cost against foreign exchange risk, the lender usually hedges his position in the forward exchange market.

Edge Act and Agreement Corporations

Edge Act and Agreement corporations are subsidiaries of American banks that operate overseas. The Edge Act allowed American banks to act as holding companies and to own stock of foreign banks. Thus, these banks are able to provide loans and other banking services for American-owned companies in most countries around the world.

Background. Section 25 of the Federal Reserve Act was amended in 1916 as a means of permitting American banks to engage in international banking. Under this amendment, banks enter into an agreement with the Board of Governors of the Federal Reserve System concerning the types of activities which they would engage in. Hence, these Edge Act subsidiaries have been given the name "Agreement Corporations."

The 1916 amendment to the Federal Reserve Act did not provide for federal chartering of international banking corporations. This omission was rectified three years later (1919) by the passage of the now famous Edge Act. The Act has come to be known as "the Edge Act" because it was sponsored by then Senator Walter Edge of New Jersey. The Act added section 25(a) to the Federal Reserve Act. Section 25(a) authorized the Board of Governors to charter the so-called Edge Act corporations "for the purpose of engaging in international or foreign banking or other international or foreign financial operations . . . either directly or through the agency, ownership, or control of local institutions in foreign countries."[4]

The activities of Edge Act corporations are governed not only by the Edge Act but also by the related Regulation K of the Federal Reserve System. This regulation was first issued in 1920 and has been revised from time to time. The primary purpose of the 1963 revision was to enable the Edge Act corporations to operate more effectively in financing international trade and commerce. Before 1963 an Edge Act corporation could not engage in both banking and financing activities. However, the 1963 revision of Regulation K made it possible for the Edge Act corporation to partially integrate both banking and financing activities.

[4] Section 25(a) of the Federal Reserve Act (12 U.S.C. 611-631).

The Principal Features of the Edge Act. The Edge Act has a number of important features. First, foreign banking corporations organized under the Edge Act must have a minimum capital of $2 million. This is in sharp contrast with the 1916 amendment to the Federal Reserve Act whereby national banks with a minimum capital of $1 million could invest a maximum of ten percent of their capital in state-chartered foreign banking corporations. Second, such corporations may engage only in international banking and financing activities, but they may have an office in the United States. Third, while Edge Act subsidiaries basically cannot engage in banking activities within the United States, they may do so if such activities are incidental to or for the purpose of carrying out their foreign operations. Fourth, the Board of Governors of the Federal Reserve System is authorized to prescribe rules and regulations governing the operation of Edge Act subsidiaries.

Types of Activities. Edge Act and Agreement corporations typically engage in three types of activities: international banking, international financing, and acting as holding companies. It has already been mentioned that the 1963 revision of Regulation K provided for one type of Edge Act corporation which may engage in both banking and financing operations.

In their capacity as international banking corporations, Edge Act and Agreement corporations may hold demand and time deposits of foreign parties. They can make loans, but such loans to any single borrower cannot exceed ten percent of their capital and surplus. They can also open or confirm letters of credit, make loans or advances to finance foreign trade, create bankers' acceptances, receive items for collection, remit funds abroad, buy or sell securities, issue certain guarantees, and engage in foreign exchange transactions.

In their capacity as international financing corporations, Edge Act and Agreement corporations invest in the stock of nonbank financial concerns, development corporations, or commercial and industrial companies. Certainly, such investments require prior specific consent of the Board of Governors under certain circumstances. Edge Act subsidiaries have financed some foreign finance companies and official development corporations. In most cases, however, they finance commercial and industrial companies directly through loans and equity contributions. The major purpose of such financing activities is to provide promising foreign companies with capital at an early or important stage.

In their capacity as holding companies, Edge Act and Agreement corporations can own shares of foreign banking subsidiaries and affiliates. Member banks of the Federal Reserve System are not permitted to own shares of foreign banking subsidiaries. A foreign banking subsidiary may be more advantageous than a branch for two reasons: (1) Foreign branches are allowed to carry on only the activities allowed to their parent banks in the United States. (2) Certain countries do not permit nondomestic banks to open branches in their territory. In other instances, Edge Act and Agreement corporations have been the instrument through which U.S. banks have acquired equity interests in well-known foreign banks.

Closing Comment. Edge Act and Agreement corporations enhance the range of American banking activities abroad. They can engage in regular international banking and financial activities. They can also own shares of foreign businesses and banks. An increased use of such corporations may be expected whenever the favorable conditions for expanded foreign trade and financial operations exist. Hence, a significant further increase in Edge Act and Agreement corporations would depend largely upon the future growth of foreign trade and investment.

DEVELOPMENT BANKS

Development banks provide multinational companies with a broad range of financing resources. They are banking organizations established to support the economic development of underdeveloped areas through intermediate- and long-term loans. There are three broad groups of development banks: worldwide, regional, and national.

World Bank Group

The World Bank Group is a group of worldwide financial institutions organized after the devastation of World War II to aid economic reconstruction. These institutions include the International Bank for Reconstruction and Development, the International Development Association, and the International Finance Corporation.

The International Bank for Reconstruction and Development (IBRD). The IBRD, commonly known as the World Bank, was established at the Bretton Woods Conference in 1944 as a companion institution to the International Monetary Fund. Because the major objective of the World Bank was to finance reconstruction and development after World War II, it made certain loans in Europe for reconstruction. It found its resources completely inadequate for this purpose and thus stopped such reconstruction loans. With the Marshall Plan providing funds for reconstruction in Europe, the World Bank was able to concentrate on lending for economic development.

In recent decades, the World Bank has placed a major emphasis on loans to less developed countries for the development of such social infrastructure projects as irrigation, schools, and roads. Such developments are essential for future industrialization. Approximately a third of its development loans have gone to electrical power, a third for transportation improvements, and the remaining third for agricultural projects and education. Loans are made only to member governments, government agencies, and private businesses whose loans are guaranteed by their governments.

Because the Bank finances only a portion of project cost, private investors must finance the remaining portion. To encourage the direct participation of private investors into its loans, the Bank has adopted high credit standards. (1) It makes loans only for projects whose cost and revenue estimates are reasonably accurate. (2) When loans are made to private companies, these loans must be guaranteed by their governments. (3) An additional one percent is added to the regular interest rate. These funds go into reserve funds which are used to meet losses in the event of default. (4) Member countries are required to pay in the unpaid portion of their quotas in the event that funds are needed to meet losses. The application of such high standards has brought private funds increasingly into international investments.

The capital subscribed by member countries represents the basic equity capital for the Bank. Member countries are assigned subscription quotas on the basis of their size and wealth. They must pay ten percent of their quota when they join the Bank and the remaining 90 percent of the quota is subject to call if required. However, a substantial portion of the Bank's capital comes from bonds sold on world markets. Because the Bank applies high credit standards, its bonds usually carry high credit ratings.

International Finance Corporation. The World Bank had a number of problems in providing financial assistance to less developed countries. (1) All loans had to be guaranteed by governments. (2) The Bank provided only loans. (3) It financed only the foreign exchange requirements for a project and ignored local expenditures or working capital requirements. (4) It typically financed only large projects of public importance. These problems led to the development of the International Finance Corporation (IFC) in 1956 primarily to finance private enterprises in less developed countries through loan or equity participation.

The IFC regards development finance companies and industrial projects as the proper outlets for its limited capital. It assists in establishing development finance companies in areas where there are gaps in the local capital and money markets. It also helps existing development finance companies expand or reorganize their operations. The IFC usually invests in those industrial projects which will contribute to improved foreign exchange position, increased employment, improved management skills, or the exploration of natural resources. It provides risk capital to companies that require funds in order to expand, modernize, or diversify existing operations. It also helps to finance the establishment of new ventures. Ordinarily, it does not invest in such infrastructure projects as hospitals, transportation, and agricultural development.

IFC funds are available for either foreign exchange or local currency expenditures to meet fixed assets or working capital requirements. It makes nonguaranteed loans to private enterprises in less developed countries. Most of these loans have maturities from seven to 12 years. All its investments are made along with private investors and its financial contribution usually accounts for much less than 50 percent of total project cost.

International Development Association. The International Development Association (IDA) was established in 1960 as an affiliate of the World Bank Group to meet the specific needs of less developed countries. The IDA's loans are designed to finance good projects that are unable to support loan repayment schedules with conventional terms. Credit terms are generally extended for 50 years with very low or no interest. Repayment begins after a ten-year grace period and can be made in local currencies.

All World Bank members are free to join the IDA and more than 100 countries have done so. IDA resources are separate from World Bank resources. Nearly 90 percent of the IDA's capital comes from subscriptions of its member countries. The second most important source of its capital is the World Bank's contribution. IDA member countries are classified into two broad categories: Part I countries which consist of relatively developed countries and Part II countries which consist of less developed countries. Part I countries pay all of their subscriptions in convertible currencies, while Part II countries pay only ten percent of their subscriptions in convertible currencies and the remainder in their own currencies. Certain nonmember countries such as Switzerland and New Zealand have made loans to the IDA on the same terms on which the IDA lends to its members.

Regional Development Banks

Regional groups of countries have established regional development banks to promote more effective economic development within the member countries. Leading regional development banks are the Inter-American Development Bank, the European Investment Bank, the Asian Development Bank, and the African Development Bank.

Inter-American Development Bank. The Inter-American Development Bank (IDB) was founded in 1959 by the United States and 19 Latin American countries to further the economic development of its member countries. IDB loans are available only when private sources are not available on reasonable terms. It usually finances no more than 50 percent of total project cost.

The IDB has three types of activity. They are:

(1) With its Ordinary Capital Resources Fund, the Bank makes development loans to both public and private institutions. These loans are earmarked for projects that promote Latin America's economic development.
(2) With its U.S. created Social Progress Trust Fund, the Bank makes loans to finance projects with high social value.
(3) With its Fund for Special Operations, the Bank makes loans whose terms are much more lenient than those available in the regular money and capital markets. Maturities may be extremely long, repayment may be made in the borrower's currency, or interest rates may be arbitrarily low.

European Investment Bank. The European Investment Bank (EIB) was established in 1958 by members of the European Economic Community. Its resources are used to support the socio-economic infrastructure of nations or basic industries. Most of these loans have maturities from 12 to 20 years. Ordinarily, three or four year intervals are established before loan repayments begin.

The EIB has three types of responsibility. These include:

(1) It assists in financing projects which involve two or more member governments. In this case, it plays an important role in coordinating the activities of different national financial agencies.
(2) It promotes the potentials of economies of scale. It helps specialize or expand the operations of plants or firms in countries with a comparative advantage in certain lines of business.
(3) It helps achieve a more uniform and high level of economic maturity within the Common Market.

Asian Development Bank. The Asian Development Bank (ADB) was formed in 1966 by several Asian countries in partnership with the United States, Canada, Britain, West Germany, and some other European countries. Approximately one-third of its subscribed capital and voting power belongs to nonregional industrial countries. The ADB makes long-term loans to private companies without government guarantees. Some ADB loans go to Asian national banks that reloan to private enterprises through their respective development agencies. Some other ADB loans are used to supply risk capital.

African Development Bank. The African Development Bank (AfDB) was established in 1964 by the Organization of African Unity. Unlike other regional development banks, the AfDB has excluded nonregional partners in an effort to avoid undue outside influence. It makes long-term loans to industrial investors and underwrites equity offerings for projects. Because it excludes nonregional participants, it suffers from severe capital limitations which in turn restrict its ability to lend.

National Development Banks

Many governments in industrial countries have their own development banks to foster international loans and investments. The three leading institutions of the United States are the Export-Import Bank, the Agency for International Development, and the Overseas Private Investment Corporation.

Export-Import Bank. The Export-Import Bank, commonly known as the Exim Bank, was founded in 1934 as an independent agency of the U.S. government. Although the Exim Bank was originally created to facilitate trade with the Soviet Union, its purpose has been expanded over the years. (1) It makes development loans to foreigners that enable them to buy American goods and services. (2) It makes short- and intermediate-term loans to finance American exports. (3) It can make loans to finance American imports. (4) It can finance exports or guarantee export credits which do not meet the traditional criteria of reasonable assurance of payment.

The Exim Bank now operates under the amended Export-Import Bank Act of 1945. However, its lending authority has been extended from time to time. Since 1953 its life or lending authority has been renewed for five-year periods by the U.S. Congress. In the Fall of 1961, it expanded its operations by stimulating the establishment of the Foreign Credit Insurance Association. Its operations were further expanded by legislation in 1968 to provide for the establishment of an Export Expansion Facility. This facility enables the Exim Bank to participate in high risk transactions. In 1974, the extension of its life was in doubt for a while because the Congress wanted to limit its lending authority to the Soviet Union, but an agreement was made to extend its life. Its direct loan limit was also changed to cover the cost of exports from 30 to 55 percent and to increase its guarantees from 45 to 85 percent.

Agency for International Development. The Agency for International Development (AID) was established in 1961 to carry out nonmilitary U.S. foreign assistance programs. The AID, as an agency of the U.S. State Department, places emphasis on assistance to friendly governments or to support programs which will make foreign friends for the United States. As the primary aid agency of the U.S. government, it performs three functions: (1) It administers the government's programs of technical cooperation with less developed countries. (2) It administers the government's economic programs for less developed countries. (3) It carries out special emergency programs as directed by the President of the United States.

Development loans are made to friendly governments and private companies may borrow these funds from their governments. To prevent heavy drain of U.S. dollars, loans are usually tied to purchases of U.S. goods and services. Moreover, these funds are generally maintained in the United States and are simply made available for use by recipient countries. All development loans are repayable in dollars and can have a maximum maturity of 50 years with a grace period of ten years. In making development loans, the AID considers the availability of funds at reasonable terms from other free-world sources. Interest rates are usually lower than international money rates.

Overseas Private Investment Corporation. The AID was responsible for the conduct of local currency loans under Public Law (PL) 480 until the Overseas Private Investment Corporation (OPIC) was established in 1969. PL 480 provides for sales of surplus agricultural products to less developed countries for local currencies. The OPIC handles the so-called Cooley Amendment Funds. The Funds are local currency funds received in payment for agricultural products sold by the United States either under the Mutual Security Act or the Agricultural Trade Development Assistance Act. The OPIC lends these Cooley Amendment Funds to U.S. firms or subsidiaries in those countries that provided the funds by purchasing agricultural products from the United States. These loans are also extended to foreign private companies whose activities facilitate the expansion of overseas markets for U.S. agricultural products.

The OPIC is also responsible for insuring American overseas investors against political risks. It has concentrated its protection in seven of the 80 eligible countries: Argentina, Brazil, Chile, the Dominican Republic, India, Jamaica, and Korea. It combines private business with the U.S. foreign policy objective of encouraging American firms to invest in less developed countries. Thus, it grants insurance for projects which are in the best interest of the United States and the host country's economy.

SUMMARY

For purposes of expansion, new investment, and day-to-day operations, the international financial manager must be familiar with various sources of funds. These sources of funds may be either internal or external. This chapter has discussed such internal sources of funds as funds provided by operations (retained earnings and depreciation), funds from the parent (equity contributions, loans, and trade credit), and loans from subsidiaries.

External sources of funds include joint business ventures with local owners and/or borrowings from financial institutions in the parent country or abroad. Commercial banks are a major financial intermediary in foreign trade and investment. The upsurge of direct foreign investment by multinational companies since the early 1950s has forced banks to follow their customers overseas. The principal instruments used by banks to accommodate multinational firms' borrowing requests are overdrafts, unsecured short-term loans, arbi loans, and link financing.

The Edge Act of 1919 allowed American banks to act as holding companies and to own stock of foreign banks. Since then many Edge Act and Agreement corporations have been established as subsidiaries of American banks which operate overseas. These Edge Act and Agreement corporations provide loans and other banking services to American companies in most countries around the world.

Development banks provide multinational companies with a variety of financing sources. They are banks established to aid in economic development through equity participations, loans, or some intermediate form of investment. They may be worldwide, regional, or national. The World Bank Group consists of the International Bank for Reconstruction and Development, the International Development Association, and the International Finance Corporation. These worldwide development banks are designed to provide financial support for less developed countries.

Regional groups of countries have established regional development banks to promote more effective economic development within the member countries. Four regional lending institutions formed to facilitate development on four continents are the Inter-American Development Bank, the Asian Development Bank, the European Investment Bank, and the African Development Bank. National Development banks perform the same general functions as worldwide and regional development banks.

REFERENCES

7-1 Anderson, Gerald L., "International Project Financing," *Financial Executive* (May 1977), pp. 40-45.

7-2 Dufey, Gunter, "Corporate Finance and Exchange Rate Variations," *Financial Management* (Summer 1972), pp. 51-57.

7-3 Eiteman, David K., and Arthur I. Stonehill, *Multinational Business Finance* (Reading, Mass.: Addison-Wesley Publishing Co., 1979), Chapters 9 and 13.

7-4 Lees, Francis A., "International Lending Strategies of Commercial Banks," *Columbia Journal of World Business* (Winter 1975), pp. 40-49.

7-5 Lessard, Donald R., ed., *International Financial Management* (New York: Warren, Gorham & Lamont, 1979).

7-6 Robbins, Sidney M., and Robert B. Stobaugh, "Financing Foreign Affiliates," *Financial Management* (Winter 1972), pp. 56-67.

7-7 Rodriguez, Rita M., and E. Eugene Carter, *International Financial Management* (Englewood Cliffs, N.J.: Prentice-Hall, Inc., 1979), Chapter 7.

7-8 Ruckdeschel, Fred B., "Risk in Foreign and Domestic Lending Activities of U.S. Banks," *Columbia Journal of World Business* (Winter 1975), pp. 50-54.

7-9 Semler, Johannes, "Advantages and Disadvantages of Forming Finance Companies Abroad," *Euromoney* (June 1974), pp. 56-59.

7-10 Suz, John, *International Development Banks* (Dobbs Ferry, N.Y.: Oceana, 1974).

7-11 Zenoff, David B., and Jack Zwick, *International Financial Management* (Englewood Cliffs, N.J.: Prentice-Hall, Inc., 1969), Chapters 8 and 9.

£¢$£¢

EIGHT

INTERNATIONAL FINANCIAL MARKETS

In this chapter we discuss both Eurodollar markets and international banking. Eurodollar markets and multinational banking operations of commercial banks are two major sources of capital which exist in international markets but are not available to purely domestic corporations. The growth of Eurodollar markets has been expanded by a parallel expansion of the world banking system.

EURODOLLAR MARKETS

The Eurocurrency market consists of banks that accept deposits and make loans in foreign currencies outside the country of issue. These deposits are commonly known as Eurocurrencies. Thus, U. S. dollars deposited in London are called Eurodollars; German marks deposited in Paris are called Euromarks; and British pounds deposited in New York are called Eurosterling.

Because Eurodollars are the predominant form of Eurocurrency, the term "Eurodollar" frequently refers to the entire Eurocurrency market.[1] Eurodollars could be broadly defined as dollar-denominated deposits in banks all over the world except the United States. These banks may be foreign banks or foreign branches of U. S. banks. However, many experts narrowly define Eurodollars as dollar-denominated deposits in Western European banks or foreign branches of U. S. banks in Western Europe. Hence, they distinguish between Eurodollars and petrodollars in the Middle East or between Eurodollars and Asiandollars in Hong Kong and Singapore.

Eurodollar markets are well organized, very efficient, and very large. They serve a number of valuable purposes for multinational business operations. Eurodollars are a convenient money market device for multinational firms to hold their excess liquidity. Eurodollars are a major source of short-term loans to finance corporate working capital needs and foreign trade. In recent years, the so-called "Eurobond markets" have developed as a major source of long-term investment capital for multinational companies.

Creation of Eurodollars

Many multinational companies and governments have learned to employ the Eurodollar market as readily as they do the domestic banking system. The major sources of Eurodollars are (1) the growing dollar reserves of oil-exporting countries, (2) foreign governments or businessmen who prefer to hold dollars outside the United States, (3) foreign banks with dollars in excess of current needs, and (4) multinational companies with excess cash balances. Since the 1974 oil crisis, oil-exporting countries have had enough leverage on the worldwide oil supply to impose a major price escalation. As a result, the Middle East, where more than half of the world's known oil reserves are located, has acquired enormous economic wealth and has become the important source of Eurodollars. Once Eurodollars come into existence, they can create themselves through the lending and investing activities of commercial banks. T-accounts may be used to illustrate such Eurodollar creation.

Example 8-1 Assume that the International Trading Company holds $1,000 on deposit in a New York bank. If the reserve requirement is 20 percent, the $1,000 deposit will be reflected in the books of the New York bank, the International Trading Company, and the Federal Reserve Bank of New York as follows:

[1] The Bank for International Settlements estimates that U. S. dollars account for about 75 percent of the total Eurocurrency market.

New York Bank

	Deposit of International Trading Company $1,000

International Trading Company

Deposit held with New York Bank $1,000	

Federal Reserve Bank of New York

	Deposit of New York bank held as part of its reserve requirement $ 200

Cash flows in a commercial bank involve four major elements of information: (1) currency, (2) institution and location, (3) maturity date, and (4) interest rate. To better understand how bank transfers take place and how Eurodollars come into existence, let us examine a few transactions.

Step 1. Assume that the International Trading Company decides to transfer its $1,000 deposit from the New York bank to a London bank. Let us further assume that the International Trading Company decides to maintain its dollars in a dollar-denominated 90-day deposit account at the going rate with the London bank. This situation will be reflected in the books of the New York bank, the London bank, and the International Trading Company as follows:

New York Bank

	Deposit of International Trading Company –$1,000
	Deposit of London bank +$1,000

London Bank

Deposit in New York bank +$1,000	Deposit of International Trading Company +$1,000

International Trading Company

Deposit in New York bank –$1,000	
Deposit in London bank +$1,000	

By this step, a Eurodollar deposit has been created. The London bank has now obtained the power to deal in dollars outside the United States. Note, however, that total deposit levels in the United States have not changed; the $1,000 liability of the London bank is matched by its $1,000 deposit in the New York bank. The only change at the New York bank was in the name of the depositor from the International Trading Company to the London bank.

Step 2. Because the London bank has to pay interest on its 90-day deposit liability to the International Trading Company, it decides to extend a Eurodollar loan of $1,000 to a Paris firm. This loan transaction will be reflected in the books of the London bank and the Paris firm as follows:

London Bank

Dollar loan to Paris firm	+$1,000	Dollar deposit of Paris firm	+$1,000

Paris Firm

Dollar deposit in London bank	+$1,000	Dollar loan repayable to London bank	+$1,000

Because the New York bank still has $1,000 deposit liability to the London bank, its balance sheet has not changed. But the London bank has increased its deposits and loans by $1,000. This expands the total Eurodollar deposit liabilities of non-U. S. banks to $2,000. The International Trading Company now holds $1,000 of Eurodollars with the London bank and the Paris firm has an additional $1,000 of Eurodollars in the London bank.

The London bank exhausted its dollar lending capacity. Thus, if the Paris firm had held its dollar deposit with the London bank, the multiple creation of Eurodollars would have stopped. However, if the Paris firm withdraws its dollar deposits from the London bank and deposits it with a Paris bank, the Eurodollar creation process could continue.

Step 3. Assume that the Paris firm withdraws its deposit from the London bank and deposits it in a Paris bank. The following set of T-accounts record the event.

New York Bank

		Deposit of London bank	–$1,000
		Deposit of Paris bank	+$1,000

London Bank

Deposit in New York bank	–$1,000	Dollar deposit of Paris firm	–$1,000

Paris Bank

Deposit in New York bank	+$1,000	Dollar deposit of Paris firm	+$1,000

Paris Firm

Dollar deposit in London bank	–$1,000		
Dollar deposit in Paris bank	+$1,000		

After Step 3 the amount of Eurodollars is still $2,000, but the Paris bank has obtained Eurodollar deposits that it can lend out. The potential expansion of Eurodollars is infinite in the case where banks do not maintain any reserves against their Eurodollar deposits.

Because there are usually no legal reserves against Eurodollar deposits, one may argue that Eurodollar deposits could expand indefinitely. Who creates this infinite expansion of Eurodollars? Three parties do so jointly: (1) public and private depositors by always keeping their money in non-U.S. banks on deposit, (2) banks by keeping none of their Eurodollar deposits in the form of cash, and (3) public and private borrowers who make it possible for the banks to find Eurodollar loans and attractive earning assets to buy with their excess cash. However, there are a number of checks to this expansion. First, public and private depositors may hold a portion of their money in the form of non-deposit cash. Second, banks may retain a part of their Eurodollar deposits as a liquid reserve. Third, borrowers may convert the dollars borrowed into local currency. This conversion will not only stop the further expansion of Eurodollar deposits, but it may actually reduce the volume of outstanding Eurodollar deposits.

Historical Development of the Eurodollar Market

In the previous section, we have seen that Eurodollars come into existence when a depositor of a U. S. bank transfers funds to a foreign bank or to a foreign branch office of an American bank. Ordinarily, transfers of funds into the Eurodollar market are prompted by the consideration that foreign banks offer higher rates of interest to their dollar depositors than American banks. Foreign banks accept dollar-denominated deposits because they can in turn lend them at higher rates.

European banks usually offer higher rates of interest to their dollar depositors than U. S. banks for several reasons. (1) Under the Regulation Q of the Federal Reserve System, U. S. banks are subject to the interest rate ceiling on time deposits. (2) They are required to hold a stipulated percentage of their deposits at a Federal Reserve bank or in vault cash. (3) They have to pay deposit insurance assessments.[2] Dollar-denominated deposits in banks outside the United States are free of these restrictions.

To understand why the Eurodollar market has grown so rapidly since the 1950s, it is useful to begin with the origin of the Eurodollar market. Perhaps ironically, the Soviet Union and other communist countries started a large volume of transactions in Eurodollar deposits shortly after World War II. Eastern European holders of dollars were afraid to deposit their dollar holdings in the United States because these dollars might become blocked in the United States.

The Eurodollar market originated in the 1950s because of the desire of Eastern European banks to leave their dollar deposits in Europe rather than in the United States. But the major reason was the strength of the U. S. dollar. In the 1950s, the U. S. dollar emerged as the leading international reserve currency. Thus, the U. S. dollar replaced the British pound as the primary instrument of exchange in the money markets of the world.

The Eurodollar market functions efficiently for the following three reasons. First, the United States imposes no restrictions on nonresident payment or transfers of dollar balances. Foreign governments, individuals, and companies are free to maintain and transfer deposits in U. S. banks. Second, European banks accept Eurodollar deposits and make Eurodollar loans at competitive rates. The absence of reserve requirements and no interest ceilings on Eurodollar time deposits make Eurobanks competitive with American banks. Third,

[2] The Federal Deposit Insurance Corporation (FDIC) was established in 1933 to insure the deposits of U. S. commercial banks. Practically all deposits are insured up to a certain amount per account by the FDIC. FDIC member banks pay their insurance premiums equal to one-twelfth of one percent of their total deposits.

there is a demand for dollar deposits and dollar loans outside the United States. In other words, there are non-Eurobank entities which are willing to deposit dollars in non-U. S. banks and to borrow from such banks for investment purposes.[3]

Growth of the Eurodollar Market. It is extremely difficult to measure the size of the Eurodollar market because of the difficulty in defining the market. Does the market include only dollars or should it also include other Eurocurrencies convertible into dollars? Should the measurement include deposits accepted by the first foreign banks or should it also include deposits all along the chain (e.g., from the Paris bank, to the London bank, to the Bonn bank, etc.)? Does the market include deposits only in European banks or should it also include deposits located outside Europe (e.g., dollar deposits in the Middle East and Asia)? Estimates of Eurodollar market size vary as widely as do criteria for computation.

Thus, it is not surprising to find that there is no statistical series covering the period from the early years to the present. The principal collectors of statistics are the Bank for International Settlements (BIS) and Morgan Guaranty Trust Company (Morgan). However, it was not until 1963 that they began to keep more or less complete track of the dollar and foreign currency transactions of European banks. In recent years, practically all articles and books on the market depend on the estimates made by BIS and Morgan.

The Eurodollar market grew quite slowly at first, as international financial managers learned of its existence and advantages. However, since the mid-1960s the market has grown at a truly phenomenal rate, which is beyond the wildest estimates of the most optimistic forecasters. Both BIS and Morgan estimate the size of the Eurodollar market in terms of both the gross size and the net size. The gross size of the market is the sum of all Eurodollar deposit liabilities. The net size of the market is the gross size of the market minus interbank deposits.

Both BIS and Morgan estimate that the net size of the market has grown at an average annual growth rate of about 30 percent. According to Morgan's estimate, the growth rate of the market in terms of the net size reached as high as 76 percent in 1976 and the growth size of the market exceeded $1,000 billion at the end of 1981. It is important to note that these data do not include deposits in banks outside Europe and thus underestimate the size of the market.

[3] Gunter Dufey and Ian H. Giddy, *Credit Creation and the Growth of the Eurodollar Market*, Research Paper No. 127 (New York: Columbia University Graduate School of Business, 1976), p. 8.

Causes for Eurodollar Expansion. Although the basic causes of Eurodollar expansion are efficiency, many writers argue that the market grew as a direct result of monetary controls imposed in the United States and exchange controls imposed in Europe during the 1950s and 1960s. In 1957, British monetary authorities attempted to strengthen their weakening pound by imposing tight controls on English banks lending in sterling to nonresidents of England. The Bank of England encouraged English banks to turn to dollar lending as the only alternative which would permit them to maintain their lending position in international finance.

In the mid-1960s, the American authorities adopted a set of regulations to control capital outflows from the United States and to reduce the balance-of-payments deficit. Although there are some differences in opinions concerning the impact of these regulations on the growth of the Eurodollar market, many assume that the market grew as a result of the regulations. They are: (1) the Interest Equalization Tax of 1963 which imposed restraints on foreign portfolio investment, (2) the Voluntary Foreign Credit Restraints of 1964 which imposed restrictions on capital outflows from U. S. banks and corporations, and (3) the Office-of-Foreign Direct-Investment Guidelines of 1965 which imposed controls on U.S.-financed foreign direct investment.

Two other regulations that contributed heavily to the rapid growth of the Eurodollar market are Regulations Q and M. The Federal Reserve's Regulation Q limited the interest rate that U. S. banks could pay on time deposits. In the 1930s, the United States imposed interest rate ceilings for time deposits and prohibited interest payments on demand deposits. The purpose of the rate ceilings was to prevent banks from paying too much interest on deposits and thus from making risky loans on which they could charge high interest rates. Because the ceilings did not apply to Eurodollar deposits, it was advantageous for U. S. bank depositors to pull funds from the United States and invest in high-yield Eurodollar deposits. In the 1960s, regulations were imposed to control such transfers by Americans, but they could not be applied to foreigners who had deposits in the United States.

By the Federal Reserve's Regulation M, U. S. banks are required to keep a stipulated percentage of their deposits at a Federal Reserve bank or in vault cash. These reserve requirements are determined by the Board of Governors of the Federal Reserve System within certain limits set by Congress. Because Eurodollar deposits had no such reserve requirements, Eurobanks were free to lend or invest against the full face amount of the account. But in 1969, Regulation M was amended to require ten percent marginal reserves on any increase in

Eurodollar loans of U. S. banks from their foreign branches above the level of May 1969. This reserve requirement was originally imposed to reduce capital inflows into the United States. In 1971, the requirement was raised to 20 percent and its purpose was to prevent capital outflows from the United States. But the reserve requirement on Eurodollar loans of U. S. banks was reduced to zero in 1978, which made Eurodollar loans more desirable.

The Federal Reserve Board in 1968-1969 adopted a tight monetary policy. This tight policy reduced the availability of funds in the United States. To evade the Federal Reserve's tight monetary policy, U. S. banks became the single biggest source of demand for Eurodollars in the history of the market in 1969. The United States was the major user of Eurodollars until 1970, while Western Europe was the major provider of Eurodollars. This pattern began to change in 1970 as the United States repaid Eurodollar loans and Western Europe emerged as a substantial user of Eurodollars.

Another set of economic factors also contributed to the rapid growth of the Eurodollar market. They include: (1) the tendency for central banks to place some of their own excess dollar reserves in the market, (2) the growth of foreign trade and investment, (3) confidence in the U. S. dollar, (4) the growing oil dollar reserves of oil-exporting countries, and (5) the growth of the Eurobond market.

Uses of Eurodollars. European banks with Eurodollars may use these funds in a number of ways. First, they may redeposit their Eurodollars in other European banks or European branches of a U. S. bank. Second, they may make loans to non-bank users such as multinational companies. These multinational companies use the dollars to meet their dollar obligations or to buy local currencies. Third, they may transfer their dollars to Eurodollars in European branches of a U. S. bank which in turn would lend these funds to the U. S. home office.

Heavy borrowers in the Eurodollar market are governments and commercial banks. Many countries have recently been suffering petroleum-related deficits. Hence, they want Eurodollars to help improve their international reserves. U. S. commercial banks have borrowed Eurodollars to rebuild their own reserve position. Many commercial banks rely on Eurodollars to grant credit to exporters and importers. Eurobanks frequently swap Eurodollars in local currencies in order to make loans to domestic companies. In addition, international development banks such as the World Bank and various regional development banks have been regular borrowers in the market.

Many of the private nonbank borrowers continue to be companies engaged in international operations as exporters, importers, and investors. They are attracted by the size of the market and the importance of the U. S. dollar as the international reserve. A second advantage of Eurodollar loans is that the funds raised in the external market have no restrictions attached about their deployment. In contrast, the funds raised in national money markets have some restrictions in almost all cases. Finally, international money markets provide multinational companies with flexibility in many ways such as terms, conditions, and covenants.

The Group of Ten countries as a whole are usually the net provider of Eurodollars, but Switzerland accounts for most of the net position. In addition, oil-exporting countries are the substantial providers of funds to the Eurodollar market. The European countries outside the Group of Ten, Eastern Europe, and Latin America are the three largest users of Eurodollars. Such Asian countries as Hong Kong, Indonesia, South Korea, and the Philippines are also well-known borrowers of Eurodollars.

Eurodollar Instruments

The two major types of instruments used in the Eurodollar market are Eurodollar deposits and Eurodollar loans.

Eurodollar Deposits. Eurodollar deposits are either fixed-time deposits or negotiable certificates of deposits (CDs). About 85 percent of Eurodollar deposits are in the form of time deposits with the funds placed in the bank for a fixed maturity at a specific interest rate. In contrast to the U. S. practice, Eurobanks do not maintain checking accounts (demand deposits) for their customers. While maturities of these time deposits range from one day to a number of days, most of them have a maturity of less than one year. Time deposits are for fixed periods, but Eurobanks are frequently flexible if the depositor desires to withdraw his deposits early.

Approximately 15 percent of Eurodollar deposits are in the form of negotiable CDs. Negotiable CDs for Eurodollars were first introduced in 1966 by the London branch of First National City Bank of New York (now Citibank). Currently, most major Eurobanks issue negotiable CDs whose safety and liquidity are assured by an active secondary market. The secondary market consists of broker/dealer firms who are members of the International CD Market Association. This Association was established in London in 1968 to provide customers with the highest quality of services.

There are two types of CDs: tap CDs and tranche CDs. Tap CDs are the more usual form of negotiable CDs and are issued in single amounts whenever banks require funds in a specific amount for a particular maturity. Tap CDs are available for maturities of less than one year. They are issued in multiples of $1,000 with a usual minimum purchase amount of $10,000 or $25,000. Tranche CDs are a series of identical tranches, each of which has a small denomination such as $10,000 or $25,000. However, all of these tranches have identical yields, interest payment dates, and maturities. Thus, tranche CDs have great appeal to those investors who prefer an instrument with smaller denominations than those of conventional tap CDs. Their maturities and their total amounts outstanding are much greater than those of tap CDs.

Eurodollar Loans. Eurodollar loans range from a minimum of $500,000 to $100 million, typically in multiples of $1 million. Their maturities range from 30 days to five or seven years. Short-term Eurodollar financings represent the major part of the Eurodollar lending business. Short-term Eurodollar loans are usually conducted under prearranged lines of credit. Under such an arrangement, the Eurobank establishes a maximum loan balance (line of credit) after investigation of its client's credit standing. Although the commitment period is typically one year, advances under a line of credit are normally made against notes with maturities of 90 or 180 days. Lines of credit are renewable after a thorough review process. These short-term Eurodollar loans are usually made on an unsecured basis and repaid at the maturity date.

Eurobanks also provide international concerns with medium-term loans. There are two major forms of medium-term Eurodollar loans: revolving Eurodollar credits and Eurodollar term loans. A revolving credit is a confirmed line of credit beyond one year. Under this arrangement, the Eurobank permits its clients to borrow a specified amount of Eurodollars for a specified period of time, usually three to five years. But actual loans are normally made against renewable notes with maturities of between 90 and 180 days. Eurodollar term loans are the less popular form of medium-term Eurodollar loans. They have such provisions as the revolving feature and an agreed-upon amortization schedule. The interest rate on these term loans is adjusted every six months. Borrowers are usually permitted to prepay the loans on the interest-adjustment date.

Interest Rates. It should be clear from the preceding discussion that there are two sets of interest rates: Eurodollar-deposit interest rates and Eurodollar-loan interest rates. In general, Eurodollar-loan interest rates are higher than Eurodollar-deposit interest rates to meet administrative costs of loans and to make profits. Interest rates on Eurodollar deposits are usually higher than those on deposits in the United States. This is because as discussed in the preceding section, governments regulate domestic money markets while Eurodollars are free of these regulations.

Eurodollar deposit and loan rates are determined by supply and demand forces. More specifically, these rates depend on the rates in the corresponding home currency, spot and forward exchange rates, domestic and Eurocurrency rates in other currencies, and the inflation rate in various countries. Many economists have presumed that Eurodollar-deposit rates depend on U. S. money market rates.[4] Figure 8-1 shows selected Eurodollar deposit and U. S. money market rates. Throughout the 1978-1981 period, the U. S. 90-day CD's rates have provided an effective floor for the three-month Eurodollar deposit rates.

Interest rates on Eurodollar loans are usually lower than similar rates in the United States. With deposit rates higher and lending rates lower in the Eurodollar market than in the U. S. market, Eurobanks must operate on a narrower margin. There are a number of factors which enable Eurobanks to operate profitably on narrower margins than domestic markets. U. S. banks are subject to statutory reserve requirements, deposit insurance fees, and other official restrictions such as Regulation Q. Eurobanks remain free of these restrictions.

Eurobanks usually establish their lending rate at some fixed percentage above the six-month London Interbank Offer Rate (LIBOR). The LIBOR is the arithmetic average of the rates at which six major banks in London are willing to borrow a substantial portion of their dollar funds at a certain time during the morning. Loans are typically made at a range of ¾ of one to three percent above the LIBOR. The actual charge to the Eurodollar borrower depends on such factors as market conditions, maturity, and credit worthiness. In addition, it is a well-established practice in the Eurodollar market to charge a commitment fee of ¼ to ½ percent on the unused portion of the loan.

In the absence of tight controls on international financial transactions, arbitrage and risk differences affect the relationship between rates in the internal market (the U. S. market) and in the external market (the Eurodollar market). The absence of government controls on international capital flows results in arbitrage between internal and external segments of the market for dollar credit. This arbitrage

[4] See Patric H. Hendershott, "The Structure of International Interest Rates: The U. S. Treasury Bill Rate and the Eurodollar Deposit Rate," *Journal of Finance* (September 1967), pp. 455-465; and George Rich, "A Theoretical and Empirical Analysis of the Eurodollar Market," *Journal of Money, Credit, and Banking*, (August 1972), pp. 616-635.

Figure 8-1 Selected Euro-Dollar and U.S. Money Market Rates.

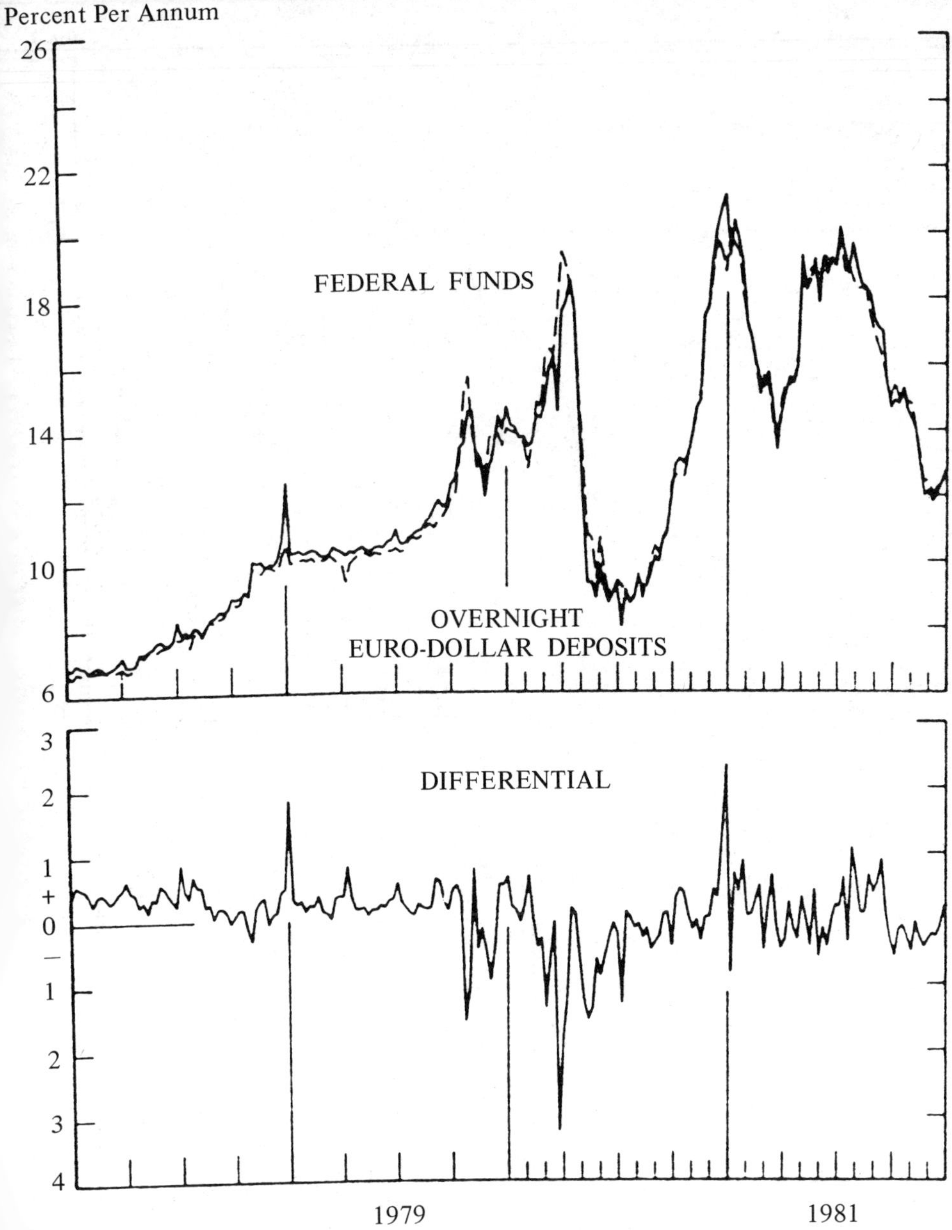

[1] Percent on differential scale = 2 percent on rate scale.

Source: Board of Governors of the Federal Reserve System, *Selected Interest and Exchange Rates* (January 4, 1982), Chapter 7.

Figure 8-1 Continued.

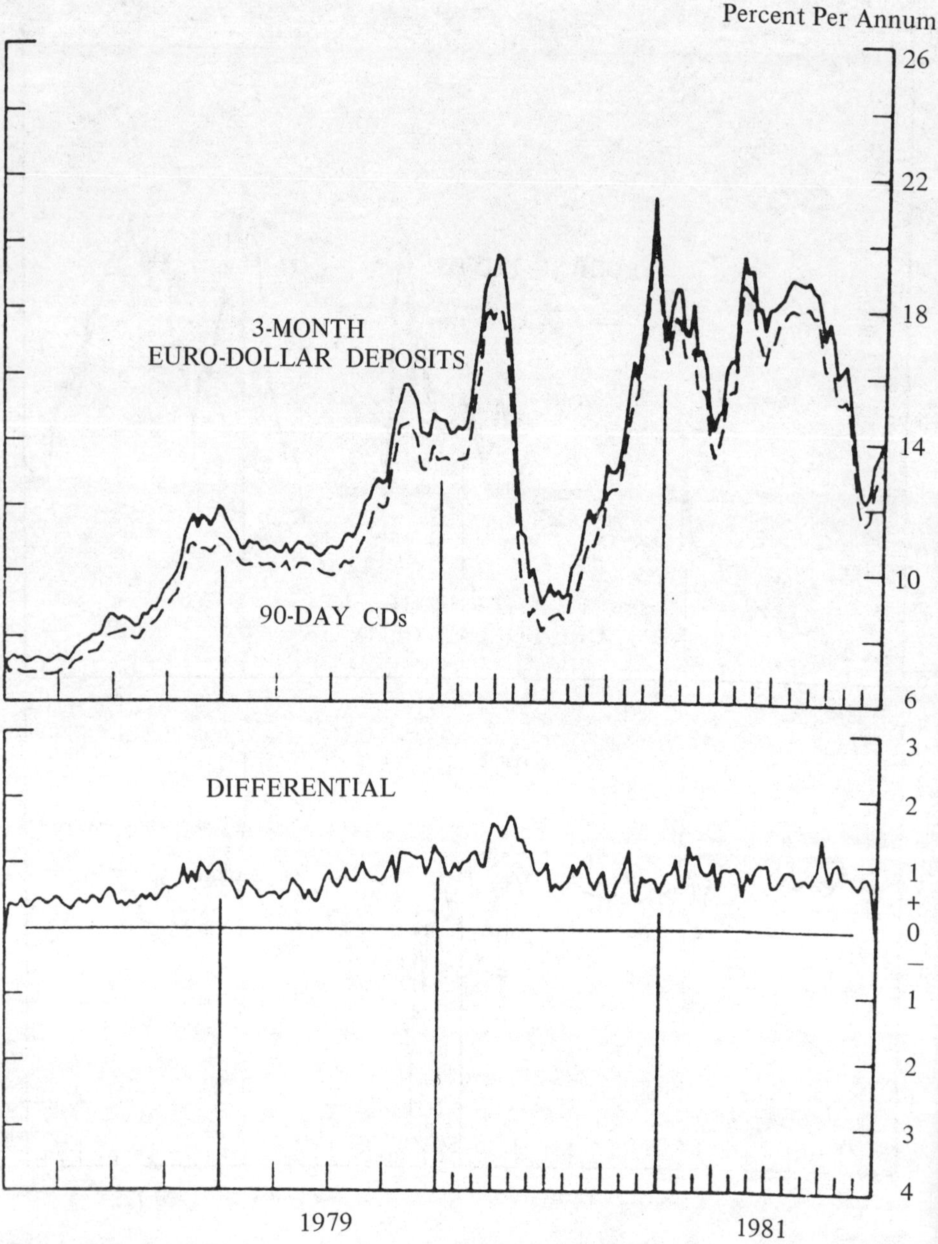

keeps the spread between internal and external rates within a narrow margin.

Risk differences between internal and external money markets represent a possible reason for the observation that deposit rates are higher and lending rates lower in the Eurodollar market than in the U. S. market. In general, risks on external dollar deposits are somewhat greater than those on internal dollar deposits and loans. The major risks in the Eurodollar market include (1) the removal of nonresident convertibility by the United States, (2) the seizure of Eurodollar assets and liabilities by the authorities where they operate, and (3) the refusal of central banks to function as lenders of last resort in the case of Eurobanks.

In addition to arbitrage and risk differences, differences in the institutional structure of the markets influence differences between U. S. rates and Eurodollar rates. These market imperfections occur because of (1) institutional factors, (2) perceptual factors, (3) regulatory restraints such as reserve requirements, and (4) oligopolistic market conditions which stem from barriers to entry in the U. S. banking system.

THE ASIAN CURRENCY MARKET

In 1968, an Asian version of the Eurodollar came into existence with the acceptance of dollar-denominated deposits by commercial banks in Singapore. Singapore was an ideal location for the birth of the Asian currency market. It had an excellent communication network, important banks, and a stable government.

The Asian currency market developed when the Singapore branch of the Bank of America proposed the Monetary Authority of Singapore relax taxes and restrictions. The Monetary Authority accepted these proposals and extended a number of important incentives to foreign banks so that dollar accounts could be held in Singapore. They include: (1) the removal of an existing 40 percent tax on interest payments on foreign currency deposits, (2) the reduction of tax rate on interest earned from offshore loans, (3) the abolition of stamp duties on CDs and bills of exchange, and (4) the abolition of the 20 percent reserve requirements for Asian Currency Units (ACUs). An ACU is a section within a bank which has authority and separate accountability for Asian currency market operations.

There are several reasons suggested for the development of the Asian currency market in Singapore. First, Asian dollar deposits would attract other deposits, increase banking activities, and earn income from these financial services. These earnings would improve its balance of payments and develop a service-oriented industry. Second, Singapore might also obtain a degree of additional political security. The existence of foreign deposits and foreign banks in Singapore might build up support for its neutrality and increase its importance as an Asian financial center. Third, the presence of the Asian currency market in Singapore would enhance its publicity and prestige. Fourth, most Southeast Asian countries need large amounts of capital for their economic development. Because Singapore is located at the center of this area, it is a logical place for the development of the Asian currency market.

Although the market is still quite small, it grew rapidly. Currently, over 70 banks or other financial institutions have licenses from the Monetary Authority of Singapore to operate ACUs. Most deposits in ACUs are in U. S. dollars, but other foreign currencies such as Swiss francs, Dutch guilders, and German marks are also accepted. Domestic residents are normally prohibited from participating in the offshore (international) market. Similarly, offshore financial institutions are restricted in their dealings with the domestic market.

There are no taxes on interest paid on foreign currency deposits and no restrictions applied to capital outflows and inflows. Regular foreign currency deposits are accepted as low as $25,000. Although the minimum deposit maturity is one month, the market offers deposit options of varying maturities. Citibank introduced negotiable CDs in 1970.

THE EUROBOND MARKET

Offshore (international) bonds are those bonds which are initially sold outside the country of the borrower. There are three types of international bonds: foreign bonds, parallel bonds, and Eurobonds. Foreign bonds are sold in a particular country by a foreign borrower, underwritten by a syndicate composed of members from that country, and denominated in the currency of that country. Parallel bonds are those bonds issued by a number of currencies simultaneously, where the borrower obtains funds from a number of countries in the currencies of those countries. Eurobonds are sold simultaneously in many countries other than the country of the currency in which the issue is denominated.

Most large foreign-bond issues had been floated in the United

States, Great Britain, and Switzerland. The weakening British pound in the late 1950s reduced the importance of the domestic British capital market for foreign firms. The Interest Equalization Tax (1963-1974) of the United States effectively stopped New York's usefulness as a capital market for new foreign bonds. Thus, international borrowers and investors shifted their activities from the United States to Europe. This shift caused the Eurobond market to develop.

Eurobonds are direct claims on leading multinational companies, governments, or governmental enterprises. Hence, they are in many respects very much like domestic bonds. They are sold simultaneously in many countries through multinational syndicates of underwriting banks. These underwriting banks include major European banks, European branches of U. S. banks, and banks from other financial centers such as Hong Kong and Japan.

Currency Denomination of Eurobonds

Eurobonds are denominated in various currencies: the U. S. dollar, the German mark, the Dutch guilder, the Canadian dollar, the Swiss franc, the French franc, and composite units of currencies. But about 60 percent is denominated in U. S. dollars, 34 percent is denominated in other single currencies, and the remaining six percent is denominated in composite units of currencies.[5] These multiple-currency bonds may be classified in the categories of currency-option bonds and currency basket bonds.

The holders of currency-option bonds are allowed to receive their interest income in the currency of their option from among two or three predetermined currencies at a predetermined exchange rate. The original bond contract contains the currencies of choice and the exchange rates. The currency option enhances the exchange guaranty for the investor. Thus, the investor will make some gain if all currencies included in the contract do not depreciate against the desired currency.

A number of currency-basket bonds have been developed to maintain the purchasing power of interest income. The value of currency-basket bonds is based on the weighted average of values of several currencies. Some popular forms of currency-basket bonds include SDRs, the European-Unit-of-Account, and the European-Composite-Unit bonds. However, there have been very few of these basket-bond issues because they spare the investor the trouble of creating a portfolio in exactly these currency proportions.

[5] M. S. Mendelsohn, *Money on the Move: The Modern International Capital Market* (New York: McGraw-Hill Book Co., 1981), p. 147.

Types of Eurobonds

There are three types of Eurobonds: straight Eurobonds, convertible Eurobonds, and floating-rate Eurobonds. Straight Eurobonds account for approximately 85 percent of Eurobonds and other types of Eurobonds account for the remaining 15 percent.

Straight Eurobonds. These bonds have fixed maturities and carry a fixed rate of interest. Straight Eurobonds are repaid by amortization or in a lump sum at the maturity date. The amortization method refers to the retirement of a long-term debt by making a set of equal periodic payments. These periodic payments include both interest and principal. Or the borrower may retire his bonds by redeeming the face value of the bonds at maturity. Under this method, the fixed interest on the face value of bonds is paid at regular intervals.

Straight Eurobonds are technically unsecured (debenture) bonds because almost all of them are not secured by any specific property of the borrower. Because of this, debenture bondholders become general creditors in the event of default; they look to the nature of the borrower's assets, its earning power, and its general credit strength.

Perhaps the greatest advantage of all types of Eurobonds for individual investors is that interest income on them is exempt from withholding taxes at source. Investors must report their interest income to their national authorities, but both tax avoidance and tax evasion are extremely widespread. Official institutions hold a large proportion of investment in Eurobonds and are not liable for tax. Another large class of investors in Eurobonds consists of private institutions. These private institutions legally avoid tax by being based in tax haven countries.

Convertible Eurobonds. These bonds are convertible into parent common stock and have become increasingly prevalent as the market for straight Eurobonds has weakened. The conversion price is usually fixed at a certain premium above the market price of the common stock on the date of the bond issue. Investors are free to convert their fixed-income securities into common stock at any time before the conversion privilege expires; the borrowing company is obliged to issue new stock for that purpose.

The convertible provision is used to make certain fixed Eurobonds more attractive to investors and consequently to increase their marketability. Convertible Eurobonds provide investors with a steady income and an opportunity to participate in rising stock prices. Thus, their interest rates have been 1.5 to 2 percent below those on straight Eurobonds. Because international investors are inflation-conscious, they prefer convertible Eurobonds which maintain the purchasing power of money.

Some Eurobonds are issued with warrants. A warrant is an option to buy a stated number of common shares at a stated price during a prescribed period. Warrants pay no dividends, have no voting rights, and become worthless at expiration unless the price of the common stock exceeds the exercise price. Convertible Eurobonds do not bring in additional funds. When they are converted, common stock increases and the convertible securities are retired. When warrants are exercised, common stock and cash increase simultaneously.

Floating-Rate Eurobonds. These bonds are frequently called floating-rate notes. The rate of return on these notes is adjusted at regular intervals, usually every six months, to reflect changes in short-term market rates. Because one of their main objectives is to provide dollar capital for non-U. S. banks, practically all floating-rate notes have been issued in dollars.

Like other Eurodollar bonds, floating-rate notes are issued in denominations of $1,000 each. They carry a margin of usually ¼ percent above the LIBOR; this margin is normally adjusted every six months. The link between the rate of return on floating-rate notes and LIBOR rates is intended to protect the investor against capital loss.

When non-U. S. banks obtain dollars by floating-rate notes, their credit lines with other banks are not eroded. However, when they obtain dollars in interbank market or by the sale of CDs to other banks, their credit lines with other banks are eroded. Because non-U. S. banks usually lend at the floating rate of interest, it makes sense for them to obtain funds on the same basis.

INTERNATIONAL BANKING AND SOVEREIGN RISK

The unprecedented expansion of global economic activity since the end of World War II has been accompanied by a parallel growth of the world banking system because banks followed their customers abroad. Another prominent characteristic of bank lending in recent years has been the increasing use of bank syndications to make extremely large loans to developing and East-bloc countries. A number of preceding chapters discussed international banking operations with respect to foreign trade and foreign direct investment by multinational companies. Thus, this section places major emphasis on syndicated loans and country risk (sovereign risk).

Types of Foreign Banking Offices

There are five major types of foreign banking offices: representative offices, correspondent banks, branch banks, subsidiaries, and banking consortia.

Representative Offices. National banks may establish their offices in foreign countries when their parent bank is doing business in these foreign countries or in neighboring countries. They do not engage in most traditional banking functions such as deposits, loans, letters of credit, drafts, and Eurodollar markets.

Representative offices obtain information, give advice, and arrange local contacts for their parent bank's business customers. They help local business executives initiate inquiries about the parent bank's services and introduce visiting executives to local banks. They put parent bank's clients in contact with government officials or local business firms. They also provide their parent bank with credit analysis of local firms and political information about the country.

Correspondent Banks. Most major national banks maintain correspondent banking relationships with local banks in many major foreign cities of the world. The correspondent banking system is an entirely informal arrangement whereby a bank in a country maintains deposit balances with banks in foreign countries and looks to them for a variety of services and assistance.

Local correspondent banks accept drafts, honor letters of credit, and provide credit information. They also collect or pay foreign funds because of import or export transactions.

Branch Banks. Foreign branch banks do not have their own corporate charter, their own board of directors, or any shares of common stock outstanding. Thus, they are an operational part of the parent bank; their assets and liabilities are in fact those of the parent bank.

Foreign branch banks provide a full range of banking services under the name and guarantee of the parent bank. Because legal loan limits depend on the size of the parent bank, they attract large local borrowers.

Banking Subsidiaries. Foreign subsidiary banks have their own charter, their own board of directors, their own stockholders, and their own managers. However, they are owned entirely or in major part by a foreign parent bank. They must comply with all of the laws of the host country.

Because foreign subsidiary banks maintain their status as local institutions with local ownership and management, they are able to attract additional local deposits and have greater access to the local business community. In addition, because they have permanent relations with their foreign part-owner, they are more likely to appeal to the foreign business community than purely local banks.

Consortium Banks. A consortium bank is a permanent group of banks to handle large international loans. It has its own charter but is a joint venture owned by two or more shareholder-parent banks with usually different nationalities.

Consortium banks develop their own business as well as take customers suggested by their parent banks. They arrange global syndicates for large international loans. Syndicates are employed in large international loans to spread the risk and to overcome the inability of a single bank to handle a large loan alone. Consortium banks also underwrite corporate securities and arrange mergers and acquisitions.[6]

Syndicated Loans

Large syndicated loans to developing and East-bloc countries have become extremely important for many U. S. and Western European banks. For some banks, international loans have become as important as their domestic banking operations. On the other hand, recent events in Poland, Iran, Iraq, Afghanistan, Libya, Mexico, and Nicaragua have raised serious questions about large loans to developing and Soviet-bloc countries.

Loan Volume. As of the end of 1980, loans from the world's private banks to developing countries were estimated to exceed $100 billion and net hard-currency debt of Soviet-bloc countries to the West were estimated to equal about $70 billion. Table 8-1 shows the net hard-currency debt of each Soviet-bloc country to the West. Net hard-currency loans to Soviet-bloc countries by Western banks and governments increased ten times between 1970 and 1980; they are expected to double from 1980 to 1985.

Evaluation of International Loans

International loans have a number of advantages for banks. (1) International loans have been very profitable for many of the world's

[6] For an extensive discussion on foreign acquisitions of U. S. banks, see Staff of the Office of the Comptroller of the Currency, *Foreign Acquisitions of U. S. Banks* (Richmond: Robert F. Dame, Inc., 1981).

Table 8-1 Soviet Bloc Debt (in billion current U. S. dollars)

Country	1970	1980	1985-f
Bulgaria	0.7	2.7	4-5
Czechoslovakia	0.6	3.4	5-6
East Germany	1.4	11.8	18-20
Hungary	0.6	7.0	10-11
Poland	1.1	21.9	30-35
Romania	1.6	9.0	19-21
USSR	1.0	9.6	30-35
COMECON Banks	0.3	4.1	6-7
Total	7.3	69.5	122-140

Source: Wall Street Journal (January 2, 1982), p. 16.
f-Forecast by Wharton Econometric Forecasting Associates.

largest banks and have had a significant impact on the earnings of such giant banks as Citicorp, Chase Manhattan, and Bank of America. (2) Diversification of international loans by country and by type of customer has enabled many banks to improve their risk-return performance. (3) Developing and Soviet-bloc countries have traditionally attempted to preserve their high credit standing with international banks. (4) There are a number of safeguards designed to reduce the risk of international loans. They include credit insurance programs in the lenders' own countries and guarantees by host governments on loans to private companies within their country.

International loans have a number of disadvantages for banks. (1) Country risk analysis is extremely complex because it depends on many variables. (2) International bankers have recently failed to anticipate dramatic increases in country risk. (3) Some bankers have relaxed their credit standards in order to compensate for weak domestic demand for loans since 1974. (4) The ability of developing and Soviet-bloc countries to service their external debt has deteriorated dramatically since 1974. (5) If borrowing countries are unable to meet their obligations on time, banks are forced to roll over their loans indefinitely.

Sovereign Risk

Recent crises in Poland and some developing countries have brought international banks under intensified questioning from analysts and investors concerned about loans to politically risky countries. Country or sovereign risk refers both to the possibility of default on foreign loans and to unanticipated restrictions of cash flows to the parent country.

There are two major differences between domestic loans and foreign loans. (1) Because repayment of international loans must go through the exchange market, international banks must assess prospects for exchange rates and for controls on capital flows. (2) A common legal system or an ultimate arbitrator does not exist to settle disputed claims. Developing and East-bloc countries are particularly unlikely to bind themselves to accept the decisions of Western-oriented international legal frameworks. Thus, country-risk assessment is critical for commercial banks to safeguard their international loans against country risk.

Nature of Country-Risk Assessment. Many international bankers have undertaken country-risk analysis for many years. They are now working on their second or third generation of country-risk models. Their original models have been modified on the basis of their experience and their knowledge of other banks' procedures. These modified models could result in more informed business decisions and less risk in international loans.

Country risk is nothing more than the assessment of economic opportunity against political odds. Thus, country-risk assessment requires analyses of both political and economic indicators. There are a number of country-risk assessment models available in either academic journals or commercially. However, the list of factors to be considered in country-risk analysis varies from forecaster to forecaster. Perhaps the most comprehensive list of factors has been provided by Davis.[7] He has subdivided these factors into external economic indicators, internal economic indicators, and political indicators.

External economic indicators include:

1. Foreign Public Debt/GNP–relates external debt to country wealth.
2. Debt Service Ratio–relates debt service requirements to export income.
3. Months of Import Coverage–relates reserve levels to potential need for reserves.
4. IMF Holdings of Domestic Currency as a Percentage of Quota–a measure of resort to IMF borrowings for balance of payments support.
5. Current Account/GNP–a measure of the country's net external borrowing relative to country size.

[7] Robert R. Davis, "Alternative Techniques for Country Risk Evaluation," *Business Economics* (May 1981), pp. 34-41.

6. Average External Debt Due in Next 3 Years/Current Exports of Goods and Services–a measure of debt bunching.
7. Lead Export/Total Exports–a measure of diversification of the export base.

Internal economic indicators include:

1. Real GNP–a measure of country wealth.
2. Real GNP/capita–a measure of country wealth.
3. Inflation Rate–a measure of economic instability, disruption, and government mismanagement.
4. Investment/GNP–a measure of potential economic growth.
5. Net Government Budget/GNP–a measure of the potential crowding out of private investment, increased government demand for external debt, the potential for inflationary money growth, and government mismanagement.
6. Money Growth Rate minus Real Economic Growth–a measure of inflationary pressure and government mismanagement.
7. Real GNP Growth–a measure of potential wealth, productivity, and return to investment.

Political indicators include:

1. Power base of current government–Indicator ranges from widespread popular support of government to unpopular control by ruling elite.
2. Mechanisms for expression of discontent–Related to the ability to effect peaceful change, alter direction of policy without wholesale structural change of the political system, and provide internal continuity.
3. Mechanisms for orderly succession of leadership–Indicator ranges from well-defined and tested succession mechanism to undefined mechanism with little history of peaceful succession.
4. Consensus regarding priorities–A measure of the degree of agreement and unity on the fundamental objectives of government policy and the extent to which this concensus cuts across party lines and ethnic division.
5. Vulnerability to external pressure–A measure of susceptibility to overt or clandestine pressure designed to alter foreign and domestic policies and the internal political structure.
6. Relationship to U. S.–Ranging from close political and commercial ties to hostile relations.

Country-risk assessment may provide international banks with a number of useful purposes. (1) It permits international banks to assess relative conditions of diverse countries based on common criteria. (2) Because it is based on a common set of criteria, it tends to offset individual biases. (3) A country's risk ranking is a useful "straw dog" rating.[8] Country risk may be assessed in two ways: the debt-service ratio and the overall country creditworthiness.

Debt-Service Ratio. The debt-service ratio is the ratio of the required payment of principal and interest to the sum of hard-currency export balance and net balance in invisibles. A debt-service ratio of 0.2 or higher is usually regarded as a danger signal for defaults on foreign loans.

In recent years, the debt-service ratios of some developing countries have been higher than 0.2. These countries include Argentina, Mexico, Peru, Uruguay, Bangladesh, and Sri Lanka.[9] Table 8-2 shows the debt-service ratios of Soviet-bloc countries. All East-block countries with an exception of the Soviet Union have the debt-service ratios of greater than 0.2 as of the end of 1981. The debt-service ratios in Table 8-2 are those calculated by the Wharton Econometric Forecasting Associates. The Wharton Econometric Forecasting Associates has not calculated a debt-service ratio for the East bloc as a whole. But the Organization for Economics Cooperation and Development, which computes a debt-service ratio on a more stringent basis, puts the East bloc at 0.4, including the Soviet Union.[10] Although no single or composite measure of debt-service ability can accurately forecast country risk, the lack of such measures would frustrate the ability of international banks to assess country risk.

Table 8-2 Debt-Service Ratios for East Bloc Countries

Country	1970	1975	1981
Bulgaria	0.30	0.44	0.29
Czechoslovakia	0.09	0.11	0.25
East Germany	0.14	0.26	0.43
Hungary	0.16	0.24	0.57
Poland	0.19	0.32	0.87
Romania	0.36	0.21	0.32
USSR	0.07	0.13	0.07

Source: Wall Street Journal (January 8, 1982), p. 16.

[8] *Ibid.*, p. 35.

[9] David K. Eiteman and Arthur I Stonehill, *Multinational Business Finance* (Reading, Mass.: Addison-Wesley Publishing Co., 1979), 486.

[10] *Wall Street Journal* (January 8, 1982), p. 16.

Overall-Country Creditworthiness. The combined impact of economic, political, and other indicators may be used to rate country risk. The better-known services of this type include Haner's Business-Risk Environment Index (BREI), Business International's Country-Assessment System (CAS), Frost and Sullivan's World Political-Risk Forecasts (WPRF), and Institutional Investor's Country-Credit Ratings.

The BREI uses 15 risk factors on which 43 countries are rated from zero (unacceptable) to four (superior conditions) by a panel of experts. These panel members are asked to assign a weight to each of these 15 factors according to their perceived importance. The scores are averaged and the countries are then ranked on the basis of these average scores.

The CAS evaluates 55 factors for 70 countries. A group of specialists rate each of the 70 nations on these 55 factors and then rank the nations under the three categories of country risks, business opportunities, and operating conditions.

The WPRF makes monthly estimates of the probability of a loss because of political developments in the short-term (18 months) and long-term (five years). Moreover, subscribers receive individual country reports which describe expected short-term and long-term conditions.

Institutional Investor introduced its country-credit ratings in 1979 and has adjusted these ratings every six months since then. Country-credit ratings developed by *Institutional Investor* are based on ratings from 75-100 leading international bankers. These bankers are asked to rate each of the countries on a scale from zero to 100. Those countries with a value of zero represent the least creditworthy countries; thus, they have the greatest chance of default on international loans. Those countries with a value of 100 represent the most creditworthy countries; thus, they have the least chance of default. "*Institutional Investor's* country credit ratings have been recognized in staff reports of both the International Monetary Fund and the World Bank."[11]

Table 8-3 shows country-by-country credit ratings conducted by *Institutional Investor*. Many East-bloc countries received not only poor credit ratings but also suffered sharp drops in ratings from September 1980 to September 1981 mainly due to the crisis in Poland. Traditionally, oil-exporting countries such as Iraq, Iran, and Libya exhibited the identical pattern in these ratings with East-bloc nations because of their political problems and the recent oil glut. Some de-

[11] "Rating Country Risk," *Institutional Investor* (March 1981), p. 234.

Table 8-3 Institutional Investor's Country Credit Ratings

Rank Sept. 1981	Rank March 1981	Country	Institutional Investor credit rating	Six-month change	One-year change
1	1	United States	98.3	0.1	0.3
2	2	Switzerland	96.2	−0.8	−1.5
3	4	Japan	95.7	0.5	0.5
4	3	West Germany	94.7	−1.6	−3.0
5	5	Canada	93.1	1.0	0.0
6	7	Australia	90.4	0.4	1.0
7	8	United Kingdom	89.0	−0.9	−1.2
8*	10	Norway	88.4	−1.0	−0.5
9*	9	Netherlands	88.4	−1.3	−2.3
10	6	France	87.8	−2.4	−3.9
11	11	Austria	85.2	−0.7	−2.4
12	13	Sweden	82.0	−1.5	−3.2
13	12	Belgium	81.0	−3.5	−5.9
14	14	Singapore	78.4	−0.2	0.9
15	15	New Zealand	77.3	−0.7	−0.5
16	17	Finland	76.5	−1.0	−0.1
17	16	Hong Kong	76.0	−1.6	−1.9
18	19	Saudi Arabia	74.3	0.8	−1.0
19	22	Malaysia	73.8	1.0	0.7
20	18	Italy	73.1	−1.6	−2.7
21	21	Denmark	72.9	−0.2	−1.5
22	25	Kuwait	71.2	0.8	−0.8
23	20	Ireland	70.8	−2.6	−2.6
24	29	Taiwan	69.1	0.4	2.4
25	23	Mexico	69.0	−2.5	−4.1
26	26	Spain	68.4	−1.8	−1.9
27	27	U.S.S.R.	68.0	−1.6	−1.7
28	24	China	67.4	−3.9	−4.8
29	28	Venezuela	66.0	−3.3	−3.4
30	32	South Africa	61.9	0.1	2.1
31	31	Greece	61.8	−0.7	−0.3
32	33	United Arab Emirates	60.7	0.9	0.4
33	37	Bahrain	59.3	1.1	0.5
34	40	Algeria	58.6	1.2	2.0
35*	35	Iceland	57.7	−1.0	−1.0
36*	34	Colombia	57.7	−1.4	−1.3
37	42	Qatar	57.6	0.7	−1.7
38	41	Indonesia	57.4	0.3	2.3
39	46	South Korea	57.1	1.7	0.2
40	43	Portugal	57.0	0.4	2.1
41	44	Trinidad & Tobago	56.5	−0.1	−1.9
42	30	Argentina	56.4	−7.0	−7.9
43	45	Nigeria	55.4	−0.4	1.4
44*	36	East Germany	55.4	−3.0	−5.0
45	38	Czechoslovakia	55.1	−2.4	−4.6
46	47	Chile	54.8	0.4	−0.1
47	39	Hungary	54.7	−2.8	−3.6

Table 8-3 continued

Rank Sept. 1981	March 1981	Country	Institutional Investor credit rating	Six-month change	One-year change
48	49	Thailand	51.7	−0.4	−0.8
49	48	Ecuador	50.4	−1.9	−1.9
50	54	Brazil	48.9	−0.8	−3.8
51	50	Libya	48.4	−3.5	−5.6
52	53	India	48.3	−1.7	−1.5
53	55	Tunisia	47.6	−0.7	−1.3
54	52	Yugoslavia	47.4	−2.9	−4.7
55	57	Oman	47.0	0.3	0.1
56	58	Papua New Guinea	45.7	−0.6	2.9
57	59	Paraguay	45.6	0.4	0.0
58	56	Bulgaria	45.5	−1.9	−2.2
59	60	Iraq	45.4	0.9	−12.3
60	51	Romania	45.1	−6.2	−6.8
61	63	Peru	43.3	−0.1	2.9
62	64	Panama	41.7	−1.0	−2.1
63	62	Ivory Coast	41.5	−2.7	−4.7
64	61	Philippines	41.4	−3.0	−5.4
65	68	Uruguay	41.2	0.1	0.3
66	66	Jordan	39.7	−2.2	−2.5
67	72	Egypt	38.8	2.8	3.9
68	67	Israel	38.1	−3.4	−5.4
69	65	Kenya	37.5	−5.0	−5.8
70	69	Morocco	36.9	−2.9	−3.9
71	73	Republic of Gabon	36.2	0.9	1.1
72	71	Cyprus	35.8	−1.1	−0.8
73	70	Costa Rica	32.2	−6.6	−8.2
74	75	Syrian Arab Republic	27.9	−4.3	−7.7
75	8	Zimbabwe	25.9	−0.4	−1.1
76	76	Dominican Republic	25.4	−4.5	−5.1
77*	77	Cuba	23.1	−5.4	−7.2
78*	79	Senegal	23.1	−2.3	−5.4
79*	80	Malawi	21.6	−3.5	–
80*	–	Guatemala	21.6	–	–
81	81	Pakistan	21.3	−0.8	1.0
82	–	Mauritius	21.0	–	–
83	84	Seychelles	19.9	−1.1	−2.4
84	74	Poland	19.5	−13.4	−17.6
85	–	Honduras	19.1	–	–
86	82	Bolivia	19.0	−2.9	−6.2
87	86	Angola	18.8	−0.8	−1.5
88	85	Liberia	16.9	−4.0	−8.7
89	90	Jamaica	16.6	1.1	0.0
90	83	Lebanon	16.4	−5.4	−6.9
91	93	Turkey	16.0	2.3	3.3
92	91	Congo	14.8	−0.6	−1.3
93	88	Zambia	13.9	−2.5	−3.8
94	87	Tanzania	13.5	−3.3	−4.7

Table 8-3 continued

Rank Sept. 1981	Rank March 1981	Country	Institutional Investor credit rating	Six-month change	One-year change
95	94	Iran	13.2	0.5	−3.2
96	–	Grenada	12.9	–	–
97	92	Sierra Leone	12.6	−2.5	−3.6
98*	96	Ethiopia	10.2	−1.0	−2.2
99*	95	Sudan	10.2	2.1	2.9
100	89	El Salvador	10.1	−5.7	–
101	97	Nicaragua	9.0	−2.2	−0.9
102	99	Zaire	6.6	−0.2	−1.3
103	98	North Korea	5.1	−1.9	−3.4
104	100	Uganda	5.0	−1.3	−3.1

Source: Institutional Investor (September 1981), pp. 284-285.

*Order determined by the actual results before rounding. Reprinted by permission of the *Institutional Investor.*

veloping countries such as Argentina, Peru, and Uruguay did not do well in these ratings primarily because of their high debt-service ratios.

Significance of Country-Risk Assessment. Recent events in Poland and several other countries have dramatized the importance of country-risk analysis. Thus, it is not difficult to understand why many international bankers have begun to search for more systematic means of assessing and managing country risk. They have recently increased their resource commitments, employed more qualified staff analysts, and adopted more sophisticated methods to assess country risk.

Although country risk can never be completely eliminated, its systematic assessment and management can significantly decrease its impact. The debt-service ratios, country-credit ratings by some institutions such as *Institutional Investor*, and other procedures established by an individual bank may be used to reduce the possibility of defaults on foreign loans and their interest.

SUMMARY

Eurodollars are dollar-denominated deposits in banks all over the world except the United States. The Eurodollar market is the truly international money market undisturbed by the rules and restrictions of any national authority. Eurodollars have become a major source of short-term loans for multinational companies to finance their working capital needs and foreign trade. With the growth in availability of Eurodollars, Eurobanks have begun to extend medium-term Eurodollar loans for multinational companies to finance their medium-term needs. Although the Eurobond market is of a more recent vantage, it is a parallel development of importance to multinational financial management. Eurobonds are mainly to facilitate expansion involving fixed asset commitments.

In this chapter, we also discussed international bank lending and country risk. A prominent feature of bank lending in recent years has been the growing use of bank syndications to make extremely large loans to developing and East-bloc countries. Recent events in Poland and a number of developing countries have brought international banks under intensified questioning from analysts and investors concerned about loans to politically risky countries. For some banks, international lending can be as important as their domestic operations. Thus, it is important for international banks to reduce the impact of country risk through its systematic assessment and management.

PROBLEMS

8-1 Fill in the following blank spaces assuming that the reserve ratio is 20 percent.

Bank	Acquired Reserves	Required Reserves	Excess Reserves	Amount Bank Can Lend
Bank 1	$100.00	$20.00	$80.00	$80.00
Bank 2				
Bank 3				
Bank 4				
Bank 5				
Bank 6				
Bank 7				
Bank 8				
Bank 9				
Bank 10				
Bank 11				
Bank 12				
Bank 13				
Other Banks				
Total Amount Loaned				

8-2 Assume that a commercial bank has the following simplified balance sheet. The reserve ratio is 20 percent.

Assets		1	2	Liabilities and Net Worth		1	2
Reserves	$44,000	____	____	Demand Deposits	$200,000	____	____
Securities	76,000	____	____				
Loans	80,000	____	____				

a. Determine the maximum amount which this bank can safely lend. Show in Column 1 how the bank's balance sheet will appear after the bank has loaned this amount.
b. By how much has the supply of money changed?
c. Show the new balance sheet in Column 2 after checks drawn for the entire amount of the new loans have been cleared against this bank.
d. To what extent, will this lending alter the supply of money?
e. Aside from the leakage of required reserves at each stage of the lending process, there are some other leakages of money from the lending process. List and discuss them.
f. Assume: (1) an American citizen transfers $2,000 of his deposits from a U. S. bank to an Eurobank and (2) Eurobanks as a whole keep five percent of their Eurodollar deposits in vault cash. Determine the maximum amount of Eurodollar supply that Eurobanks can create on the basis of $2,000 deposit.

8-3 a. A German multinational company acquires $2,000 on demand deposit in a Los Angeles bank. How will the $2,000 deposit be reflected in the books of the Los Angeles bank, the German company, and the Federal Reserve Bank of San Francisco? Assume the reserve ratio is 20 percent.
b. The German company transfers its $2,000 deposit from the Los Angeles bank to an Italian bank. Moreover, it decides to deposit its $2,000 in a dollar-denominated time deposit account. How will this transaction be reflected in the T-accounts for the Los Angeles bank, the Italian bank, and the German company?
c. The Italian bank retains $200 of its deposit in the Los Angeles bank and extends a Eurodollar loan of $1,800 to a British firm. What are the transactions to record the loan?
d. The British firm withdraws its deposit from the Italian bank and deposits it in a London bank. Record the event in the appropriate accounts.
e. The London bank lends its $1,800 demand deposit to a Swiss firm. How will this loan be reflected in the T-accounts for the London bank and the Swiss firm?
f. After transaction e, what is the total amount of Eurodollars?

REFERENCES

8-1 Bhattachary, Anindya, *The Asian Dollar Market* (New York: Praeger, 1977).

8-2 Clasper, Stephen, "How the Asian Dollar Bond Market Has Developed," *Euromoney* (January 1977), pp. 90+.

8-3 Coats, Warren L., "The Weekend Eurodollar Game," *Journal of Finance* (June 1981), pp. 649-660.

8-4 Davis, Robert R., "Alternative Techniques for Country Risk Evaluation," *Business Economics* (May 1981), pp. 34-41.

8-5 Dufey, Gunter, and Ian H. Giddy, *Credit Creation and the Growth of the Eurodollar Market* (New York: Columbia University Graduate School of Business, 1976).

8-6 Dufey, Gunter, and Ian H. Giddy, "Innovation in the International Financial Markets," *Journal of International Business Studies* (Fall 1981), pp. 9-32.

8-7 Feiger, George, and Bertrand Jacquillat, *International Finance* (Boston: Allyn and Bacon, Inc., 1982), Chapters 8, 9, 10, and 11.

8-8 Hendershott, Patric H., "The Structure of International Interest Rates: The U. S. Treasury Bill Rate and the Eurodollar Deposit Rate," *Journal of Finance* (September 1967), pp. 455-465.

8-9 Khoury, Sarkis J., "International Banking: A Special Look at Foreign Banks in the U. S.," *Journal of International Business Studies* (Fall 1979), pp. 36-52.

8-10 Lusztig, Peter, and Bernhard Schwab, "Units of Account and the International Bond Market," *Columbia Journal of World Business* (Spring 1975), pp. 74-79.

8-11 Mendelsohn, M. S., *Money on the Move: The Modern International Capital Market* (New York: McGraw-Hill Book Co., 1981).

8-12 "Rating Country Risk," *Institutional Investor* (September 1981), pp. 231-290.

8-13 Quinn, Brian S., "The International Bond Market for the U. S. Investor," *Columbia Journal of World Business* (Fall 1979), pp. 85-90.

8-14 Rich, George, "A Theoretical and Empirical Analysis of the Eurodollar Market," *Journal of Money, Credit, and Banking* (August 1972), pp. 616-635.

8-15 Riehl, Heinz, and Rita M. Rodriguez, *Foreign Exchange Markets* (New York: McGraw-Hill Book Co., 1977).

8-16 Santomero, Anthony M., "The Error-Learning Hypothesis and the Term Structure of Interest Rates in Eurodollars," *Journal of Finance* (June 1975), pp. 773-883.

8-17 Staff of the Office of the Comptroller of the Currency, *Foreign Acquisitions of U. S. Banks* (Richmond: Robert F. Dame, Inc., 1981).

PART FOUR

Asset Management

NINE

WORKING CAPITAL MANAGEMENT

Chapters 6 through 8 have described the various sources of funds necessary to finance foreign trade and investment. Chapters 9 through 12 will discuss asset management. Chapter 9 deals with working capital management which involves the use of certain prescribed aids such as the risk-return tradeoff, credit standards, and inventory models. Working capital management is important not only because it involves a major portion of management time but also because there is a close relationship between sales growth and the need to finance current assets.

Management of working capital can be viewed as either a static (stock) responsibility or a dynamic (flow) process. The static approach focuses on individual processes such as management of cash, accounts receivable, and inventories. The important aspect of this approach is how to determine appropriate levels of cash balances, accounts receivable, and inventories. On the other hand, the dynamic approach focuses on transfers of liquid funds from one geographic location or currency to another. These transfers involve many constraints and uncertainties.

OBJECTIVES AND CONSTRAINTS

The objective of working capital management is to determine the optimal amount of investment in various current asset accounts. The optimal amount of investment in current assets is the level of current asset holdings that maximizes return on investment.

Gentry and several others conducted a survey to collect information on working capital management from a sample of 579 top executives in large corporations in Belgium, France, India, and the United States.[1] Table 9-1 shows the survey results. These writers isolated

Table 9-1 Most Important Working Capital Management Objectives of Companies in Belgium, France, India and the United States

	Objectives (percent of total respondents)				
	Belgium	France	India	U. S.	Total
(Number of respondents)	(37)	(54)	(38)	(450)	(579)
Supporting Sales					
To provide the cash, accounts receivable, inventories, and short-term credit necessary to support the anticipated sales in a defined planning period	45.9	53.7	50.0	55.6	54.4
Financial Buffer					
To provide a financial buffer in order to minimize the effect of surprises in sales or materials, production, labor, credit, and transportation	35.1	7.4	18.4	6.4	9.2
Minimization					
To minimize the balances in cash, receivables, inventories and short-term debt	13.5	25.9	18.4	21.3	21.2
Investment Decision					
To evaluate changes in each current asset as an investment decision and to minimize the cost of short-term credit	5.4	11.1	13.2	15.1	14.0

Source: Gentry, Mehta, Bhattacharyya, Cobbaut, and Scaringella, "An International Study of Management Perceptions of the Working Capital Policies," *Journal of International Business Studies* (Spring/Summer 1979), p. 31.

[1] James A. Gentry, Dileep R. Mehta, S. K. Bhattacharyya, Robert Cobbaut, and Jean L. Scaringella, "An International Study of Management Perceptions of the Working Capital Process," *Journal of International Business Studies* (Spring/Summer 1979), pp. 28-38.

four objectives of working capital management and ranked them according to the responses of the 579 international managers from different countries. Approximately 55 percent of these managers reported that the most important objective of working capital management was to provide various current assets and short-term credit necessary to support the anticipated sales. Another 21 percent indicated that the most important objective of working capital management was to minimize the investment in current assets.

Because multinational companies operate across national borders, they face political, tax, foreign exchange, and other economic constraints.[2] To achieve the predetermined objective of working capital management, the financial manager must give special consideration to these constraints.

Political constraints can block dividend repatriation or other forms of fund remittances. This blockage occurs because of restrictions on the international movement of funds and other exchange controls. Tax constraints limit the free flow of affiliate funds to the parent or to sister affiliates. These may occur because higher taxes on all corporate earnings or extra taxes on dividends may be imposed to curb inflation. Foreign exchange constraints are a third limiting factor on fund flows from one country to another. International fund flows involve foreign exchange transaction costs and exchange rate fluctuations. Other economic factors such as inflation and interest rates also have an important impact on the international mobility of corporate funds.

CASH MANAGEMENT

Cash provides the multinational company with the ability to pay bills as they come due, but it is not an earning asset. Thus, it is very important to determine an optimal level of investment in cash. The major sources of cash inflow are dividends, royalties and fees, cash sales and collections on accounts receivable, depreciation, sales of new securities, loans from banks or nonbank financial institutions, and advance cash payments on contracts. In contrast, cash outflows are necessary for interest and dividend payments, retirement of debt

[2] For a good discussion of this topic, see David A. Ricks, *International Dimensions of Corporate Finance* (Englewood Cliffs, N.J.: Prentice-Hall, Inc., 1978), Chapters 2, 3, 4, and 5; and David K. Eiteman and Arthur I. Stonehill, *Multinational Business Finance* (Reading, Mass.: Addision-Wesley Publishing Company, 1979), Chapters 10 and 12.

and other securities, income tax payments, payments on accounts payable, wages and salaries, and purchases of fixed assets.

Keynes suggested that there are three main reasons why companies prefer to hold cash rather than other forms of assets: the transaction motive, the precautionary motive, and the speculative motive.[3] The transaction motive states that cash balances are held partly in anticipation of day-to-day cash disbursements. The precautionary motive suggests that cash balances are held partly as protection against deviations from budgeted cash flows. The speculative motive relates to the holding of cash in order to take advantage of profit-making opportunities.

These general principles that apply to cash management on an international basis are frequently similar to those utilized by many companies domestically. The overall cash management objective for any corporation is to minimize the cash within the company with the goal of optimizing corporate fund utilization. However, the parameters within which multinational companies operate are much broader and much more complex. Furthermore, the relationships among these parameters are constantly changing. Hence, cash management on an international basis must consider a host of new variables such as tax concepts, governmental restrictions on such things as intracompany fund flows, differences in cultures, and foreign exchange rates.

The Flow of Funds

Multinational business operations require a steady flow of funds from parent to subsidiary, from subsidiary to parent, and between subsidiaries. Because these fund flows are unique, we will consider one at a time.

The largest flow of funds from parent to subsidiary is the initial investment. The subsidiary may also receive additional funds in the form of loans or added investments. The purchases of goods from the subsidiary offers another form of fund flows from parent to subsidiary. This form of fund flows involves transfer pricing. A *transfer price* is the price on goods sold between related entities.

The major components of fund flows from subsidiary to parent consist of dividends, interest on loans, principal reduction payments, royalty payments, license fees, technical service fees, management fees, export commissions, and payments for goods received from the

[3] John M. Keynes, *The General Theory of Employment, Interest, and Money* (New York: Harcourt, Brace & Jovanovich, 1936), pp. 170-174.

parent. The parent does not have total control in the size of the flow of funds because of foreign exchange controls, tax constraints, etc. For example, many governments impose a withholding tax when dividends are remitted to foreign owners.

Funds flow from one subsidiary to another when they lend funds to each other or buy goods from each other. Loans between subsidiaries result in interest and principal reduction payments passing from the debtor subsidiary to the creditor subsidiary. Funds from one subsidiary may also be used to establish another subsidiary. When such investments are made, all dividends and principal payments may go directly to the home office. However, it is possible for these two subsidiaries to have cash flows similar to parent company cash flows.

To carry out its operations, the multinational company causes a steady flow of funds to take place between its family members. These fund flows cannot avoid the problem of float. *Float* refers to the status of funds in the process of collection. Float from a domestic point of view represents only the temporary losses of income of these funds that are tied up in the process of collection. In international operations, however, the problem of float is twofold: (1) the loss of income on the funds tied up during the longer transfer process and (2) their exposure to foreign exchange rate risk during the transfer period.

Multilateral Netting. Large multinational corporations involve a highly coordinated interchange of material, parts, work-in-process, and finished goods among the various units of the multinational companies because they are accompanied by a large volume of intracorporate fund flows. These crossborder fund transfers involve the foreign exchange spread, the opportunity cost of the float, and other transaction costs such as cable charges. Netting has been frequently suggested as one method of minimizing the total volume of interaffiliate fund flows.[4]

Multilateral netting is an extension of bilateral netting. For example, if subsidiary A purchases $10 million worth of goods from subsidiary B and B in turn buys $11 million worth of parts from A, the combined flows are $21 million. But on a net basis, subsidiary A would pay subsidiary B only $1 million. Bilateral netting would be useless where internal sales are more complex. Think of a situation where subsidiary A sells $10 million worth of goods to subsidiary B, subsidiary B sells $10 million worth of goods to subsidiary C, and subsidiary C sells $10 million worth of goods to subsidiary A. In

[4] Alan C. Shapiro, "Payments Netting in International Management," *Journal of International Business Studies* (Fall 1978), pp. 51-58.

this case, bilateral netting would be of no use, but multilateral netting would eliminate interaffiliate fund transfers completely.

While netting is not practiced widely, its value has been recognized by a number of multinational companies. The 1977 survey of 197 multinational companies by Business International found that 28 percent of the U. S. firms and 33 percent of the European firms use multilateral netting.[5]

Leads and Lags. Multinational companies can accelerate (lead) or delay (lag) the timing of foreign-currency payments in order to reduce foreign exchange exposure or to increase working capital available. These leads and lags can be achieved by modifying the credit terms extended by one unit to another. In order to reduce foreign exchange exposure, companies should accelerate the payments of hard-currency payables and delay the payment of soft-currency payables. If subsidiary X buys goods worth $10 million monthly from subsidiary Y on 60-day credit terms, Y is in effect financing $20 million of working capital for X. The extension of the terms to 120 days would enable subsidiary X to have an additional $20 million of working capital.

Leads and lags are used by many U. S. and non-U. S. multinational companies in order to minimize foreign exchange exposure and to shift the burden of financing from one unit to another. This technique has a number of advantages over direct loans. First, leading and lagging do not require a note that officially recognizes an obligation to the seller. Moreover, the amount of credit can be adjusted up or down by shortening or lengthening the credit terms. Second, indications are that governments interfere less with payments on intracompany accounts than on intracompany loans. Third, under Section 482 of the U. S. tax code, U. S. firms do not have to pay interest on intracompany accounts up to six months, but they have to pay interest on all intracompany loans.

As with all other transfer mechanisms, many governments impose controls on intracompany credit terms and netting. Table 9-2 shows the various restrictions imposed on leading and lagging as well as on netting by a set of selected countries.

Cash Centers

Cash management can be centralized, regionalized, or decentralized on a company level. Decentralization permits subsidiaries to use

[5] Business International, *Computerized Corporate Statistical Tables, New Techniques in International Exposure and Cash Management* (New York: Business International Corporation, 1977), p. 237.

Table 9-2 Limits on Leads and Lags and Netting

Limits on Leads and Lags and Netting in Selected Countries*
(Periods given below are maximum possible terms)

Country	Export lag	Export lead	Import lag	Import lead	Netting
Argentina	180 days	Allowed-no limit	Allowed-no limit	Not allowed	Not permitted
Australia	180 days[1]	30 days	180 days[2]	30 days[2]	Permission required
Belgium	180 days[3]	90 days[3]	180 days[3]	90 days[3]	Permission required
Brazil	Not allowed	Allowed-no limit	180 days	Not allowed[4]	Not permitted
Canada	Allowed-no limit	Allowed-no limit	Allowed-no limit	Allowed-no limit	Permitted
Denmark	30 days[5]	Allowed-no limit[6]	Allowed-no limit[6]	30 days[5]	Permitted
France	180 days[7]	Allowed-no limit	Allowed-no limit	Permission required[8]	Permission required but difficult
Germany	Allowed-no limit	Allowed-no limit	Allowed-no limit	Allowed-no limit	Permitted
Ireland	180 days	Allowed-no limit	Allowed-no limit[9]	Not allowed[10]	Permission required but readily available
Italy	120 days[11]	360 days	360 days	60 days	Not permitted[12]
Japan	180 days	180 days[13]	120 days[14]	120 days[14]	Not permitted[15]
Korea	Permitted but not encouraged	Permission required	Permitted but not encouraged	Permission required but rare	Permitted
Malaysia	180 days[16]	Allowed-no limit[16]	Allowed-no limit	Allowed-no limit	Permitted[17]
Mexico	Allowed-no limit	Allowed-no limit	Allowed-no limit	Allowed-no limit	Permitted
Netherlands	Allowed-no limit	Allowed-no limit	Allowed-no limit	Allowed-no limit	Permitted

Table 9-2 continued

Country	Export lag	Export lead	Import lag	Import lead	Netting
New Zealand	180 days	Allowed-no limit[18]	Allowed-no limit[19]	Not allowed[20]	Permission required[21]
Pakistan	120 days	Allowed-no limit	Not allowed	Not allowed	Not permitted
Philippines	60 days[32]	Allowed-no limit	90 days	Not allowed	Permission required
Singapore	180 days[22]	Allowed-no limit	Allowed-no limit	Allowed-no limit	Permitted[23]
South Africa	180 days[24]	Allowed-no limit	Allowed-no limit	Not allowed[25]	Not permitted except with special permission
Spain	90 days	180 days	180 days[26]	Not allowed[27]	Permission required but difficult
Sweden	Commercial practice[28]	Allowed-no limit	180 days[28]	Permission required[29]	Permission required[30]
Taiwan	Generally not permitted[31]	Tolerated[31]	Tolerated[31]	Permitted in some cases[31]	Not possible
UK	180 days	Allowed-no limit	Allowed-no limit	Not allowed	Permitted
US	Allowed-no limit	Allowed-no limit	Allowed-no limit	Allowed-no limit	Permitted

*Based on information primarily obtained locally from finance ministries, central and commercial banks.

Footnotes: [1] Deferred terms are approved for export of capital equipment and in some instances where goods are sent abroad on consignment; foreign currency proceeds are permitted to be held overseas for a maximum of one month to meet firm commitments falling due abroad; [2] Longer periods may be granted by Reserve Bank if normal commercial practice with goods is involved; [3] Belgium/Luxembourg Exchange Institute requires permission for all commercial payments above Bfr10 million; [4] Except with special permission from exchange department of central bank for a maximum of 25% of value of imports; [5] Maximum allowed deviation from original date of payment stipulated by trading partners in the contracts, which must be in conformity with normal commercial practices for the particular line of business involved; [6] When customary within the trade; [7] Receipts must now be converted into francs within 8 days, although in practice an extension of a few days is tolerated; [8] Allowances are made for 30% down payment on imported capital goods and 10% down payment for noncapital goods; [9] Officially

Table 9-2 continued

there is a 9-month limitation, but this is never followed in practice; [10] Sometimes allowed for capital goods; [11] Once payment is received, Italian exporters must convert proceeds into lira within 15 days; [12] Italian exchange office of Foreign Trade Ministry can authorize exceptions; for firms that are both importers and exporters, "compensations" can be effected between their exchange receipts and payments, allowing more flexibility in leads and lags; [13] But exporters are allowed to receive advances for up to 12 months on export contracts of less than $500,000; [14] But importers are usually bound by the contracted time of payment; [15] Except for "invisible" trade-related items, such as harbor charges, warehouse fees, etc.; [16] Payments must be in certain specified currencies; [17] Except for payment of exports as noted and for receipt of loan funds by Malaysian companies; [18] But not customary, except in the wool trade; [19] If more than 12 months, consent of the Overseas Investment Commission must be obtained; [20] In special cases, the Reserve Bank will allow early deposits–down payments–on capital equipment where called for by usual trade practice; [21] But is not usual–in general, exceptions or qualifications to the above rules are unusual and authorities are reluctant to make concessions; [22] Permission of the Monetary Authority of Singapore necessary if proceeds are expected to be received more than 6 months after shipment date; [23] For transactions relating to payments for goods and services; offsetting in relation to loans requires specific MAS approval; [24] Once payment is received, exporter can hold foreign exchange for 7 days; [25] Except with special exchange control approval, and after specifically designed equipment is ordered; [26] Includes a 90-day grace period; permission may be obtained for lags up to a year rather easily, but is more difficult for longer periods; [27] Special permit may allow down payment of up to 25% when the order is placed; higher down payments may at times be negotiated; [28] Normally follows customary conditions of payment; otherwise 180 days maximum; [29] Allowed only for normal one-third down payment on machinery and related goods, and consignments of under Skr50,000; [30] Must be based on current payments, and is authorized only if it involves balancing out of accounts between Swedish parents and their foreign subsidiaries; [31] Technically these practices are allowed, since there are no specific regulations concerning leads and lags; however, the country's all-embracing exchange control system ordinarily makes leads and lags impractical; [32] The full value of exports is normally required to be remitted within 60 days, but lags of up to 180 days are allowed for new exports or sales to new markets.

Source: Business International, *The State of the Art in International Exposure and Cash Management* (New York: Business International Corporation, 1977), p. 183. Reprinted by permission of the publisher, Business International Corporation.

excess cash in any way they see fit. While this is popular among subsidiary managers, decentralization does not allow the multinational company to utilize its most liquid asset on a widespread basis. Effective cash management requires the predetermination of cash flow centers. For example, the multinational company should not choose to hold cash in a country which has violent political upheavals and rampant inflation. Rather, it should transfer idle local cash balances as quickly as possible to a more stable environment.

Centralized cash management calls for each local subsidiary to hold at the local level the minimum cash balance for transaction purposes. All funds not needed for transaction purposes are channeled to a central cash center. This cash center has responsibility for placing the central pool of funds in such currencies and money market instruments which will best serve the needs of the multinational company on a worldwide basis.

Centralized cash management has a number of advantages over decentralized cash management. (1) The central cash center can collect information more quickly and make better decisions as to the relative strengths and weaknesses of various currencies. Such information and decisions are necessary to invest the central pool of funds most profitably. (2) Funds held in the cash center can quickly be returned to a subsidiary with cash shortages by wire transfer or by providing a worldwide banking system with full collateral in hard currency. The central pool of funds eliminates the possibility that one subsidiary will borrow at higher rates while another holds surplus funds idle or invests them at lower rates. (3) By holding all precautionary balances in a central cash center, the multinational company can reduce the total pool in size without any loss in the level of production. This is due to the synergistic effect, which is said to exist when the whole is worth more than the mere sum of its parts. This effect has been frequently defined as "2 + 2 = 5."

Before any cash is remitted to a central cash center, local cash needs must be properly assessed. The proper assessment of local cash needs in relation to the cash center involves the following six steps: (1) Cash budgets should be prepared to know anticipated cash outflows and inflows at key future dates. (2) Each subsidiary must have effective cash collection procedures which would speed cash flows into the company. (3) Each subsidiary must also have systematic cash disbursement procedures which would delay cash flows out of the company. (4) Each subsidiary should estimate when and how much surplus cash it will have. (5) Each subsidiary should also estimate when and how much shortages it will have. (6) The multinational company must develop necessary steps for cash mobilization such as a management information system, a cash transfer system, and clear responsibility for making cash transfer decisions.

Many factors affect the location of cash centers. From an economic point of view, idle funds should move toward those locations which would provide the highest profitability and safety. These funds are accumulated in cash centers for temporary investments prior to reassignment elsewhere. Thus, the multinational company must choose those locations from which the funds can again be readily assigned to other places of the world.

Perhaps the most important factor affecting the location of cash centers is the local government's political stability and its attitude toward foreign-based companies. Local laws may require partial ownership of alien companies by nationals of the host country or by the government itself. Hostility of the courts toward foreign business claims and disclosure requirements may all work against the operation of a subsidiary as a cash center. Aggregate tax levels and penalty rates on excessive dividend remittances also play an important role in the selection of cash centers.

The multinational company must also consider a variety of economic factors in the selection of cash centers. These cash centers should be located in countries whose currencies are stable in value and readily convertible into other currencies. It is extremely difficult for the financial manager to predict exact timing of a change in the exchange rate. Most governments take all possible measures to avoid speculation against their currencies. It is critical, therefore, to engage in hedging operations to assure that foreign exchange losses can be minimized. Thus, the existence of an active forward market and the availability of suitable money market instruments for the deployment of temporary excess resources are important.

Cash centers are usually located in the major financial centers of the world such as New York and London. Brussels has become popular as a cash center for companies operating in Europe. Additional popular locations for cash centers include such tax haven countries as Luxembourg, the Bahamas, Bermuda, and the Netherlands. These countries offer most of the prerequisites for a corporate cash center: political and economic stability, freely convertible currency, access to international communications, and well defined legal procedures.

ACCOUNTS RECEIVABLE MANAGEMENT

The level of accounts receivable depends upon the volume of credit sales and the average collection period. These two variables in turn depend upon credit standards, credit terms, and collection policy. As management moves from customers who are more likely to pay their bills to customers who are less likely to pay their bills, sales tend to increase. However, the lenient credit policy is also likely to increase bad debt losses and investments in accounts receivable. In theory, the company should liberalize its credit standards to the point where the marginal profit on its increased sales equals the marginal cost of credit.

Because money has a time value, accounts receivable have a cost in terms of foregone interest. Nevertheless, many multinational companies frequently decide to sell for credit in order to expand sales volume and profits. If sales are made on the basis of drafts on importers, trade acceptances or bankers' acceptances are created and these may be discounted at banks or sold in the money market. In addition, in many countries, government agencies extend export credit at preferential interest rates which make the accumulation of accounts receivable even more desirable.

Multinational accounts receivable are created by two separate types of transaction: sales to outside the corporate group and intracompany sales. These two types of transactions must be considered separately because their economic consequences are different. One truly unique problem area of multinational accounts receivable management has to do with the risk of currency value changes. The accounts receivable manager should understand this risk and take all necessary actions to minimize such a risk.

Sales to Independent Customers and Intracompany Sales

Management of accounts receivable from independent buyers involves two types of decision: the denomination of currency to be used for payments and the terms of payment. Domestic sales are always denominated in the local currency. In contrast, export sales can be denominated in the currency of the exporter, the currency of the importer, or a third country currency. The exporter would prefer to price and to invoice in the strongest currency, while the importer would prefer to pay in the weakest currency. Competition or custom will frequently resolve the problem, but the usual result is a tradeoff between the term of payment and the denomination of currency. For example, the exporter may grant a longer credit period in exchange for the importer's promise to pay its purchase in a hard currency.

Many factors affect the terms of payment, but perhaps one of the most important is the strength of the currency denominated in the transaction. If payments are to be made in a soft currency, accounts receivable should be collected as quickly as possible in order to minimize the possibility of exchange losses between the sale date and the collection date. Sales made in a hard currency may be permitted to remain outstanding somewhat longer. If the devaluation of its home currency is imminent, the exporter might want to encourage slow payment of its hard currency receivables.

Intracompany sales differ from sales to independent customers in that little concern is given to credit standing and that the timing of the payments may depend upon the company's desire to allocate resources rather than normal payment schedules. Such sales are necessary for many reasons. Subsidiaries produce different products and often sell to each other. Like the location of cash balances, the location of intracompany receivables and their amount are a policy problem of the multinational company in the allocation of its resources on a global basis. If the parent company desires to transfer funds to its affiliate, it may do so by having the affiliate delay the payment of intracompany purchases.

Because intracompany sales usually cross national boundaries, governments are concerned about such sales. If subsidiaries are located in countries whose currencies are likely to devalue or to float downward, the parent company may instruct its subsidiaries to pay their purchases more quickly. In contrast, if subsidiaries are located in countries whose currencies are expected to upvalue or to float upward, the parent company may instruct its subsidiaries to delay payments. It is important to note that early payments and later payments in conjunction with intracompany sales are feasible only when the parent company owns 100 percent of its various affiliates.

Currency Value Problems

Accounts receivable risks result from changes in exchange rates between the sales date and the collection date. There are several ways that the accounts receivable manager may be able to reduce these risks. The seller may require that all payments are to be made in hard currencies. This requirement would assure the seller that payments are to be made in currencies likely to face little or no devaluation on the foreign exchange market. In certain instances, the multinational company refuses credit sales denominated in foreign currencies altogether. It is often possible for multinational companies to buy currency credit insurance. For example, American exporters can purchase protection from the Foreign Credit Insurance Association described in Chapter 6.

The use of factors is another way to minimize accounts receivable risks from changes in exchange rates between the sale date and the collection date. Factoring is a process whereby a company sells its accounts receivable on a nonrecourse basis. Nonrecourse means that the factor takes the loss if the customers of its client do not pay their accounts. In addition to risk bearing, the factor performs a number of additional services such as credit checking, bookkeeping, and the collection of accounts. U. S. banks have been responsible for the rapid expansion of international factoring. In 1963, the Comptroller of the Currency ruled that factoring is a proper area for national bank expansion. Since then many American banks have entered the factoring business not only in the United States but also in Europe and gradually into the rest of the world.

INVENTORY MANAGEMENT

The overall efficiency of inventory management is extremely important for two reasons. (1) Inventories represent a significant segment of total assets for most business firms. (2) They are the least liquid of current assets and thus errors in inventory management are not quickly remedied. Hence, it is not surprising to note that for the last few decades the greatest improvements within the area of current asset management have been made in the area of inventory control and investment. With the application of computers and mathematical models, the size of inventories in relation to sales has been greatly reduced.

The level of sales, the length of the production cycle, and the durability of the product are the major determinants of investment in inventory. In domestic or one-country operations, companies attempt to balance their inventory level in such a way that both carrying costs and stockout costs are minimized. However, differentials in the costs of production and storage in different countries allow the multinational company to maintain more flexible inventory policies. For instance, multinational companies can take advantage of the cheaper costs that may exist in a particular country by shifting its production or storage function to that country. These advantages are offset by such disadvantages as tariff levels and other forms of import restrictions used by governments.

Given the fact that many foreign affiliates operate under inflationary economic conditions, it is important for a multinational company to determine whether to buy inventory in advance or to delay purchase until the inventory is actually needed. Advance purchase involves such carrying costs as interest on funds tied up in inventory, insurance premiums, storage costs, and taxes. Later purchase increases the possibility of higher costs either through inflation or devaluation. Inflation increases the costs of locally purchased items and devaluation increases the costs of imported items.

Despite the desire for optimization of inventory levels, many companies that rely on imported inventories maintain over-stocked inventory accounts.[6] "The fears of continued inflation, raw materials shortages, and a number of other environmental constraints . . . are inducing companies to maintain high overseas inventory levels rather than risk curtailment of their overseas operations."[7] The additional environmental constraints include anticipated import bans in foreign countries, anticipated delivery delays caused by dock strikes and slowdowns, the lack of sophisticated production and inventory control systems, and increased difficulty in obtaining foreign exchange for inventory purchases.

Protective Measures Against Inflation

Many foreign affiliates operate under inflationary economic conditions. Thus, it is important for multinational companies to determine the effects of an increasing local price level or devaluation on their inventory management policies. The type of inventory normally stocked by subsidiaries is of importance to this decision. Some subsidiaries rely heavily on imported inventories, while other subsidiaries depend heavily upon locally acquired inventories. Some other subsidiaries may rely almost equally on imported and locally acquired inventories.

If a subsidiary relies heavily on imported goods, it should seek to build up its inventory of supplies, equipment, and components in advance of an expected devaluation. This is because devaluation at a later date effectively increases the costs of imported goods. For example, if the host country should declare a ten percent devaluation of its currency in relation to the dollar, the subsidiary should pay ten percent more local currency for the same amount of imported goods from the United States.

On the other hand, if a subsidiary depends heavily upon locally purchased goods, it should seek to minimize its inventory of supplies, equipment, and components. This is because devaluation at a later date effectively reduces the dollar value of inventories acquired

[6] Alan C. Shapiro, "Optimal Inventory and Credit Granting Strategies Under Inflation and Devaluation," *Journal of Financial and Quantitative Analysis* (January 1973), pp. 34-46.

[7] Business International, *How Inflation, Shortages, Tight Money Affect Global Corporate Investment Policies* (New York: Business International Corporation, 1974), p. 273.

locally. If inventories are translated at current rather than historical exchange rates, a ten percent devaluation of the local currency against the dollar would reduce the dollar value of its inventory by ten percent.

Finally, if a subsidiary relies almost equally on imported inventories and locally purchased inventories, it should seek to reduce its locally acquired inventories and to increase its imported inventories in advance of an expected devaluation. However, if accurate forecasts of devaluation are not possible, the company should maintain the same amount of imported goods and locally purchased goods to avoid foreign exchange risks. This is because a devaluation would affect both types of inventories equally and thus the subsidiary would experience neither a gain nor a loss.

Pricing

Up to this point, our discussion has centered on preventive measures that multinational companies may take to reduce the risks associated with devaluation. Additional action can be taken in the area of pricing to reduce these risks.

> ***Example 9-1*** Assume that 10 American-made radios have been imported into Korea which subsequently devalues its wons by 100 percent. The original exchange rate was KW50 per $1, the original cost was KW1,000 per radio, and the original selling price was KW1,500 per radio.

The Korean subsidiary has two basic policies with respect to price: (1) it can maintain the original price of its inventory in an effort to undercut competition and (2) it can increase the price of its inventory in order to earn all or part of the original dollar profit expected. Table 9-3 shows the effects of both policies to the Korean subsidiary. Maintenance of the old price will result in a dollar loss of $50 on the sale of the 10 radios even if local figures indicate a profit of KW5,000. If the subsidiary increases its selling price to the dollar equivalent of the original selling price, it will earn a profit of $100. However, it is important to note that this assumes the Korean government does not maintain price controls. Although there are no price controls imposed by the Korean government, a price increase of the magnitude indicated in Policy (2) would perhaps discourage some sales. If the price elasticity of demand for the merchandise is extremely high, the local market may not bear the higher price. Nevertheless, a certain

Table 9-3 Effect of Pricing on Profits

			(1) Maintain old price		(2) Adjust price	
Exchange Rate			Korean Currency	Dollars (current value)	Korean Currency	Dollars (current value)
KW100	(now)	Sold for	KW15,000	$150	KW30,000	$300
KW50	(old)	Cost	KW10,000	$200	KW10,000	$200
		Profit	KW 5,000	($50)	KW20,000	$100

level of price rise is required to prevent a deterioration of converted earnings.

Another important question is whether the subsidiary should continue to import that type of merchandise. If local sales prices can be raised to cover the now higher dollar import prices, imports should continue. If not, imports should cease. Although the decision not to import the merchandise does not cause any translation loss, it may result in idle production capacity and an eventual operating loss due to the surrender of that particular foreign market. If possible, multinational companies should price their inventory goods in such a way that sales revenues include the sum of the increase in replacement cost of the inventory sold, plus the loss in real value of the monetary profit expected, plus the increased income taxes.

REDUCING VULNERABILITY TO INFLATION AND DEVALUATION

When it becomes clear that inflation will continue and devaluation is imminent, it is advisable that managers consider the following adaptations. Cash balances should be minimized and foreign debts denominated in convertible currencies should be liquidated. When the host government appears likely to impose foreign exchange controls, remittances should be accelerated. If controls are already in effect, any excess funds should be reinvested in assets which are not so vulnerable as cash. At the same time, the subsidiary must be careful at a sensitive time. Remittances through the black market may result in serious economic reprisals.

It is worthwhile to take all the normal procedures of speeding up the collection process and delaying payments. If the subsidiary needs funds on a short-term basis, it should obtain them from local banks. However, under conditions of an imminent devaluation and/or a rapid increase in price levels, bank loans are usually not obtainable. It then becomes necessary to obtain local currency loans by factoring receivables or by pledging inventories. If the subsidiary has preestablished overdraft facilities with local banks, it is desirable to exhaust them before it secures its assets for loans. This is because overdraft facilities are normally the cheapest local credit available.

Unless local buyers will ignore higher prices and respond to credit offerings positively, accounts receivable should be reduced to the extent that local operating circumstances permit. Investments in locally purchased goods should be minimized and investments in imported goods should be maximized under inflationary conditions. Such prepaid expenses as deposits on materials and insurance premiums should be kept as small as possible. Forward contracts may be necessary to protect the convertible currency value of funds between accumulation and transfer.

SUMMARY

International working capital management techniques are essentially similar to those employed domestically, but additional variables are involved. In domestic operations all transactions are subject to the same rules of movement, accumulation, and reinvestment, but these rules vary when these transactions occur across national boundaries. These additional variables include political tax, foreign exchange, and other economic constraints.

To manage working capital from a global perspective, the multinational company must carefully evaluate various constraints such as foreign exchange rate fluctuations and base ultimate decisions about the transfer of funds on this evaluation. The company then must establish clear lines of accountability for asset deterioration and exchange losses. Finally, a workable system of controls must be developed to help measure the performance of working capital management.

Cash management can be centralized or decentralized on a company level. Although decentralization is popular among subsidiary managers, it does not permit the multinational company to use its most liquid asset on a widespread basis. Effective cash management requires the establishment of cash centers. This sytem calls for each local subsidiary to hold at the local level the minimum cash balance for transaction purposes. All funds not needed for transaction purposes are channeled to a central cash center. This cash center has responsibility for placing the central pool of funds in such currencies and money market instruments which will best serve the needs of the multinational company on a worldwide basis.

Multinational accounts receivable are created by two separate types of transaction: sales to independent customers and intracompany sales. Management of accounts receivable from independent customers involves the denomination of currency to be used for payments and the terms of payment. Intracompany sales differ from sales to independent customers in that little concern is given to credit standing and that the timing of the payments may depend upon the company's desire to allocate resources rather than normal payment schedules. One truly unique area of multinational accounts receivables management has to do with the risk of currency value changes. The accounts receivable manager should understand this risk and take all necessary actions to minimize such a risk.

The overall efficiency of inventory management is extremely important for two reasons: (1) Inventories represent a significant segment of total assets for most business firms. (2) They are the least liquid of current assets and thus errors in inventory management are not quickly remedied.

When foreign subsidiaries operate under inflationary conditions, it is important to determine whether to purchase inventory in advance or to delay purchase until the inventory is actually needed. Advance purchase involves such carrying costs as interest on funds tied up in inventory, insurance premiums, and storage costs. Later purchase involves the possibility of higher costs either through inflation or devaluation. Thus, the inventory manager should compute the optimal tradeoff between higher carrying costs and higher purchase costs for inventory.

REFERENCES

9-1 Arpan, Jeffrey S., "Multinational Firm Pricing in International Markets," *Sloan Management Review* (Winter 1972-1974), pp. 1-9.

9-2 Eiteman, David K., and Arthur I. Stonehill, *Multinational Business Finance* (Reading, Mass.: Addison-Wesley Publishing Co., 1979), Chapters 10 and 11.

9-3 Gentry, James A., Dileep R. Mehta, S. K. Bhattachayya, Robert Cobbaut, and Jean L. Scaringella, "An International Study of Management Perceptions of the Working Capital Process," *Journal of International Business Studies* (Spring/Summer 1979), pp. 28-38.

9-4 Goeltz, Richard K., "Managing Liquid Funds Internationally," *Columbia Journal of World Business* (July-August 1972), pp. 59-64.

9-5 Nalin, Domenico F., "Cash Planning and Managing Corporate Finance," *Euromoney* (February 1976), pp. 76+.

9-6 Ricks, David A., *International Dimensions of Corporate Finance* (Englewood Cliffs, N.J.: Prentice-Hall, Inc., 1978), Chapters 3, 4, and 5.

9-7 Rutenberg, David P., "Maneuvering Liquid Assets in a Multinational Company: Formulation and Deterministic Solution Procedures," *Management Science* (July 1970), pp. 671-684.

9-8 Seed, Allen H., "Measuring Financial Performance in an Inflationary Environment, *Financial Executive* (January 1982), pp. 40-51.

9-9 Shapiro, Alan C., "Optimal Inventory and Credit-Granting Strategies Under Inflation and Devaluation," *Journal of Financial and Quantitative Analysis* (January 1973), pp. 37-46.

9-10 Wunderlisch, Karl, "Centralized Cash Management Systems for the Multinational Enterprise," *Management International Review* (June 1973), pp. 43-57.

TEN

CAPITAL EXPENDITURE ANALYSIS

The basic principles of analysis are the same for foreign and domestic investment projects. However, the foreign investment decision results from a complex process which differs in some key aspects from the domestic investment decision. The cash flow analysis for foreign direct investment projects is much more complex than that for domestic investment projects. The cost of capital for foreign investment projects is typically higher than that for domestic investment projects.

The relevant cash flows are the dividends and royalties that would be repatriated by each subsidiary to the parent firm. Since these net cash flows must be converted into currency of the parent company, they are subject to future exchange rate changes. Normally, foreign projects are more risky than domestic projects. Hence, the cost of capital for a foreign project is higher than that for a similar domestic project. This higher risk comes from two major sources: exchange risk and political risk.

In this chapter, we examine the use of capital budgeting analysis for foreign direct investment projects. In Chapter 11 we describe the nature of political risk and some techniques to minimize it. In Chapter 12 we consider the nature of foreign exchange risk and some methods to reduce it.

FOREIGN DIRECT INVESTMENT AND HOST COUNTRIES

Host countries can benefit from foreign direct investment in many ways. (1) Foreign investment induces the transfer of technology and skills which are frequently in short supply. (2) It increases both national employment and domestic wages. (3) It provides local workers with an opportunity to learn managerial skills. (4) It also contributes to tax revenues and helps balance international payments.

Although foreign investment tends to contribute much needed resources to host countries (developing countries in particular), it is viewed by many with misgivings.[1] Arguments against foreign investment range from excessive cost of resources transferred, a loss of political and economic sovereignty, decreases in competitivenesses of domestic markets, and increases in exploitations. Some charge that foreign investment undermines indigenous cultures and societies by imposing Western values and lifestyles on developing countries.

It would thus seem apparent that while foreign direct investment has the potential to contribute positively to development, there is no guarantee that it would have no harmful impact on host countries. But the question of foreign investment need not be a zero sum game. What is needed is to set up a feasible framework for investment to define the rights and responsibilities of both parties. This framework should allow both a reasonable return to the investor and a positive contribution to development goals of the host country.

FOREIGN DIRECT INVESTMENT POSITIONS

U. S. multinational companies dominated foreign direct investment for the last two decades (1960s and 1970s). In fact, over much of the past two decades there had been two familiar stereotypes. (1) The multinational company tended to be based in the United States. (2) Most foreign direct investment was made by these U. S. multinational companies.

However, recent statistics indicate that these two stereotypes may no longer be the case. For example, "whereas in 1963 U. S. multinational companies accounted for two-thirds of the world's 100

[1] Dirk W. Stikker, *The Role of Private Enterprise in Investment and Promotion of Exports in Developing Countries*, United Nations Conference on Trade and Development (New York: 1968), p. 14.

largest companies and for three-fifths of the 500 largest, by 1979 their share had dropped to below one-half of each group."[2] In another instance, recent takeover attempts of some U. S. firms by foreign companies have once again captured media headlines across the country and heightened concern that the U. S. economy is being bought by foreigners.

Thus, it is not difficult to understand why in 1976 the U. S. Department of Commerce conducted a comprehensive study on foreign investment in the United States.[3] The study found that: (1) while foreign investment in the United States was growing, it was relatively insignificant; (2) the foreign investors operated in basically the same ways as domestic companies; and (3) existing U. S. laws were sufficient to protect U. S. interests. More specifically, the study came to the following basic conclusions:

1. Foreign investment was present in almost all sectors but was relatively insignificant except in newsprint, dyes, pharmaceuticals, and synthetic fibers; foreign investment was concentrated in industrial states but the more recent investors had located in the South and had come largely from Europe.
2. Most foreign investors were not large by U. S. standards, operated only in one state from one plant, and were regularly involved in international trade (24 percent of all U. S. merchandise exports and 30 percent of U. S. imports). U. S. citizens comprised 95 percent of their workforce.
3. The major reasons for investing in the U. S. were: (a) the size of the U. S. market; (b) U. S. political stability and fewer governmental controls; (c) the U. S. lead in marketing and management know-how; (d) the efficiency and skill of U. S. labor; (e) the highly developed capital markets in the U. S.; (f) the R&D capabilities of the U. S.; (g) the receptiveness of Americans to new ideas and products; and (h) the relatively large supply of natural resources.[4]

Table 10-1 shows the breakdown of the world's 100 largest companies by country of origin. The country list increased from nine countries in 1963 to 14 countries in 1979, including three companies

[2] John Hein, *The World's Multinationals: A Global Challenge* (New York: The Conference Board, 1981), p. 5.

[3] U. S. Department of Commerce, *Foreign Direct Investment in the United States* (Washington, D. C.: Government Printing Office, 1976).

[4] Jeffrey S. Arpan, Edward B. Flowers, and David A. Ricks, "Foreign Direct Investment in the United States: The State of Knowledge in Research," *Journal of International Business Studies* (Spring/Summer 1981), pp. 140-141.

Table 10-1 The World's 100 Largest Industrial Corporations

Country of Origin	1963	1971	1979
United States	67	58	47
Germany	13	11	13
United Kingdom	7	7	7
France	4	5	11
Japan	3	8	7
Italy	2	3	3
Netherlands-United Kingdom	2	2	2
Netherlands	1	2	3
Switzerland	1	2	1
Canada	–	–	2
Australia	–	1	–
Belgium	–	–	1
Brazil	–	–	1
Mexico	–	–	1
United Kingdom-Italy	–	1	–
Venezuela	–	–	1

Source: John Hein, *The World's Multinationals: A Global Challenge* (New York: The Industrial Conference Board, 1981), p. 5.

from Latin America. This increase reflects the emergence of national oil companies into the top ranks mainly because of sharply higher oil prices. Although the number of U. S. multinational companies in this list decreased from 67 in 1963 to 47 in 1979, no other country is even close to the United States in the number of the world's top 100 companies. Furthermore, by 1979 U. S. multinational companies still accounted for almost one-half of the world's 100 largest companies. It is important to recognize the fact that in 1979 the United States accounted for only about two-fifths of the total output of the world's industrial countries.

Table 10-2 shows U. S. direct investment position abroad and foreign direct investment position in the United States for a selected number of years. U. S. direct investment abroad increased from \$31.9 billion in 1960 to \$78.2 billion in 1970, a 2.5 times increase. Foreign direct investment in the United States rose from \$6.9 billion in 1960 to \$13.2 billion in 1970, almost a two-fold increase. In contrast, U. S. direct investment abroad increased by almost three times from 1970 to 1980 and foreign direct investment in the United States rose by almost five times during the same period. This means that while in the 1960s U. S. direct investment abroad increased at a faster rate than foreign direct investment in the United States, in the 1970s the trend reversed. It is also important to observe that foreign invest-

Table 10-2 United States: Foreign Direct Investment Positions (in billions of dollars)

Year	U. S. Investment Abroad	Foreign Investment in U. S.
1960	31.9	6.9
1965	49.5	8.8
1970	78.2	13.2
1973	101.3	20.5
1974	110.1	25.1
1975	124.1	27.7
1976	136.8	30.8
1977	149.9	34.6
1978	167.8	42.5
1979	186.8	54.5
1980	213.5	65.5

Source: U. S. Department of Commerce, *Survey of Current Business*, various issues.

ment in the United States had been under 30 percent of the U. S. foreign investment over the past two decades.

These statistics are essentially consistent with the findings of the Commerce Department's study on foreign investment in the United States: foreign investment in the United States is growing but still insignificant. As Lotti and Tomai put it, "estimates indicate that the nation (the United States) has not yet been acquired by foreigners."[5] Although some recently suggested that the United States impose restrictions on foreign investment in this country, it is unlikely that additional restrictions will be instituted on foreign investment in the near future. Moreover, many empirical studies have found that foreign investors bring many benefits to the United States.[6] Thus, it seems undesirable to place additional restrictions on foreign investment in the United States at the present time.

THE INVESTMENT DECISION MAKING PROCESS

The foreign investment decision involves the allocation and commitment of funds to foreign investment projects.[7] The rational use

[5] Marcello Lotti and James V. Tomai, "Foreign Investors Bring Many Benefits to U. S. Companies," *Management Focus* (November/December 1981), p. 19.

[6] *Ibid.*, pp. 19-21.

[7] For an excellent discussion of the foreign investment decision process, see Yair Aharoni, *The Foreign Investment Decision Process* (Boston: Graduate School of Business Administration, Harvard University, 1968).

of capital resources is critical for the future well-being of the multinational company. This is because such an investment usually requires a very large sum of money and is made in expectation of benefits to be realized over a number of years.

The foreign investment decision process involves the entire process of planning expenditures in foreign countries beyond one year. The choice of one year is arbitrary, but the one-year boundary is rather widely accepted. There are many steps and elements in the entire process of planning capital expenditures in foreign countries. Each element is a subsystem of the capital budgeting system. Thus, the foreign investment decision process may be viewed as an integral unit of many elements which are directly or indirectly interrelated. Here we assume that the entire foreign investment decision process consists of seven phases: (1) the decision to search for foreign investment, (2) an assessment of the political climate in the host country, (3) an examination of the company's overall strategy, (4) cash flow analysis, (5) the required rate of return, (6) economic evaluation, and (7) risk adjustment.

Search for Foreign Investment

A system should be established to stimulate ideas for capital expenditures abroad and to identify good investment opportunities. This is because the availability of good investment opportunities provides the foundation for a successful investment program. Moreover, good investment opportunities do not just appear. A continuous stream of attractive investment opportunities comes from hard thinking, careful planning, and frequently large outlays for research and development.

The first phase in the foreign investment decision process is an analysis of the forces that lead some company officials to focus attention on the possibilities of foreign investment. If the company recognizes foreign investment as a legitimate program, its search for foreign investment opportunities will start. The economic and political forces in the host countries are largely responsible for the expansion of foreign investment. Many companies also desire foreign investment to seek new markets, raw materials, and production efficiency. Chapter 2 described these and other motives for foreign investment in detail.

In any particular case it is not easy to pinpoint one motive for a decision to invest abroad or to find out exactly who was the originator of a foreign project. The decision to search for foreign investment results from a series of events, a combination of several motivating forces, and activities of different persons. Typically, the decision to look abroad depends on the interaction of many forces. Considerations such as profit opportunities, tax policy, and diversification strategies are economic variables which may affect a decision to look overseas. In addition, environmental forces, organizational factors, and a drive by some high-ranking officials inside the company could be the major forces which lead a company to look abroad.

Essentially, advantages of superior knowledge and economies of scale determine direct foreign investment.[8] These two types of advantages permit a multinational company to operate its subsidiary more profitably than local competitors. The term "knowledge" is used here to mean production technologies, managerial skills, industrial organization, knowledge of product, and foreign markets.

In addition to superior knowledge, foreign direct investment allows the multinational company to obtain economies of scale. Vertical foreign investment reduces the costs and uncertainties that exist when subsequent stages of production are handled by different producers. Horizontal foreign investment provides the multinational company with opportunities to eliminate duplicate facilities as well as to consolidate the functions of production, marketing, and purchasing.

Political Climate

One major concern of multinational companies is the possibility that the political climate of the host country may deteriorate. The multinational financial manager must analyze the political environment of the proposed host country and determine whether or not the economic environment would be receptive to the proposed project. In general, those projects designed to reduce the country's need for imports and thus save foreign exchange are given the highest priority by the host government.

Political actions such as government takeovers and operational restrictions adversely affect company operations. Thus, the emphasis of the analysis must center on such factors as the host government's attitudes toward foreign investment, the desire of the host government for national rather than foreign control, and its political stability. It is also important to determine that adequate and prompt compensation is guaranteed if nationalization becomes desirable in the public interest.

[8] Charles P. Kindleberger, *American Business Abroad: Six Lectures on Direct Investment* (Yale University Press, 1969).

Company's Overall Strategy

If the initial screening of the political climate is favorable, the multinational company can move on to the next stage of the decision process. An assessment of the company's overall strategy is useful to determine whether and which foreign operations would allow the company to use its strength or to strengthen its weakness. This approach allows the company to reduce the number of alternatives to a manageable number. At this stage, the company must check whether the suggested project conflicts with company policies and resources. The emphasis of analysis must also center on such factors as whether the company has the experience to handle the project and how the project could be integrated into existing projects.

Cash Flow Analysis

The fourth stage of the screening process involves a standard cash flow analysis. The after-tax cash outflows and inflows directly associated with each project must be estimated to evaluate capital investment alternatives. The multinational company must forecast its expected expenditures for the proposed project. Ordinarily, these forecasts can be obtained from the historical data of similar ventures. They may also be estimated by such forecasting techniques as the percent of sale method or a linear regression analysis. An important difference in the application of cash flow analysis for foreign investment is that there are two sets of cash flow analyses: cash flows for the project itself and cash flows available to the parent company.

Demand Forecast. The first step in the analysis of cash flows for any investment proposal is a forecast of demand. Such usage estimates are highly correlated with such factors as historical demands, population, income, alternative sources of products, competition, the feasibility of serving nearby markets, and general economic conditions.

There are a number of obvious reasons for the strong emphasis on the market size in the investment decision process. First, the expected market size can be used as an indication of profit possibility for the proposed investment project. Second, small markets tend to have high uncertainty. If the market is small, the multinational company has little or no leeway left in case of error of estimate. Third, small markets are not worth the effort. Because one of the scarce resources in the company is management, the proposed project should be large enough to support the management time that would have to be spent on project analysis.

Duties and Taxes. Because foreign investment cuts across national boundaries, a unique set of tax laws and import duties may be applicable. The multinational company must review the tax structure of the host country. Analysis would include the definition of a taxable entity, statutory tax rates, tax treaties, the treatment of dual taxation, and tax incentive programs. It is also important for the multinational company to know whether the host government would impose any customs duties on imported production equipment and materials that could not be obtained from local sources.

Exchange Rate. Another important feature of foreign investment analysis is that project inflows available to the investor are subject to foreign exchange rates and restrictions. When the host country has a stable exchange rate, no problems are presented. However, if the exchange rate is expected to change or allowed to float, cash flow analysis becomes more complicated. This is because it is necessary to forecast the exchange rate which may be applicable to convert cash flows into hard currencies.

It is equally important to recognize that many host governments have various exchange control regulations. Under these regulations, permission may be required to buy foreign exchange with local currency for payment of loan interest, management fees, royalties, and most other billings for services provided by foreign suppliers. Applications for permission to purchase foreign exchange may be subject to considerable delay. The granting of permission to buy foreign exchange does not guarantee the availability of the related exchange in time. This is because commercial banks can allocate to their customers only such amounts as are made available by the central bank.

There are many factors that affect the blockage of funds to nonresidents. They include an unexpected shortage of foreign exchange, a long-run deficiency of the foreign exchange, and certain types of domestic political pressures. If all funds are blocked in perpetuity, the value of the project to the parent is zero. However, in actuality funds are likely to be only partially blocked because multinational companies have many ways to remove blocked funds. These methods include transfer price adjustments, loan repayments, royalty adjustments, and fee adjustments. Furthermore, most host countries limit the amount of fund transfer to nonresidents or block the transfer of funds only on a temporary basis. Nevertheless, multinational companies must analyze the impact of blocked funds on project return. It is critical to determine the amount of blocked funds, their reinvestment return, and ways in which funds can be transferred under the host country's law.

Project vs. Parent Cash Flows. To yield the after-tax profits from the proposed project, the multinational company must develop a demand forecast, forecast its expected expenditures, and review the tax structure of the host country. The estimated sales less the estimated expenses plus non-cash outlays such as depreciation give the cash inflows from operations.

Typically, the multinational company desires to maximize the utility of project cash flows on a worldwide basis. The parent multinational company must value only those cash flows which can be repatriated because only these funds can be used to reinvest in other subsidiaries, pay dividends, pay debt obligations, or invest in new ventures. Project cash flows would have little value if they could not be used for these alternatives.

Project cash flows and parent cash flows can have substantial differences mainly due to tax regulations and exchange controls. Moreover, some project expenses such as management fees and royalties are returns to the parent. In general, incremental cash flows to the parent are worldwide parent cash flows after investment minus worldwide parent cash flows before investment. The existence of such differences raises the question of which cash flows should be used as the relevant cash flows in project evaluation. Because the value of a project is determined by the net present value of future cash flows to the investor, cash flows available for repatriation should be used as the relevant cash flows in foreign investment analysis. Hence, the multinational company must analyze the impact of taxation, expropriation, and exchange controls on cash flows to the parent.

The Cost of Capital

The cost of capital is the minimum rate of return that a project must yield in order to be accepted by a company. This minimum rate of return is sometimes called the discount rate or the required rate of return. The actual required rate of return applied by a multinational company may be the cost of capital adjusted for political and exchange risks.

The weighted average cost of capital is normally used as the firm's cost of capital for a number of reasons. First, if a single component cost is used as the acceptance criterion, it is possible to accept projects with a low rate of return while rejecting projects with a high rate of return. Some low-return projects may be accepted because they can be financed with a cheaper source of capital such as debt. Some high-return projects would be rejected because they have to be financed with an expensive source of capital such as equity. Second, if the firm accepts those projects that yield more than its weighted average cost of capital, it is able to increase the market value of its common stock. This increase occurs because these projects are expected to earn more on their equity-financed portion than the cost of equity.

The weighted average cost of capital is the cost for each type of capital multiplied by its proportion of the total amount of all capital issued by the firm:

$$k = \frac{S}{B + S}(k_e) + \frac{B}{B + S}(k_t) \qquad (10\text{-}1)$$

where k = weighted average cost of capital, k_e = cost of equity, k_t = after-tax cost of debt, B = market value of the firm's debt, and S = market value of the firm's equity.

Optimum Capital Structure. The optimum capital structure is defined as the combination of debt and equity that yields the lowest cost of capital or that maximizes the overall value of the company. Evidence indicates that companies seek the optimum capital structure. For instance, financial ratios published by Dun & Bradstreet, Robert Morris Associates, and other organizations show considerable similarities in the capital structure among companies in the same industry.

These considerations may not be equally applicable to the multinational case because we cannot ignore the modifying effects of environmental variables peculiar to international operations. Evidence suggests that the capital structure of companies in the same industry varies widely from country to country.[9] For example, the debt ratio for most Japanese companies is much higher than the comparable debt ratio for American companies in the same industry. This additional debt is partly because: (1) the Bank of Japan provides major industries with loans through commercial banks and (2) lenders know that the government protects their business. Debt ratios for Germany, Italy, Japan, and Sweden are considerably higher than those for the United States or the United Kingdom. This may be due to the fact that the former group of countries has thinner equity markets than the latter group of countries.

Actual measurement of the values of each capital assumes that companies are concerned with the marginal cost of new funds. Com-

[9] David K. Eiteman and Arthur I. Stonehill, *Multinational Business Finance* (Reading, Mass.: Addison-Wesley Publishing Co., 1979), pp. 366-371.

panies should always expand their capital budget by raising funds in the same proportion as their optimum capital structure. However, as their capital budget expands in absolute terms, their marginal cost of capital will eventually increase. This means that companies can only tap the capital market for some limited amount in the short-run before their marginal cost of capital goes up, even though the same optimum capital structure is maintained.

Multinational companies are able to raise funds in a number of capital markets: the Euromarkets, local foreign capital markets, and their own domestic capital market. This enables multinational firms to expand their capacity to raise funds in the short-run over the amount of capital that could be raised in their home capital market, even if the firm's optimum capital structure is preserved.

Cost of Equity. The cost of equity for a firm is the minimum rate of return necessary to attract investors to buy or hold the firm's common stock. This required rate of return is the discount rate that equates the present value of all expected future dividends per share with the current price per share. If dividends per share are expected to grow at a constant growth rate indefinitely, we can measure the cost of equity by the following formula:

$$k_e = \frac{D_1}{P} + g \tag{10-2}$$

where D_1 = expected dividends per share to be paid at the end of one year, P = current market price per share, and g = annual dividend growth rate.

An alternative approach to the dividend valuation model for common stock is the capital asset pricing model (CAPM). This model assumes that the total risk of a security consists of systematic (undiversifiable) risk and unsystematic (diversifiable) risk. Examples of systematic risk include changes in the overall economy, tax reform by Congress, and a change in the world energy situation. Examples of unsystematic risk include a wildcat strike affecting only the company, a new competitor producing essentially the same product, and a technological breakthrough of making an existing product obsolete.

Within the framework of international context, systematic risk relates to such global events as worldwide recessions, world wars, and changes in the world energy supply. Unsystematic risk relates to such national events as expropriation, currency controls, inflation, and exchange rate changes.

If the market is in equilibrium, the expected return of an individual security (j) is stated as follows:

$$\bar{R}_j = R_f + (\bar{R}_m - R_f)\beta_j \tag{10-3}$$

where $\bar{R}_j$ = expected return of security j, R_f = riskless rate of interest, $\bar{R}_m$ = expected return of the market portfolio, which is a group of risky securities such as Standard & Poor's 500 Stocks, and β_j = systematic risk of security j. This equation is known as the security market line, which consists of the riskless rate of interest (R_f) and a risk premium $[(\bar{R}_m - R_f)\beta_j]$.

One potential problem with using the CAPM is how to compute beta. Beta may be estimated solely on the basis of subjective probability distributions. But it is the common practice to use past data to estimate future betas. If the beta computed from historical data is a reliable surrogate for the future beta, the financial manager has an important new tool to assist him in the formulation of profitable investment decisions. Some empirical surveys indicate that past betas are useful in predicting future betas.[10] It is important to note that betas tend to have greater stability when the number of securities in a portfolio is larger and when the time intervals being studied are longer.

The main difference between the two approaches to the cost of equity is that the dividend valuation model emphasizes the total risk of expected returns while the CAPM emphasizes only the systematic risk of expected returns. In any case, it is important to note that the cost of equity is some function of the market's preference for return and risk.

Cost of Debt

The explicit cost of debt for a domestic firm can be defined as the discount rate that equates the net proceeds of the debt issue with the present value of interest plus principal payments. If we want to express all cost-of-capital rates on an after-tax basis, we must adjust this explicit cost of debt for taxes, because interest charges are usually tax deductible. If we denote the after-tax cost of debt by k_t, it can be approximated by

$$k_t = k_i(1 - t) \tag{10-4}$$

where k_i = before-tax cost of debt and t = tax rate.

[10] Marshall E. Blume, "On the Assessment of Risk," *Journal of Finance* (March 1971), pp. 1-10; Robert A. Levy, "On the Short-Term Stationarity of Beta Coefficients," *Financial Analysts Journal* (November-December 1971), pp. 55-62; Frank J. Fabozzi and Jack C. Francis, "Stability Tests for Alpha and Betas Over Bull and Bear Market Conditions," *Journal of Finance* (September 1977), pp. 1093-1099.

Multinational companies must overcome a number of complicated factors to measure the cost of debt. First, multinational companies can borrow in Eurocurrency markets, international bond markets, or national capital markets. Hence, they must estimate interest rates and the proportion of debt to be raised in each market in order to measure the before-tax cost of debt. Second, in order to measure the after-tax cost of debt, multinational companies must estimate tax rates in each market in which they intend to borrow and determine the deductibility of interest by each national tax authority. Third, when multinational companies issue debt denominated in a foreign currency, the nominal cost of principal and interest in foreign currency terms must be adjusted for foreign exchange gains or losses.

The Appropriate Cost of Capital. If multinational companies make a separate allowance for different levels of risk in foreign projects, they must use the weighted average cost of capital as an appropriate cost of capital. They have three choices in deciding their appropriate cost of capital: (1) the parent cost of capital, (2) the subsidiary cost of capital, and (3) some weighted average of the two.

If the parent company should finance the entire cost of its foreign project by itself, the parent cost of capital can be used as the appropriate cost of capital for the project. If the company obtains all of the capital for the project overseas, the foreign cost of capital can be used as the appropriate cost of capital. In most cases, however, the multinational company uses the whole world as a combined source of funds. Thus, the appropriate cost of capital usually is an overall weighted average of the two.

The inflation adjusted discount rate may have to be used as an appropriate cost of capital in order to reflect local inflation for local projects. However, it is important to recognize that inflation tends to be built into the cost of debt and equity for the company. That is, the weighted average of the parent cost of capital and the subsidiary cost of capital reflects such anticipated price changes. When lenders and equity holders anticipate price increases, they would demand the higher rate of return than otherwise would be the case so that the weighted average cost of capital could reflect inflation. Thus, the multinational company should not add an extra increase to the discount rate derived from the cost of capital in order to adjust for inflation.

Economic Evaluation

Once cash flows and the required rate of return have been determined, the company begins the formal process of evaluating investment projects. Many techniques have been developed for project evaluation under conditions of certainty. They range from simple rules of thumb to sophisticated mathematical programming methods. The four most commonly used methods for an economic evaluation of individual projects are payback, average rate of return, internal rate of return, and net present value.

The capital budgeting literature favors the use of the net-present-value and internal-rate-of-return methods, which are sometimes called the discounted cash-flow approaches. Because the payback and average-rate-of-return methods have various limitations, the two discounted cash-flow-approaches provide a more sophisticated basis for ranking and selecting investment projects. They clearly recognize that money has a time value and that money in the near future is more valuable than money in the distant future. They also use the cash flows of a project over its entire life span. The use of cash flows avoids difficult problems underlying the measurement of income, thus eliminating such irrelevant influences as depreciation methods and inventory valuation.

The net present value of a project is the present value of its expected cash inflows minus the present value of its expected cash outflows. The internal rate of return is the discount rate that equates the present value of expected cash inflows with the present value of expected cash outflows. The decision rule tells us to: (1) accept a project if its net present value is positive and (2) accept a project if its internal rate of return is greater than the firm's cost of capital.

In many situations the net-present-value and internal-rate-of-return methods lead to the same decision. However, there are also situations where they may lead to different decisions. These two rules lead to the same decision if the following conditions hold:

1. Investment proposals under consideration are mutually independent and they are free of capital rationing constraints.
2. All projects are equally risky so that the acceptance or rejection of any project does not affect the cost of capital.
3. A meaningful cost of capital exists to the extent that the company has access to capital at this cost.
4. A unique internal rate of return exists; every project has just one internal rate of return.

In the absence of these assumptions, the two discounted cash-flow approaches may lead to different decisions, thus making the capital budgeting decision much more complex.

When the net-present-value and internal-rate-of-return methods produce different answers, the former is better than the latter for a number of reasons.[11]

1. The net present value is easier to compute than the internal rate of return.
2. If the primary goal of the firm is to maximize the value of the firm, the net-present-value method leads to the correct decision, while the internal rate of return may lead to the incorrect decision.
3. A single project may have more than one internal rate of return under certain conditions, whereas the same project has just one net present value at a particular discount rate.
4. Once computed, the internal rate of return remains constant over the entire life of the project. This static assumption is less than realistic during a period of rising interest rates and inflation. Uneven discount rates present no problems when the net present value method is used.
5. With the net-present-value method, the implied reinvestment rate reflects an approximation of the opportunity cost for reinvestment. But with the internal-rate-of-return method, the implied reinvestment assumption does not approximate the opportunity cost for reinvestment at all.

Example 10-1 In December 1982 the International TV Corporation was approached by the government of Samson in West Africa with a request that the company establish a plant in Samson to assemble television sets. In return for an increase in tariffs against other companies in the industry, the company wishes to invest a total of 1,500 Samson liras in the proposed plant. The SL1,500 will be financed with only common stock, all of which will be owned by the parent. The plant is to be depreciated over a five-year period on a straight line basis for tax purposes. It is expected to have a salvage value of SL750 at the end of five years. The company will pay income taxes at 20 percent on net income earned in Samson and no withholding taxes on dividend repatriated. The United States also has a 50 percent tax rate

[11] Suk H. Kim and Henry J. Guithues, *Finance Principles: An Introduction* (Richmond: Robert F. Dame, Inc.: 1982), pp. 153-167. Although the net-present value method is superior theoretically, the internal-rate-of-return method has certain advantages. The internal rate of return is identical with the yield rate to the maturity of bonds or other securities. Thus, the internal rate of return is directly comparable with the firm's cost of capital in the computation. The prior determination of the cost of capital is frequently cited as one of the advantages for the net-present-value method. But it is in fact the method's most controversial and difficult aspect.

with direct credit for Samson's taxes. This means that net income earned in Samson by U. S. companies will be subject to a total tax of 50 percent. Expected revenues, operating costs, and applicable exchange rates are given in Tables 10-3 and 10-4. There is no restriction on dividend repatriation, but depreciation cash flows may not be repatriated until the company is liquidated. These cash flows can be reinvested in Samson's government bonds to earn tax-exempt interest at the rate of eight percent. The company's cost of capital is 15 percent.

Table 10-3 shows the projected cash flows for the proposed plant. It is important to recognize that for the first year a total tax of 50 percent (SL225) will be levied: 20 percent of the Samson tax (SL90) and 30 percent of the U. S. tax (SL135).

Table 10-4 shows the depreciation cash flows and interest-compounded depreciation cash flows at the termination of the project at the end of five years. Thus, a total of SL880 will be repatriated to the United States along with the plant's fifth year earnings of SL375 at the end of five years.

The last two steps in the analysis are: (1) to convert the cash flows from liras to dollars and (2) to determine the net present value of the plant. Table 10-5 shows these two computation steps. It should be noted that the fifth year cash flow of SL2,005 consists of dividends (SL375), the estimated salvage value of the plant (SL750), and the interest-accumulated depreciation cash flows (SL880).

The current exchange rate of five liras to the dollar is expected to hold during the first year. But the lira is expected to depreciate at a rate of five percent per year after the first year. The expected cash flows in dollars are obtained by dividing the cash flows in liras by the exchange rates. The dollar cash flows are then discounted at the firm's cost of capital (15%) to arrive at a present value figure for each year. Cumulative net present values are the final amounts given in Table 10-5. We see that from the parent's point of view, the plant would break even on a discounted cash flow basis during the fifth year.

Table 10-3 Projected Earnings After Taxes for the Proposed Plant

	Year 1	Year 2	Year 3	Year 4	Year 5
Revenues	SL1,500	SL1,650	SL1,800	SL1,950	SL2,100
Operating costs	900	900	1,050	1,050	1,200
Depreciation	150	150	150	150	150
Taxable income	SL 450	SL 600	SL 600	SL 750	SL 750
Total tax at 50%	225	300	300	375	375
Earnings after tax	SL 225	SL 300	SL 300	SL 375	SL 375

Table 10-4 Depreciation Cash Flows

Year	Depreciation	Interest Factor at 8%	Terminal Value Year 5
1	SL150	1.360	SL204
2	150	1.260	189
3	150	1.166	175
4	150	1.080	162
5	150	1.000	150
			SL880

Because the net present value of the project is positive ($19), the International TV Corporation should accept the proposed plant in order to maximize the market value of the company. The project's internal rate of return is approximately 17 percent. Because the internal rate of return (17%) is greater than the cost of capital (15%), the internal rate of return criterion also indicates acceptance.

Risk Analysis

Thus far the analysis has assumed that the dollar cash flows are certain to occur. In reality all foreign investment projects are subject to various risks such as business and financial risks, inflation and currency risks, and political risks. A change in some of these risks may have a deciding effect on the financial consequences of a particular project. Moreover, the risks vary widely from country to country.

Only a few of the financial variables are normally known in advance with a fair degree of accuracy. Investors are basically risk averters. If we do not know in advance exactly which future events will occur, we will have to determine the risk-return tradeoff in order to choose more attractive projects.

The risk-adjusted discount rate and the certainty equivalent ap-

Table 10-5 The Parent's Net Present Value

Year	Cash Flows	Exchange Rate	Cash Flows	Present Value at 15%	Cum. Net Pres. Value
0	–SL1,500	5.00	–$300	–$300	–$300
1	225	5.00	45	39	– 261
2	300	5.25	57	43	– 218
3	300	5.51	54	36	– 182
4	375	5.79	65	37	– 145
5	2,005	6.08	330	164	19

proach are used by many multinational companies to adjust for project estimates. Assume that the cost of capital for a firm is ten percent when the riskless rate of return is seven percent. The three percent difference between the cost of capital and the riskless rate of return reflects the degree of risk for the company. The company may increase its discount rate by one percent to a total of 11 percent for a mildly risky project, by three percent to a total of 13 percent for a more risky project, and so on. Hence, the risk-adjusted discount rate accounts for the time value of money and the relative risk of the project in terms of a risk premium.

The certainty equivalent approach is an alternative to the risk-adjusted discount rate. It incorporates the manager's preference for return and risk directly into the capital budgeting decision. While the risk-adjusted discount rate adjusts for risk in the denominator of the net-present-value formula, the certainty equivalent approach adjusts for risk in the numerator of the same equation.

When the certainty equivalent approach is used, the annual cash flows are multiplied by a certainty equivalent coefficient, which is a certain cash flow divided by an uncertain cash flow. If management is indifferent between a certain \$140 and an uncertain \$200, its coefficient is 0.70 (\$140 ÷ \$200). The coefficient assumes a value of between 0 and 1. It varies inversely with risk. If the firm perceived greater risk, it would use a lower coefficient which would deflate the dollar return value. Once all the risky cash flows are adjusted downward to reflect uncertainty through the use of the coefficient, these certain cash flows are then discounted at the risk-free rate to determine the certain net present value.

Evaluation of the Two Risk Adjustment Methods. While the risk-adjusted discount rate is appealing for its simplicity, it has a number of practical problems. First, it is extremely difficult to determine the appropriate discount rate for each project or project class. Second, it does not adjust for the variability of the cash flows which are subject to risk. Third, it applies the same discount-rate risk premium to the project throughout its useful life.

The certainty equivalent approach may be able to more accurately adjust for risk than the risk-adjusted discount rate. First, the certainty equivalent approach adjusts for risk in the expected cash flows which are subject to risk. Second, the certainty equivalent coefficient represents a probability factor reflecting the degree of confidence that the decision maker has in obtaining a particular cash flow. Third, this method requires us to use a different certainty equivalent coefficient for each year.

PORTFOLIO THEORY[12]

In the real world, practically no company or individual invests everything in a single project. Thus, it is useful to consider the risk and return of a particular project in conjunction with its counterparts in existing assets or new investment opportunities. Portfolio theory deals with the selection of investment projects that would minimize risk for a given rate of return or that would maximize the rate of return for a given degree of risk. Such a portfolio is sometimes called the *optimum portfolio*.

Markowitz and Tobin developed a powerful technique for a simultaneous risk-return analysis of multiple projects.[13] Although the technique was applied first for the selection of portfolios of common stocks, it is also applicable to the evaluation of capital investment projects. This approach employs two basic measures: an index of expected value and an index of risk. The expected value for a portfolio of investments is simply the sum of the individual present values for the projects that make up the portfolio. The standard deviation as a measure of risk for the portfolio, however, is not so easily measured. There are many business situations where the risks of individual projects tend to offset each other. Thus, successful diversification makes it possible for the company to have the risk of a portfolio less than the sum of the risks of the individual projects.

> ***Example 10-2*** Project A has a cost of \$800, while Project B has a cost of \$1,000. These two projects are mutually independent and their possible net cash flows at the end of one year are given in Table 10-6. Assume that the cost of capital is five percent.

Because the expected net cash flow for both projects is \$1,000 (\$2,000 × 0.5 + \$0 × 0.5), their net present values (NPV) are computed as follows:

$$NPV_A = \frac{\$1,000}{(1.05)^1} - \$800 = \$152$$

$$NPV_B = \frac{\$1,000}{(1.05)^1} - \$1,000 = -\$48$$

[12] For a comprehensive discussion of portfolio, see Suk H. Kim and Henry J. Guithues, *Capital Expenditure Analysis* (Lanham, Maryland: University Press of America, 1981), Chapter 9.

[13] Harry Markowitz, *Portfolio Selection: Efficient Diversification of Investment* (New York: John Wiley & Sons, Inc., 1959); and James Tobin, "Liquidity Preferences as Behavior Toward Risk," *Review of Economic Studies* (February 1958), pp. 65-86.

Table 10-6 Net Cash Flows Under Different Economic Conditions

Economic Condition	Probability	Net Cash Flows Project A	Net Cash Flows Project B
Boom	0.50	$2,000	$ 0
Recession	0.50	0	2,000

The standard deviation of a project (σ) is computed as follows:

$$\sigma = \sqrt{\sum_{i=1}^{n} (R_i - \bar{R})^2 P_i}$$

where R_i = net cash flow associated with the ith event (i.e., a particular economic condition such as boom or recession), $\bar{R}$ = expected net cash flow, and P_i = probability of the ith event. Thus, the standard deviations of Projects A and B can be obtained as follows:

$$\sigma_A = \sqrt{(\$2{,}000 - \$1{,}000)^2 (0.50) + (\$0 - \$1{,}000)^2 (0.50)} = \$1{,}000$$

$$\sigma_B = \sqrt{(\$0 - \$1{,}000)^2 (0.50) + (\$2{,}000 - \$1{,}000)^2 (0.50)} = \$1{,}000$$

Project A has a net present value of $152 and Project B has a net present value of –$48. Both projects have an equal standard deviation of $1,000. Project B would have no chance to be accepted because its expected net present value is negative. Project A has a positive net present value of $152, but most investors are likely to reject the project because its risk is too high.

We can completely eliminate risk by combining these two projects. Whether a boom occurs or a recession occurs, the expected net cash flow of this combination is $2,000 and their combined net present value is $104 ($152 – $48). The standard deviation of this two-project portfolio is zero (0) because the portfolio always produces a net present value of $104. When we consider Projects A and B separately, both projects are clearly undesirable. However, when we treat them as a portfolio, we find the portfolio acceptable.

Portfolio effect is defined as the extent to which the risks of individual projects tend to offset each other. The portfolio effect depends on the degree of correlation that exists between two or more projects. The correlation coefficient measures the degree of correlation between two projects and varies from zero (no correlation or independence) to ±1.0 (perfect correlation).

A correlation coefficient of –1.0 means that the two sets of returns for two projects tend to move in exactly opposite directions.

For example, if a boom occurs, Project A is expected to return $2,000, while Project B is expected to return nothing. In contrast, if a recession occurs, Project A would earn nothing, whereas Project B would earn $2,000. Thus, these two projects are perfectly negatively correlated. We have seen that when two projects are perfectly negatively correlated, diversification can totally eliminate risk.

A correlation coefficient of +1 means that the two sets of returns for two projects tend to move in exactly the same direction. Suppose that if a boom occurs, Projects A and B would yield an equal amount of $2,000, but if a recession occurs, they would earn an equal amount of $100. Then we can say that these two projects are perfectly positively correlated. In this case, diversification would not reduce risk at all.

A correlation coefficient of zero (0) means that the two sets of returns for two projects are uncorrelated or independent of each other. If two projects are uncorrelated, diversification would reduce risk considerably.

Because the degree of correlation among projects depends on economic factors, most pairs of domestic projects have a correlation coefficient of between 0 and +1.0. The argument is that most projects are likely to earn more during a boom, while they are likely to earn less during a recession. If so, diversification can reduce the overall risk somewhat but not much. But different product lines and different geographic markets tend to have a relatively low degree of correlation to each other, thereby making it possible to reduce the overall risk considerably by diversification.

FOREIGN CAPITAL BUDGETING THEORY AND PRACTICE

It has been fifteen years since Stonehill and Nathanson[14] surveyed 110 U. S. and non-U. S. multinational companies to determine their foreign capital budgeting practices. Since then, research on the subject not only refined its theoretical base but also expanded the knowledge of actual capital budgeting practices.

A review of the literature on foreign direct investment theory reveals the following:[15]

[14] Arthur I. Stonehill and Leonard Nathanson, "Capital Budgeting and the Multinational Corporation," *California Management Review* (Summer 1968), pp. 39-54.

[15] Eiteman and Stonehill, *Multinational Business Finance*, Chapters 8 and 10; and Alan C. Shapiro, "Capital Budgeting for the Multinational Corporation," *Financial Management*

1. Multinational companies should value only those cash flows which can be repatriated because only these funds can be used to reinvest in other subsidiaries, pay dividends, pay debt obligations, or invest in new ventures.
2. Multinational companies should use discounted cash-flow methods for ranking and selecting foreign investment projects because these methods clearly recognize the time value of money and also employ the cash flows of a project over its entire life span.
3. Multinational companies should use their weighted average cost of incremental capital for evaluating foreign projects because those projects that yield more than the firm's weighted average cost of capital will increase the value of the firm.
4. Multinational companies should use either the certainty equivalent approach or the risk-adjusted discount rate in order to adjust project estimates for different levels of risk in foreign projects.

Independent surveys have shown that the art and science of overseas capital budgeting have vastly improved since 1966. Two recent surveys found that large U. S. multinational companies measure their foreign project income in terms of cash flows, use discounted cash-flow techniques, compute the cost of capital in a variety of ways, and adjust for risk subjectively.[16] Thus, there is reason to believe that large U. S. multinational companies follow the theoretically prescribed approach in the areas of income measurement and capital budgeting techniques. But they are yet to adopt the techniques favored by academia in the areas of the selection of the discount rate and of risk analysis.

SUMMARY

Foreign investment projects involve many complex variables which do not exist in domestic projects. In this chapter we discussed the benefits and drawbacks of foreign investment for the host country,

(Spring 1978), pp. 7-16; and Alan C. Shapiro, *Multinational Financial Management* (Boston: Allyn and Bacon, Inc., 1982), Chapters 13-15.

[16] Vinod B. Bavishi, "Capital Budgeting Practices at Multinationals," *Management Accounting* (August 1981), pp. 32-35; and David J. Oblak and Roy J. Helm, Jr., "Survey and Analysis of Capital Budgeting Methods Used by Multinationals," *Financial Management* (Winter 1980), pp. 37-41.

the U. S. foreign investment position, the foreign investment position in the United States, and the foreign investment decision process.

Project cash inflows and outflows are analyzed after first identifying foreign investment alternatives. Parent cash flows are then obtained by dividing the project cash flows by the exchange rates. Within this context the net present value of parent cash flows must be positive for a foreign project to be acceptably profitable. In conjuction with the earlier stages of analysis, some adjustments should be made to facilitate risk.

PROBLEMS

10-1 Assume that the American Electrical Corporation (AEC) is considering the establishment of a freezer manufacturing plant in Spain. AEC wants to invest a total of 10,000 Spanish pesetas in the proposed plant. The Pts10,000 will be financed with only common stock, all of which will be owned by the parent company. The plant is to be depreciated over a five-year period on a straight-line basis for tax purposes. It is expected to have a salvage value of Pts5,000 at the end of five years. Spain has 35 percent corporate income tax and no withholding taxes on dividend paid. The United States has 50 percent corporate income tax with direct credit for Spanish taxes. Spain does not impose any restriction on dividend repatriation, but it does not allow the parent company to repatriate depreciation cash flows until the plant is liquidated. These depreciation cash flows may be reinvested in Spanish government bonds to earn eight percent tax exempt interest. The cost of capital used to analyze the project is 15 percent. The current exchange rate of Pts5.00 per U. S. dollar is expected to hold during year one, but the Spanish peseta is expected to depreciate thereafter at a rate of five percent a year. Assume the following revenues and operating costs in terms of Spanish pesetas.

	Year 1	Year 2	Year 3	Year 4	Year 5
Revenues	10,000	11,000	12,000	13,000	14,000
Operating Costs	6,000	6,000	7,000	7,000	8,000

a. Determine the projected earnings after taxes for the proposed plant.
b. Determine the interest-compounded depreciation cash flows at the end of five years.
c. Determine the net present value of the plant, the profitability index, and the internal rate of return for the plant in terms of the U. S. dollar.

10-2 The Wayne Company currently exports 500 calculators per month to Jordan at a price of $60 and the variable cost per calculator is $40. In May

1983, the company was approached by the government of Jordan with a request that it establish a small manufacturing plant in Jordan. After a careful analysis the company decided to make an equity investment of $1 million, half of which would represent working capital and the other half fixed assets. The company would sell the plant to a local investor for the sum of $1 at the end of five years and the central bank of Jordan would repay the company for the working capital of $500,000. In return for an increase in tariffs against other companies, the Wayne Company is willing to sell its calculators in Jordan for $50 per unit. In addition, the company will have to buy certain raw materials from local suppliers and to use local managers. Total costs of local managers and materials would be $15 per calculator. Other materials would be purchased from the parent at $10 and the parent would receive a direct contribution to overhead after variable costs of $5 per unit sold. Under this arrangement, the company expects that it can sell 1,000 calculators per month. The fixed assets are to be depreciated on a straight-line basis over a five-year period. The company will have to pay income taxes at 50 percent on profits earned in Jordan. The United States also has 50 percent tax rate with direct credit for Jordanian taxes. The current exchange rate is ten Jordanian dinars per dollar and it is expected to stay the same for the next five years. There is no restriction on cash flow repatriation.

a. Determine the net present value of the project at ten percent.
b. The Wayne Company has been informed that, if it decides to reject the project, it would lose its entire export sales. How does this affect the decision by the Wayne Company?

10-3 Problems 10-1 and 10-2 highlight the complexities involved in foreign investment decisions. Identify these problems.

10-4 A project with an initial cost of $15,000 is expected to produce net cash flows of $8,000, $9,000, $10,000, and $11,000 for each of the next four years. The firm's cost of capital is 12 percent, but the financial manager perceives the risk of this particular project to be much higher than 12 percent. The financial manager feels that a 20 percent discount rate would be appropriate for the project.

a. Compute the net present value of the project at the firm's cost of capital.
b. Compute the risk-adjusted net present value of the project.

10-5 A project has a cost of $1,400. Its net cash flows are expected to be $900, $1,000, and $1,400 for each of the next three years. The respective certainty equivalent coefficients are estimated to be 0.75, 0.55, and 0.35. With a six percent risk-free discount rate, determine the certain net present value.

10-6 At present, the riskless rate of return is ten percent and the expected rate of return on the market portfolio is 15 percent. The expected returns for five stocks are listed below, together with their expected betas.

Stock	Expected Return	Expected Beta
A	0.22	1.5
B	0.30	1.3
C	0.12	0.8
D	0.15	0.7
E	0.14	1.1

On the basis of these expectations, which stocks are overvalued? Which stocks are undervalued?

10-7 Assume that a company wishes to sell $6 million worth of bonds and $14 million worth of common stock. The bonds have 13 percent before-tax cost of capital and the stock is expected to pay $1.4 million in dividends. The growth rate of dividends has been eight percent and is expected to continue at the same rate. Determine the weighted average cost of capital if the tax rate on income is 50 percent.

REFERENCES

10-1 Aggarwal, Raj, "Investment Performance of U. S. Based Multinational Companies: Comments and a Perspective in International Diversification of Real Assets," *Journal of International Business Studies* (Spring/Summer 1980), pp. 98-104.

10-2 Arpan, Jeffrey S., Edward B. Flowers, and David A. Ricks, "Foreign Direct Investment in the United States: The State of Knowledge of Research," *Journal of International Business Studies* (Spring/Summer 1981), pp. 137-154.

10-3 Baker, James C., and Laurence Beardsley, "Multinational Companies' Use of Risk Evaluation and Profit Measurement for Capital Budgeting Decisions," *Journal of Business Finance* (Spring 1973), pp. 38-43.

10-4 Brewer, Thomas L., "Political Risk Assessment for Direct Investment Decisions: Better Methods for Better Results," *Columbia Journal of World Business* (Spring 1981), pp. 5-11.

10-5 Calvet, A. Louis, "A Synthesis of Foreign Direct Investment Theories and Theories of the Multinational Firm," *Journal of International Business Studies* (Spring/Summer 1981), pp. 43-60.

10-6 Cao, A. D., "Social Pricing in Foreign Direct Investment Evaluation," *Business Economics* (January 1980), pp. 53-60.

10-7 Davidson, William H., "The Location of Foreign Direct Investment: Country Characteristics," *Journal of International Business Studies* (Fall 1980), pp. 9-22.

10-8 Kim, Suk H., and Edward J. Farragher, "Capital Rationing and Binary Integer Programming for Investment Projects Abroad," *Southern Business Review* (Fall 1979), pp. 6-17.

10-9 Kim, Suk H., and Henry J. Guithues, *Capital Expenditure Analysis* (Lanham, Maryland: University Press of America, 1981), Chapter 12.

10-10 Lotti, Marcello, and James V. Tomai, III, "Foreign Investors Bring Many Benefits to U. S. Companies," *Management Focus* (November/December 1981), pp. 19-21.

10-11 Oblak, David J., and Roy J. Helm, Jr., "Survey and Analysis of Capital Budgeting Methods Used by Multinationals," *Financial Management* (Winter 1980), pp. 37-41.

10-12 Shapiro, Alan C., "Capital Budgeting for the Multinational Corporation," *Financial Management* (Spring 1978), pp. 7-16.

10-13 Stanley, Mariejorie T., "Capital Structure and Cost of Capital for the Multinational Firm," *Journal of International Business Studies* (Spring/Summer 1981), pp. 103-120.

10-14 Stonehill, Arthur I., and Leonard Nathanson, "Capital Budgeting and the Multinational Corporation," *California Management Review* (Summer 1968), pp. 39-54.

10-15 Tong Hsin-Min, and C. K. Walter, "An Empirical Study of Plant Location Decisions of Foreign Manufacturing Investors in the United States," *Columbia Journal of World Business* (Spring 1980), pp. 66-74.

$£$£¢$£¢$£¢$£¢$£¢$£¢$£$£¢$£¢$£¢$£¢$£¢$£¢$£$£¢$£¢$£¢$£¢$£

ELEVEN

POLITICAL RISKS

Potential conflict between the goals of multinational companies and their host countries causes a variety of political risks for multinational companies. The primary goal of the multinational company is to maximize the wealth of its stockholders. On the other hand, most host countries desire to develop their economy through greater utilization of local factors of production, to maintain more control over key industries through less reliance on foreign capital and know-how, and to strengthen their international position through less imports and more exports.

Foreign investment projects have always been subject to political risks. However, recent events have dramatized the importance of political risk assessments for foreign investment decision-making. The developments in Iran, Afghanistan, Libya, and Poland have surely reinforced attitudes toward political risk assessment which had been prevalent among business managers.

Multinational investors should understand the forces at work when political uncertainty occurs so that they can forecast the future business climate, establish appropriate objectives, and take the precautionary measures when necessary. In this chapter, we discuss the nature of political risks, the types of political risks, political risk forecasting, and responses to political risks.

NATURE OF POLITICAL RISKS

Traditionally, conflicts have occurred over such issues as conversion of an economy to the style of a specific political system, joint ventures, control of export markets, control of key industries, contribution to balance of payments, national sovereignty, and economic development. Such conflicts are not limited to developing countries. Much more subtle but very real conflicts exist between multinational companies and developed host countries. In recent years, Canada and France have imposed various restrictions on foreign companies. Even within the United States the same kinds of political risks exist. Some congressmen have recently proposed that the United States establish a national foreign investment control commission to protect vital economic and national resources.

It is frequently difficult to separate political and economic risks. While government decisions are political by definition, the underlying forces behind the decisions may be purely economic. For example, the blockage of funds to nonresidents may be imposed because of an unexpected shortage of foreign exchange or a long-run deficiency of the foreign exchange instead of certain types of domestic political pressures. Some government decisions are partly political and partly economic. For instance, the 1980 U. S. government decision to freeze all Iranian assets in the United States had a twofold objective: the release of American hostages held in Iran and the protection of U. S. economic interest in Iran.

Countrywide political risks can be conveniently divided into three broad categories: political climate, economic climate, and foreign relations. The level of political violence may be measured by tendencies toward subversions, rebellion or political turmoil. Multinational investors should consider such factors as levels of political violence, the existence of extreme tendencies among political parties, and recurring governmental crises.

An overall assessment of economic climate is also important to protect foreign investment from political risks. Relevant economic factors include the likelihood of government intervention in the economy, levels of interest and inflation rates, persistent balance-of-payments deficits, levels of foreign debts, and worsening monetary reserves.

Finally, multinational investors should determine the extent to which host countries manifest hostilities toward other countries. Important factors here are the incidence of conflict with their neighbors, the evidence of an arms race, and the size of the defense budget.

TYPES OF POLITICAL RISKS

"Political risks arise from the actions of national governments which interfere with or prevent international business transactions, or change the terms of agreement, or cause the confiscation of wholly or partly foreign owned property."[1] This definition suggests that political risks can be divided into two broad categories: actions that restrict the freedom of a foreign company to operate in a given host environment and actions that result in the takeover of alien assets. The former category includes operational restrictions such as employment policies and locally shared ownership, loss of transfer freedom, financial, personal, or ownership rights, breaches or unilateral revisions in contracts and agreements, discrimination such as taxes and compulsory joint ventures, and damage to property or personnel from riots, revolutions and wars. The second category includes compulsory sales of business assets to local shareholders, compulsory sales of business assets to local and federal government units, and confiscation of business assets with or without compensation.

When operational restrictions are imposed, funds are usually blocked in the host country. There are a number of ways to remove blocked funds. The most obvious way is to arrange swaps between corporations. Here each corporation lends to the other in the country where its own funds are restricted. Other methods include transfer price adjustments and some other adjustments such as fees, royalties, and loan repayments. Of course, most of these methods raise some serious ethical and legal questions. Moreover, black market operations may not be available for the relatively large size and highly visible transactions such as an attempt to terminate company operations in a small developing country.

Expropriation

Although there are many types of foreign environmental risks, much of the literature on this subject matter has concentrated on the extreme cases of expropriation or nationalization. Business operations in foreign countries are subject to the power of the host countries. It is customary that alien assets are seized for a public purpose, without discrimination, and with adequate compensation. Although

[1] J. Fred Weston and Bart W. Sorge, *International Management Finance* (Homewood, Ill.: Richard D. Irwin, Inc., 1972), p. 60.

these three rules are in accordance with the traditional principle of international law, they have been often ignored by many of the less-developed countries.

According to a 1980 study by Jodice, since 1960 a total of 1535 foreign companies from 22 industrial countries have been nationalized in 511 separate actions by 76 countries. Almost 12 percent of all foreign investment made in 1967 was expropriated in the subsequent nine years.[2]

No comprehensive listing of foreign takeovers of American companies exists because such records are not compiled by an official source at the time of the event. Nevertheless, there are several surveys of foreign takeovers which shed some light on the number of expropriations and the total value of American assets expropriated. Perhaps the most comprehensive survey of this type was conducted by Hawkins, Mintz, and Provissiero.[3] Table 11-1 shows a categorization of foreign takeovers of American companies since World War II. The categories observed include the frequency by subperiod, industry of the company, region of the host country, the form of the takeover, the selectivity of the host country, and the political circumstances in the host country at the time of the takeover.

As shown in Table 11-1, foreign governments took over 170 U. S. foreign affiliates during the period 1946-1973. These 170 takeovers are grouped as follows: 12 during 1946-1960, 22 during 1961-1966, 79 during 1967-1971, and 57 during 1972-1973. It is obvious that takeovers of U. S. firms since World War II have increased consistently in annual number. For the entire sample, the most number of takeovers occurred in the extractive industry (69), followed by manufacturing (51), financial (32), and utilities (18). The proportion of takeovers in manufacturing has increased dramatically, whereas the proportion of takeovers in utilities has decreased dramatically. The breakdown by region of host country shows that Latin America accounted for the largest proportion of takeovers.

Table 11-1 also shows that well over half of the takeovers have been expropriations, while the remainder are distributed among three other forms of takeovers. The data suggest that the proportion of expropriations fell in the 1970s over the 1960s, as contract renego-

[2] David A. Jodice, "Sources of Change in Third World Regimes for Foreign Direct Investment, 1968-1976," *International Organization* (Spring 1980), pp. 177-206.

[3] Robert G. Hawkins, Norman Mintz, and Michael Provissiero, "Government Takeovers of U. S. Foreign Affiliates," *Journal of International Business Studies* (Spring 1976), pp. 3-15. For other similar surveys, see *Economic and Sovereignty over Natural Resources* (New York: United Nations, September 1974), pp. 1-3; and J. Frederick Truitt, *Expropriation of Private Foreign Investment,* International Business Series No. 3 (Bloomington, Ind.: Indiana University, 1974).

Table 11-1 Summary Distribution of the Sample Foreign Takeovers of U. S. Firms

	Entire Post-War Period					
	Number	Percent	1946-60	1961-66	1967-71	1972-73
Total–All Industries & Regions	170	100	12	22	79	57
			(percent of the total for period indicated)			
By Industry:						
Extractive	69	41	50	50	39	37
Financial	32	19	–	5	28	18
Manufacturing	51	30	–	27	27	40
Utilities	18	10	50	18	6	5
By Region:						
Latin America	93	55	83	59	44	61
Africa	51	30	17	–	51	16
Middle East	14	8	–	32	4	7
Asia	12	7	–	9	1	16
By Form of Takeover:						
Expropriation	103	60	67	95	63	42
Intervention/Requisition	25	15	–	–	14	25
Renegotiation of Contract	20	12	–	–	8	25
Forced Sale	22	13	33	5	15	8
By Selectivity of Takeover:						
Entire Industry: Mixed	21	12	33	–	8	19
Entire Industry: Foreign	68	40	42	68	38	28
Selected Firms: No Industry Spec.	25	15	8	–	21	16
Selected Firms Within Spec. Ind.	56	33	17	32	33	37
By Political-Economic Circumstances:						
Leftist Change in Government	81	48	17	41	65	33
Right or Center Nationalist	7	4	17	–	6	2
Natural Resource Sovereignty	35	20	33	41	4	32
Nature and Standardized Product	47	28	33	18	25	33

Source: Robert G. Hawkins, Normal Mintz, and Michael Provissiero, "Government Takeovers of U. S. Foreign Affiliates," *Journal of International Business Studies* (Spring 1976), p. 9.

tiations and intervention have become more attractive. The breakdown by selectivity of takeover indicates that the largest number of takeovers has occurred when the entire industry was nationalized but the entire industry included only foreign companies. Finally, the categorization of the takeovers by political-economic motive shows that left-wing changes in government accounted for almost half of the takeovers in the sample.

The numbers and values of takeovers may well continue to increase for years to come, because "the modern wave of nationalism and the heightened competition among multinational companies all combine to make expropriation both feasible and politically desirable for host governments."[4] Furthermore, "these same factors also make the trend competitively and legally beyond the effective resistance of the multinational companies themselves."[5]

FORECASTING POLITICAL RISK

Once the nature of political risks and their implications have been examined, the focus should shift to the manager's task of forecasting these risks in foreign countries where his company has business interest. As multinational companies have become more experienced and more diversified, they are beginning to maintain political forecasting staffs on the similar levels as economic forecasting staffs.

Political risk assessment enables multinational companies to classify foreign countries into at least the following three categories.[6] (1) It identifies those countries which have the potential to become the Irans and Cubas of tomorrow. (2) It isolates those countries whose political risks have decreased or which have been unnecessarily discounted for political risks. (3) It helps multinational companies identify those countries whose political risks are significant but not bad enough to automatically rule them ineligible for foreign investment.

The task of political risk forecasting involves four basic steps. (1) The multinational company should investigate the present administration's attitudes and policies toward foreign investment. (2) It

[4] Hawkins, Mintz, and Provissiero, "Government Takeovers of U. S. Foreign Affiliates," p. 15.

[5] *Ibid.*

[6] Joseph V. Micallef, "Political Risk Assessment," *Columbia Journal of World Business* (Summer 1981), p. 48.

should assess the country's political stability. (3) It should integrate the political risk assessment into the company's strategic planning. (4) It should develop strategies to reduce the company's exposure to political risks.

Government's Attitudes Toward Foreign Investment

The first step in forecasting political interference is to understand the attitudes and policies of the present administration to private foreign companies. The key here is to identify favorable or unfavorable trends affecting the climate in which the subsidiary will operate. There has always been evidence of a change in the government's attitudes toward foreign direct investment prior to the overt act of confiscating alien assets. Other important factors to be considered include the dependency of the host country on the foreign investor's country for economic aid or political support, the types of pressures exerted on the chief governmental policy-makers, the existence of leftist groups at the highest levels of government, and the government's economic development plan in relation to foreign investment.

Political Stability

The second step in evaluating the vulnerability of a company to political risks is to understand the type of government currently in power, its patterns of political behavior, and its norms for stability. All these factors can be used to assess political stability of the host country. Political stability is in fact one of the principal preconditions for foreign direct investment by large multinational companies. The background information on the political environment of the host country goes far beyond an understanding of the administration's attitudes and policies toward foreign investment. The multinational company should understand the path along which all policies toward foreign investment have been made in the past.

A Conference Board study of investors from the 12 major capital exporting countries found that many investors had eliminated countries and even entire geographical regions from their investment considerations for political reasons. Political instability was the most frequently cited political obstacle.[7]

[7] The 12 major capital exporting countries are Belgium, Canada, Denmark, France, Germany, the Netherlands, Sweden, Switzerland, United Kingdon, and United States. For details of this study, see National Industrial Conference Board, *Obstacles and Incentives to Private Foreign Investment* (New York, 1969).

Because political factors are subject to constant changes, it is also important to institute an intelligence system to monitor and evaluate political developments. The intelligence system should be concerned with two things: (1) it should develop reliable in-house expertise about the host country and (2) it should allow the company to collect and distribute necessary information to all relevant parties.

Political Risk and Strategic Planning

The third step in the process of political risk assessment is to integrate the assessment into the company's strategic planning. There are two ways to integrate political risk factors into strategic planning. The multinational company may establish cutoff points for foreign projects under different conditions of political risk. In addition, the multinational company may design capital budgeting plans to reflect changes in the level of political risk.

The existence of various political risks requires multinational companies to introduce modifications into investment analysis. Because political risks are extremely high in some countries, multinational companies may have to use a high risk premium in the cost of capital to compensate for these risks. This extra risk premium may eliminate consideration of new projects in these countries.

If foreign projects are divisible, different capital budget plans can be established to reflect different degrees of political risk. For example, oil companies may allocate their funds for oil exploration among countries with different levels of political risk. In addition, multinational companies can diversify their investment into projects with varying degrees of risk. For example, oil companies may invest a portion of their funds on safe projects such as pipeline projects and the remaining portion of the funds on risky projects such as oil exploration projects.

Strategies for Decreasing Political Risks

The fourth step is to assess the relative strengths and security of the subsidiary itself. The multinational company must appraise the environment in which it operates as well as its bargaining power. This appraisal enables the multinational company to learn how its foreign affiliate can become a good citizen of the host country and to determine whether the host government will continue to need its presence.

To become a good citizen of the host country, the multinational company may use the greatest possible amount of locally supplied raw materials, hire local people for managerial positions, and make the equity of the subsidiary available to the host country's investors. The subsidiary's ability to retain an essential status in the host country depends on its competitive edge, the degree to which its product is valued by the host government, and the cost to the economy of local production of the product as opposed to importation.

RESPONSES TO POLITICAL RISKS

Political risk forecasting is critical to the multinational company in reaching a decision on a particular project. The multinational company is not helpless in the case of political risk. One broad group of protections against political risks are government insurance policies and guarantee programs. Chapters 6 and 7 described these programs in some detail.

Defensive Measures Before Investment

There are three types of defensive measures before investment: concession agreements, planned divestment, and adaptation to host-country goals.

Concession Agreements. Many host countries have recently increased their surveillance of foreign operations within their borders. To minimize subsequent political risks, it is desirable for the multinational company to negotiate concession agreements with host-country governments. The concession agreement spells out a contractual obligation on the part of both foreign investor and host country. Careful negotiations may result in contracts that address such critical issues as provision for arbitration of disputes, funds remittances, transfer prices, local equity participation, method of taxation, price controls, the right to exports, limitations on nationality of personnel, and so on.

Planned Divestment. Planned divestment has been frequently suggested as one of the most important preinvestment strategies in order to avoid subsequent expropriation. It provides for the sale of majority ownership in foreign affiliates to local nationals during a previously agreed-upon period of time. Planned divestment is often a necessary condition for entry into foreign markets or has been imposed on already existing companies.

The major argument for planned divestment is that host countries benefit from foreign direct investment in the early years, but successful foreign firms replace potential local firms in the later years. These benefits include new capital, entrepreneurship, new management techniques, and new technology. Foreign investment makes it possible for local firms to develop their own capital, entrepreneurship, management, and technology. If successful foreign companies continue to dominate all the profitable growth areas, host countries tend to ask foreign companies the question of what have you done for us.

Adaptation to Host-Country Goals. The concession agreement specifies specific rights and responsibilities of both the foreign company and host country, but it is often revised to adapt to changing host-country priorities. When the foreign company sticks to the legal interpretation of its concession agreement, the host-country government uses pressures in areas not covered by the agreement. If these pressures do not work, the host-country government reinterprets the agreement as necessary to obtain desired changes from the foreign company. Thus, it is advisable for multinational companies to voluntarily adapt to changing host-country priorities whenever possible.

Defensive Measures After Investment

Once the decision to invest is made and preinvestment defensive measures have been taken, several operating strategies can be used to cope with political risks. These are grouped for convenience into two types: strategies necessary to be a good citizen of the host country and strategies which make expropriatory actions difficult or unfeasible.

Many foreign affiliates often attempt to harmonize their policies with their host-country goals and priorities. They may hire an increasing number of local persons for positions initially held by representatives of the parent company management. They may share ownership with host-country private or public companies. They may develop and use local sources of supply for their raw materials and component requirements. They may try to export their products in order to bolster host-country reserves of foreign exchange.

There are many operational policies and organizational approaches which make expropriatory actions extremely difficult or unfeasible. A number of these arrangements, collectively known as working capital management, have been described in Chapter 9.

There are several examples of other techniques that can be used to make expropriatory actions very difficult. Foreign firms may maintain technological superiority over local companies and other competing foreign firms. The challenge here is to introduce technological improvements on a continuing basis into the host country. They may organize international operations in such a way that individual subsidiaries are integrated into a worldwide production and logistical system. Under such an integration, a subsidiary would not be able to operate or compete successfully, as is done in the petroleum industry. Control of key patents and processes, joint-venture arrangements, capitalization with a thin equity base and a large local debt proportion, and control of key export markets for a subsidiary's products are examples of policy actions in this respect.

Remedies After Expropriation

The resolution of the controversy prior to confiscation is far more attractive than recovery of value for assets lost through expropriation. However, certain remedies or counter-actions may be adopted after an expropriation has taken place. William R. Hoskins has suggested four action phases that typically follow an expropriation: rational negotiation, negotiation flavored with power tactics, exploration of legal remedies, and surrender by management and decision to seek only salvage value.[8]

Rational Negotiation. Because most expropriations occur with some warnings for the involved enterprise, there are opportunities to dissuade the host-country government from its intended takeover. During the period of rational negotiation, the foreign company may offer some additional concessions to the host country. It may promise to invest more capital for expansion, hire national managers, accept the local company as a minority partner, contribute to political campaigns, and change expatriate management.

Power Tactics. If rational negotiations do not work, the foreign company may rely on power tactics. They include an offer to release the government from existing concessions or support government programs, solicitation of political support from opposition parties or from friendly neighboring countries, and the intercession of the parent country's government on an informal basis. Such power tactics

[8] William R. Hoskins, "How to Counter Expropriation," *Harvard Business Review* (September-October 1970), pp. 102-112.

should be used carefully because their misuse may well bring about stronger negative reaction from the host country rather than the desired result.

Legal Remedies. The traditional view of the capital exporting countries assumes that expropriation is valid if the host country provides the foreign company with full, prompt, and effective compensation. But this traditional view of expropriation has been mostly ignored by the less-developed countries. At some point following Phases 1 and 2, the foreign company may begin to explore legal redress of its grievances. It will first exhaust all local legal remedies. It will then seek legal redress in the parent country's court system. The government of the parent company often uses the promise of aid or the threat to withhold aid as means of settling the dispute. The foreign company may have the government of its parent company present a claim through the International Court of Justice.

In addition to these legal remedies, multinational companies can take their grievances to the International Center for Settlement of Investment Disputes, which was established under the auspices of the World Bank in 1966. Most industrial countries, most African countries, and many Asian countries have signed the Convention of Settlement of Investment Disputes. Although the International Center was established to provide a conciliation and arbitration mechanism to settle investment disputes, examples of settlement by the International Center are extremely rare. Because such settlements require a relinquishment of sovereignty by host-country governments over activities within their own borders, there is a considerable doubt about the extensive use of the organization in the future.

Management Surrender. If Phases 1, 2, and 3 all fail to produce a satisfactory solution, management of the expropriated company concedes defeat and seeks to salvage what it can from the situation. Hoskins suggests three possible avenues for a continued economic relationship without excessive concern for legal ownership. (1) The foreign company handles exports under a commission arrangement. (2) It signs a management contract to provide the host country with technical and managerial skills. (3) It sells raw materials and components to the host country.

SUMMARY

Losses from political risks may arise because of governmental action that interferes with the completion of contractual obligations between the foreign company and its host government. Political risks cannot be predicted in the same way as credit losses and thus cannot precisely be offset in measurable ways. Thus, multinational companies must understand the types of political risks which they can expect to encounter, assess the likelihood of encountering these risks, and take various protective measures to minimize the risks.

Political risks range from moderate actions such as exchange controls to extreme actions such as expropriation. Although there are many types of foreign environmental risks, much of the literature on this subject has concentrated on the extreme cases of nationalization. Business operations in foreign countries are subject to the power of the host countries. Foreign assets can be seized for a public purpose, without discrimination, and with adequate compensation. Although these three rules are in accordance with a traditional principle of international law, they have been frequently ignored by many of the less-developed countries.

Once the nature of political risks and their implications have been assessed, multinational companies should focus on forecasting these risks in foreign countries where they have business interests. The forecasting of political risks involves four basic steps. (1) The multinational company should examine the present administration's attitudes and policies toward foreign investment. (2) It should assess the country's political stability. (3) It should integrate the political risk assessment into the company's strategic planning. (4) It should develop strategies to reduce the company's exposure to political risks.

The multinational company is not helpless in the event of political risks because there are a variety of protections against them. These are grouped for convenience into three categories: defensive measures before investment, defensive protective measures after investment, and remedies after expropriation. Protective measures prior to investment include concession agreements, planned divestment, and voluntary adaptation to host-country goals. Defensive measures after investment involve various ways and actions for the foreign company to be a good citizen of the host country. After expropriation has occurred, the foreign company may use four-phase actions suggested by Hoskins: rational negotiation, negotiation flavored with power tactics, exploration of legal remedies, and surrender by management and decision to seek only salvage value.

REFERENCES

11-1 Amerasinghe, C. F., "Model Clauses for Settlement of Foreign Investment Disputes," *The Arbitration Journal* (December 1973), pp. 232-257.

11-2 Bradley, David, "Managing Against Expropriation," *Harvard Business Review* (August 1977), pp. 75-83.

11-3 Brewer, Thomas L., "Political Risk Assessment of Direct Foreign Investment Decisions: Better Methods for Better Results," *Columbia Journal of World Business* (Spring 1981), pp. 5-11.

11-4 Davis, Robert R., "Alternative Techniques for Country Risk Evaluation," *Business Economics* (May 1981), pp. 34-41.

11-5 Davidson, William H., "The Location of Foreign Direct Investment: Country Characteristics," *Journal of International Business Studies* (Fall 1980), pp. 9-12.

11-6 Green, Robert T., and Christopher M. Korth, "Political Instability and the Foreign Investor," *California Management Review* (Fall 1974), pp. 23-31.

11-7 Hawkins, Robert G., Norman Mintz, and Michael Provissiero, "Government Takeovers of U. S. Foreign Affiliates," *Journal of International Business Studies* (Spring 1976), pp. 3-15.

11-8 Hoskins, William R., "How to Counter Expropriation," *Harvard Business Review* (September-October 1970), pp. 102-112.

11-9 Jodice, David A., "Sources of Change in Third World Regimes for Foreign Direct Investment, 1968-1976," *International Organization* (Spring 1980), pp. 177-206.

11-10 Knudsen, Harold, "Explaining the National Propensity to Expropriate: An Ecological Approach," *Journal of International Business Studies* (Spring 1974), pp. 51-71.

11-11 Micallef, Joseph V., "Political Risk Assessment," *Columbia Journal of World Business* (Spring 1981), pp. 47-52.

11-12 Rummel, R. J., and David A. Heenan, "How Multinations Analyze Political Risk," *Harvard Business Review* (January-February 1978), pp. 67-76.

11-13 Sachdev, Jagdish C., "Disinvestment: A Corporate Failure or a Strategic Success?" *International Studies of Management and Organization* (Spring-Summer 1976), pp. 23-35.

11-14 Wright, Richard W., and Colin S. Russel, "Joint Ventures in Developing Countries: Realities and Responses," *Columbia Journal of World Business* (Summer 1975), pp. 74-80.

TWELVE

FOREIGN EXCHANGE RISK

Foreign exchange risk is the risk of loss due to changes in the international exchange value of national currencies. Assume that a Japanese exporter sells TV sets on a three-month credit to U. S. citizens and invoices them in dollars. If the dollar declines in value relative to the Japanese yen three months later, the exporter suffers a loss in foreign exchange that may well wipe out the trade gain. If the dollar increases in value relative to the Japanese yen, it works to the advantage of the exporter.

So long as we do not have a single world currency, some degree of exchange risk exists in any system. Currency value fluctuations had been quite frequently pronounced in the past. During the 20-year period from 1948 to 1968, 96 countries devalued their currencies three or more times. Sixty-two countries devalued their currencies by more than 40 percent and 24 countries devalued their currencies by more than 75 percent.[1]

Two recent developments have made this problem more complicated. First, most industrial countries have permitted their currencies to float since 1973. Daily currency fluctuations have become a way of life since then. Second, the Financial Accounting Standards Board

[1] Margaret G. DeVries, "The Magnitude of Exchange Devaluation," *Finance and Development*, No. 2 (1968), pp. 10-11.

(FASB) issued its Statement No. 8 in Autumn 1975 about foreign exchange gains and losses. This statement required companies to report their exchange gains and losses in a uniform way. It eliminated the reserves that companies previously used to smooth fluctuations in earnings and losses due to exchange rate changes. Because SFAS No. 8 caused most investors to be confused about the implications of translation gains and losses, the FASB issued its Statement No. 52 in 1981 to replace SFAS No. 8.

This chapter has four major sections. The first section describes three major exchange exposures: translation, transaction, and economic. The second section discusses a number of translation methods, placing major emphasis on SFAS Nos. 8 and 52. The third section examines several economic indicators which are widely used to forecast currency devaluation. The fourth section covers some techniques designed to minimize foreign exchange risk.

FOREIGN EXCHANGE EXPOSURES

Every company faces an exposure to foreign exchange risk as soon as it chooses to maintain a physical presence in a foreign country. Foreign exchange exposure refers to the possibility that a firm will gain or lose due to changes in exchange rates. By the same token, the firm faces an exposure to exchange risk when it chooses to finance its operations in foreign currencies. Both exchange risks are ordinarily analyzed in the context of the investing and financial decisions. An important task of the international financial manager is to compare potential losses with the cost of avoiding these losses. The three basic types of exchange exposure are translation exposure, transaction exposure, and economic exposure.

Translation Exposure

Companies may wish to translate financial-statement items from a foreign currency into their home currency in order to prepare consolidated financial statements or to compare financial results. It is important to note that the term "conversion" should not be used in this case because we are not considering the actual conversion of one currency into another. Here values of financial-statement items are simply restated.

Translation exposure, sometimes called accounting exposure, measures the effect of an exchange rate change on published financial statements of a firm. The difference between exposed assets and exposed liabilities is frequently called net exposure by accountants. Under U. S. generally accepted accounting principles, the net-monetary-asset position of a subsidiary is used to measure its parent's foreign-exchange exposure. The net-monetary-asset position is monetary assets such as cash and accounts receivable minus monetary liabilities such as accounts payable and long-term debt.

Example 12-1 A U. S. parent company has a single-wholly-owned subsidiary in France. This subsidiary has monetary assets of 100 million francs and monetary liabilities of 50 million francs. The exchange rate declines from FF4 per dollar to FF5 per dollar.

The potential-foreign-exchange loss on the company's exposed net monetary assets of 50 million francs would be $2.5 million:

Monetary assets	FF100 million	
Monetary liabilities	50 million	
Net exposure	FF 50 million	
Predevaluation rate (FF4 = $1)	FF50 million =	$12.5 million
Postdevaluation rate (FF5 = $1)	FF50 million =	$10.0 million
Potential exchange loss		$ 2.5 million

It is important to note that these translation gains and losses do not involve actual cash flows. They are purely of a paper nature. Some companies are concerned about this risk because of "the desire to have a steady earnings per share, the need to link corporate incentive and profit-sharing systems with reported profits, and a fear that such swings will affect stock price, as well as the ability of the firm to raise capital and the cost of doing so."[2]

Transaction Exposure

Gains or losses may result from the settlement of transactions whose payment terms are stated in a foreign currency. Transaction exposure measures the effect of an exchange-rate change on outstanding obligations which existed before exchange rates changed but were settled after the exchange-rate change. Transactions subject

[2] S. L. Srinivasulu, "Strategic Response to Foreign Exchange Risks," *Columbia Journal of World Business* (Spring 1981), p. 13.

to transaction exposure include credit purchases or sales of goods or services whose prices are stated in foreign currencies, borrowed or loaned funds denominated in foreign currencies, and a party to an open (*i.e.*, uncompleted) forward-exchange contract.

Example 12-2 Assume that an American firm purchased machinery from a British firm through its U. K. subsidiary for 10,000 pounds with terms of 180 days. Let us further assume that the spot rate for pounds is $1.70 and the 180-day forward rate for pounds is $1.80. The payment must be made in pounds.

There are two alternative ways of payment available to the American firm. (1) It could buy pounds in the spot market 180 days from today and use these pounds to pay the credit. If the spot rate for pounds rises to $2.00 during this time, the American firm should spend $20,000 to buy the sum of 10,000 pounds. But this alternative is subject to foreign exchange risk because the spot rate 180 days from today is uncertain. (2) It can buy 10,000 pounds in the forward market for $18,000 and use these pounds to pay the credit 180 days from today. The second alternative would allow the American firm to avoid the risk of $2,000 ($20,000 – $18,000). But if the spot rate declines to $1.60 180 days from today, the American firm would incur a transaction loss of $2,000 ($16,000 – $18,000) under the forward contract.

Economic Exposure

Economic exposure measures the impact of an actual conversion on the net present value of expected future cash flows. Future effects of exchange rate changes occur under the general category of economic risk. A multinational company may have established its subsidiary in a country with price stability, readily available funds, favorable balance of payments, and low rates of taxation. These positive features may disappear over time as the economic situation of the country deteriorates. Eventually the local currency will devalue or depreciate. The subsidiary is likely to immediately face operational problems if it has to pay its imports in hard currencies or if it has borrowed from abroad. Exchange-rate changes may also affect such economic factors as inflationary forces, price controls, the supply of loanable funds, and local labor availability.

Example 12-3 For the coming year, a French subsidiary of an American firm is expected to earn 35 million francs after taxes and its depreciation charge is estimated at 5 million francs. The exchange rate is expected to decrease from FF4 = $1 at present to FF5 = $1 for the next year.

The difference between first-year cash flows with and without devaluation is computed as follows:

Profit after taxes	FF35 million	
Depreciation	5 million	
Cash flows from operation	FF40 million	
Predevaluation rate (FF4 = $1)	FF40 million =	$10 million
Postdevaluation rate (FF5 = $1)	FF40 million =	$ 8 million
Potential exchange loss		$ 2 million

The subsidiary's economic loss is a decline in French-franc cash flows equal to $2 million over the next 12 months. It is important to recognize that the translation loss is a one-time loss while the economic loss is an open-end event. If the anticipated business activity were to stay the same for the next five years, the decrease in annual cash flows of $2 million would continue for five years.

Transaction Exposure Versus Economic Exposure

The management of foreign-exchange risk based on translation exposure is basically static and historically oriented. By definition, translation exposure does not look to the future impact of an exchange rate that has occurred or may occur in the future. In addition, it does not involve actual cash flows. In contrast, both transaction and economic exposures look to the future impact of an exchange rate change which has occurred or may occur in the future. They also involve actual or potential cash-flow changes.

Transaction risk and economic risk are the same in kind, but they differ in degree. For example, economic risk is essentially subjective because it depends on estimated future cash flows for an arbitrary time horizon. Transaction risk, on the other hand, is essentially objective because it depends on outstanding obligations which existed before changes in exchange rates but were settled after the changes in exchange rates. Table 12-1 illustrates major differences between these two exposures.

Table 12-1 Comparison of Characteristics of Transaction Exposure and Economic Exposure

Transaction Exposure	Economic Exposure
1. Contract-specific	General; relates to the entire investment
2. Cash flow losses due to an exchange rate change are easy to compute. Simple financial accounting techniques can be used to compute losses due to transaction exposure.	Opportunity losses caused by an exchange rate change are difficult to compute. A good variance accounting is needed to isolate the effect of exchange rate change on sales volume, costs, and profit margins.
3. Firms generally have some policies to cope with transaction exposure.	Firms generally do not have policies to cope with economic exposure.
4. Avoidance sometimes requires third-party cooperation (e. g., changing invoice currency)	Avoidance requires good strategic planning (e.g., choice of markets, products, etc.)
5. The duration of exposure is the same as the time period of the contract.	The duration of exposure is the time required for the restructuring of operations through such means as changing products, markets, sources and technology.
6. Relates to nominal contracts whose value is fixed in foreign currency terms.	Relates to cash flow effects through changes in cost, price and volume relationships.
7. The only source of uncertainty is the future exchange rate.	The many sources of uncertainty include the future exchange rate, and its effect on sales, price and costs.
8. *A summary definition:* Transaction exposure is an uncertain domestic currency value of a cash flow which is *known and fixed* in foreign currency terms; e.g., a foreign currency receivable.	Economic exposure is an uncertain domestic currency value of a cash flow whose value is *uncertain* even in foreign currency terms; e.g., cash flows from a foreign subsidiary.

Source: S. L. Srinivasulu, "Strategic Response to Foreign Exchange Risks," *Columbia Journal of World Business* (Spring 1981), p. 15.

TRANSLATION OF FOREIGN CURRENCY FINANCIAL STATEMENTS

Financial statements are intended to present information about the performance, financial position, and cash flows of a company. To meet this purpose, the financial statements of separate entities within a business enterprise are consolidated and presented as though they were the financial statements of a single economic entity. Financial statements are frequently restated or translated from one currency into another to assist the users of the financial statements such as investors and creditors.

In this section, two terms are used extensively: parent currency and functional currency. The parent currency, sometimes called the reporting currency, is the currency of the country where the parent company is located. For example, the parent currency of U. S.-based multinational companies is the dollar. The functional currency, sometimes called the foreign currency or the local currency, is the currency of the country where the foreign operation of a multinational company is located. The functional currency of an entity as defined in SFAS No. 52 (paragraph 39) is "the currency of the primary economic environment in which the entity operates; normally, that is the currency of the environment in which an entity primarily generates and expends cash."

The four translation methods most widely used by multinational companies are temporal, current rate, current/noncurrent, and monetary/nonmonetary.

Temporal Method (SFAS No. 8) and Current Rate Method (SFAS No. 52)

In October 1975, the FASB issued Statement of Financial Accounting Standards No. 8 (SFAS No. 8), *Accounting for the Translation of Foreign Currency Transactions and Foreign Currency Financial Statements*. SFAS No. 8 formally required U. S. companies to translate their foreign-currency financial statements into dollars by applying the exchange rate in effect at the time to which the measurement basis of each account relates. This statement also required companies to show all foreign-exchange gains or losses in their quarterly and annual reports, regardless of whether these gains or losses were realized or unrealized.

SFAS No. 8 was a product of considerable effort by the FASB to resolve the currency translation issue, which included an extensive exposure draft and discussion memorandum. However, from its inception in the Fall 1975, SFAS No. 8 was the subject of extensive debate. Most of the criticism of SFAS No. 8 centered around the recognition of foreign exchange gains or losses. Companies said that SFAS No. 8 grossly distorted their earnings because of the sharp fluctuations in foreign exchange rates. Early in 1976, the FASB acknowledged the criticism but concluded that it did not need to revise the statement. In February 1979, a 22-member task force was established to advise the FASB on its recommendation of SFAS No. 8. A substantial portion of the FASB's time and effort was devoted to this project after February 1979. On August 18, 1980, the FASB issued an Exposure Draft to replace SFAS No. 8. The FASB held public hearings on its proposed draft on December 17, 18, 19, and 22, 1980; issued a revised Exposure Draft on June 30, 1981; and issued SFAS No. 52, *Foreign Currency Translation*, on December 7, 1981. SFAS No. 52 supersedes SFAS No. 8 which superseded SFAS No. 1.

SFAS No. 52 requires use of the current exchange rate in translating foreign-currency financial statements into U. S. dollars. Such translation adjustments are placed directly in stockholders' equity rather than income. Thus, SFAS No. 52 is expected to greatly reduce fluctuations in many companies' reported earnings caused by gyrations in foreign exchange rates under SFAS No. 8.

Differences Between SFAS No. 8 and SFAS No. 52. According to SFAS No. 8, the objectives of translation were as follows:

> For the purpose of preparing an enterprise's financial statements, the objective of translation is to measure and express (a) in dollars and (b) in conformity with U. S. generally accepted accounting principles the assets, liabilities, revenue, or expenses that are measured or denominated in foreign currency.

The new objectives of translation, as stated in SFAS No. 52 are to:

> a. Provide information that is generally compatible with the expected economic effects of a rate change on an enterprise's cash flows and equity.
> b. Reflect in consolidated statements the financial results and relationships of the individual consolidated entities as measured in their functional currencies in conformity with U. S. generally accepted accounting principles.

The change in the objectives of translation is significant. The underlying assumption of SFAS No. 8 was that consolidated financial statements should reflect the transactions of the consolidated group as though all operations, including foreign operations, were extensions of the parent's domestic operations. This premise failed to recognize the fact that in many cases the operations of foreign subsidiaries exist in other environments and involve foreign currency cash flows in those other environments. Thus, the accounting results after translation did not portray the foreign currency cash flows.

SFAS No. 52 is intended to portray the foreign currency cash flows. Use of the functional currency approach and the current rate method enables companies to maintain compatibility in terms of income and cash flows before and after translation. Financial summary indicators such as profit margin, gross profit, and debt-to-equity ratio are almost the same after translation into the reporting currency as they are in the functional currency. In addition, the volatility of the company's reported earnings should be reduced under SFAS No. 52 because companies' foreign exchange gains or losses will be reported in a separate component of equity, not income. In order to achieve such new objectives of translation, some provisions of SFAS No. 8 were changed. Table 12-2 compares the major provisions of SFAS No. 8 with the same provisions of SFAS No. 52.

Translation of Foreign-Currency Financial Statements. SFAS No. 8 had formally required U. S. firms to use the temporal method since 1976 until the FASB replaced it with SFAS No. 52 issued in December 1981. According to this method, balance-sheet items carried at current or future prices should be translated at the current exchange rate while balance-sheet items carried at historical prices should be translated at the applicable historical rate. Table 12-3 shows currency-translation treatment recommended by SFAS No. 8 for various assets and liabilities. Under the temporal method, sales revenue and operating expenses are translated at the average exchange rate while cost of goods sold and depreciation are translated at the applicable historical rate. Exchange gains or losses from the translation of the balance sheet should be included in the income statement.

Under SFAS No. 52, the current exchange rate method is used to translate foreign-currency balance sheets from their functional currency into the reporting currency. The current exchange rate method is the easiest to apply because under this method, all assets and liabilities are translated at the current exchange rate (*i.e.*, the rates in effect at the balance sheet date). Only owners' equity is translated at the historical exchange rate. Unlike the controversial SFAS No. 8, SFAS No. 52 does not require companies to include translation adjustments in net income. Instead, these translation adjustments will be reported separately and accumulated in a separate component of equity until the sale or the complete or substantially complete liquidation of the foreign net investment.

Under SFAS No. 52, all income-statement elements are translated in a manner that produces approximately the same result as using the exchange rate in effect on the dates on which these elements are recognized. However, SFAS No. 52 (paragraph 12) provides that "because translation at the exchange rates at the dates the numerous revenues, expenses, gains, and losses are recognized is generally impractical, an appropriately weighted average exchange rate for the period may be used to translate those elements."

Table 12-2 Comparison of the Major Provisions of SFAS No. 8 and SFAS No. 52

Provision	SFAS No. 8	SFAS No. 52
Translation method	Temporal method	Current rate method
Functional currency	Not used	That is the currency of the primary economic environment in which an entity generates and expends cash
Foreign-exchange gains or losses from balance-sheet translations	Included in current income	Placed directly in stockholders' equity on the balance sheet
Translation of operations in highly inflationary economies	Normally not serious under the temporal method	The financial statements of a foreign entity are remeasured as if the functional currency were the reporting currency
Gains or losses from foreign currency transactions	Included in current income	Included in current income
Realization of the separate component of equity	Not applicable	Upon sale or upon complete or substantial liquidation of the investment
Gains or losses from transactions intended to hedge a net investment	Included in current income	Placed directly in stockholders' equity on the balance sheet
Gains or losses from intercompany transactions	Included in current income	Accumulated as a separate component of stockholders' equity for all intercompany transactions that are of a long-term nature. Included in current income for other intercompany transactions

Source: Peat, Marwick, Mitchell and Company, *Statement of Financial Accounting Standards No. 52: Foreign Currency Translation* (December, 1981), p. 4.

Table 12-3 Rates Used to Translate Accounts Under FASB No. 8

Assets	Translation Rate: Current	Translation Rate: Historical
Cash on hand and demand and time deposits	X	
Marketable equity securities:		
Carried at cost		X
Carried at current market price	X	
Accounts and notes receivable and related unearned discount	X	
Allowance for doubtful accounts and notes receivable	X	
Inventories:		
Carried at cost		X
Carried at current replacement price or current selling price	X	
Carried at net realizable value	X	
Carried at contract price (produced under fixed price contracts)	X	
Prepaid insurance, advertising, and rent		X
Refundable deposits	X	
Advances to unconsolidated subsidiaries	X	
Property, plant, and equipment		X
Accumulated depreciation of property, plant, and equipment		X
Cash surrender value of life insurance	X	
Patents, trademarks, licenses, and formulas		X
Goodwill		X
Other intangible assets		X
Liabilities		
Accounts and notes payable and overdrafts	X	
Accrued expenses payable	X	
Accrued losses on firm purchase commitments	X	
Refundable deposits	X	
Deferred income		X
Bonds payable or other long-term debt	X	
Unamortized premium or discount on bonds or notes payable	X	
Convertible bonds payable	X	
Accrued pension obligations	X	
Obligations under warranties	X	

Source: Financial Accounting Standards Board, *Accounting for the Translation of Foreign Currency Transactions and Foreign Currency Financial Statements*, Statement of Financial Accounting Standards No. 8 (Stamford, Conn.: FASB, 1975), p. 20.

Example 12-4 The Canadian subsidiary of a U. S. multinational corporation with a Canadian dollar functional currency started business and acquired fixed assets on January 1, 1983 when the Canadian \$/U. S. \$ exchange rate was 0.85. Table

12-4 applies the temporal method and the current exchange rate method to hypothetical financial statements which are affected by 11.8 percent devaluation and revaluation. For devaluation, the exchange rate on December 31, 1983 was 0.75 and the weighted average rate for the period was 0.80. For revaluation, the exchange rate on December 31, 1983 was 0.95 and the weighted average for the period was 0.90.

Table 12-4 shows that fluctuations in reported earnings in this example are reduced significantly under SFAS No. 52 because of both the use of a single rate in translating balance-sheet items and the reporting of translation adjustments in equity. Moreover, net income of the U. S. parent firm under the new standard is the same as what is expected based on the level of earnings in Canadian dollars.

Under SFAS No. 52, a translation loss of $11 is the expected economic effect of the Canadian dollar whose value declined against the U. S. dollar. This translation loss is reported in the balance sheet as "equity adjustments from translation." On the other hand, SFAS No. 8 requires the U. S. parent to report a translation gain of $70 in the income statement.

In contrast, a translation gain of $11 under the new standard is the expected economic effect of the Canadian dollar whose value increased against the U. S. dollar. This gain is placed directly in stockholders' equity on the balance sheet. On the other hand, the old standard requires the U. S. parent to recognize a translation loss of $58 in the income statement.

Under SFAS No. 52, key Canadian-dollar ratios, such as net income to revenue, gross profit, and long-term debt to equity, are maintained after translation from the Canadian dollar to the U. S. dollar. However, these ratios in the Canadian dollar are significantly different from those in the U. S. dollar under SFAS No. 8.

There were numerous reports that SFAS No. 8 had caused many companies' reported earnings to widely fluctuate by changes in foreign exchange rates. For example, "In 1978 Exxon suffered foreign exchange losses of $318 million, which were larger than the profits of Chase Manhattan Corporation, U. S. Steel, or Goodyear Tire and Rubber Company."[3] "The experience of the Japanese electronics producer, Sony, which follows United States accounting rules because its shares are traded on the New York Stock Exchange, is illustrative. In 1979, Sony's consolidated second-quarter earnings were reduced by a $49.3 million foreign exchange loss; whereas, in 1978,

[3] Alan C. Shapiro, *Multinational Financial Management* (Boston: Allyn and Bacon, Inc., 1982), p. 115.

		After Devaluation of Can. $				After Revaluation of Can. $			
		SFAS No. 8		SFAS No. 52		SFAS No. 8		SFAS No. 52	
	Canadian Dollars	Rates Used	U. S. Dollars	Rates Used	U. S. Dollars	Rates Used	U. S. Dollars	Rates Used	U. S. Dollars
Balance Sheet									
Cash and receivables	100	.75	75	.75	75	.95	95	.95	95
Inventory	300	.81*	243	.75	225	.91*	273	.95	285
Fixed assets, net	600	.85	510	.75	450	.85	510	.95	570
Total	1000		828		750		878		950
Current liabilities	180	.75	135	.75	135	.95	171	.95	171
Long-term debt	700	.75	525	.75	525	.95	665	.95	665
Common stock	100	.85	85	.85	85	.85	85	.85	85
Retained earnings	20		83		16		(43)		18
Equity adjustments from translation	–		–		(11)		–		11
Total	1000		828		750		878		950
Income Statement									
Revenue	130	.80	104	.80	104	.90	117	.90	117
Cost of goods sold	(60)	.83*	(50)	.80	(48)	.93*	(56)	.90	(54)
Depreciation	(20)	.85*	(17)	.80	(16)	.95*	(19)	.90	(18)
Other expenses	(10)	.80	(8)	.80	(8)	.90	(9)	.90	(9)
Exchange Gain (loss)	–		70		–		(58)		–
Income before tax	40		99		32		(25)		36
Income tax	(20)	.80	(16)	.80	(16)	.90	(18)	.90	(18)
Net income	20		83		16		(43)		18
Ratios									
Net income to revenue	0.15		0.80		0.15		negative		0.15
Gross profit	0.54		0.52		0.54		0.52		0.54
Long-term debt to equity	5.83		3.13		5.83		15.83		5.83

*Historical rates for inventory, cost of goods sold, and depreciation of fixed assets.

the second-quarter net was restated to include a $19.3 million gain on currency conversion, a $68.6 million swing in pretax income that might never be realized."[4] Many financial executives applaud the new rule because it is expected to significantly reduce such large fluctuations in companies' earnings caused by changes in foreign exchange rates.

Current/Noncurrent and Monetary/Nonmonetary Methods

The current/noncurrent method is perhaps the oldest approach used in the translation of balance-sheet accounts from the foreign currency into the parent currency. This method was most widely used in the United States from the early 1930s until SFAS No. 8 was issued in 1975.

The current/noncurrent method is based on the assumption that financial-statement accounts should be grouped according to maturity. Under this method, all current assets and current liabilities of foreign affiliates are translated into the parent currency at current exchange rates. All noncurrent assets, noncurrent liabilities, and owners' equity are translated at historical exchange rates.

The monetary/nonmonetary method produces essentially the same results as the temporary method under generally accepted accounting principles of historical accounting in the United States. The only difference is that under the monetary/nonmonetary method, inventory is always translated at the historical rate. Under the temporal method, inventory is usually translated at the historical rate, but it could be translated at the current rate if inventory is carried at market prices.

According to this method, monetary assets and monetary liabilities are translated at current exchange rates. Nonmonetary assets, nonmonetary liabilities, and owners' equity are translated at historical exchange rates. Monetary assets include cash, accounts receivable, and notes receivable. Nonmonetary assets include inventory and fixed assets. In general, all liabilities are monetary liabilities.

The proponents of this method argue that monetary assets and liabilities of foreign affiliates represent fixed amounts of money whose parent equivalents change each time the exchange rate changes. Thus, these monetary accounts should be translated at the current exchange rate. Although under the current/noncurrent method some current assets are monetary and some others are nonmonetary, all of them are translated at the current-exchange rate. However, the

[4] Jeffrey S. Arpan and Lee H. Radebaugh, *International Accounting and Multinational Enterprises* (Boston: Warren, Gorham & Lamong, 1981), p. 88.

monetary/nonmonetary method raises a serious problem when companies have more liabilities than monetary assets at the time of a functional-currency devaluation because this results in an exchange gain from translation.

Comparison of Four Translation Methods

All financial-statement items restated in terms of the parent currency are the functional-currency amount multiplied by the appropriate exchange rate. Table 12-5 compares the four-translation methods in terms of the exchange rate for each balance-sheet item: current/noncurrent, monetary/nonmonetary, temporal, and current rate.

Example 12-5 Assume that a foreign subsidiary of a U. S. multinational company has the following: (1) cash = FC100; (2) account receivable = FC150; (3) inventory = FC200; (4) fixed assets = FC250; (5) current liabilities = FC100; (6) long-term debt = FC300; and (7) net worth = FC300. Let us further assume that the historical exchange rate is \$2 = FC1, the current exchange rate is \$1 = FC1, and inventory is carried at market prices.

Table 12-6 illustrates the effect of each translation method on the balance sheet. Exchange gains or losses are shown here as a separate plug (balancing) account to show how they would be derived. However, in actual practice net worth would be used as a plug figure or exchange gains and losses would be closed out to retained earnings.

Under the current/noncurrent method, an exchange loss of \$350 is recorded because current assets are greater than current liabilities. On the other hand, under the monetary/nonmonetary method, an exchange gain of \$150 is recorded because monetary liabilities exceed

Table 12-5 Exchange Rates Used to Translate Balance-Sheet Items

Balance-Sheet Accounts	Current/ Noncurrent	Monetary/ Nonmonetary	Temporal	Current Rate
Cash	C	C	C	C
Receivables	C	C	C	C
Payables	C	C	C	C
Inventory	C	H	C or H	C
Fixed assets	H	H	H	C
Long-term debt	H	C	C	C
Net worth	H	H	H	H

Table 12-6 Comparison of Four Translation Methods

Accounts	Functional Currency	Current/ Noncurrent		Monetary/ Nonmonetary		Temporal		Current Rate	
Cash	FC100	1	$ 100	1	$ 100	1	$ 100	1	$ 100
Accounts receivable	150	1	150	1	150	1	150	1	150
Inventory	200	1	200	2	400	1	200	1	200
Fixed assets	250	2	500	2	500	2	500	1	250
Total	FC700		$ 950		$1150		$ 950		$ 700
Current liabilities	FC100	1	$ 100	1	$ 100	1	$ 100	1	$ 100
Long-term debt	300	2	600	1	300	1	300	1	300
Net worth	300	2	600	2	600	2	600	2	600
Gains (losses)	–		(350)		150		(50)		(300)
Total	$700		$ 950		$1150		$ 950		$ 700

monetary assets. Under the current rate method, the exchange loss is $300 because all accounts except net worth are translated at the current exchange rate.

Worldwide Translation Practices

In 1979 Price Waterhouse International published a survey of translation practices covering 64 countries. Table 12-7 presents their findings. They evaluated translation principles and practices for these 64 countries on the basis of the following criteria: required by law, insisted upon, predominant practice, minority practice, rarely or not found, not accepted, and not permitted.

This survey found that practically all countries initially record financial-statement accounts at the exchange rate in effect on the transaction date. Most of the responding countries reported that at subsequent balance-sheet dates it is required, insisted upon, or the predominant practice to translate receivables or payables of a foreign currency at the current exchange rate.

FORECASTING CURRENCY DEVALUATION

Currencies are rarely devalued without prior indication of weakness. Most researchers in this area have attempted to forecast cur-

Table 12-7 Translation Methods Required, Insisted Upon, or Predominant Practice

Current/ Noncurrent	Monetary/ Nonmonetary	Temporal	Current Rate
El Salvador	Bahamas	Argentina	Australia
Greece	Costa Rica	Austria	Botswana
Iran	Guatemala	Bermuda	Colombia
Malawi	Honduras	Bolivia	Denmark
New Zealand	Korea	Canada	Fiji
Pakistan	Nicaragua	Chile	France
South Africa	Philippines	Dominican Republic	Germany
Zambia	Sweden	Ecuador	Hong Kong
	Taiwan	Jamaica	India
		Panama	Ireland
		Peru	Ivory Coast
		United States	Japan
		Venezuela	Jersey
			Kenya
			Malaysia
			Netherlands
			Norway
			Paraguay
			Senegal
			Singapore
			Switzerland
			Trinidad and Tobago
			United Kingdom
			Uruguay
			Zimbabwe

Source: R. D. Ritzgerald, A. D. Stickler, and T. R. Watts, *International Survey of Accounting Principles and Practices* (Price Waterhouse International, 1979), pp. 248-252.

rency devaluation on the basis of some key economic indicators.[5] Some of these indicators are balance-of-payments deficits, international monetary reserves, inflation, money supply, and exchange spread between official versus market rates. These economic indicators are also used to forecast foreign exchange controls. The use of such economic statistics depends on the purchasing-power-parity theory described in Chapter 5. Under this theory in combination with a freely flexible-exchange-rate system, if the United States had an inflation rate of ten percent while Italy had an inflation rate of 15 percent, the Italian lira should decline in value by five percent rela-

[5] Richard J. Rogalski and Joseph D. Vinso, "Price Variations as Predictors of Flexible Exchange Rates," *Journal of International Business Studies* (Spring-Summer 1977), pp. 71-81; and Ian H. Giddy, "Exchange Risk: Whose View?" *Financial Management* (Summer 1977), pp. 23-33.

tive to the dollar. Under a fixed-exchange-rate system, the difference between the forecasted and actual rates of exchange measures a currency's basic disequilibrium. Political factors and other economic factors such as relative interest rates are also considered in forecasting currency devaluation.

The Balance of Payments

Trends and forecasts for the balance of payments indicate the direction that the value of a currency is to be adjusted. If a country spends more abroad than it obtains from abroad over a sustained period of time, the possibility of devaluation increases. If the country receives more from abroad than it spends abroad, the probability of re-evaluation increases.

In the long run, the balance-of-payments deficit is most unhealthy. A trend toward a deficit position in international trade and investment is a strong indication of troubled times ahead. If foreigners expect a country to have the balance-of-payments deficit over a sustained period of time, they will build up monetary claims against that country. The country's currency will not need devaluation if foreigners are willing to hold these monetary claims. This is because interest rates and the cost of forward cover will adjust to the expected exchange rates in the absence of artificial constraints on the operation of foreign exchange markets.

However, if government interference with interest rates or intervention in the foreign exchange market exists, markets become inefficient. Such inefficient markets may preclude the country from earning sufficient foreign exchange to support its weakened currency. They may also discourage foreigners to hold and invest locally the net funds obtained due to the country's balance-of-payments deficit. If these foreigners rush to sell their foreign currency holdings, the possibility of devaluation rises.

International Reserves

International monetary reserves are assets held by central banks or governments which can be used to settle international payments. They are composed of gold, Special Drawing Rights, and convertible foreign exchange. For most countries, the principal convertible currencies are the U. S. dollar, the British pound, the German mark, the Swiss franc, and the French franc.

International reserves reflect the solvency of a country with respect to its ability to meet international obligations. Debt repayment obligations, profit and royalty remittances, and payments of purchases on credit represent international obligations. Continued balance-of-payments deficits may lead to a decrease in international reserves of a country that maintains fixed exchange rates, unless these deficits are offset by increased short-term loans or investment. As international reserves of countries with flexible exchange rates decrease, they are likely to be judged in economic trouble. Both situations increase the likelihood of devaluation or depreciation.

Inflation

Many economic forces link the prices of real assets (inflation rates) with the prices of money (exchange rates). The relationship between inflation rates and exchange rates is provided by the purchasing power doctrine. According to this doctrine, currencies of countries with higher inflation rates than the United States tend to depreciate in value against the dollar. By the same token, currencies of countries with lower inflation rates than the United States tend to appreciate in value against the dollar.

It should be emphasized that inflation and devaluation may not necessarily have a causal relationship, but they may rather have a partial correlation. In some cases, both inflation and devaluation occur due to a dramatic increase in the cost of some other factor such as the cost of imported petroleum. In other situations, their relationship is circular. For example, domestic inflation leads to a price disadvantage for exported goods and a price advantage for imported goods. These two forces cause balance-of-payment problems, which in turn lead to devaluation or depreciation. It is also interesting to note that devaluation in its turn leads to a rise in the price of such essential imports as raw materials or foodstuffs, thereby creating another round of domestic inflation.

Money Supply

Money supply consists of currency in circulation and demand deposits. The classical economic theory assumes that a country should experience an increase in output to match increases in demand at home. Increases in output cause unemployment to fall and a level of real income to rise. Theoretically, all this can happen without inflation. But evidence indicates that wages and other forms of payment tend to increase at a faster rate than output. This creates a situation where the supply of money grows faster than is warranted by real economic growth. Because such an economic situation leaves too much money available to purchase too few goods, prices begin to rise and eventually this leads to inflation. Simply stated, inflation is the consequence of a country's spending beyond its capacity to produce. As the economy approaches full employment, any additional increase in money supply can only serve to make prices spiral upward. Some foreign exchange forecasters use the money supply as a timely indicator for price changes and thus evidence of exchange rate changes to maintain the purchasing power parity.

Official Versus Market Rates

Many foreign exchange forecasters use the exchange spread between official and market rates as a valid indicator of currency health. The purpose of the comparison is to observe the value placed on a particular currency by outsiders. Under a freely flexible exchange-rate system, no spread exists between these two exchange rates. However, some spread is practically inevitable where currencies are pegged and exchange controls are imposed on the convertibility of local currency into hard currencies. Under such a situation, the widening spread between official and free market rates measures the falling confidence in a local currency.

Many less developed countries have exchange controls, but they also have a free market rate for certain types of transactions. Payments for imports, dividend remittances, and some other international fund transfers may be required to be made at an official exchange rate. However, such remittances as those for foreign tourists entering the country or for local residents going overseas may be allowed to convert their currency holdings into a hard currency or a local currency at the free market rate. The rise in the spread between official and market rates would serve as an indication of increasing apprehension over the near future. Thus, the increasing excess of a free market rate over an official rate can be used as a valuable piece of evidence to forecast devaluation.

Other Indicators

There are a number of exchange rate forecasting models available in either academic journals or commercially. However, the list of factors to be considered in forecasting devaluation or revaluation varies from forecaster to forecaster. In addition to the five economic indicators described above, such economic factors as government spending, relative interest rates, national incomes, and business cycles have been suggested as variables relevant to exchange rate forecasting.

Perhaps the most comprehensive list of factors has been provided by Korth. This list includes: level of reserve assets, sudden imbalance in the balance of payments, level of foreign indebtedness, wide fluctuations in the balance of payments, extraordinary factors such as wars, domestic rate of inflation, anticipated changes in trading partners' economies, exchange and capital controls, importance of the currency in international use, importance of the country in international trade, elasticities of supply and demand for trade and other balance of payments items, past history of changes in the value of the currency, personal philosophies of high-ranking government officials, economic philosophies of the political party in power, proximity of elections, opinions of bankers and leading businessmen, large forward exchange discounts or premiums, unusually low or high interest rates, significant change in domestic investment and spending, and trend of domestic real estate values.[6]

HEDGING DEVICES

The two preceding sections focused on the types of foreign exchange exposure and currency value forecasting. Before a multinational company decides on when and by what techniques it should seek protection against exchange risk, it should identify the types of exchange exposure and then forecast devaluation or revaluation. These techniques are loosely grouped together as covering or hedging. Covering is narrowly defined as the purchase or sale of foreign exchange forward to protect a foreign exchange loss in the conversion from one currency to another. Hedging is broadly defined as all actions taken to protect the value of a company's exposed assets and financing.[7]

The traditional concept of exchange risk management assumes that only financial items on the current balance sheet are exposed to exchange risk. In order to reduce foreign exchange exposure, the company must increase hard-currency assets and reduce soft-currency

[6] Christopher M. Korth, "The Future of Currency: A Four-Step Procedure for Forecasting Change," *Business Horizons* (June 1972), pp. 67-76.

[7] Andreas R. Prindl, *Foreign Exchange Risk* (New York: John Wiley & Sons, 1976), p. 58.

assets, whereas at the same time it should decrease hard-currency liabilities and increase soft-currency liabilities. When a devaluation appears likely, the company must determine whether it has an unwanted net exposure to exchange risk. When the company finds that it has an unwanted net exposure to exchange risk, there are a variety of techniques it can take in order to reduce this net exposure. They include balance sheet hedge, financial market hedge, and swap.

Balance-Sheet Hedge

A balance-sheet hedge involves the selection of the currency in which monetary assets and liabilities are denominated so that an exchange rate change would make exposed assets equal to exposed liabilities. While balance-sheet hedges are generally employed to minimize translation exposure, they can also be used to reduce transaction and economic exposures. If the basic hedging purpose is to offset translation exposure, the company must maintain the same amount of monetary assets in a particular currency and monetary liabilities in that currency. This is because a devaluation would affect both types of balance-sheet accounts equally and thus the company would suffer neither a gain nor a loss. If the basic hedging purpose is to reduce transaction exposure or economic exposure, the company must have debt denominated in a currency which will change in value by an amount that will offset the change in value of future cash receipts.

There are two types of balance-sheet hedge in the event of a devaluation: operations with third parties and intercompany operations. In the context of the subsidiary's relationship with other firms, the reduction of undesirable exposures would involve such procedures as the sale of local currency in the forward market, the reduction of local currency holdings, the more dependence on local sources of debt capital, and so on. When the parent company has several subsidiaries, intercompany accounts can also be used to reduce foreign exchange exposure. These methods include transfer price adjustments, the accelerated payments of dividends, and adjustments for royalty remittances. These hedging methods for devaluations would be reversed for revaluations. In other words, the basic balance-sheet hedge requires multinational firms to increase hard currency (likely to appreciate) assets and reduce soft currency (likely to depreciate) assets, while it requires them to reduce hard currency liabilities and increase soft currency liabilities. Table 12-8 presents a comprehensive list of basic hedging procedures for devaluations and revaluations.

Table 12-8 Basic Hedging Techniques

Devaluation	Revaluation
Buy parent currency (sell local currency) forward	Sell parent currency (buy local currency) forward
Decrease local currency cash holdings and marketable securities	Increase local currency cash holdings and marketable securities
Increase credit standards to decrease local accounts receivable	Relax credit standards to increase local accounts receivable
Postpone collection of hard currency accounts receivable	Accelerate collection of soft currency accounts receivable
Increase imports of hard currency goods and services	Reduce imports of soft currency goods and services
Increase local debt	Reduce local debt
Delay payment of local accounts payable	Accelerate payment of local accounts payable
Speed up remittances to parent	Postpone remittances to parent
Accelerate payment of intersubsidiary accounts payable	Postpone payments of intersubsidiary accounts payable
Postpone collection of intersubsidiary accounts receivable	Accelerate collection of intersubsidiary accounts receivable
Invoice exports in foreign currency and imports in local currency	Invoice exports in local currency and imports in foreign currency

Source: Alan C. Shapiro, and David P. Rutenberg, "Managing Exchange Risks in A Floating World," *Financial Management* (Summer 1976), p. 49.

Financial Market Hedge

There are two types of financial market hedge: forward exchange-market hedge and money-market hedge.

Forward Exchange-Market Hedge. A forward exchange-market hedge involves a contract and a source of funds to fulfill that contract. The contract permits the exchange of one currency for another at a fixed rate on some future date. A purchase of a forward contract substitutes a known cost for the uncertain cost due to foreign exchange risk caused by the possible devaluation of one currency in terms of another. Although the cost of a forward contract is usually smaller than the uncertain cost, the forward contract does not always assure the lowest cost due to foreign exchange rate change. The forward contract simply fixes this cost in advance and thus eliminates the uncertainty which may be caused by foreign exchange rate change. For example, an American company may have a German mark import payable in nine months. The American company can cover this risk by a simple purchase of marks for the same date forward as the payment maturity at a certain price.

A forward exchange-market hedge as a source of funds involves two types of funds: funds already available and funds due because of some business operation. An example of funds already available would be pounds held in the United Kingdom for an airplane being built in the United States, payment for the airplane being due in nine months in dollars, and the U. K. company already having bought dollars forward. The available pounds will be utilized to pay the forward contract. An example of funds due because of some business operation would be revenues from an export sale by a British company to the United States billed in dollars. The dollar export proceeds may be committed to fulfill a forward purchase of pounds for dollars.

Money-Market Hedge. Like a forward exchange-market hedge, a money-market hedge involves a contract and a source of funds to carry out that contract. In this case, the contract represents a loan agreement. Assume an American company has a French franc import payable in 90 days. It may borrow in dollars, convert the proceeds into French francs, buy a 90-day French Treasury bill, and pay the import bill with the funds derived from the sale of the Treasury bill. Of course, it can buy French francs in the foreign exchange spot market when the import bill becomes due.

The structure of a money-market hedge is similar to that of a forward exchange-market hedge. The difference is that the cost of the money-market approach is determined by differential interest rates while the cost of the forward exchange-market approach is determined by forward premium or discount. If foreign exchange markets and money markets are in equilibrium, the forward market or the money market approach to cover the proceeds from an international transaction does not make much difference in terms of cost.

Example 12-6 To see how forward exchange-market and money-market hedges may be utilized to protect against transaction exposure, assume that an American firm has sold an airplane to a German firm for 100,000 marks with terms of 90 days. Let us further assume that the spot rate for marks is \$0.5233, the 90-day forward rate for marks is \$0.5335, the German 90-day interest rate is ten percent, and the U. S. 90-day interest rate is 17.8 percent. It should be noted that interest rates are in equilibrium with forward exchange quotations and this is confirmed by the following computation using Equation 5-2:

$$\frac{\text{n-day forward rate} - \text{spot rate}}{\text{spot rate}} \times \frac{360}{90} = \text{domestic rate} - \text{foreign rate}$$

$$\frac{\$0.5335 - \$0.5233}{\$0.5233} \times \frac{360}{90} = 17.8\% - 10.0\%$$

$$7.8\% = 7.8\%$$

The U. S. company's bank believes that the spot rate in 90 days will rise to \$0.6000, which is higher than the implicit unbiased forecast of \$0.5335 that exists in the currency forward quotation.

There are three alternatives available to the U. S. company: do not hedge (take the transaction risk), hedge in the forward exchange market, and hedge in the money market. If the U. S. company decides to accept the transaction risk, it would receive 100,000 marks in 90 days and sell them in the foreign exchange market for dollars. If the bank's forecast is accurate, the U. S. company would receive \$60,000 (\$0.6000 × 100,000 marks) in 90 days. However, that receipt is subject to foreign exchange risk. If the mark should decline to \$0.4000, the U. S. company would receive only \$40,000, which is \$20,000 less than expected. The \$40,000 could in fact be insufficient to cover the manufacturing cost of the airplane. On the other hand, if the mark should increase in value even more than the bank's forecast, the U. S. company would receive substantially more than \$60,000.

If the U. S. company wishes to hedge its transaction exposure in the forward market, it would sell 100,000 marks in the forward market for \$53,350. This is known as a covered transaction in which the U. S. company no longer has foreign exchange risk. In 90 days, the U. S. company would receive 100,000 marks from the German importer, deliver the proceeds to the bank against its forward sale, and receive \$53,350. It should be recognized that the certain \$53,350 is less than the uncertain \$60,000 expected from the unhedged position because the forward market quotation is not identical with the bank's forecast.

In addition to the forward exchange market approach, the U. S. company can also cover its transaction against foreign exchange risk through the money-market approach. The money-market approach works as follows: (1) borrow 97,561 marks from a Bonn bank at ten percent per annum (2.5% per quarter) in exchange for a promise to pay 100,000 marks (97,561 marks × 1.025); (2) receive \$51,054 by exchanging the 97,561 marks for dollars at the current spot rate of \$0.5233; (3) invest this sum in the U. S. money market at 17.8 percent per annum (4.45% per quarter) and receive \$53,326 (\$51,054 × 1.0445) at the end of three months. This sum should be equal to the sum received in the forward exchange market hedge described earlier. The small difference between these two sums is due to a compounding error.

Swaps

When exchange rates and interest rates fluctuate too widely, the risks of forward market and money market positions are so great that the forward exchange market and the money market may not function properly. In such cases, swap arrangements may be used by governments or private traders to stimulate international transactions. They are used to protect the value of both export sales and direct foreign investment. Currency swaps can be divided into two general categories: foreign currency swap and credit swap.

Foreign Currency Swap. A foreign currency swap is an agreement between two parties to exchange local currency for hard currency at a specified future date. In other words, the company purchases the specified amount of local currency in the foreign exchange market and simultaneously buys a forward contract to sell this amount of local currency for hard currency at a future date. The former transaction is a spot transaction and the latter transaction is a forward transaction. Thus, the swap is a simultaneous spot and forward transaction. This arrangement allows the company to recover the foreign exchange at a predetermined exchange rate.

Credit Swap. A credit swap is another hedging device that is similar to the foreign currency swap. This arrangement is a simultaneous spot and forward loan transaction between a private company and a bank of a foreign country. The U. S. company deposits a given amount of dollars in the New York office of the Colombian bank. In return for this deposit, the bank lends a given amount of pesos to the company's subsidiary in Colombia. The same contract provides that the bank would return the initial amount of dollars to the company at a specified date and the subsidiary would return the original amount of pesos to the bank. By so doing, the American company recovers the original dollar amount of its deposit and the Colombian bank obtains a free hard currency loan in the United States.

Example 12-7 A subsidiary in France requires the French

> franc equivalent of \$1 million at the current exchange rate of FF4 per dollar or FF4 million. To obtain FF4 million for the subsidiary in France, the parent must open a \$1 million credit in favor of a French bank. The French bank charges the parent ten percent per annum on the FF4 million made available to the subsidiary and pays no interest on the \$1 million that the parent has deposited in the bank. The parent's opportunity cost on the \$1 million deposit is 20 percent.

The total cost of this swap consists of the parent's opportunity cost and the interest charge on the local currency loan. The opportunity cost at 20 percent on the \$1 million is \$200,000 and the ten percent interest on the FF4 million (FF400,000) is \$100,000 at the prevailing rate of FF4 per dollar. Thus, the total swap cost is \$300,000 on a loan equivalent of \$1 million or 30 percent. This example suggests that a direct loan costs the parent 20 percent while the credit swap costs it 30 percent. The parent cannot choose between these two alternatives solely on the basis of comparative costs because the direct loan is unhedged while the credit swap is hedged. The meaningful comparison of the two lending alternatives requires the parent to explicitly consider foreign exchange fluctuations. The direct loan is ten percent cheaper only if the exchange rate stays the same.

If the multinational company is unable to predict future exchange rate changes with a fair degree of accuracy, it may attempt to identify the future exchange rate that equates the cost of the credit swap with the cost of the direct loan. That is, the exchange rate where the multinational company would be indifferent between the two financing alternatives. Assume that this exchange rate is denoted by y. The cost of the direct loan from the parent consists of 200,000y = the French franc cost equivalent of the direct loan (\$1 million × 20%) and (1,000,000y – 4,000,000) = the potential foreign exchange loss. The cost of the credit swap consists of 200,000y = the French franc cost equivalent of the \$1 million deposited in favor of the French bank and 400,000 = the interest paid on the FF4 million loan extended by the French bank at ten percent per annum. Because the cost of the direct loan and the cost of the credit swap are the same at the exchange rate of y, we obtain:

$$\underbrace{200{,}000y + (1{,}000{,}000y - 4{,}000{,}000)}_{\text{Direct Loan Cost}} = \underbrace{200{,}000y + 400{,}000}_{\text{Credit Swap Cost}}$$

$$y = 4.4$$

If the multinational company believes that the foreign exchange rate will not deteriorate to the equilibrium exchange rate of FF4.4 per dollar, it should choose the unhedged alternative which will be less costly. It should select the hedged alternative whenever its subjective assessment indicates that there is a significant change for the foreign exchange rate to deteriorate beyond FF4.4 per dollar.

SUMMARY

This chapter has discussed foreign exchange exposures, currency value forecasting, and hedging devices. A gain or a loss on foreign operations can occur because of a change in exchange rates. Thus, every company faces an exposure to gain or loss from changes in exchange rates as soon as it chooses to finance its operations in a foreign country. Translation exposure occurs when companies translate financial statement accounts from a foreign currency to their home currency. Economic exposure measures the impact of an actual conversion on the net present value of expected future cash flows. Transaction exposure refers to possible gains or losses which may result from the settlement of transactions whose payment terms are stated in a foreign currency.

Exchange rate forecasts are required to apply some hedging techniques. Currencies are rarely devalued or revalued without prior indication of weakness or strength. Most researchers in this area have attempted to forecast currency devaluation or revaluation on the basis of some key economic indicators. They include the balance of payments deficit, international reserves, inflation, money supply, exchange spread between official versus market rates, and interest rates. The use of such economic indicators depends largely upon the purchasing-power parity doctrine. This doctrine indicates that in the long run exchange rates reflect the relative purchasing power of currencies. In other words, it relates equilibrium changes in the exchange rate to changes in the ratio of domestic and foreign prices.

In essence, a hedge is a type of insurance which provides protection against the risk of loss from a change in foreign exchange rates. When a devaluation appears likely, the multinational company must determine whether or not it has any unwanted net exposure to foreign exchange risk. When the company finds that it has an unwanted net exposure to exchange risk, there are a variety of techniques it can take in order to reduce this net exposure. They include balance sheet hedge, forward exchange market hedge, money market hedge, foreign currency swap, and credit swap. These techniques are essentially employed to minimize translation and transaction exposures.

PROBLEMS

12-1 The current exchange rate of Swedish krona is SKr4 per $1. The Exton Company, the Swedish subsidiary of a U. S. multinational company, has the following balance sheet:

Assets		Claims on Assets	
Cash	SKr 500	Accounts payable	SKr 100
Accounts receivable	600	Notes payable	200
Inventory (Cost)	400	Other payables	1,000
Inventory (Market Price)	800	Total current liabilities	SKr1,300
Total current assets	SKr2,300	Long-term debt	800
Plant and equipment	2,400	Common stock	1,000
Accumulated Depreciation	1,400	Retained earnings	200
Net plant and equipment	1,000	Exchange loss or gain	—
Total assets	SKr3,300	Total claims on assets	SKr3,300

If the krona devalues from Skr4 per $1 to SKr5 per $1, what would be the translation loss (gain) under each of the following methods: current/non-current, monetary/nonmonetary, temporal, and current rate.

12-2 The current exchange rate of the Swedish krona is SKr4 per $1. The krona is expected to devalue from SKr4 per $1 on January 1 to SKr5 per $1 on December 31. Assume that the following events transpire during the ensuing 12 months.

(1) Inventory on hand at the beginning of the year is sold for SKr8,000. (2) The cost of goods sold is SKr4,500 and the company uses the FIFO method of accounting. (3) Selling, general, and administrative expenses of SKr900 are incurred and paid during the year. (4) Annual depreciation expenses are SKr500. (5) Annual interest expenses are SKr100 and paid at the end of the year. (6) The marginal tax rate of the company is 50 percent and payable at the end of the year. (7) The exchange loss of $15 under the temporal method and the exchange loss of $10 under the current rate method arise from the translation of the balance sheet.

Prepare the income statement in terms of Swedish kronas and then translate the income statement items into dollars under the temporal method and the current rate method.

Note: Depreciation charges are translated at the historical rate (SKr4 per $1) under the temporal method and the average rate (SKr4.5 per $1) under the current rate method. If the company uses the FIFO inventory method of accounting, the cost of goods sold is translated at the historical rate under the temporal method, but it is translated at the average rate under the current rate method. Because interest expenses and taxes are paid at the end of the year, they are translated at the current rate (SKr5 per $1) under both methods. Sales and other operating expenses are translated at the average rate under both methods.

12-3 A U. S. company buys ¥ 100,000 worth of goods from a Japanese firm. This payment must be made in 180 days in Japanese yens. The following quotations and expectations exist:

Present spot rate	$0.0050
180-day forward rate	$0.0051
Japanese interest rate	7.00%
U. S. interest rate	11.00%
Highest expected spot rate 180 days hence	$0.0052
Lowest expected spot rate 180 days hence	$0.0046

The U. S. company does not have any idle dollar balances at present, but it expects to have adequate cash in 180 days. Identify the alternatives available for making payment.

12-4 Assume that a subsidiary in Germany needs GM500,000 and that the credit swap has been proven to be the least costly hedged alternative. Further assume that the best unhedged alternative is the direct loan from the parent and the cost of the parent advance (direct loan) is 20 percent. The current exchange rate is $0.5000 per GM1. To obtain GM500,000 for the subsidiary in Germany, the parent must open a $250,000 credit ($0.5000 × GM500,000) in favor of a French bank. The French bank charges ten percent per year on the GM500,000 made available to the subsidiary and pays no interest on the $250,000 deposit that the parent has deposited in the bank.

What is the exchange rate which would make the parent advance and the credit swap equally attractive?

12-5 The Exton Company, the Swedish subsidiary of a U. S. multinational company, has just received "inside" information that the Swedish krona will devalue 20 percent against the dollar during the coming week. The current exchange rate is $0.25 per SKr1. The current assets of the subsidiary and its monetary liabilities are expressed in kronas but classified by the actual currency of denomination as follows:

		Currency of Actual Denomination	
	Total	Swedish Kronas	U. S. dollars
Cash	SKr1,000	SKr 600	SKr 400
Accounts receivable			
from U. S. parent	400	0	400
from Swedish customers	800	800	0
Inventory	600	600	0
Total current assets	SKr2,800	SKr2,000	SKr 800
Accounts payable			
to U. S. parent	SKr1,200	SKr 0	SKr1,200
to Swedish suppliers	800	800	0
Long-term debt	2,000	1,000	1,000
Total monetary liabilities	SKr4,000	SKr1,800	SKr2,200

a. Determine the net translation exposure as well as the net transaction exposure in terms of Swedish kronas.

b. Determine the translation gain (loss) and the transaction gain (loss) on the assumption that the krona will devalue by 20 percent next week.

c. What basic hedging techniques are available to minimize potential loss or to maximize potential gain should the krona devalue next week?

REFERENCES

12-1 Aggarwal, Raj, "FASB No. 8 and Reported Results of Multinational Operations: Hazard for Managers and Investors," *Journal of Accounting, Auditing and Finance* (Spring 1978), pp. 197-216.

12-2 Arpan, Jeffrey S., and Lee H. Radebaugh, *International Accounting and Multinational Enterprises* (New York: Warren, Gorham & Lamont, 1981), Chapters 4, 5, 6, and 7.

12-3 Arthur Anderson & Co., *Interpretations of Statement of Financial Accounting Standards No. 13* (1979).

12-4 Bernstein, Edward M., "The Dollar Under the Regime of Floating Exchange Rates," in Mark B. Winchester, ed., *The International Essays for Business Decision Makers* (Houston: The Center for International Business, 1980), pp. 244-249.

12-5 Brittain, Bruce, "Tests of Theories of Exchange Rate Determination," *Journal of Finance* (May 1977), pp. 519-529.

12-6 Cornell, Bradford, and Marc R. Reinqanum, "Forward and Future Prices: Evidence from the Foreign Exchange Market," *Journal of Finance* (December 1981), pp. 1035-1046.

12-7 Devris, Margaret G., "The Magnitude of Exchange Devaluation," *Finance and Development*, No. 2 (1968), pp. 7-18.

12-8 Dince, Robert R., and Peter N. Umoth, "Foreign Exchange Risk and the Portfolio

Approach: An Example for West Africa," *Columbia Journal of World Business* (Spring 1981), pp. 24-28.

12-9 Evans, Thomas G., William R. Folks, Jr., and Michael Jilling, *The Impact of Statement of Financial Accounting Standards No. 8 on the Foreign Exchange Risk Management Practices of American Multinationals* (Stamford, Conn.: FASB, 1978).

12-10 Everett, Robert M., Abraham M. George, and Aryeh Blumberg, "Appraising Currency Strengths and Weaknesses: An Operational Model for Calculating Parity Exchange Rates," *Journal of International Business Studies* (Fall 1980), pp. 80-91.

12-11 Jacque, Laurent L., "Management of Foreign Exchange Risk: A Review Article," *Journal of International Business Studies* (Spring/Summer 1981), pp. 81-102.

12-12 Feiger, George, and Bertrand Jacquillat, *International Finance* (Boston: Allyn and Bacon, Inc., 1982), Chapters 5, 6, and 7.

12-13 Financial Accounting Standards Board, Statement of Financial Accounting Standards No. 8, *Accounting for the Translation of Foreign Currency Transactions and Foreign Currency Financial Statements* (Stamford, Conn.: FASB, October 1975).

12-14 Financial Accounting Standards Board, Statement of Financial Accounting Standards No. 52, *Foreign Currency Translation* (Stamford, Conn.: FASB, December 1981).

12-15 Flanders, June M., and Asher Tishler, "The Role of Elasticity Optimism in Choosing an Optimal Currency Basket with Application to Israel," *Journal of International Economics* (August 1981), pp. 379-394.

12-16 Frenkel, Jacob A., "The Forward Exchange Rate, Expectations, and the Demand for Money: German Hyperinflation," *American Economic Review* (September 1977), pp. 653-670.

12-17 Frenkel, Jacob A., and Richard M. Levich, "Transaction Costs and Interest Arbitrage: Tranquil Versus Turbulent Periods," *Journal of Political Economy* (November/December 1977), pp. 1209-1226.

12-18 Galliot, Henry J., "Purchasing Power Parity as Explanation of Long-Term Changes in Exchange Rates," *Journal of Money, Credit, and Banking* (August 1970), pp. 348-357.

12-19 Giddy, Ian H., "Exchange Risk: Whose View?" *Financial Management* (Summer 1977), pp. 23-33.

12-20 Korth, Christopher M., "The Future of Currency: A Four-Step Procedure for Forecasting Change," *Business Economics* (June 1972), pp. 67-76.

12-21 Officer, Lawrence H., "The Purchasing-Power-Parity Theory of Exchange Rates," *IMF Staff Papers* (March 1976).

12-22 Rogalski, Richard J., and Joseph D. Vinso, "Price Level Variations as Predictors of Flexible Exchange Rates," *Journal of International Business Studies* (Spring/Summer 1977), pp. 71-81.

12-23 Srinivasulu, S. L., "Strategic Response to Foreign Exchange Risks," *Columbia Journal of World Business* (Spring 1981), pp. 13-23.

12-24 Wilby, William L., "Interest Rates and Exchange Rates Under the Fed's New Operating Procedure," *Economic Perspectives* (Federal Reserve Bank of Chicago, September/October 1981), pp. 3-13.

PART FIVE

Multinational Accounting and Taxation

THIRTEEN

MULTINATIONAL ACCOUNTING: REPORTING AND CONTROLLING

A reporting system measures the assets, liabilities, and owners' equity of a business unit at a particular time (the balance sheet). It also matches expenses to revenues in order to determine the net income or net loss for a period of time (the income statement). A control system relates actual performance to some predetermined goal. If a multinational company is to function in a coordinated manner, it must measure the performance of its foreign affiliates. It is equally important for managers of the affiliates to run their operations according to clearly defined objectives.

Multinational accounting is complicated by two types of problems. First, because multinational companies operate in many countries, they face different economic conditions. Thus, satisfactory accounting practices in one country may not be satisfactory in other countries. Second, there are many special problems in accounting for multinational operations. These problems include transfer pricing, taxes and tariffs, varying rates of inflation, the significance of debt ratio in the context of different capital markets, inventory valuation problem, and the related problem of currency translation.

ACCOUNTING SYSTEMS

Three basic types of economic systems are the free market system of most industrial countries, the controlled market system of developing countries, and the tightly controlled system of communist countries. If accounting is to maintain its social usefulness, each economic system should have a unique accounting pattern unlike the other two. Hence, essentially different economic systems should develop and employ different accounting systems. However, the accounting system adopted by a foreign subsidiary must be consistent with one established by host country reporting and tax regulations. It must also be consistent with the system established by the parent company for consolidation, tax, and managerial decisions.

Choi and Mueller, in their pioneering book in the field of international accounting, identified four approaches to accounting development which can be observed among industrial countries with the free market system.[1] They are the macroeconomic pattern, the microeconomic pattern, the independent-discipline approach, and the uniform accounting approach. This section describes the nature of each approach and its philosophies.

Macroeconomic Approach

A group of countries, including Sweden, have adopted a macroeconomic approach to accounting. The underlying hypothesis is that national economic policies *lead* rather than *follow* company goals. These countries have adopted policies designed to mitigate the disturbing effects of business cycles. Their accounting rules have been tailored to facilitate these policies through such requirements as some averaging of reported corporate income over the length of the typical business cycle.

Such accounting views are based on three postulates. (1) Business is the essential unit in the economic structure of a country. (2) Business best achieves its goals through close coordination of its activities with the national economic policies of its environment. (3) To best serve public interest, enterprise accounting must interrelate closely with national economic policies.

Under the macroeconomic approach, the purpose of accounting is to measure economic transactions of the business sector so that eco-

[1] Frederick D. S. Choi and Gerhard C. Mueller, *An Introduction to Multinational Accounting* (Englewood Cliffs, N.J.: Prentice-Hall, Inc., 1978), pp. 37-46.

nomic planners are better prepared to monitor and direct national economic activities in desired directions. Thus, companies have been required to publish financial statements and information on the position of the company, its future plans, employment, and total remuneration paid. In addition, many of our newer accounting concepts clearly fit into the macroeconomic framework of accounting development. Human resource accounting and accounting for corporate social responsibilities fit into the macroeconomic pattern of accounting.

Microeconomic Approach

Accounting practices in another group of countries, including the Netherlands, have been heavily influenced by microeconomic theory. Under the free enterprise system, private business activities are the cornerstones of the economic affairs and accounting performs a service function for business and business enterprises. Thus, it appears reasonable that accounting should orient itself to the same micro considerations that reflect its environment.

A microeconomic-oriented accounting system depends upon four postulates. (1) Business companies are focal points of business activities. (2) Their policies are designed to ensure their continued existence. (3) The company's best policy for survival is optimization in an economic sense. (4) Because accounting is a branch of business economics, it derives its concepts and applications from economic analysis.

The most important concept of microeconomic-oriented accounting is that the accounting process must focus on maintaining the purchasing power of monetary capital invested in the firm. Replacement value accounting fits microeconomic concepts best. The value of any good is its replacement value because the sale of something or its loss means the loss of a value for the company that can generally be regained only by purchase or production of an identical good. The microeconomic approach to accounting also assumes that replacement costs are based on the present value of income stream expected to be obtained from the use of an asset.

Independent-Discipline Approach

The accounting systems in the United States, Canada, and the United Kingdom are treated as an independent discipline. Accounting and business practices follow the same pattern of development because accounting provides business with an effective service. Just like business can produce its concepts from experience and practice, accounting can develop its own concepts from practice. Thus, existing accounting practices are the foundation for creation of accounting concepts. Generally accepted accounting principles represent accounting concepts and practices based on the independent discipline.

Under the independent-discipline approach to accounting, the accounting principles used by a particular company must be consistent from year to year. However, the principles used by one company need not be used by another company. One company may use FIFO to determine the cost of goods sold, while another may use LIFO. One company may depreciate an asset on a straight-line basis, while another company may depreciate the same asset on a double declining-balance method.

Uniform Accounting Systems

Germany, France, and Argentina have adopted uniform accounting systems which involve identical terminology and account classifications for all companies. There are a number of reasons why some countries have adopted a uniform accounting system. (1) It appears to make accounting more scientific. (2) It presents itself as a convenient device for economic and business control by government. (3) It affords a relatively simple way to achieve uniformity among companies.

Typically, uniform accounting systems have been developed in countries where national corporate laws regulate various matters of company operations. These matters include rights of stockholders, rules concerning disclosure of financial information, and rules for preparation of financial statements. Unfortunately, uniform accounting systems do not recognize basic differences among different industries. Moreover, they tend to restrict the development of new accounting concepts and practices.

FINANCIAL REPORTING

Multinational companies cross national boundaries in search for resources or markets. Thus, it is important to recognize that financial statements issued by companies in various countries differ in the form of presentation and in the degree of detail disclosed.

Dual Reporting System

In its 1975 study, the Accountants International Study Group recommended that primary and secondary financial statements would be recognized as part of formal generally accepted accounting standards and principles.[2] Primary financial statements are prepared in accordance with the accounting and reporting standards of a company's country of domicile. They are also expressed in the language and currency of that country. Secondary financial statements are prepared according to the accounting and reporting standards of another country. Such secondary financial statements are translated into a foreign currency, they are expressed in a foreign language, and they accompany the independent auditor's report expressed in a form commonly used in a foreign country.

Secondary statements may not be necessary if the primary statements satisfy the information requirements of financial reporting audiences in other countries. However, the majority of multinational companies with reporting audiences in more than a single country prepare secondary statements for interested parties in other countries. Such a dual reporting system may produce corporate financial information of a high quality, it may be more responsive to the perceived financial information needs of distinct users, and it may better serve international money and capital markets. The dual reporting system also has some problems. (1) It creates some problems when mergers and investment decisions are made with an eye to their financial statement effects. (2) Another problem occurs in the translation process when the treatment of foreign exchange gains or losses, inventory valuation, and the like may limit the validity of the secondary statements.

Areas of Major Differences

There are a number of major differences in accounting principles worldwide. In some countries such as the United States, the income statement is regarded as the most important statement, whereas in

[2] Gerhard G. Mueller, "The Dual System for Transnational Financial Reporting," *The Accounting Forum* (May 1975), pp. 17-25.

most European and Latin American countries, the balance sheet is regarded as the financial statement of prime interest. U. S. focus on the income statement is primarily due to the fact that most large U. S. corporations are publicly held. U. S. stockholders prefer increased wealth, which is measured by increasing stock prices and/or increased dividends. In contrast, stockholders in European and Latin American countries are primarily concerned with the ownership of wealth and the strength of the company in relation to claims of creditors.

Because many European countries are more conservative than the United States in their presentation of financial statements, they establish various reserves to smooth out income fluctuations from year to year. Reserves for contingencies may be established in years when earnings are high and they may be used in years when earnings are low. Such reserves sometimes arise due to statutory requirements that a certain portion of annual profits be set aside as reserves.

Consolidation of accounts is another area of difference. Companies in such developed countries as the United States and the United Kingdom follow the practice of consolidated financial statements. However, many developing and European countries do not require companies to consolidate foreign subsidiaries. The source of concern is that the parent company may decide to consolidate only profitable affiliates. This would make it difficult for the outsider to evaluate the company's overall performance.

Financial Disclosure

One important purpose of financial reporting is to supply information for decision making. This purpose may be achieved by requiring companies to disclose proper financial data and other relevant information. Before companies disclose any financial data, they should determine the users of the information, the amount of the information to be disclosed, and the purpose of the information. The users of disclosed financial data include stockholders, creditors, employees, customers, governmental agencies, and the general public. The amount of the information to be disclosed depends not only upon the expertness of the user but also upon the desirable standard. Three generally proposed disclosure standards are adequate, fair, and full disclosure. The proper financial data are disclosed for investors so that they can use the information for their investment decisions.

Because multinational companies have financial reporting obligations to diverse audiences, multinational financial disclosure is required by FASB Statement No. 14 in cases where multinational operations account for at least ten percent of total operations. However, such disclosure varies widely among countries. Most U. S. companies disclose their financial information to their stockholders and the public as a whole. This disclosure is largely because of the pressure of the U. S. Securities and Exchange Commission and the New York Stock Exchange's listing requirements.

European countries tend to disclose less financial data and provide less information about how assets are valued than U. S. companies. Income statements often fail to disclose sales or the cost of goods sold. Because trends in sales and in gross profit margins cannot be detected, it is extremely difficult for the reader of the income statement to determine the comparative strength of a company. In addition, methods of calculating depreciation and the degree of consolidation are often not explained.

European secrecy is traditional. Beyond tradition, there are a number of reasons why European companies disclose only a minimum amount of information. These reasons include the lack of legal requirements; the lack of pressures from creditors such as banks and stockholders; the lack of need for public equity financing; and the lack of extensive equity markets. European companies also tend to understate earnings for several reasons. Higher reported earnings may encourage stockholders to demand higher dividends or unions to seek pay increases. Tax avoidance is another reason why European companies tend to hide earnings.

Auditing

The opinion of a competent, professional, and independent auditor is essential to maintain the high reliability of international financial statements because of the great diversity of accounting practices in various countries. Auditors review financial statements and then attest their reliability, fairness, and other aspects of the information. Thus, auditing establishes and maintains the integrity of published financial information.

Although auditing standards are less diverse than accounting standards, they still differ by country. Auditing standards are pretty much alike in many countries such as the United States, Canada, Germany, the Netherlands, the United Kingdom, Japan, Norway, and Sweden. The financial statements of all or most public companies in these countries are required to be audited by independent public accountants. However, companies in Belgium and France are required to appoint one or more statutory examiners who need not be independent public accountants. Moreover, some countries such as the

Bahamas, Indonesia, Panama, and Uruguay have no auditing requirements for most companies.[3]

Most U. S. public accounting firms have opened offices in many countries. Thus, U. S. subsidiaries in Kenya and Honduras may be audited by the same firms that audit parent books in the United States. The increasing use of their services by companies in foreign countries may lead to greater uniformity of auditing standards among countries. Another reason why auditing standards are more uniform than accounting standards is because professional auditors are the only parties involved in establishing such standards.

Auditing procedures are somewhat more diverse internationally relative to auditing standards. In the United States, trade accounts receivable are confirmed and physical inventory counts are frequently taken. In contrast, these procedures are not practiced in many European countries. Trade accounts payable are not confirmed in the United States, while they are confirmed in a number of other countries. Companies in many European and Latin American countries have difficulty of verifying their disbursements because cancelled checks become the property of the bank and are not returned to the issuing companies.

CONSOLIDATION OF ACCOUNTS

Consolidated financial statements present the results of both foreign and domestic operations as if they were a single economic unit. Thus, such statements tend to disregard legal distinctions that exist among the separate corporate entities organized under different national laws. They are most useful to the shareholders and creditors of the parent company. The parent company consolidates its accounts with those of its subsidiaries on a line-by-line basis by adding together assets, liabilities, net worth, revenues, and expenses.

U. S. multinational companies are required to consolidate the financial statements of affiliates into those of the parent if the parent owns more than 50 percent of the affiliate's voting shares. But consolidation is not required if the subsidiary is engaged in a completely different line of business or in the process of liquidation or expropriation. Companies account for their foreign investments on the basis

[3] George C. Watt, Richard M. Hammer, and Marianne Burge, *Accounting for the Multinational Corporation* (New York: Financial Executives Research Foundation, 1977), pp. 214-215.

of the equity method if the parent owns between 20 and 50 percent of the affiliate. Under the equity method, the parent carries its affiliates at the initial cost of the investment plus its proportionate share of profits or losses. Companies are required to carry their foreign affiliates on the basis of the cost method if the parent owns less than 20 percent of the affiliate. Under the cost method, the parent carries its affiliates at the initial investment plus its dividends received.[4]

The practice of consolidation varies from country to country. U. S. multinational companies disclose only consolidated financial results. Separate financial statements of either the parent or its subsidiaries are not disclosed. According to *A Survey in 46 Countries: Accounting Principles and Reporting Practices* (1975) by Price Waterhouse International, both parent and consolidated financial statements are required in Australia, Canada, Denmark, Ethiopia, Germany, Jamaica, Japan, Kenya, Malaysia, Mexico, New Zealand, Nigeria, Republic of Ireland, Rhodesia, Singapore, South Africa, the United Kingdom, and Venezuela. Consolidation is optional in other countries.[5]

Within every country there are many users of financial information. Principal users of consolidated financial statements of multinational companies are stockholders and creditors of the parent company, stockholders and creditors of the affiliate, and management of the parent company.

Stockholders of the parent company need consolidated financial statements to judge their share of total asset values and total income represented by the group of companies which they own through the medium of parent company stock. From a practical standpoint, however, the consolidated statement may distort the real position of the stockholder if a substantial portion of a particular firm's foreign assets and its earnings are in weak or nonconvertible currencies. Stockholders of an affiliate are not likely to have a direct interest in consolidated financial statements because their welfare depends upon the financial success of the single affiliate whose shares they hold. However, they may have an indirect interest in consolidated financial statements because such statements indicate the financial strength of the parent and its subsidiaries as a whole.

Because short-term obligations are paid from the cash flow of the parent, the parent's short-term creditors have a genuine interest in the financial statements of the parent alone. However, long-term

[4] Jeffrey S. Arpan and Lee H. Rodebaugh, *International Accounting and Multinational Enterprises* (Boston: Warren, Gorham & Lamont, 1981), p. 212.

[5] Price Waterhouse International Executives Services, *A Survey in 46 Countries: Accounting Principles and Reporting Practices* (October 1975), Tables 207 and 211.

creditors of the parent are primarily interested in consolidated financial statements because the satisfaction of their claims depends primarily upon the profitability of the enterprise as a whole. Creditors of a foreign subsidiary are mainly concerned with the financial statements of the subsidiary. However, consolidated financial statements are useful to creditors of the subsidiary in cases where the debts of the subsidiary are guaranteed by the parent.

Consolidated financial statements are used for two purposes by management. (1) They are used to report to stockholders on management's stewardship of the company. (2) They are used as a foundation for international judgment of its performance. Management also uses financial statements and other information to make decisions concerning production, marketing, pricing, and dividend policies.

MULTINATIONAL CONTROL SYSTEM

A multinational company consists of the parent and its subsidiaries in foreign countries. To operate the multinational company as a system, the parent and its subsidiaries need continuing flows of data. Hence, the key element in the control system is the company's system for collection and dissemination of data on a worldwide basis. The company's information system generally consists of two types of communications between the parent and its subsidiaries: (1) impersonal communications such as budgets, plans, programs, and regular reports; and (2) personal communications such as meetings, visits, and telephone conversations.[6]

Communications essential to evaluating enterprise performance usually follow established organization channels. The effective communication system requires an effective reporting system for collecting information on results of actual operations and disclosing deviations from predetermined standards so that corrective actions may be taken.

The financial results of profits have traditionally provided a standard to evaluate the performance of business operations. However, as multinational companies expand their operations across national boundaries, the standard itself is affected by the environment in which they operate. Inflation and foreign exchange fluctuations affect all the financial measures of performance for multinational companies.

[6] Stefan H. Robock, Kenneth Simmonds, and Jack Zwick, *International Business and Multinational Enterprises* (Homewood, Ill.: Richard D. Irwin, Inc., 1977), p. 521.

To compare the results of various affiliates of the multinational company, multinational financial managers must understand the various ways in which inflation and exchange fluctuations affect operations as measured by traditional financial statements.

Every control system establishes a standard of performance and compares actual performance with the standard. The most widely used standards are budgeted financial statements. The preparation of the statements is a planning function, but their administration is a controlling function. To determine the impact of inflation and exchange rate fluctuations on financial statements, we will compare budgeted financial statements with actual financial statements. The budgeted statements are prepared without any anticipated inflation or exchange fluctuations, while the actual statements are prepared after these phenomena have occurred.

The Impact of Inflation on Financial Statements

Table 13-1 presents the impact of two rates of inflation (10% and 20%) on the major accounts of both the balance sheet and the income statement. The approximate annual inflation rates reflected on sales are five percent and ten percent instead of ten percent and 20 percent because of the following two assumptions: (1) one unit is sold every month and (2) prices increase at an even rate throughout the year.

If we follow the results of the case with a total annual inflation rate of ten percent or 0.83 percent per month, annual sales increase to 2,100, a five percent increase over the budgeted sales of 2,000. If one unit is sold every month, the first unit is sold at 0.83 percent over the budgeted price; the second unit is sold at 1.66 percent over the budgeted price; and so on until the 12th unit is sold at a price of ten percent over the budgeted price. It should be noted that the cost of goods sold increases by only four percent from the budgeted cost of 1,500 to the actual cost of 1,560 because the cost of goods sold is based on historical costs. Interest expenses are assumed to remain constant. The budgeted depreciation charge is identical with the actual depreciation charge because depreciation charges are based on historical costs. The combination of higher prices in sales and the use of historical costs in the two major accounts will increase the profits after taxes by 20 percent from 100 to 120.

The effects of inflation on the balance sheet accounts depend upon the date when assets were acquired or liabilities incurred. Fixed assets and inventory are carried at cost, while accounts receivable and payable are carried at the prices prevailing at the time of the transac-

Table 13-1 The Impact of Inflation on Financial Statements

Income Statement (in foreign currency)

	Budget	Actual with Annual Inflation Rate of: 10%	20%
Sales	2,000	2,100	2,200
Cost of goods sold	1,500	1,560	1,620
Gross margin	500	540	580
Depreciation	200	200	200
Operating income	300	340	380
Interest expense	100	100	100
Profit before taxes	200	240	280
Taxes (50%)	100	120	140
Profit after taxes	100	120	140

Balance Sheet (in foreign currency)

	Initial	Budget	Actual with Annual Inflation Rate of: 10%	20%
Cash	0	400	440	480
Accounts receivable	200	200	220	240
Inventory	100	100	110	120
Total current assets	300	700	770	840
Plant and equipment	350	350	350	350
Less: Depreciation	–	(200)	(200)	(200)
Total assets	650	850	920	990
Accounts payable	300	300	330	360
Notes payable	300	300	300	300
Taxes payable	–	100	120	140
Total current liabilities	600	700	750	800
Equity	50	50	50	50
Retained earnings	–	100	120	140
Total liabilities & equity	650	850	920	990

tions. The budgeted cash of 400 consists of profits after taxes (100), taxes payable (100), and depreciation (200).

The Impact of Exchange Fluctuation on Financial Statements

Let us assume that the subsidiary purchases all of its raw materials from Country A and sells all of its finished products to Country B. Thus, both exports and imports are denominated in foreign currencies. In this case, exchange rate fluctuations affect the level of both revenues and costs measured in terms of the domestic currency. Table 13-2 shows that an appreciation in the revenue currency (Country B's currency) raises profits assuming that costs remain constant. In contrast, an appreciation in the cost currency (Country A's currency) reduces profits after taxes unless selling prices are adjusted to reflect the increase in costs.

There are similarities between the impact of inflation and the impact of exchange fluctuations on reported profits. If prices in the local currencies are increased by the same percentage as the increase in the cost of imports, the impact of exchange fluctuations on profits is identical with the impact of a comparable local inflation rate. A ten percent increase in export prices accompanied by a proportional increase in import prices produces profits of 120, which is identical with the profit obtained when the local inflation rate was ten percent in the example in Table 13-1.

We cannot determine the true impact of exchange fluctuations on foreign operations unless the parent's accounts and those of its subsidiaries are expressed in terms of a homogeneous currency unit. When financial statements expressed in the local currency are translated into the currency of the parent company, any changes in the value of the local currency relative to the parent currency will affect the reported profits. The translation procedure is regulated by the accounting profession and this was discussed in Chapter 12.

FOREIGN CORRUPT PRACTICES ACT[7]

The Securities and Exchange Commission (SEC) first investigated illegal foreign payments in 1974 with its probe of questionable contributions by U. S. companies to the reelection campaign of former President Nixon. Subsequent inquiries by the SEC, the Department of Justice, and the Senate Foreign Relations Committee disclosed questionable payments exceeding $300 million by 450 companies. Consequently, Congress passed the Foreign Corrupt Practices Act (FCPA) on December 19, 1977 as an amendment to the Securities Exchange Act of 1934. The FCPA consists of two separate sections: antibribery and accounting.

The antibribery section was the first piece of legislation in U. S.

[7] This section draws heavily upon Suk H. Kim, "On Repealing the Foreign Corrupt Practices Act," *Columbia Journal of World Business* (Fall 1981), pp. 75-80.

Table 13-2 Impact of Exchange Fluctuations on Export Revenues and Import Costs

	Budget	B's Currency Appreciates 10%	A's Currency Appreciates 10%	Both Currencies Appreciates 10%
Sales	2,000	2,100	2,000	2,100
Cost of goods sold	1,500	1,500	1,560	1,560
Gross margin	500	600	440	540
Depreciation	200	200	200	200
Operating income	300	400	220	340
Interest expense	100	100	100	100
Profit before tax	200	300	120	240
Taxes (50%)	100	150	60	120
Profit after tax	100	150	60	120

history making it a criminal offense for U. S. companies to corruptly influence foreign officials or to make payments to any person when they have "reason to know" that part of these payments will go to a foreign official. The accounting section establishes two interrelated accounting requirements. First, public companies must "keep books, records, accounts, which, in reasonable detail, accurately and fairly reflect the transactions and dispositions" of their assets. Second, corporations are also required to "devise and maintain a system of internal accounting controls sufficient to provide reasonable assurance" that transactions have been executed in accordance with management's authorized procedures or policies. Congress concluded that the antibribery and accounting sections would effectively prevent payments of foreign bribes and off-the-book slush funds. Penalties for violations include fines of up to $1 million for corporations and $10,000/or five years in jail for individuals.

From its inception in December 1977, the FCPA has been the subject of extensive debate. Corporate executives and chief officers of accounting firms have argued that the FCPA constitutes a further encroachment on legitimate and necessary management prerogatives. Some members of Congress and enforcement officers of government agencies, on the other hand, have countered that the FCPA has made U. S. executives aware of their responsibilities and immense influence in the international business community. Basically, there are three possible alternatives: (1) repeal the FCPA, (2) modify it, and (3) sustain it unmodified.

Repealing the FCPA

Critics of the FCPA argue that it should be repealed for a number of good reasons. (1) It has forced U. S. companies to increase their audit cost substantially. (2) The Department of Justice and the SEC have failed to establish a set of clear guidelines. (3) It has put U. S. companies at a competitive disadvantage. (4) In many countries, not only foreign payments are not outlawed, but they are encouraged. (5) It was unnecessary because U. S. law enforcement agencies have many statutes at their disposal to prevent illegal foreign payments by U. S. companies.

Increased Internal Control Costs. Because the FCPA monitors accounting procedures and levies heavy penalties for violations, it has compelled U. S. companies to revise internal controls. A number of surveys found that many companies expanded their documentation effort to comply with the FCPA. For example, a 1981 survey of 185 U. S. major corporations conducted by the General Accounting Office (GAO) found that 80 percent of the responding companies have substantially revised their existing codes of conduct.[8] According to a 1980 survey of 673 U. S. executives conducted by the Financial Executives Institute (FEI), 65 percent reported that their companies have undertaken extensive programs to document their present internal control practices and 75 percent said that their companies have introduced a code of conduct in response to the FCPA.[9]

The FCPA's accounting section recognizes that the cost of internal accounting control should not exceed the benefits received. However, there are many indications that compliance programs burden companies with additional costs though they receive no commensurate benefits in terms of improved controls and record keeping. The 1981 GAO survey reported that 55 percent of the responding companies have increased costs that exceeded benefits.[10] According to the 1980 FEI survey, most respondents perceived changes in their internal control system as cost burdens. This study also noted that some corporate officials believed that their increased documentation was a paper-gathering exercise to serve as a defense against SEC inquiries.[11]

There are a number of reasons why the cost of internal accounting control has exceeded the benefits received. First, two interrelated accounting requirements–record keeping and internal control requirements–contain ambiguous terms such as "in reasonable detail" and "reasonable assurance." Because the language is difficult to inter-

[8] The General Accounting Office, *Impact of the Foreign Corrupt Practices Act on U. S. Business* (March 4, 1981), pp. 6-7.

[9] Robert K. Mautz, et al., *Internal Control in U. S. Corporations: The State of Art* (New York: The Financial Executives Research Foundation, 1980), pp. 42-43 and p. 89.

[10] The General Accounting Office, *Impact of the Foreign Corrupt Practices Act on U. S. Business*, p. 29.

[11] Robert K. Mautz, et al., *Internal Control in U. S. Corporations: The State of Art*, p. 83.

pret, companies have enlarged the scope of their compliance effort in the belief that literal compliance is virtually impossible. Second, many corporate executives fear that the FCPA's accounting section "will be interpreted as broadly as possible and used by the SEC as a weapon against business."[12] Third, the SEC has repeatedly stated that it would enforce the accounting requirements for both domestic and foreign transactions.

Failure of Enforcement Agencies to Clarify the FCPA. The law has been severely criticized from its inception on the ground that it was vague and difficult to interpret. Nevertheless, the Department of Justice and the SEC have failed to establish a set of clear guidelines.

The 1981 GAO survey found that over 50 percent of its respondents rated the terms of "reason to know" in the antibribery section and "reasonable assurance" in the accounting section as inadequate or very inadequate.[13] As described earlier, the unclear concept of the "reasonable assurance" provision has forced U. S. companies to increase a substantial amount of their accounting and auditing costs. Furthermore, the ambiguity of the "reason to know" provision has caused U. S. companies to: (1) withdraw from joint ventures for fear that they later could be held responsible for the acts of their foreign partners; (2) incur substantial legal and investigative costs to check the backgrounds of their sales agents abroad; (3) not obtain the services of effective sales agents; (4) lose contracts simply because of the time needed to investigate sales agents and institute safeguards; (5) withdraw from existing markets; and (6) give up their efforts to enter new markets.[14]

The Justice Department released the Act Review Procedure in March 1980 to clarify the Act's antibribery provision. Under this procedure, the Justice Department will give its opinion on the legality of a contemplated transaction within 30 days after receiving the necessary information. The department would also provide companies with the maximum protection from disclosure of sensitive information submitted under the procedure. However, the September 1980 report on exports, prepared by the Department of Commerce and the Office of the U. S. Trade Representative, stated that businessmen are not optimistic that the review procedure will prove very useful because: (1) the Justice Department's response will ordinarily

[12] Ibid., p. 302.

[13] Jack G. Kaikati and Wayne A. Label, "American Bribery Legislation: An Obstacle to International Marketing," *Journal of Marketing* (Fall 1980), p. 39.

[14] The Department of Commerce and the Office of the U. S. Trade Representative, *Report to the President on Export Promotion Functions and Potential Export Disincentives* (Washington, D. C.: The Government Printing Office, 1980).

come after the business decision must be made; (2) foreign agents will often be reluctant to give the information needed by the Justice Department to evaluate the proposed transaction; (3) confidential information in letters might be disclosed; and (4) the mere fact that they have sought guidance will become known and cause adverse publicity.[15] These major concerns were confirmed by the fact that the Justice Department had received only three review requests in one year's existence of the review procedure.[16]

The SEC, which shares enforcement responsibility with the Justice Department, has further undercut the impact of this review procedure. The SEC has refused to be bound by the Justice Department's decisions under the review procedure. So, even though the Justice Department may assure companies that their foreign payments do not violate the antibribery provision of the Act, the SEC could conceivably initiate civil action against them.

The SEC has made a series of efforts to convince the business community that it will not use the Act's accounting provision as a weapon of further encroachment on legitimate internal management processes. In April 1979, the SEC proposed rules to clarify the accounting provision. The SEC withdrew its proposal in June 1980 after receiving almost 1,000 hostile letters from accounting firms, corporate executives, and business organizations.[17] In February 1980, the SEC asked all SEC registered companies and others to submit their comments on the Act in order to determine the substance of the criticisms and necessary actions to take in response to these concerns. The SEC received only 14 comments despite the four-month comment period. Consequently, it did not have enough information to properly evaluate the concerns expressed by the business community.[18] On January 13, 1981, SEC's Chairman, in a speech before an AICPA conference, delivered a policy statement on the accounting provision. However, he repeated the agency's previous positions that (1) the accounting provision contains a "reasonableness" standard rather than the traditional standard of materiality and (2) the concept of "reasonable assurance recognizes that the cost of internal control should not exceed the benefits received."[19]

[15] Ibid.

[16] Department of Justice, Foreign Corrupt Practices Act Review Procedure Release," Nos. 80-01, 80-02, and 80-03.

[17] Wanda A. Wallace, "Internal Control Reporting: 950 Negative Responses," *CPA Journal* (January 1981), p. 33.

[18] Robert N. Holt and Rebecca E. Fincher, "The Foreign Corrupt Practices Act," *Financial Analyst Journal* (March-April 1981), p. 75.

[19] Harold M. Williams "The Accounting Provisions of the Foreign Corrupt Practices Act: An Analysis," SEC Release No. 34-17500 (February 9, 1981).

Despite its attempts to help the business community on the accounting section, the SEC has failed to establish a set of clear guidelines. Legal, accounting, and corporate officials complained about the FCPA's broad and catch-all accounting section which ignores cost/benefit considerations. In fact, many of them fear that the accounting section will be used as a wedge into internal management processes. Thus, it is not difficult to understand why some companies prepared "FCPA defense files which are loaded with legal briefs, review forms, and related documentary evidence of compliance, all collected in anticipation of a fateful day in court."[20]

Competitive Disadvantage. Critics of the FCPA have charged that the FCPA placed U. S. companies at a competitive disadvantage, thereby contributing to an unfavorable U. S. balance of payments. Hard verifiable data neither support nor reject the belief that the FCPA has caused U. S. companies to lose foreign sales. But American business executives have complained that U. S. companies have lost foreign sales worth millions of dollars because of the FCPA.

According to the 1981 GAO survey of 185 U. S. major companies, more than 30 percent of those questioned stated that they had lost millions of dollars in foreign sales due to the FCPA. In addition, 60 percent felt that American companies could not successfully compete against other companies abroad.[21] In a 1979 survey of major U. S. multinational companies conducted by Peat, Marwick, Mitchell & Co., 71 percent indicated that the FCPA would result in a significant loss of business by U. S. companies to foreign competitors.[22] The Export Disincentives Task Force, created in the Fall of 1979 but abolished in 1981, estimated that U. S. firms may lose foreign sales by as much as $1 billion a year as a result of the FCPA.[23]

Furthermore, specific case examples suggest that the FCPA has caused the loss of millions of dollars in exports. In one instance, a partner in a prominent law firm, located in Washington, D. C., received an urgent phone call from Cairo. A U. S. client, negotiating with the Egyptians, requested legal advice so that his proposed contract would preclude any bribes. After a marathon 20-hour negotiating session at the Nile Hilton, the lawyer failed to "sanitize" the deal. In the end, the Egyptians became angry, walked out of the negotia-

[20] Robert K. Mautz, et al., *Internal Control in U. S. Corporations: The State of Art*, p. 302.

[21] The General Accounting Office, *Impact of the Foreign Corrupt Practices Act on U. S. Business*, p. 14.

[22] Peat, Marwick, Mitchell & Co., "Survey of Business Attitudes Toward the Foreign Corrupt Practices Act," (January 16, 1979).

[23] William T. Coleman, Jr., "Government Regulations of Foreign Business Practices: A Reassessment," *Financial Executives* (September 1980), p. 39.

tions, and the U. S. company lost the contract.[24] In another instance, a Saudi Arabian businessman, an agent of American companies, complained that the FCPA prevented American manufacturers from winning a three billion-dollar communications contract that went, instead, to European companies.[25] Ernest Johnston, Jr., a State Department's representative disclosed in a Congressional testimony, "in 1980 our embassy in Muscat reported that a U. S. firm lost a $20 to $30 million deal largely because of delays caused by lengthy internal review to determine the application of the FCPA to the proposed transaction.[26] Many American executives in Asia have complained that they lost a significant amount of foreign sales to European and Japanese competitors because such foreign companies were not subject to similar antibribery laws.[27]

The FCPA's adverse impact on U. S. corporate foreign sales has been attributed to a number of factors. First, both U. S. executives and government officials charge that U. S. companies forego legitimate export opportunities because certain aspects of the FCPA's antibribery section are ambiguous. Second, the FCPA does not recognize the cold fact that payments are an accepted business practice in many countries. The FCPA has insulted other governments which have antibribery laws while it disrespects those countries whose standards differ from ours. Third, foreign companies are not similarly restricted as U. S. companies.

National Legislation on Foreign Payments. National legislation on foreign payments and monitoring agencies such as the SEC in this country do not exist in most countries. Canadian law stipulates that private Canadian companies should comply with the laws of each foreign country. It is not a criminal offense under British law to commit bribery overseas.[28] In many countries, foreign payments are in fact legalized and encouraged.[29]

The FCPA is viewed as a unilateral mandate, "a futile attempt to

[24] "Senate to Begin Debate on Administration's Plan to Ease Rules Against Paying Bribes Overseas," *The Wall Street Journal* (May 20, 1981), p. 48.

[25] David C. Gustman, "The Foreign Corrupt Practices Act of 1977: A Transactional Analysis," *The Journal of International Law and Economics* (1979), p. 380.

[26] Ernest B. Johnston, Jr., "Testimony Before a Joint Hearing of the Subcommittee on International Finance and the Subcommittee on Securities of the Senate Banking, Housing and Urban Affairs Committee," (May 20, 1981).

[27] "The U. S. Law Barring Bribes Blamed for Millions in Lost Sales in Asia," *New York Times* (June 26, 1979), p. 1.

[28] Jack G. Kaikati and Wayne A. Label, "The Foreign Antibribery Law: Friend or Foe?" *Columbia Journal of World Business* (Spring 1980), p. 49.

[29] For example, Italy in 1980 legalized payments to foreign officials who obtained business for Italian companies. A confidential West German Memorandum by the Federal Office

legislate the moral code under which foreign government officials behave." Because U. S. companies must obey the aws in each foreign country, critics argue that these nations establish in reality the legal standards for business practices. They suggest that to put U. S. exporters on an equal competitive footing with foreign companies, Congress should scrap the FCPA and seek an international forum to solve a worldwide problem of corrupt business practices. Over 50 percent of the 1981 GAO survey questionnaire respondents felt that an international antibribery agreement would strengthen American companies' competitive position.[30]

Of course, the United States alone cannot solve international payments problems. Perhaps the most effective way to regulate foreign business practices is an approach of "shared morality," such as one attempted by the United Nations. In August 1976, the United Nations Economic and Social Council adopted a resolution calling for a working group of representatives from 18 nations to draft an international treaty on illicit payments. Although the council's working group developed a draft agreement in the Spring of 1979, the United Nations General Assembly failed to adopt any agreement on illicit payments. At a June 1980 economic summit in Venice, seven industrial nations, including the United States, supported the U. N. effort but decided to undertake independent action if U. N. efforts were delayed. The United States has made a good faith effort to obtain an U. N. agreement since the economic summit, but the State Department is not optimistic that an effective agreement can be reached in the near future.[31]

Other Statutes. Critics point out that the FCPA was unnecessary because there are many statutes which can be used to prevent illegal foreign payments by U. S. companies. They include the Securities Act of 1933, the Securities Exchange Act of 1934, the Security Assistance and Arms Control Act of 1976, the Tax Reform Act of 1976, the Bank Secrecy and Reporting Act of 1970, the Federal Trade Commission Act of 1934, the Sherman Antitrust Act of 1890, the Clayton Antitrust Act of 1914, and various mail and wire fraud laws.

These and some other existing laws in their view could be used to determine prosecutable offenses. In fact, many government cases

for Foreign Trade advised companies to provide as much as 25 percent of the contract price to corrupt foreign officials. See "Big Profits in Big Bribery," *Time* (March 16, 1981), pp. 66-67.

[30] The General Accounting Office, *Impact of the Foreign Corrupt Practices Act on U. S. Business*, p. 45.

[31] "GIST: Multinational Corporations" (Bureau of Public Affairs, Department of State, March 1981).

against foreign payoffs have been based on laws other than the FCPA. For example, the Justice Department sued McDonnell Douglas on the grounds that the company violated the mail and wire fraud laws. Allegedly, McDonnell Douglas defrauded the government of Pakistan by failing to report to the U. S. Export-Import Bank $2 million in payments to Pakistani agents on four DC10s sold to Pakistan International Airlines between 1972 and 1977.[32]

Modifying the FCPA

The Reagan Administration and some U. S. Senators such as John Chafee have launched a major effort to amend the FCPA since January 1981. Those who advocate the modification of the FCPA argue that the United States should not completely scrap the law as we await a viable international solution to a worldwide problem of corrupt business practices. In order to make the FCPA more equitable, effective, and understandable, they suggested that the U. S. Congress should remove criminal sanctions from the FCPA, end dual enforcement by the SEC and the Department of Justice, end the dual burden of record keeping for both domestic and foreign transactions, and limit its accounting requirements.

In December 1981, the U. S. Senate passed a bill which clears up some of the ambiguity that U. S. executives had complained about the FCPA. The bill gives sole enforcement authority for the antibribery section of the FCPA to the Justice Department. It eliminates criminal liability for failure to set up adequate internal accounting controls. It spells out conditions under which bribes not specifically authorized by corporate officials may be illegal. It also eliminates the current "reason to know" provision in the antibribery section of the FCPA. Finally, the bill changes the name of the law from the Foreign Corrupt Practices Act to the Business Records and Practices Act. At the time of writing this chapter, Representative Timothy Wirth, chairman of the House Finance subcommittee, was conducting hearings on the FCPA.

Retaining the FCPA

Proponents of the FCPA contend that if U. S. companies are allowed to corruptly influence foreign officials, in all likelihood they

[32] In September 1981 the U. S. Department of Justice dropped illicit-payment charges against four McDonnell Douglas executives. Under the settlement, McDonnell Douglas agreed to pay $55,000 in criminal fines and $1.2 million in damages. For details, see "McDonnell Douglas Admits Fraud Charge in Payoffs Case, Fined Maximum $55,000," *The Wall Street Journal* (September 9, 1981), p. 22.

would wish to do the same in the United States. Because the FCPA bans illegal payments to foreign officials, monitors accounting procedures, and levies heavy penalties for violations, the FCPA has encouraged U. S. companies to introduce corporate policies against corrupt foreign payments and to improve internal controls.

Both the 1981 GAO survey and the 1980 FEI survey found that an overwhelming majority of the companies have undertaken a variety of positive steps to prevent illegal payments to foreign officials and to improve their internal controls. In addition, according to the 1981 GAO survey, more than 70 percent of the respondents felt that the FCPA had been effective in reducing questionable foreign payments.[33] Some believe that the reduction of questionable foreign payments by U. S. companies is essential to upgrade the image of U. S. business. Thus, a strong argument can be made for the retention of the FCPA because the basic purpose of the FCPA was to improve the image of U. S. business and institutions tarnished by Watergate and related scandals.

There is no documentary evidence to support that U. S. companies have lost a substantial amount of export sales as a direct result of the FCPA. U. S. exports have increased significantly since the FCPA became effective in 1977. For example, exports of non-agricultural products alone had almost doubled to $179.8 billion in 1980 from $96.5 billion in 1977.[34] In addition, many large U. S. companies such as IBM, General Electric, and Eastman Kodak have successfully sold their products abroad without payments because their market positions and their advanced technology are strong.[35]

Conclusion

The international business community will experience dramatic fluctuations and keener competition in this decade. Many U. S. executives believe that the huge U. S. trade deficit and the rapidly weakening competitive advantage of the United States are signals that this country cannot afford to ignore. To overcome such problems, there must be a process of mutual cooperation and involvement between the federal government and the business community. There has been such a cooperation since the U. S. Congress began its deliberations

[33] The General Accounting Office, *Impact of the Foreign Corrupt Practices Act on U. S. Business,* pp. 6-17.

[34] U. S. Department of Commerce, *Survey of Current Business* (June 1981).

[35] Jack G. Kaikati and Wayne A. Lable, "American Bribery Legislation: An Obstacle to International Marketing," p. 41.

on the possible revision of the FCPA and on removal of U. S. export disincentives in late 1980.

SUMMARY

Accurate financial reports on operations must be prepared for stockholders and creditors to make decisions about the value of existing operations. They are especially important in international business where operations are typically supervised from a distance. Hence, meaningful financial reports are the cornerstone of effective international financial management. To check performance against standards on a worldwide basis, financial control systems must fit international circumstances.

World accounting systems can be classified into four basic types. A macroeconomic approach assumes that the accounting system should facilitate government economic policies. A microeconomic approach assumes that accounting performs a service function for business and thus it should orient itself to the same micro considerations that reflect its environment. An independent-discipline approach assumes that accounting can develop its concepts from practice. A uniform accounting system involves identical terminology and account classifications for all companies.

Because multinational companies cross national boundaries in search for markets or resources, their financial statements differ in the form of presentation and in the degree of detail disclosed. In the United States, the income statement is more important than the balance sheet, while in Europe, the balance sheet is treated as the financial statement of prime interest. European companies establish various reserves to smooth out income fluctuations from year to year. In contrast, such reserves are quite rare in the United States. The United States follows the practice of consolidation, but many European countries do not follow the practice of consolidation for foreign operations.

Companies must disclose proper financial data and other relevant information for their stockholders and other potential investors. The amount of disclosure depends on the expertness of the user and the desirable standard. The three major standards generally proposed are adequate, fair, and full disclosure. U. S. multinational companies are required to disclose appropriate financial data if their foreign operations account for more than ten percent of total operations. European companies tend to disclose less financial data than U. S. companies.

Consolidated financial statements present the results of both foreign and domestic operations as if they were a single economic unit. U. S. multinational companies are required to consolidate the financial statements of the parent and those of its subsidiaries if the parent owns more than 50 percent of the subsidiary's voting shares. Principal users of consolidated statements are stockholders of the parent company, stockholders of the foreign subsidiaries, creditors of the parent, creditors of the foreign subsidiaries, and managers of the parent.

A financial control system is used to make sure that financial goals and objectives are being met. Control decisions affect financial plans, just as planning decisions affect controls. Budgeted financial statements are the most widely used standards. Thus, it is important to measure the impact of inflation and exchange fluctuations on financial statements.

The Foreign Corrupt Practices Act of 1977 intended to stop the erosion of international confidence in U. S. business and institutions. The FCPA makes it unlawful for U. S. companies to influence foreign officials through payments and requires these firms to maintain strict accounting controls over their assets. Many U. S. executives would like the U. S. Congress to repeal the FCPA because: (1) it has compelled U. S. companies to increase their audit cost substantially; (2) the Department of Justice and the SEC have failed to establish a set of clear guidelines; (3) it placed U. S. companies at a competitive disadvantage; (4) in many foreign countries, foreign payments are in fact encouraged and legalized; and (5) it was unnecessary because there are many other laws which may be used to prevent illegal foreign payments by U. S. companies. If the U. S. House of Representatives goes along with the Business Records and Practices Act passed in December 1981 by the U. S. Senate, some of the FCPA's ambiguity will be clarified.

REFERENCES

13-1 Accounting Standards Committee, "Statement of Standard Accounting Practice No. 16: Current Cost Accounting," *Accountancy* (April 1980), pp. 99-110.

13-2 Aggarwal, Raj, "FASB No. 8 and Reported Results of Multinational Operations: Hazard for Managers and Investors," *Journal of Accounting, Auditing and Finance* (Spring 1978), pp. 197-216.

13-3 Arpan, Jeffrey S., and Lee H. Radebaugh, *International Accounting and Multinational Enterprises* (New York: Warren, Gorham & Lamont, 1981).

13-4 Baker, H. Kent, Robert H. Chenhall, John A. Haslem, and Roger H. Juchau, "Disclosure of Material Information: A Cross-National Comparison," *International Journal of Accounting Education and Research* (Fall 1977), pp. 1-18.

13-5 Baruch, Hurd, "The Foreign Corrupt Practices Act," *Harvard Business Review* (January-February 1979), pp. 32-49.

13-6 Choi, Frederick D. S., and Gerhard G. Mueller, *An Introduction to Multinational Accounting* (Englewood Cliffs, N.J.: Prentice-Hall, Inc., 1978).

13-7 Coleman, William T., "Government Regulations of Foreign Business Practices: A Reassessment," *Financial Executives* (September 1980), 36-40.

13-8 da Costa, Richard C., James Fisher, and William M. Lawson, "Linkages in the International Business Community: Accounting Evidence," *Journal of International Business Studies* (Fall 1980), pp. 92-102.

13-9 Danos, Paul, and Eugene A. Inhoff, "Factors Affecting Reasonableness Judgement," *Accounting Review* (January 1982), pp. 39-54.

13-10 The General Accounting Office, *Impact of the Foreign Corrupt Practices Act on U. S. Business* (March 4, 1981).

13-11 Gray, Sidney, J., Jack C. Shaw, and Brendan McSweeney, "Accounting Standards and Multinational Corporations," *Journal of International Business Studies* (Summer/Spring 1981), pp. 121-136.

13-12 Holt, Robert N., and Rebecca E. Fincher, "The Foreign Corrupt Practices Act," *Financial Analyst Journal* (March-April 1981), pp. 73-79.

13-13 Kaikati, Jack and Wayne A. Label, "The Foreign Antibribery Law: Friend or Foe?" *Columbia Journal of World Business* (Spring 1980), pp. 46-51.

13-14 Kim, Suk H., "On Repealing the Foreign Corrupt Practices Act: Survey and Assessment," *Columbia Journal of World Business* (Fall 1981), pp. 75-80.

13-15 Mautz, Robert K., et al., *Internal Control in U. S. Corporations: The State of Art* (New York: The Financial Executive Research Foundation, 1980).

13-16 Mueller, Gerhard G., "The Dual System for Transnational Financial Reporting," *The Accounting Forum* (May 1975), pp. 17-25.

13-17 Price Waterhouse International Executives Services, *A Survey in 46 Countries: Accounting Principles and Reporting Practices* (October 1975).

13-18 Shank, John K., and Gary S. Shamis, "Reporting Foreign Currency Adjustment: A Disclosure Perspective," *The Journal of Accountancy* (April 1979), pp. 56-65.

13-19 Schoenfield, Hanns-Martin, "International Accounting: Development Issues, and Future Directions," *Journal of International Business Studies* (Fall 1981), pp. 83-100.

13-20 Wallace, Wanda A., "Internal Control Reporting: 950 Negative Responses," *CPA Journal* (January 1981), pp. 30-38.

13-21 Watt, George C., Richard M. Hammer, and Marianne Burge, *Accounting for the Multinational Corporation* (New York: Financial Executives Research Foundation, 1977).

13-22 Williams, Harold M., "The Accounting Provisions of the Foreign Corrupt Practices Act: An Analysis," SEC Release No. 34-17500 (February 9, 1981).

FOURTEEN

INTERNATIONAL TAXATION

Usually one of the most important variables to consider in multinational operations is the area of taxation. Perhaps no environmental variable, with the possible exception of foreign exchange, has such a pervasive influence on all aspects of multinational operations as taxation: (1) the choice of location in the investment decision, (2) the form of the new enterprise, (3) method of finance, and (4) method of transfer pricing.[1]

International taxation is a complicated variable because tax laws differ among countries and are constantly changing. Hence, it is not accidental to note that international taxation still remains somewhat of a mystery for many international executives. For example, multinational financial managers need to understand the following:[2] (1) Shareholders of foreign and domestic corporations are subject to different rules. (2) Accounting for foreign taxes on foreign operations is not identical with that on domestic operations. (3) Bilateral tax treaties and foreign tax credits exist to avoid double taxation of

[1] Albert J. Radler, "Taxation Policy in Multinational Companies," in *The Multinational Enterprise in Transition*, ed., A. Kapoor and Philip D. Grubb (Princeton, N. J.: The Darwin Press, 1972), p. 30.

[2] Frederick D. S. Choi and Gerhard G. Mueller, *An Introduction to Multinational Accounting* (Englewood Cliffs, N. J.: Prentice-Hall, Inc., 1978), pp. 282-283.

income. (4) Many countries offer a number of tax incentives in an effort to attract foreign capital and know-how. (5) Tax savings realized in low tax countries may be offset by taxes on undistributed earnings.

There are many such added complexities because governments have failed to come to any general agreement on tax policies. Each country has its own tax philosophies, tax incentives, transfer pricing policies, etc. Multinational financial managers must sort them out in order to maximize profitability and cash flow. In order for them to do so, they must acquaint themselves with the overall tax environment. Thus, this chapter covers such general topics as national tax environments, avoiding double taxation, tax incentives, and taxation of U. S. citizens abroad.

NATIONAL TAX ENVIRONMENTS

Each country has its own array of taxes. This makes it imperative that the multinational company seek local tax counsel in each country that it operates. Differences among national tax systems include assessment philosophies, collection purposes, tax computations, and tax procedures. This section describes various manifestations of these differences such as tax philosophies, types of taxes, tax morality, and tax burdens.

Tax Philosophies

A country can claim the right to tax income either on a global basis or on a territorial basis. Global claims assume that countries have the right to tax a firm and all its foreign subsidiaries. Such a firm may be domiciled, incorporated, or otherwise headquartered within their borders. Under this system, overseas earnings could be taxed twice. A German subsidiary of an American company may have to pay both U. S. and German taxes on income earned in Germany. Fortunately, some relief from double taxation is granted by most countries whose tax systems are based on global claims. Nevertheless, most multinational companies feel that global claims put them at a competitive disadvantage. Tax treaties and/or tax credit for taxes paid to foreign governments do not completely eliminate double taxation, while local companies pay only local taxes.

Under the principles of national sovereignty, countries claim the right to tax income earned within their own territory. These territorial claims are very popular with multinational companies, but not as popular with governments. Such financial centers as Hong Kong and Switzerland plus many Latin American countries do not tax their firms' income earned overseas.[3]

Types of Taxes

Multinational companies face a variety of direct and indirect taxes. Direct taxes include corporate income and capital gains taxes. Indirect taxes include value-added taxes, tariffs, and withholding taxes. In addition to these direct and indirect taxes, multinational companies may have to pay property taxes, payroll taxes, stamp and registration taxes, taxes on registrations of agreements of various types, sales and excise taxes (excluding value-added taxes), and taxes on undistributed earnings.

Income and Capital Gains Taxes. As with individual income taxes, corporate income taxes are an important source of revenue for many countries. Because most developing countries have low per capita income, individual income taxes or sales taxes are not very appropriate. Thus, developing countries obtain a larger share of government revenues from corporate income taxes than industrial countries.

Gains and losses on sales of capital assets are called capital gains and losses. Capital assets are generally defined as those assets that are not primarily for resale and that are not acquired in the ordinary course of business. These assets include stocks and bonds. If capital assets are held longer than a specified period of time, gains on sales of these assets may be subject to preferential tax treatment.

Value-Added Taxes. Value-added taxes are a special type of sales taxes. Sales taxes are those taxes assessed at one or more stages in the production process. In Canada, sales taxes are levied when production is complete; in England, when products are wholesaled; in the United States, when products are retailed; and in Germany, at all stages in the production cycle.

To avoid the compounding effect of sales taxes, many European

[3] David A. Ricks, *International Dimensions of Corporate Finance* (Englewood Cliffs, N. J.: Prentice-Hall, Inc., 1978), p. 9.

countries have adopted the value-added tax as the major source of revenue. This tax is levied at each stage of development in production to the value added during that particular stage. For example, if a car dealer purchased a car for $10,000 from a car manufacturing company and then sold it for $15,000, the value added would be $5,000 and the tax levied on this increment.

Tariffs. Tariffs are simply taxes assessed on imported goods which parallel excise and other indirect taxes paid by domestic producers of similar goods. They may be imposed for purposes of revenue or protection. When tariffs are employed to increase revenues, they are usually modest. However, when tariffs are used to protect domestic companies from foreign competition, they are typically high. Although protective tariffs do not eliminate the importation of foreign products completely, they clearly put foreign sellers at a comparative disadvantage. In this instance, consumers must pay more for foreign goods, which in turn would reduce their consumption of imported commodities.

Withholding Taxes. Withholding taxes are those taxes imposed by host governments on dividend and interest payments to foreign investors and debtholders. These taxes are collected before receipt of the income. In other words, they are usually withheld at the source by the paying corporation. For example, a 20 percent withholding tax on $10,000 interest payments to foreigners means that the tax proceeds of $2,000 are deducted from the interest payment made to the lender and collected by the borrower on behalf of the government. Hence, the purchaser of the bonds would receive only $8,000 or 80 percent of the $10,000 interest payment. Withholding taxes frequently restrict the international movement of long-term investment capital. Hence, they are generally modified by bilateral tax treaties.

Tax Morality

The issue at stake is the conflict between economics (profits) and ethics (corporate morality). Some businessmen think that profits are one thing and corporate morality is another. This assumption leads them to conclude that they have to make a choice. It is well known that in many countries both corporate and individual taxpayers are not completely honest with their tax authorities. Multinational companies must decide whether to voluntarily comply with the tax laws. Although most multinational companies comply fully with the tax laws, some companies feel that to protect their competitive position, they should evade taxes to the same extent as their competitors. Because business ethics are partly a function of cultural patterns and historic development, ethical standards vary greatly among people, companies, and societies. Therefore, there is obviously no universally accepted answer to the problem.

Host governments also have a similar morale problem. Two of the most basic tax principles are that taxes should be equitable and neutral. In other words, taxes should be fair to everyone and they should not affect decisions in the economic system. Nevertheless, many countries have imposed some arbitrary tax penalties on multinational companies for presumed violations of local tax laws. Many developing countries have various tax incentive programs for private foreign investments. These tax incentive programs abandon the principle of an economically neutral system. Under a neutral tax system, supply and demand should be left alone to determine prices and economic activity if we want the most efficient economic system.

Tax Burdens

Because different countries have varying statutory rates of income tax, differences in overall tax burdens are another natural feature of international business operations. The corporate tax rate ranges from as low as zero in such tax haven countries as the Bahamas to as high as 60 percent in such countries as Libya.

Differences in definitions of taxable corporate income create greater disparities than differences in nominal corporate tax rates. Thus, differential tax rates tell us only part of the story. In one country taxable income may be computed on a cash basis while in another country it may be determined on an accrual basis. Investment allowances and credits, reserves, the timing of depreciation deductions, and asset valuations vary greatly from country to country. Some countries provide companies with full credit for taxes on the income paid in other countries.

Tax systems also affect relative tax burdens internationally. In general, there are three classes of systems: single tax, double tax, and partial double tax. Under the single tax system, income is taxed only once. If corporations pay no taxes, their stockholders pay taxes on dividends. Under the double tax system, corporations pay taxes on profits at a given rate and dividends are then taxed as income to stockholders at their personal income tax rates. Under the partial double tax system, taxes are levied on corporate income, but dividends are taxed at a lower rate than other forms of personal income.

Or distributed corporate earnings are taxed at a lower rate than undistributed earnings (retained earnings).

Table 14-1 lists statutory income and withholding tax rates that foreign investors may be subject to if they conduct a business or make an investment in the named countries. It should be noted that all listed corporate income and withholding tax rates represent the highest possible tax rate in each category. It is also important to recognize that all these tax rates were in effect as of November 30, 1981.[4]

Table 14-1 Foreign Income and Withholding Tax Rates

Country	Domestic Income	Foreign Income	Dividends	Interest	Royalties
Europe					
Belgium	48%	54%	20%	20%	20%
Denmark	37	37	30	0	0
France	50	50	25	33	33
Germany	56	50	25	0	25
Greece	43	43	47	43	17
Ireland	45	45	35	35	35
Italy	25	25	30	20	14
Netherlands	48	48	25	0	0
Norway	51	51	25	0	0
Spain	33	33	15	15	15
Sweden	40	40	30	0	0
Switzerland	10	10	35	0	0
United Kingdom	52	52	0	33	33
The Americas					
Argentina	33	45	17	11	18
Brazil	32	32	25	25	25
Canada	46	46	25	25	25
Colombia	40	52	20	0	47
Mexico	42	42	21	42	46
U. S. A.	46	46	30	30	30
Venezuela	50	50	20	15	90
Others					
Australia	46	46	30	10	46
Hong Kong	17	17	0	15	17
Japan	40	20	20	20	20
Korea	40	25	25	25	25
Singapore	40	40	0	40	40
South Africa	42	42	15	10	13

Source: Ernst & Whinney, *Foreign and U. S. Corporate Income and Withholding Tax Rates* (December 1981).

[4] Ernst and Whinney, *Foreign and U. S. Corporate Income and Withholding Tax Rates* (January 1982).

AVOIDING DOUBLE TAXATION

Corporate foreign earnings are frequently taxed both in the country of origin and in the country that the company has its headquarters. Tax treaties and foreign tax credits are widely used to avoid double taxation of income.

Tax Treaties

Countries enter into bilateral tax treaties to avoid double taxation and thus to encourage the free flow of investments internationally. Treaty countries agree on how taxes will be imposed, shared, or otherwise eliminated on business income earned in one taxing jurisdiction by nationals of another.

Over the last 50 years, international organizations have drafted models to standardize the treaties. The League of Nations drafted the first model in 1929 and this model was followed by the so-called Model Conventions of Mexico (1943) and London (1946).[5] The Organization for Economic Coorporation and Development (OECD) developed the recent model called "the Draft Double Taxation Convention on Income and Capital" in 1963 and this model was revised in 1974. The OECD is a governmental body which consists of 24 member countries, most of which are industrial countries. The purpose of the OECD is to encourage economic growth of its members and nonmembers in the field of international trade and investment. The 1963 Draft Model Convention has become an essential document in guiding tax treaty negotiators and tax advisors.

Most tax treaties now in effect are agreements between industrial countries. Because most industrial countries are both capital exporting and importing countries, they have common interests in such areas as reduction of withholding taxes on corporate foreign income and royalties. Fewer treaties have been signed between developed and developing countries. To overcome this problem, in 1967 the United Nations established a Group of Tax Experts on Tax Treaties. In 1974 they issued Guidelines on Tax Treaties between developed and developing countries. Recent U. S. tax treaties are based on the OECD model. In May 1976, the U. S. Treasury Department pub-

[5] George C. Watt, Richard M. Hammer, and Marianne Burge, *Accounting for the Multinational Corporation* (New York: Financial Executive Research Foundation, 1977), p. 404.

lished its own Model Income Tax Treaty which represents the provisions of future U. S. tax treaties.[6]

The provisions of most tax treaties override the provisions of national income tax laws. For example, Section 894 of the U. S. Internal Revenue Code states that "income of any kind, to the extent required by any treaty obligation of the United States, shall not be included in gross income and shall be exempt from taxation under this subtitle." Thus, U. S. tax treaties provide that profits earned by U. S. companies in a foreign country are exempt from taxation unless they have permanent establishment in the foreign country. Tax treaties also reduce withholding taxes on dividends, interest, and royalties.

Table 14-2 shows various rates of withholding taxes imposed by countries with which the United States has a tax treaty. The with-

Table 14-2 Foreign Withholding Rates Under U. S. Income Tax Treaties

Country (1)	Dividends %	Interest %	Patent and Know-How Royalties (2) %
Australia	15	N/A	N/A
Austria	10(3)	E	E
Belgium	15	15	E
Canada	15(9)	15	15(9)
Denmark	15(3)	E	E
France	15(3)(10)	10(11)	5
Germany (West)	15(4)	E	E
Greece	N/A	E(5)	E
Ireland (Republic of)	N/A	E(5)	E
Italy	15(3)	N/A	E
Japan	15(3)	10	10
Korea (South)	15(3)	12	15
Luxembourg	7.5(3)	E	E
Netherlands	15(3)	E	E
New Zealand	N/A	15	15(7)
Norway	15(3)	E	E
Sierra Leone	15(3)	N/A	E
South Africa (Republic of)	N/A	N/A	N/A
Sweden	15(3)	E	E
Switzerland	15(3)	5	E
Trinidad & Tobago	25(3)	15(8)	15
United Kingdom	N/A(6)	E	E

Definitions: E–The income is exempt from withholding tax under the treaty. N/A–The treaty does not limit the tax applicable to this type of income.

Notes:

(1) The U. S. also has income tax treaties with the following countries: Barbados, Congo,

[6] For details, see *Ibid.*, pp. 406-409.

Table 14-2 continued

Finland, Hungary, Iceland, Jamaica, Malawi, Netherlands Antilles, Pakistan, Poland, Romania, Rwanda, U.S.S.R., and Zambia.

(2) The term royalties means income derived from the use of such property as patents, designs, secret processes and formula, trademarks, and know-how.

(3) The treaty withholding tax rate is reduced to 5% (10% in the case of Japan, Korea (South), Norway, and Trinidad and Tobago) if, among other conditions, the recipient is a corporation owning a specified percentage of the voting power of the distributing corporation.

(4) The treaty withholding tax rate increases to 25% if the recipient (a) owns at least 10% of the voting shares of the distributing corporation, and (b) reinvests more than 7.5% of the amount received in the distributing corporation.

(5) Exemption does not apply if the recipient corporation controls directly or indirectly more than 50% of the voting power of the paying corporation, and in the case of Greece if interest is in excess of 9% per annum.

(6) Dividends from U. K. corporations are subject to Advance Corporation Tax (ACT), a portion of which is refunded to U. S. shareholders.

(7) Election may be made to be taxed in country of origin. U. S. taxpayer could elect to be assessed in New Zealand if deductions for expenses mean a smaller liability than the 15% withholding tax. If know-how payment is wholly covered by deductible expenses, no liability exists for withholding tax.

(8) Applies only for interest paid to banks and other financial institutions.

(9) Under the new Canada-U. S. tax treaty awaiting ratification in both countries, withholding tax on dividends will be reduced to 10% where the recipient company owns at least 10% of the voting shares of the payor company, and the withholding tax on royalties will be reduced to 10%.

(10) Tax on profits of French branch limited to 10%.

(11) No withholding on bank loan interest.

(12) As of November 30, 1981, new or revised treaties with the following countries have been ratified by the U. S. Senate but had not yet become effective: Bangladesh, Egypt, Israel, Norway, Malta, and Morocco. New or revised treaties with the following countries were awaiting ratification by the U. S. Senate on that date: Argentina, Canada, Jamaica, and the Philippines.

Source: Ernst & Whinney, *Foreign and U. S. Corporate Income and Withholding Tax Rates* (December 1981), p. 30.

holding tax rates may not apply if the U. S. corporation has a permanent establishment in the treaty country. It should be noted that all withholding tax rates were in effect as of November 30, 1981 and these withholding tax rates are considerably lower than the statutory rates in Table 14-1.

Foreign Tax Credit

The purpose of the foreign tax credit is to avoid international double taxation when profits earned abroad become subject to the full tax levies of two or more countries. Under the foreign tax credit system, the United States relinquishes tax on profits earned abroad up to the amount of the foreign tax. Thus, the foreign government takes the first bite of profits earned in its jurisdiction. In addition, taxes subject to these credit provisions include withholding taxes on dividends, interest, and other income.

Example 14-1 Assume: (1) a U. S. corporation has $1,000 of foreign income; (2) the foreign country's tax rate is 40 percent; and (3) the U. S. tax rate is 50 percent. The net U. S. tax of $100 is computed as follows:

Foreign income	$1,000
Foreign tax (40%)	400
Net income after tax	$ 600
U. S. taxable income	$1,000
U. S. tax (50%)	$ 500
Foreign tax credit	400
U. S. tax payable	$ 100
Total foreign and U. S. taxes	$ 500
Effective tax rate	50%

As this example illustrates, the purpose of the foreign tax credit is to limit the total foreign income to the higher tax rate of the two countries. If the foreign tax on income earned abroad and remitted to the United States is less than or equal to the U. S. tax rate, that income will be subject to a total tax of 50 percent. Thus, if the foreign tax rate is lower than the U. S. rate, the U. S. government receives some tax revenues on the foreign income. If the foreign tax rate is higher than the U. S. rate, the U. S. government receives no tax revenues on the foreign income.

As an alternative to the foreign tax credit, U. S. companies can treat any foreign tax paid directly as a deductible expense. Because both a credit and deduction cannot be claimed in the same year, the U. S. company must decide whcther to claim the credit or deduction for foreign income taxes. In general, it is advantageous to claim a credit against federal income tax rather than a deduction.

Example 14-2 Assume: (1) a U. S. corporation has $1,000 of foreign income; (2) the foreign country's tax rate is 50 percent; and (3) the U. S. tax rate is 50 percent. The following computation shows that the credit is better than the deduction:

	Foreign Tax Credit	Foreign Tax Deduction
Foreign income	$1,000	$1,000
Foreign tax (50%)	500	500
Net income after tax	500	500
U. S. taxable income	$1,000	$ 500
U. S. tax (50%)	$ 500	$ 250
Foreign tax payable	500	0
U. S. tax payable	$ 0	$ 250
Total foreign and U. S. taxes	$ 500	$ 750
Effective tax rate	50%	75%

TAX INCENTIVES FOR FOREIGN INVESTMENT

Many countries, especially developing countries, offer a number of tax incentives in an effort to attract foreign capital and know-how to their countries. The two basic forms of tax incentive programs are government concessions and tax havens.

Government Concessions

Many concessions are offered by developing countries in order to attract multinational companies. Most concessions are in the form of a complete tax exemption for the first few years, known as "tax holidays." Some other forms of temporary tax concessions include reduced income tax rates, tax credits on new investments, tax deferrals, and reduction or elimination of various indirect taxes. These concessions, along with lower labor costs in relation to developed countries, have made many developing countries attractive for assembly and manufacturing operations.

Tax Havens

Some countries promise permanent tax inducements in order to attract multinational companies. Such countries are known as tax havens and have few natural resources. In addition to low tax rates, tax havens must have a stable government, good communication facilities, freedom of currency movements, and the availability of financial services. Tax havens may be classified into four broad categories: (1) the Bahamas, Bermuda, and the Cayman Islands, which have no taxes; (2) the British Virgin Islands and Gibraltar, which have very low taxes; (3) Hong Kong, Liberia, and Panama, which assess taxes on income from domestic sources but impose no taxes on income from foreign sources; and (4) countries that permit special privileges to make them suitable as tax havens for very limited purposes.[7]

A large number of non-U. S. multinational companies have foreign affiliates which act as tax havens for corporate funds. These corporate funds are held in the tax havens until they are reinvested or repatriated elsewhere. Tax-haven affiliates are the outgrowth of tax-deferral features on foreign earnings allowed by some parent countries to their multinational companies. Normally, parent companies can defer taxes on their foreign earnings until these earnings are received as dividends.

The U. S. government originally permitted U. S. companies to defer taxes on their foreign earnings so that they could invest abroad and compete on an equal footing with foreign companies. Unfortunately, these tax-deferral features were frequently used by U. S. companies to avoid U. S. taxes. Typically, U. S. parent companies established a foreign holding company with a tax haven domicile. The major purpose of such a tax-haven corporation was to receive tax free the profits earned by its operating subsidiaries. For example, these holding companies would receive the exclusive right to export the products of the parent company. This makes it possible for a portion of the profits to shift from the parent to the foreign holding company. Similar mechanisms were often used by some U. S. companies to avoid taxes on royalties and other foreign-source income.

The U. S. Revenue Act of 1962 introduced Subpart F to prevent U. S. multinational companies from using tax havens in order to avoid U. S. and foreign taxes. The Revenue Reduction Act of 1975 and the Revenue Reform Act of 1976 tightened the Subpart F rules. Under this provision, taxes are imposed on undistributed foreign base company income or Subpart F income (defined below) of controlled foreign corporations. A controlled foreign corporation is a foreign corporation in which more than 50 percent of the voting shares are owned by U. S. shareholders. For the purpose of arriving at the per-

[7] Jean Doucet and Kenneth J. Good, "What Makes a Good Tax Haven," *Banker* (May 1973), p. 493.

centage of control, only shareholders holding more than ten percent of the voting power are counted.

The term "foreign base company" is used to describe a corporation whose base or registration is in a country in which it does not conduct active operations. Foreign base company income includes foreign personal holding company income, foreign base company sales income, foreign base company service income, and foreign base company shipping income.

There are a number of exceptions to the general rule. (1) If controlled foreign corporations domiciled in developing countries reinvest their earnings in these countries, Subpart F provisions do not apply. (2) If the combination of U. S. and foreign taxes paid on all income of the controlled foreign corporation is close to the U. S. tax rate, Subpart F provisions do not apply. (3) If foreign base company income is less than ten percent of the controlled foreign company's gross income, Subpart F provisions do not apply.

U. S. Tax Incentives

To encourage certain business activities in specific areas of the world, the United States has introduced a number of tax incentives into its tax provisions over the years. The U. S. tax incentives involve five types of operations: (1) operations in the Western Hemisphere (Western Hemisphere Trade Corporation), (2) operations in U. S. possessions (Possessions Corporation), (3) export operations (Domestic International Sales Corporation), (4) export operations (Export Trade Corporation), and (5) operations in developing countries (Less Developed Country Corporation). The first three types of operations involve operations by domestic corporations and the last two types of operations involve foreign operations. Operations (1), (4), and (5) have been phased out during the last few years.

Possessions Corporation. A U. S. firm engaged in business within a United States possession obtains tax advantages if it meets certain requirements: (1) It is a domestic U. S. corporation. (2) At least 80 percent of its gross income for the last three years is derived from sources within a possession of the United States. (3) At least 50 percent of its gross income results from the active conduct of a trade or business within a possession of the United States. A possessions corporation is a U. S. corporation that meets these three requirements. Possessions of the United States are the Panama Canal Zone, Guam, American Samoa, Wake and Midway Islands, and Puerto Rico. The Virgin Islands are specifically excluded.

Possessions corporations exclude from U. S. gross income amounts earned outside the United States unless the income is received in the United States. Hence, they would arrange to receive their income initially outside the United States even though they may subsequently transfer the income from foreign bank accounts to bank accounts in the United States. When possessions corporations pay dividends to their U. S. parent company, the parent treats the dividends as if they were received from foreign corporations and can claim direct and deemed paid foreign tax credits.

Possessions corporations are treated in most ways as foreign corporations, but there are two important exceptions. (1) They are treated as domestic corporations for purposes of organization, reorganization, and liquidation. (2) They are not treated as controlled foreign corporations for Subpart F purposes.

Domestic International Sales Corporation. To provide a tax incentive for U. S. companies to increase their exports, the Revenue Act of 1971 introduced a system of tax deferral for a new type of U. S. corporation called a Domestic International Sales Corporation (DISC). Under these new rules, the DISC's earnings are not taxed to the DISC but instead are taxed to the stockholders when distributed or deemed distributed. Essentially, the DISC can defer U. S. tax on 50 percent of its taxable income, while the other half is deemed distributed and taxed as a dividend to the shareholder. The shareholders of a DISC are entitled to the foreign tax credit for foreign taxes on the DISC.

To qualify as a DISC, a U. S. corporation must satisfy a number of requirements. (1) At least 95 percent of its gross income must be qualified export receipts. Qualified export receipts are income from exports, receipts from the lease of export property for use by the lessee outside the United States, and certain related income. (2) At least 95 percent of its assets at the end of the taxable year must be qualified export assets. Qualified export assets are export property produced in the United States and held for exports, assets used in relation to export activities, accounts receivable arising in connection with exports, and working capital reasonably needed for operations. (3) It must have at least $2,500 of capital on each day of the taxable year and only one class of stock. (4) It must make an election during the 90-day period immediately before the beginning of the taxable year.

The 1976 Tax Reform Act substantially eliminated the DISC tax deferral for all except new DISCs and DISCs which increase their exports over a four-year base period. DISC tax benefits from 1976 to 1979 are available for the gain in average annual export profits over a

1972-1976 base period. After 1976, the base period moves to be the fourth, fifth, sixth, and seventh preceding years. Under this incremental approach, the export profit base level is 67 percent of the annual export profit over the four-year period. Because new DISCs have no effective base period for the first four years, all export income qualifies for DISC tax benefits. In the fifth year the fourth preceding year becomes the base period. After the fifth year the fourth and fifth preceding years become the base period. Table 14-3 shows base-period years for various taxable years.

Although there are many kinds of DISC, they are most commonly formed by U. S. manufacturers to export merchandise. In addition to deferring income tax, the Internal Revenue Code allows DISCs to use more liberal transfer pricing policies. In order to concentrate profits in the DISCs, they are allowed to buy export inventory from their parent at a price lower than the arm's-length price. DISCs are also allowed to lend some of their deferred profits to their shareholder (the producer company) for a variety of export-related activities. Such loans are not considered as dividends and thus are not taxed.

TAXATION OF U. S. CITIZENS ABROAD

Every country has the right to tax earnings of its citizens. But the United States goes far beyond most industrial countries by taxing the worldwide income of its citizens. According to a 1979 survey of Business International, the United States was the only industrial country that taxed its expatriates on worldwide income.[8] This has

Table 14-3 Base Period Years for Various Taxable Years

Taxable Year	Base Period	
	Existing DISC	New DISC Formed in 1976
1976	1972-1975	–
1977	1972-1975	–
1978	1972-1975	–
1979	1972-1975	–
1980	1973-1976	1976
1981	1974-1977	1976-1977
1982	1975-1978	1977-1978
1983	1976-1979	1978-1979
1984	1977-1980	1979-1980

[8] *Wall Street Journal* (February 8, 1979), p. 2.

compelled U. S. multinational companies to pay their expatriates more or to replace their expatriates with local people.[9]

Some tax reliefs for U. S. citizens abroad were provided by the Foreign Earned Income Act of 1978, which allowed the deductions for cost of living, housing, schooling, home leave travel, and hardship area. These deductions are repealed for 1982 and thereafter, because the Economic Recovery Tax Act of 1981 completely overhauls the U. S. tax treatment of U. S. citizens working abroad.

Perhaps the most significant feature of the 1981 Act is the reintroduction of an exclusion of foreign earned income which existed prior to 1978. The new earned income exclusion is equal to $75,000 beginning in 1982 and increasing $5,000 annually to $95,000 in 1986:

Tax Year	*Earned Income Exclusion*
1982	$75,000
1983	80,000
1984	85,000
1985	90,000
1986	95,000

For 1982 and subsequent years, U. S. taxpayers will be able to exclude and/or deduct foreign housing costs in excess of a base amount (currently $6,059).

In high tax countries such as Belgium and Germany, the overall tax cost will be almost the same under both the new law and the old law because the employee will have no U. S. tax liability under either law. Under the old law, his earned income will be reduced by the deductions for excess foreign living costs and his U. S. tax liability will be completely offset by the high foreign taxes he pays to foreign countries. Under the new law, he may have no foreign earned income in excess of the annual exclusion and thus no U. S. tax liability. Expatriates who reside in low tax countries such as Saudi Arabia and Hong Kong will pay less U. S. tax under the 1981 Act.[10] Table 4-4 compares the old and new laws affecting U. S. citizens abroad.

SUMMARY

Multinational taxation has a significant impact on the choice of location in the initial investment decision, form of the new enterprise,

[9] Jeffrey S. Arpan and Lee H. Radebaugh, *International Accounting and Multinational Enterprises* (Boston: Warren, Gorham & Lamont, Inc., 1981), p. 282.

[10] Ernst and Whinney, *The New Tax Law for U. S. Citizens Abroad* (November 1981), pp. 1-2.

Table 14-4 Comparison of Old and New Laws Affecting U. S. Citizens Abroad

Provision	Old Law	New Law
Deduction for Excess Foreign Living Costs	Deductions allowed for housing, cost of living, schooling, home leave travel and hardship area.	None
Earned Income Exclusion	$20,000 exclusion of foreign earned income for employees residing in a hardship area camp or performing charitable services in a lesser-developed country.	$75,000 exclusion of foreign earned income in 1982 increasing $5,000 a year to $95,000 for 1986 and thereafter. Exclusion and/or deduction for foreign housing expenses in excess of a base housing amount (currently $6,059).
Bona Fide Residence Test	U. S. citizen must be bona fide resident of foreign country or countries for an entire tax year.	Same
Physical Presence Test	U. S. citizens and resident aliens must be physically present in a foreign country or countries for 510 full days during any 18 consecutive-month period.	U. S. citizens and resident aliens must be physically present in a foreign country or countries for 330 full days during any 12 consecutive-month period.
Election Provision	Election not to claim the exclusion applies to all future years and cannot be revoked without consent of IRS Commissioner.	Election made separately for annual foreign earned income and housing exclusions. Election applies to all subsequent years and can be revoked with or without consent of IRS Commissioner. If election revoked without consent, it may not be reelected for the next 5 years.
Denial of Double Benefits		
Credits	Foreign taxes attributable to excluded earned income are not allowed as a credit.	Same
Deductions	Deductions (such as unreimbursed employee business expenses) attributable to excluded income are not allowed. Moving expense deduction specifically exempt from this disallowance rule.	All deductions (including moving expenses) attributable to excluded and earned income are not allowed.

Table 14-4 continued

Provision	Old Law	New Law
Exclusions	None	Exclusions (such as the exclusion of meals and lodging furnished for the convenience of an employer) attributable to excluded earned income are not allowed.
Exclusion of Camp Meals and Lodging	Taxpayers electing the earned income exclusion and residing in foreign camps in designated hardship areas can exclude value of employer furnished meals and lodging provided the lodging is substandard.	Taxpayers residing in foreign camps may exclude value of employer furnished meals and lodging. No election required and the hardship area and substandard lodging requirements no longer apply.

Source: Ernst & Whinney, *The New Tax Law for U. S. Citizens Abroad* (November 1981), p. 4.

method of finance, and many other international financial decisions. Tax planning for multinational operations involves complex problems such as national tax environments, double taxation, and various tax incentive programs. Thus, it is highly desirable that multinational companies seek the inputs of experienced tax and legal counsel in both parent and host countries. Nevertheless, to preserve profit opportunities abroad and receive special tax incentives, it is important for the financial manager of a multinational company to be acquainted with the national tax environments and other tax problems in the host countries in which the company operates.

REFERENCES

14-1 Arpan, Jeffrey S., and Lee H. Radebaugh, *International Accounting and Multinational Enterprises* (New York: Warren, Gorham and Lamont, 1981), Chapter 11.

14-2 Bruece, Charles M., "New Rules Taxing Americans Working Abroad," *Taxes* (February 1979), pp. 79-84.

14-3 Burns, Jane O., "Exports and the Tax Reform Act of 1976," *International Tax Journal* (February 1978), pp. 810-823.

14-4 Choi, Federick D. A., and Gerhard G. Mueller, *An Introduction to Multinational Accounting* (Englewood Cliffs, N. J.: Prentice-Hall, Inc., 1978), Chapter 8.

14-5 Cliff, Walter C., "Pairing: A Technique for Avoiding CFC Status and Other Burdens of U. S. Taxation," *Taxes* (August 1979), pp. 530-537.

14-6 Ernst and Whinney, *Foreign and U. S. Corporate Income and Withholding Tax Rates* (December 1981).

14-7 Ernst and Whinney, *Hypothetical Tax Tables for U. S. Citizens Abroad* (December 1981).

14-8 Feiger, George, and Bertrand Jacquillat, *International Finance* (Boston: Allyn and Bacon, Inc., 1982), Chapter 12.

14-9 Kalish, Richard H., "Intercompany Pricing: How to Handle an International Tax Examination," *Tax Adviser* (April 1978), pp. 196-218.

14-10 Patrick, Robert J., Jr., "A Comparison of the U. S. and OECD Model Income Tax Conventions," *Law and Policy in International Business* (1978), pp. 613-718.

14-11 Sanden, B. Kenneth, "VAT: What, How, Where," *Tax Adviser* (March 1973), pp. 150-157.

14-12 Watt, George C., Richard M. Hammer, and Marianne Burge, *Accounting for the Multinational Corporation* (New York: Financial Executives Research Foundation, 1977), Part IV.

FIFTEEN

INTERNATIONAL TRANSFER PRICING*

The advent of U. S.-based multinational corporations and their continued growth have added another, more complicated dimension to transfer pricing. The complications arise because international transfer pricing must meet not only the objectives of the management control process, but also a wide variety of other objectives. These other objectives are sometimes so important that the objectives of goal congruence (profit maximization) and performance evaluation are considered secondary or unachievable. Thus, it is important that the type of objectives involved in international transfer pricing and their effect on transfer prices be understood thoroughly.

This chapter is divided into two closely related sections. The first section is a discussion of additional objectives a company might consider when establishing prices for transfers across national boundaries. The second section elaborates on one of these objectives, tax minimization, with a discussion of Section 482 of the Internal Revenue Code and its implications for international transfer pricing.

*Ralph L. Benke, Jr. and James Don Edwards, *Transfer Pricing: Techniques and Uses* (New York: National Association of Accountants, 1980), Chapter 6. Reprinted with the permission of the National Association of Accountants, © 1980.

INTERNATIONAL TRANSFER PRICING OBJECTIVES

In establishing international transfer prices, a firm must try to satisfy a number of objectives not relevant to domestic transfer pricing. For example, the firm wants to minimize taxes and at the same time win approval from the government of the host country. Yet the basic objectives of profit maximization and performance evaluation also are important. Often it is not possible to satisfy all these objectives simultaneously, so a company must decide which objectives are the most important. As a result, a particular transfer price, rather than evolving from a transfer pricing technique, may be established arbitrarily to fulfill an objective involving international considerations. The discussion that follows examines some of these objectives.[1]

Income Tax Minimization

By far the most persuasive objective in international transfer pricing is tax minimization. The economic advantages are obvious and immediate if a transfer price shifts profit from a country with a high tax rate to a country with a low tax rate. For example, if a product is being manufactured in a country with a favorable tax structure, a high transfer price will result in more of the profit from the sale of the product being taxed at the favorable rate. An example of using transfer pricing to minimize income taxes is shown in Exhibit 15-1.

As the example in Exhibit 15-1 has shown, tax minimization via transfer pricing is a simple process. When a firm minimizes taxes by shifting profit between countries, however, other objectives of transfer pricing, such as performance evaluation and profit maximization, may become harder, if not impossible, to attain.

On the surface it would appear that tax minimization would meet the objective of profit maximization, but whether it does or not depends upon the specific circumstances. It is unlikely, however, that a transfer price which minimizes taxes also will guide a company toward profit-maximizing decisions such as whether to sell a product internally or externally or whether to invest in additional productive facilities. Furthermore, a program of tax minimization may result in different transfer prices for the same product transferred to different countries, so foreign affiliates in different countries will have differ-

[1] This section is influenced by James S. Shulman, *Transfer Pricing in Multinational Business*, Soldiers Field Press, Massachusetts, 1975, pp. 18-33.

Exhibit 15-1
Tax Minimization

	Manufacture in Country A		Sell in Country B		Company View
Sales Price			$ 200		$ 200
Transfer Price	$ 100	→	($ 100)		
Variable Costs	(60)	+	(30)	=	(90)
Contribution Margin Per Unit	$ 40	+	$ 70	=	$ 110
Number of Units	×1,000		×1,000		×1,000
Total Contribution Margin	$40,000	+	$70,000	=	$110,000
Fixed Costs	(10,000)	+	(4,000)	=	(14,000)
Profit	$30,000	+	$66,000	=	$96,000
Tax Rate	×.2		×.4		
Tax Payable	$ 6,000	+	$26,400	=	(32,400)
Company Profit					$63,600

In the example above, the transfer price of $100 per unit results in $30,000 of the ultimate profit of $96,000 remaining in the country with the 20 percent tax rate. Clearly, it is to the economic benefit of the company to raise the transfer price as high as the government in Country B will allow. In so doing, more of the profit is shifted into Country A and taxed at a lower rate.

For example, if the government of Country B will allow a transfer price of $150 per unit, $50,000 of the $70,000 contribution margin in Country B will be shifted back to Country A, giving Country A a total contribution margin of $90,000 with tax of $16,000. The tax in Country B will decline from $26,400 to $6,400. Thus, a transfer price of $150 per unit gives the same before-tax profit of $96,000 but increases the after-tax profit from $63,600 to $73,600 because of the $10,000 reduction in total tax.

ent transfer prices with which to make other profit maximizing decisions.

The other objective, performance evaluation, is even more difficult to attain when the objective of tax minimization is pursued. The profit in one country will be greater than the profit in another country, not because of better management but because of the transfer price. One way around this problem is to establish a separate reporting system for control purposes so performance evaluation is based on more realistic reports.

The tax rate is not the only factor to consider in tax minimization because countries have different requirements for calculating taxable income. Even though Country A has a tax rate of 20 percent on all taxable income and Country B has a 40 percent rate, total taxes may be lower in Country B if, for example, Country A severely restricts deductions for depreciation while Country B does not.

Although income taxation is the most persuasive objective to influence transfer prices, other objectives will from time to time assume a position of importance or perhaps dominance. Among these factors are import duties, avoidance of financial problems, and currency fluctuations.

Import Duties

Import duties, as well as income taxes, can be minimized. For example, a company benefits economically if it transfers products at low prices to a country with high import duties. All other things being equal, the company can reduce the total cost for import duties through transfer pricing.

Although import duty minimization sounds easy, frequently it is complicated because "all other things" are rarely equal. For example, a country with low import duties may have high income taxes, or a country with high import duties may have low income taxes. Another factor is the tax rate of the country from which the product is shipped. Thus, the company must consider import duties along with income taxes in both the shipping and receiving countries. This is a delicate process, as James S. Shulman has noted:

> Adjusting transfer prices for the effects of import and income taxes is a delicate balancing act. For example, the higher the import tax assessed to the importer, the lower the profit remaining as a basis for income taxes. Since there is virtually no coordination of the two revenue-collecting departments in [most countries], the income-tax collecting branch may be unduly exercised. An added difficulty results from the attempt of the parent to balance the extra cost of duty resulting from a high import price paid by its affiliate against the lower income taxes that the affiliate will be charged with, as well as the potentially higher income taxes that the exporting affiliate may be required to remit.[2]

Balancing import duties and income taxes is more complicated than simply minimizing taxes. In order to minimize import duties and income taxes in Belgium, the receiving country, and income taxes in two shipping countries, one company in this study invoiced identical goods into Belgium at different prices. The different prices drew the attention of customs officials and income-tax authorities. The result was a comprehensive review of pricing practices used by

[2] James S. Shulman, "When the Price Is Wrong–By Design," *Columbia Journal of World Business*, May-June 1967, pp. 69-76.

the company in Belgium, which led to required changes in pricing practices and higher total income taxes. In addition, the investigation had a ripple effect. Other countries learned of the investigation, and several started comprehensive reviews of the company's pricing practices in their countries. In addition to all-around higher income taxes, the company suffered a great deal of bad publicity.

Minimization of income taxes and import duties is an important goal. Recently, however, taxing authorities in many countries have begun to pay closer attention to attempts by companies to transfer profit to countries with lower taxes. As one unfortunate company discovered, overzealous efforts to minimize import duties and taxes may result in short-run gains but long-run losses.

Avoiding Financial Problems

Transfer pricing often can be used to circumvent economic restrictions placed on multinational companies by host countries. For example, Israel places severe restrictions on the amount of profit that can leave the country. A way around this is to charge high prices for imports. Of course, a country that imposes such a restriction probably will watch import and export prices closely.

A second economic restriction by some countries is disallowing certain expenses against taxable income. For example, some general administrative expenses or research and development expenses may be disallowed if they are performed elsewhere. Another example is royalty fees charged by management against subsidiary income. To the extent these are disallowed by the host country, the amounts can be recaptured by increasing the price of goods shipped into the country.

Transfer pricing also can be used to improve the financial condition of an affiliate, thereby presenting a favorable profit picture to satisfy earnings criteria by foreign lenders. In this manner the parent company can avoid committing capital to a foreign affiliate, even though the affiliate may be required to secure the loan. Furthermore, besides improving the affiliate's financial picture, low transfer prices provide the affiliate a competitive edge that can be very useful during the startup period of a new venture.

Currency Fluctuations

During periods of currency instability, the performance reports of foreign affiliates can be affected dramatically by exchange rate fluctuations. Many United States-based multinational companies find it convenient to evaluate the performance of foreign affiliates with reports stated in U. S. dollars. If currency exchange rates fluctuate during the performance period, however, it may be difficult to evaluate the performance of the affiliate. At the same time, management of the affiliate often finds it more convenient to evaluate its performance with reports stated in local currency rather than U. S. dollars.

This performance evaluation problem is compounded by transfer pricing unless the transfer price changes with changes in currency values. The difficulties that arise when the transfer prices are not adjusted for currency exchange fluctuations and a proposed solution have been illustrated by Duane Malmstrom and are shown in Exhibits 15-2 and 15-3, respectively.[3]

As a simple solution to the difficulties illustrated in Exhibit 15-2, Malmstrom proposes an indexing formula. The formula, which he refers to as dollar indexing, is shown below:

$$NTP = OTP \times \frac{CER}{PER}$$

where NTP = new transfer price, OTP = old transfer price, CER = current exchange rate, and PER = planned exchange rate. This formula is applied in Exhibit 15-3.

Malmstrom's dollar indexing formula is both simple and effective. The formula is similar to formula used for price-level adjustments in inflation accounting. Furthermore, just as inflation accounting can isolate price-level gains and losses, Malmstrom's dollar indexing formula can isolate operational results and exchange fluctuation results. It also should be noted that the indexing formula shifts the burden of foreign currency fluctuation to Subsidiary A who is in the best position to make decisions that are affected by the fluctuations.

SUMMARY OF INTERNATIONAL OBJECTIVES

A number of international objectives have been discussed–income tax minimization, import duty minimization, adjusting for currency fluctuations, avoiding economic restrictions, and presenting a favor-

[3] Duane Malmstrom, "Accommodating Exchange Rate Fluctuations in Intercompany Pricing and Invoicing," *Management Accounting*, September 1977, pp. 24-28.

Exhibit 15-2

Transfer Prices Not Adjusted for Currency Exchange Fluctuations

Under fixed United States dollar transfer pricing, performance measurement is distorted whenever the actual exchange rates for the producing or purchasing country deviate from the planned exchange rate. For example, suppose Subsidiary A (a manufacturing location) plans to produce and sell 1,000 devices to its affiliated subsidiaries at $10 per unit, the approved transfer price. Suppose also that Subsidiary A's total local currency cost to produce these devices is LCA 18,000 and that the planned exchange rate is $1.00 = LCA2. Thus, the planned P&L's for Subsidiary A, measured in United States dollars and in local currency, will be:

Subsidiary A–Plan

	United States dollars	Exchange rate	Local currency
Sales (intercompany)	$10,000	$1.00 = LCA2	LCA 20,000
Costs	9,000	LCA1 = $.50	18,000
Profit	$ 1,000		LCA 2,000
Percent of sales	10		10

Now suppose that the year actually progresses exactly as planned, except that the United States dollar devalues so that $1.00 = LCA1. Thus, the actual P&L results for Subsidiary A measured in United States dollars and in local currency will be:

Subsidiary A–Results

	United States dollars	Exchange rate	Local currency
Sales (intercompany)	$10,000	$1.00 = LCA1	LCA 10,000
Costs	18,000	LCA1 = $1.00	18,000
Profit	$ (8,000)		LCA (8,000)
Percent of sales	(80)		(80)

As you can see, even though Subsidiary A actually achieved planned device volume and controlled its local currency manufacturing costs precisely as planned, its profit performance was completely obliterated by the exchange rate change. This "distortion" occurred in both the United States dollar P&L and in the local currency P&L.

able financial picture of a foreign affiliate in order to enhance borrowing opportunities or provide a temporary competitive edge. These objectives are not always compatible with the objectives of the management control process, goal congruence (profit maximization) and performance evaluation, so a firm sometimes must maintain one set

Exhibit 15-3

Transfer Prices Adjusted for Currency Exchange Fluctuation

Consider what would happen if all suppositions were the same as in [Exhibit 15-2], except that dollar indexing was in effect. Since Subsidiary A's planned exchange rate was LCA1 = $.50, but the actual exchange rate was LCA1 = $1.00, its dollar transfer prices would be increased through the use of the formula:

$$\text{NTP} = \text{OTP} \times \frac{\text{CER}}{\text{PER}}$$

$$= \$10 \times \frac{\$1.00}{\$\ .50}$$

$$= \$20.00 \text{ per device}$$

Assuming that actual volumes were achieved, at planned local currency costs, Subsidiary A's actual P&L results would be:

Subsidiary A–Results

	United States dollars	Exchange rate	Local currency
Sales (intercompany)	$20,000	$1.00 = LCA1	LCA 20,000
Costs	18,000	LCA1 = $1.00	18,000
Profit	$ 2,000		LCA 2,000
Percent of sales	10		10

As you can see, Subsidiary A actually achieves its planned profit rate, measured in dollars and local currency. Thus, under dollar indexing, factory performance is not distorted due to exchange rate fluctuations.

of books for foreign authorities and another set for parent company performance evaluation purposes.

Sometimes the practice of maintaining two sets of books causes problems. The books used for foreign authorities are likely to be the best known set both inside and outside the company. Managers of foreign affiliates that are profitable by virtue of favorable transfer prices may assume an unjustified aura of superiority over managers of affiliates that are subject to less favorable transfer prices. The parent company management also may overlook, at least temporarily, the source of a profit of a foreign affiliate that enjoys favorable transfer prices. If these situations occur, and they are likely to at least to a small degree, they can cause hard feelings between foreign affiliates or between the parent and foreign affiliates.

In addition, a company must be at least prudent and probably cautious in establishing and changing transfer prices. Authorities in other countries are becoming increasingly sophisticated, and even among third world countries, blatant efforts to shift profit to the obvious detriment of a country will be detected quickly and dealt with swiftly. A considerable amount of goodwill may be lost. On the other hand, a company that consistently pursues policies designed to satisfy to the greatest extent possible the taxing authorities of all host countries, even at some economic sacrifice, can build up goodwill. One company in this study, in order to be as even-handed as possible, established all transfer prices so that the profit on transferred products was split 50-50 between the sending country and the receiving country. This policy ended the many difficulties the company had with taxing authorities, particularly in Europe.

As noted earlier, in spite of the varied international objectives that can be accomplished by transfer pricing, income tax and import duty minimization seem to dominate international transfer pricing decisions.

SECTION 482 OF THE INTERNAL REVENUE CODE AND TRANSFER PRICING

As noted previously, tax minimization is one of the most persuasive objectives in international transfer pricing because of the immediate economic benefits involved. Tax minimization, however, must be pursued cautiously. Host country governments understandably are very sensitive to transfer prices, so a thorough understanding of tax regulations of host countries is necessary to avoid difficulties.

In the United States, transfer pricing is covered by Section 482 of the Internal Revenue Code; that in any case of two or more companies owned or controlled by the same interest, the Internal Revenue Service (IRS) may distribute, apportion or allocate gross income or deductions between or among the businesses if it determines that it is necessary to do so in order to prevent evasions of taxes or reflect clearly the income of the businesses involved. Section 482 sets forth allocation rules for specific items:

1. Imputed interest on intercompany loans and advances;
2. Services performed by one member for another;
3. Use of tangible property;
4. Pricing of intercompany sales of tangible property;
5. Transfers of intangible property.

Of these five specific items, this chapter is concerned with only (4), which covers transfer pricing of tangible property.

How does Section 482 affect transfer pricing of tangible property? In a typical case, a United States parent company sells goods to its foreign affiliate for resale. If the IRS finds that the price to the affiliate was below an arm's-length price, it adjusts the taxable income of the parent to reflect the higher arm's-length price. The result is an increase in the parent's U. S. tax liability. The foreign affiliate, however, will have taken the lower price into account in computing its cost of goods sold and its foreign tax. Therefore, unless the foreign government allows the affiliate to correspondingly adjust its foreign taxes, double taxation will occur. While the foreign tax credit provisions of the U. S. Internal Revenue Code can offset the double taxation to some extent, only in rare cases will it do this completely.

The threat of double taxation is no longer as great as it once was, however, because the United States government has entered into a number of tax treaties with foreign governments. These treaties contain a provision, generally referred to as the Related Persons Article, that mitigates the problem of double taxation. This provision, which is similar to Section 482 of the U. S. IRC, expresses mutual recognition of the principle of allocation of income and deductions among related persons when their dealings have not been at arm's-length; the provision also recognizes the right of the countries to continue to propose and make allocations which will reflect arm's-length dealings pursuant to their domestic laws.

The important feature of pursuing tax minimization is to ensure that transfer prices reflect arm's-length transactions as much as possible. In determining the arm's-length price for the sale of tangible property between a U. S. parent and foreign affiliate, Section 482 and related regulations allow three pricing methods. These methods are the comparable uncontrolled price method, resale price method, and cost-plus method. Each of these methods will be examined in detail, followed by methods that might be allowed by the IRS.

Comparable Uncontrolled Price Method

Reg. 1.482-2(3) (l) (i) defines an arm's-length price as the price an unrelated party would have paid under the same set of circumstances for the property involved in the controlled sale. The IRS views the comparable uncontrolled price method as the most reliable indication of an arm's-length price because it reflects (1) the price of sales made by a controlled group to an unrelated party, (2) the price of sales made by an unrelated party to a controlled group, or (3) the price of sales between parties that are not members of the same controlled group and, therefore, are unrelated to each other.[4] Thus, the comparable uncontrolled price method is actually the prevailing market price transfer pricing technique.

However, the prevailing market price rarely can be used because perfectly competitive markets are necessary. Recognizing this constraint, the IRS allows the use of the adjusted market price transfer price when the market is slightly imperfectly competitive. The IRC reads:

> Uncontrolled sales are considered comparable to controlled sales if the physical property and circumstances involved in the uncontrolled sales are identical to the physical property and circumstances involved in the controlled sales, or if such properties and circumstances are so nearly identical that any differences either have no effect on price, or such differences can be reflected by a reasonable number of adjustments to the price of uncontrolled sales.[5]

Some adjustments that are allowed are for differences in the quality of the product, terms of sale, intangible property associated with the sale, time of sale, terms of delivery, and the level of the market (*i.e.*, wholesale, retail) and the geographic market in which the sale takes place. These adjustments are a reflection of a slightly imperfectly competitive market. Thus, Section 482 allows the prevailing market price to be adjusted for identifiable and quantifiable market imperfections when small dollar amounts are involved.[6] In other words, Section 482 sanctions use of the adjusted market price, which is derived from the general rule for transfer pricing proposed by this chapter.

On the other hand, Section 482 places a rather severe restriction on the determination of the adjusted market price because it allows only as many adjustments as are used with sales requiring the fewest and simplest adjustments. See the following example.

> Thus, for example, if a taxpayer makes comparable uncontrolled sales of a particular product which differ from the controlled sale only with respect to the terms of delivery, and makes other compar-

[4] A controlled sale is one between related parties. An uncontrolled sale is an arm's-length sale between unrelated parties. A controlled group is one of the related parties making an internal transfer of tangible property.

[5] Reg. 1.482-2(c)(2)(ii).

[6] The IRC uses the words "definite and reasonably ascertainable effect." The point at which a difference is no longer definite or reasonably ascertainable is likely to be difficult to determine and is the source of many taxpayer-IRS disputes. Reg. 1-482-2(e)(2)(ii).

> able uncontrolled sales of the product which differ from the controlled sale with respect to both terms of delivery and terms of payment, the comparable uncontrolled sales differing only with respect to terms of delivery should be selected as the comparable uncontrolled sale.[7]

There is no evidence that Section 482 allows adjustments for economies from selling internally, probably because it is difficult to verify the accuracy of the amounts. The principal internal economy is selling expenses, which would be difficult to determine precisely. A fairly accurate estimate could be made, however, that would not be too different in nature from some of the estimates already allowed by the IRC.

One effect of not allowing adjustments for internal economies is the additional tax revenues accrued to the United States. Not adjusting the transfer price downward for internal economies results in higher profit and higher U. S. taxes.

In addition, Section 482 allows transfers at less than the uncontrolled price for a short period if the primary purpose is to establish or maintain a market for the product transferred. For example, a company might want to make transfers at less than the comparable uncontrolled price in order to meet competition or introduce a new product.[8]

In summary, Section 482 specifies that when establishing transfer prices, a company first must attempt to apply the comparable uncontrolled price method. This method is similar to the prevailing market price transfer pricing technique, but the Section 482 implicitly recognizes that the perfectly competitive markets necessary to support the use of the prevailing market price rarely occur. Therefore, it allows the use of the adjusted market price, which is used with slightly imperfectly competitive markets, but restricts the number of adjustments that can be made to the prevailing market price. If a comparable uncontrolled price cannot be found, the Section specifies that the next method the company must attempt to apply is the resale price method.

Resale Price Method

The resale price method is explained best by an example from Section 482:

[7] Reg 1.482-2(e)(2)(iii).
[8] Reg. 1.482-2(e)(2)(iv).

> Thus, where one member of a group of controlled entities sells property to another member which resells the property in uncontrolled sales, if the applicable resale price of the property involved in the controlled sale is $100 and the appropriate markup percentage for resales by the buyer is 20%, the arm's length price of the controlled sale is $80 ($100 minus 20% X 100).[9]

The arm's-length price is equal to the sales price received for the property by the reseller less an appropriate markup. Although this seems fairly simple, there are at least two problems that must be addressed before the method can be used. The first problem involves the circumstances under which this method must be used. The section lists four circumstances that must exist:

1. There are no comparable uncontrolled sales.
2. An applicable resale price . . . is available with respect to resales made within a reasonable time before or after the time of the controlled sale.
3. The buyer (reseller) has not added more than an insubstantial amount to the value of the property by physically altering the product for resale. For this purpose packaging, repacking, labeling or minor assembly of property does not constitute physical alteration.
4. The buyer (reseller) has not added more than an insubstantial amount to the value of the property by the use of intangible property.[10]

Circumstances (3) and (4) would severely curtail the use of this method, but the section allows the resale price method to be used even though circumstances (3) and (4) do not exist, if the method is more feasible and is likely to result in a more accurate determination of an arm's-length price than would the use of the cost-plus method. This exception is allowed because there may be conditions under which a buyer (reseller) might add more than an insubstantial amount to the value of the property, but the amount may be determined with reasonable precision. Thus, the resale price method might be preferable to the cost-plus method if the appropriate gross profit percentage under the cost-plus method is more difficult to determine than the appropriate markup percentage under the resale price method.

The second problem involves determining the appropriate markup percentage, which is defined as follows:

[9] Reg. 1.482-2(e)(3)(i).
[10] Reg. 1.482-2(c)(3)(ii).

> The appropriate markup percentage is equal to the percentage of gross profit (expressed as a percentage of sales) earned by the buyer (reseller) or another party on the resale of property which is both purchased and resold in an uncontrolled transaction, which resale is most similar to the applicable resale of property involved in the controlled sale.[11]

The resale price method is essentially a work-back method of establishing an arm's-length price. The final sales price, referred to in the IRC as the applicable resale price, is determined first. Working backward from the final sales price involves subtracting an appropriate markup percentage, which is the percentage of gross profit (expressed as a percentage of sales) earned by the buyer (reseller) or others on the resale of similar property bought from and resold to unrelated parties under similar circumstances. This might be characterized as an arm's-length markup.

The markup percentages should be derived from uncontrolled purchases and sales of the buyer (reseller) in the controlled sale because of the probability that the buyer (reseller) will sell the same or similar items under uncontrolled circumstances. If resale by the buyer (reseller) is not a good indication of the markup percentage, the markup percentage of a competitor engaged in a similar business may be used although this figure rarely would be available. In the absence of more precise information, industry averages might be used.

The resale price method is a means of allocating the profit on products purchased internally and resold by the buyer, using the markup percentage as the allocation method. For example, assume that a product produced by a company for $60 is sold for $100. If the appropriate markup percentage is 15%, the buyer (reseller) is allocated $15 of the profit with the remainder going to the manufacturing division.

In summary, Section 482 requires the use of the resale price method if the comparable uncontrolled price method cannot be used and if the resale price method is more appropriate than the cost-plus method. The resale price method is based on the belief that after a buyer (reseller) subtracts the appropriate markup percentage from the resale price, the resulting balance should be an approximation of an arm's-length transaction. The method can be used only if the appropriate markup percentage can be determined and if an accurately determinable or insubstantial amount is added to the value of the property by the buyer (reseller). If neither the comparable uncontrolled price method nor the resale price method is appropriate, the cost-plus method should be used.

[11] Reg. 1.482-2(e)(3)(vi).

Cost-Plus Method

The cost-plus method is a work-forward method of constructing an arm's-length price. The cost-plus method is used when the buyer (reseller) adds *substantial* value to property before resale. For example, the cost-plus method will be used when the seller is merely engaged in purchasing property for resale and delivery to a buyer who further processes the property in a manufacturing activity or incorporates it into another product in a major assembly operation.

Essentially, the cost-plus method is an alternative to the resale price method. Generally it is more suitable than the resale price method if the cost and profit factors associated with the seller's functions are easier to evaluate than the cost and profit factors associated with the buyer's functions. In general, the approach to the cost-plus method is fairly liberal, as can be seen by the following statement:

> The cost of producing the property involved in the controlled sale and the costs which enter into the computation of the appropriate gross profit percentage [the plus] shall be computed in a consistent manner in accordance with sound accounting practices for allocating or apportioning costs, which neither favors nor burdens controlled sales in comparison with uncontrolled sales.[12]

The passage implies that the calculation of cost for property in a controlled sale should be the same as for property in an uncontrolled sale. Furthermore, a company is not constrained to one method of determining cost, such as full actual cost. Although the regulations do not define the phrase "cost of producing," it is probably safe to assume that cost of producing includes all costs associated with manufacturing and distributing the product, including the cost of acquiring property used in production.

The means of finding the appropriate gross profit percentage are similar to finding the appropriate markup percentage under the resale price method. If possible, the gross profit percentage should be based on uncontrolled sales of the same or similar products made by the producer of the product. If this method cannot be used, the gross profit percentage of a competitor can be used, or, as a final resort, industry figures can be used.

In the case of *Eli Lilly and Co. v. U. S.*,[13] the IRS used the gross profit percentage on domestic sales, which were deemed to be arm's-length sales, as the appropriate gross profit percentage for international sales. Ultimately, however, the IRS reduced the proposed

[12] Reg. 1.482-2(e)(4)(ii).

[13] *Eli Lilly and Co. v. U. S.*, 372 F.2d 990 (Ct. Cl. 1967).

markup on cost of goods sold by 50 percent while leaving the gross profit percentage for other expenses the same. This process was accepted by the court, even though it was somewhat arbitrary, because it was not considered to have reached unreasonable results. In *Frank v. International Canadian Corp.*,[14] the Commissioner argued that the standard to be applied was whether the price arrived at was an arm's-length price and not whether the price was a reasonable one.

These two cases illustrate the arbitrary nature of the cost-plus method. The appropriate gross profit percentage is often a subjective figure even under the best of circumstances, but subsequent manipulations of this figure only serve to move the cost-plus price further away from reality. The result is often simply arbitration between the taxpayer and the IRS over the amount of the plus.

When these three methods of establishing transfer prices—the comparable uncontrolled price method, the resale price method, and the cost-plus method—were first specified, many taxpayers complained that none of the three methods was suitable for their companies. As a result the IRS allowed a fourth alternative as described by the following passage from the IRC:

> Where the standards for applying one of the three methods of pricing . . . are met, such method must, for the purposes of this paragraph, be utilized unless the taxpayer can establish that, considering all the facts and circumstances, some method of pricing other than those described . . . is clearly more appropriate. Where none of the three methods of pricing described . . . can reasonably be applied under the facts and circumstances as they exist in a particular case, some appropriate method of pricing other than those described . . . , or variations on such methods, can be used.[15]

Some methods that might be allowed by the IRS are described briefly in the next section.

Other Methods

How far the IRS is willing to go in allowing other methods is difficult to determine, but it is likely that the method proposed by the taxpayer will be analyzed to determine whether it resulted in an arm's-length transfer price. Some methods that might be accepted by the IRS are described briefly.[16]

[14] *Frank v. International Canadian Corp.*, 308 F.2d 520 (9th Cir. 1962).

[15] Reg. 1.482-2(e)(1)(iii).

[16] This list is based on T. M. 230-2rd, "Allocations (Sec. 482)—Specific Transactions," (Tax Management, Inc., 1978), p. A-35-37.

1. *Pricing Component Parts*—The arm's-length price of a manufactured product could be estimated by adding the prices charged by unrelated parties for the various components of the completed product.
2. *Supply Substitute Material Method*—Rather than using the final selling price or gross profit percentages of the products involved in the controlled sale, the price or gross profit percentages of products in the same general class are used if they are the result of uncontrolled sales and the products in these uncontrolled sales are substituted for the products in the uncontrolled sale without a significant change in the taxpayer's resources.
3. *Appraisal Method*—The arm's-length price is the price at which an unrelated party would agree to buy the products in an uncontrolled sale.
4. *Proportionate Profits Method*—The total profit on the product is allocated between the segments, using full cost as the allocation basis.
5. *Rate of Return on Investment Methods*—The profit factor in the markup percentage or gross margin percentage is based on receiving a certain rate of return on invested assets. This method is a variation of the resale price and cost-plus methods.

Without judging any of these techniques, one can see that they range from simple variations of one of the three specified techniques to wholesale departures from any known technique. Actually, the techniques mentioned above probably have little applicability to the taxpayer. The IRS has for the most part preferred that the taxpayer use one of the three specified methods.

An important question, then, is the extent to which the specified methods proposed by the IRS are compatible with the general rule for transfer prices proposed in this study.

THE IRS METHODS AND THE GENERAL RULE

The fundamental differences between the objectives of the tax authorities and the objectives of corporate transfer pricing cause rather severe discrepancies between the transfer pricing methods allowed by the IRS and the general rule.[17] For example, recall that the objectives of transfer pricing in organizations are to promote goal congruence (profit maximization) and to enhance performance evaluation. The IRS, on the other hand, has the objective of determining a fair means of allocating the total profit of a sale between the United States and other countries. As long as the means are deemed fair and acceptable to the parties involved, it makes little difference to the IRS whether profit maximization is promoted or performance evaluation is enhanced.

A further problem is that in order for the IRS to assess taxes, a company must determine a profit. Thus, when the general rule would lead to using cost centers, a profit would have to be added, thereby resulting in a pseudo-profit center. With cost centers, the cost-plus method probably would be used to determine transfer prices for tax purposes, but such prices would not necessarily promote profit maximization or enhance performance evaluation.

In spite of the differences between the objectives of the IRS and the objectives of transfer pricing in corporations, there are occasions where the general rule and the comparable uncontrolled price method will result in identical or nearly identical transfer prices. These occasions occur when there is a prevailing market price in a perfectly competitive market or one that can be revised to an adjusted market price when the market is slightly imperfectly competitive. Although Section 482 does not specifically allow for adjustments of economics from selling internally, a strong argument for its use as part of the comparable uncontrolled price probably could be made. If so, the general rule and comparable uncontrolled price method would result in virtually the same transfer price.

It is possible that a transfer price determined by the general rule and an IRS-determined transfer price could be equal or nearly so for a profit/cost center if the proportionate profits method were used to maintain the profit concept. The proportionate profits method however, is recommended as a means of expediently maintaining the motivation of a profit center by removing a potential source of low motivation, *i.e.*, a product transferred at cost. Because the proportionate profits method results in an arbitrary profit split, it is recommended that when this technique is used, performance evaluation be based on cost analysis rather than profit analysis. Hence,

[17] The general rule is a procedure for establishing the transfer price that will promote profit maximization while enhancing performance evaluation. The general rule is not a single rule transfer pricing technique; it is a rule that ties together a number of techniques. To use the general rule, a company first must determine the type of competitive market it faces. When it is determined, application of the general rule will lead the company to the appropriate transfer price and the type of responsibility center that can be used.

while the IRS and the general rule may result in the same transfer price because both are using the contribution margin technique, the determination of taxes will be arbitrary.

In summary, although the general rule and IRS methods sometimes will result in the same transfer price, there is no reason why this always should be so. The determination of taxes is not always compatible with promoting profit maximization and enhancing performance evaluation, so separate transfer prices often will be necessary for the separate objectives of the IRS and the management control process.

DOMESTIC INTERNATIONAL SALES CORPORATION (DISC)

Although domestic international sales corporations are not discussed in detail in this chapter, they are mentioned here because they are affected by Section 482 and have significant tax advantages.

The purpose of a DISC is to encourage U. S. manufacturers to increase exports by providing them with substantial tax benefits. The basic tax advantage is the deferral of federal income tax on a significant portion of the DISC's earnings. The benefit is enhanced by favorable transfer pricing rules that increase the amount of taxable income of the DISC.[18] The transfer pricing rules are quoted next.

> In the case of a sale of export property to a DISC by a person described in Section 482, the taxable income of such DISC and such person shall be based upon a transfer price which would allow such DISC to derive taxable income attributable to such sale (regardless of the sales price actually charged) in the amount which does not exceed the greatest of (1) 4% of the qualified export receipts on the sale of such property by the DISC plus 10% of the export promotion expenses of such DISC attributable to such receipts, (2) 50% of the combined taxable income of such DISC and such person which is attributable to the qualified export receipts on such property derived as the result of a sale by the DISC plus 10% of the export promotion expenses of such DISC attributable to such receipts, or (3) taxable income based upon the sales price actually charged (but subject to the rules provided in Section 482).[19]

[18] See Reg. 1.943-1 for a list of qualifications necessary to establish a DISC.

[19] Reg. 1.944(a).

When rules (1) or (2) are used, Section 482 does not apply. Under these rules, which are designed to simplify compliance, the transfer price from the related supplies to the DISC is computed only after the DISC sells the goods to a customer. The DISC and its supplier may make adjustments upward or downward following the close of the taxable year in which the DISC sells the goods in order to obtain the most favorable allocation of income permitted by these rules.

The favorable tax aspects and transfer pricing rules have made DISCs very popular.

SUMMARY

There are a number of objectives involved in international transfer pricing besides fulfilling the objectives of the management control process. Often these objectives are so important that they override the objectives of the management control process, resulting in transfer prices that neither promote profit maximization nor enhance performance evaluation.

One of the most influential objectives is the minimization of income taxes, which is achieved by an allocation of profit among the countries involved in the manufacture and sale of the product. In the United States, the allocation of profit is regulated by Section 482 of the Internal Revenue Code. Section 482 specifies three methods of determining transfer prices: the comparable uncontrolled price method, the resale price method, and the cost-plus method. In addition, the Section allows the use of any other method that the taxpayer can show is more appropriate.

REFERENCES

15-1 Arpan, Jeffrey S., and Lee H. Radebaugh, *International Accounting and Multinational Enterprises* (New York: Warren, Gorham and Lamont, 1981), Chapter 10.

15-2 Benke, Ralph L., Jr., and James Don Edwards, *Transfer Pricing: Techniques and Uses* (New York: National Association of Accountants, 1980).

15-3 Burns, Jane O., "Transfer Pricing Decisions in U. S. Multinational Corporations," *Journal of International Business Studies* (Fall 1980), pp. 23-39.

15-4 Business International Corporation, *Decision Making in International Operations* (New York: Business International Corporation, March 1980).

15-5 Choi, Frederick D. S., and Gerhard G. Mueller, *An Introduction to Multinational Accounting* (Englewood Cliffs, N. J.: Prentice-Hall, Inc., 1978), Chapter 8.

15-6 Chown, John, *Taxation and Multinational Enterprises* (London: Longman, 1974).

15-7 Greene, James, and Michael G. Duerr, *Intercompany Transactions in the Multinational Firm* (New York: Conference Board, 1970).

15-8 Keegan, W. J., "Multinational Pricing: How Far Is Arm's-Length?" *Columbia Journal of World Business* (May/June 1969), pp. 57-66.

15-9 Kim, Seung H., and Stephen W. Miller, "Constituents of the International Transfer Pricing Decisions," *Columbia Journal of World Business* (Spring 1979), pp. 69-76.

15-10 Obersteiner, Erich, "The Management of Liquid Fund Flow Across National Boundaries," *International Journal of Accounting* (Spring 1976), pp. 91-101.

15-11 Organization for Economic Cooperation and Development Committee on Fiscal Affairs, *Transfer Pricing and Multinational Enterprises* (Paris: OECD, 1979).

15-12 Sharav, Itzhak, "Transfer Pricing: Diversity of Goals and Practices," *Journal of Accountancy* (April 1974), pp. 56-62.

15-13 United Nations Conference on Trade and Development, *Dominant Positions of Market Power of Transnational Corporations* (New York: United Nations, 1978).

[illegible] Crucial [illegible]. [illegible]

[illegible] (Pittsburgh [illegible]) [illegible]

[illegible] and the [illegible]

[illegible] York: [illegible]

[illegible]

[illegible] (1961), [illegible]

[illegible] John W. [illegible] of the [illegible]

[illegible] the [illegible] 30 [illegible]

[illegible]

[illegible]

[illegible]

[illegible] Frank. [illegible]

[illegible]

[illegible] New York: [illegible] 1958.

$£¢$£¢$£$£¢$£$£¢$£¢$£¢$£¢$£¢$£¢$£¢$£¢$£¢$£¢$£¢$£¢$£¢$£¢$£¢

APPENDIX A

INTEREST TABLES

TABLE A COMPOUND VALUE OF $1

Period	1%	2%	3%	4%	5%	6%	7%	8%	9%	10%
1	1.010	1.020	1.030	1.040	1.050	1.060	1.070	1.080	1.090	1.100
2	1.020	1.040	1.061	1.082	1.102	1.124	1.145	1.166	1.188	1.210
3	1.030	1.061	1.093	1.125	1.158	1.191	1.225	1.260	1.295	1.331
4	1.041	1.082	1.126	1.170	1.216	1.262	1.311	1.360	1.412	1.464
5	1.051	1.104	1.159	1.217	1.276	1.338	1.403	1.469	1.539	1.611
6	1.062	1.126	1.194	1.265	1.340	1.419	1.501	1.587	1.677	1.772
7	1.072	1.149	1.230	1.316	1.407	1.504	1.606	1.714	1.828	1.949
8	1.083	1.172	1.267	1.369	1.477	1.594	1.718	1.851	1.993	2.144
9	1.094	1.195	1.305	1.423	1.551	1.689	1.838	1.999	2.172	2.358
10	1.105	1.219	1.344	1.480	1.629	1.791	1.967	2.159	2.367	2.594
11	1.116	1.243	1.384	1.539	1.710	1.898	2.105	2.332	2.580	2.853
12	1.127	1.268	1.426	1.601	1.796	2.012	2.252	2.518	2.813	3.138
13	1.138	1.294	1.469	1.665	1.886	2.133	2.410	2.720	3.066	3.452
14	1.149	1.319	1.513	1.732	1.980	2.261	2.579	2.937	3.342	3.797
15	1.161	1.346	1.558	1.801	2.079	2.397	2.759	3.172	3.642	4.177
16	1.173	1.373	1.605	1.873	2.183	2.540	2.952	3.426	3.970	4.595
17	1.184	1.400	1.653	1.948	2.292	2.693	3.159	3.700	4.328	5.054
18	1.196	1.428	1.702	2.026	2.407	2.854	3.380	3.996	4.717	5.560
19	1.208	1.457	1.753	2.107	2.527	3.026	3.616	4.316	5.142	6.116
20	1.220	1.486	1.806	2.191	2.653	3.207	3.870	4.661	5.604	6.727
21	1.232	1.516	1.860	2.279	2.786	3.399	4.140	5.034	6.109	7.400
22	1.245	1.546	1.916	2.370	2.925	3.603	4.430	5.436	6.658	8.140
23	1.257	1.577	1.974	2.465	3.071	3.820	4.740	5.871	7.258	8.954
24	1.270	1.608	2.033	2.563	3.225	4.049	5.072	6.341	7.911	9.850
25	1.282	1.641	2.094	2.666	3.386	4.292	5.427	6.848	8.623	10.834
30	1.348	1.811	2.427	3.243	4.322	5.743	7.612	10.062	13.267	17.449
40	1.489	2.208	3.262	4.801	7.040	10.285	14.974	21.724	31.408	45.258

TABLE A COMPOUND VALUE OF $1 (continued)

Period	11%	12%	13%	14%	15%	16%	17%	18%	19%	20%
1	1.110	1.120	1.130	1.140	1.150	1.160	1.170	1.180	1.190	1.200
2	1.232	1.254	1.277	1.300	1.322	1.346	1.369	1.392	1.416	1.440
3	1.368	1.405	1.443	1.482	1.521	1.561	1.602	1.643	1.685	1.728
4	1.518	1.574	1.630	1.689	1.749	1.811	1.874	1.939	2.005	2.074
5	1.685	1.762	1.842	1.925	2.011	2.100	2.192	2.288	2.386	2.488
6	1.870	1.974	2.082	2.195	2.313	2.436	2.565	2.700	2.840	2.986
7	2.076	2.211	2.353	2.502	2.660	2.826	3.001	3.185	3.379	3.583
8	2.305	2.476	2.658	2.853	3.059	3.278	3.511	3.759	4.021	4.300
9	2.558	2.773	3.004	3.252	3.518	3.803	4.108	4.435	4.785	5.160
10	2.839	3.106	3.395	3.707	4.046	4.411	4.807	5.234	5.695	6.192
11	3.152	3.479	3.836	4.226	4.652	5.117	5.624	6.176	6.777	7.430
12	3.498	3.896	4.334	4.818	5.350	5.936	6.580	7.288	8.064	8.916
13	3.883	4.363	4.898	5.492	6.153	6.886	7.699	8.599	9.596	10.699
14	4.310	4.887	5.535	6.261	7.076	7.987	9.007	10.147	11.420	12.839
15	4.785	5.474	6.254	7.138	8.137	9.265	10.539	11.974	13.589	15.407
16	5.311	6.130	7.067	8.137	9.358	10.748	12.330	14.129	16.171	18.488
17	5.895	6.866	7.986	9.276	10.761	12.468	14.426	16.672	19.244	22.186
18	6.543	7.690	9.024	10.575	12.375	14.462	16.879	19.673	22.900	26.623
19	7.263	8.613	10.197	12.055	14.232	16.776	19.748	23.214	27.251	31.948
20	8.062	9.646	11.523	13.743	16.366	19.461	23.105	27.393	32.429	38.337
21	8.949	10.804	13.021	15.667	18.821	22.574	27.033	32.323	38.591	46.005
22	9.933	12.100	14.713	17.861	21.644	26.186	31.629	38.141	45.923	55.205
23	11.026	13.552	16.626	20.361	24.891	30.376	37.005	45.007	54.648	66.247
24	12.239	15.178	18.788	23.212	28.625	35.236	43.296	53.108	65.031	79.496
25	13.585	17.000	21.230	26.461	32.918	40.874	50.656	62.667	77.387	95.395
30	22.892	29.960	39.115	50.949	66.210	85.849	111.061	143.367	184.672	237.373
40	64.999	93.049	132.776	188.876	267.856	378.715	533.846	750.353	1051.642	1469.740

TABLE A COMPOUND VALUE OF $1 (continued)

Period	21%	22%	23%	24%	25%	26%	27%	28%	29%	30%
1	1.210	1.220	1.230	1.240	1.250	1.260	1.270	1.280	1.290	1.300
2	1.464	1.488	1.513	1.538	1.562	1.588	1.613	1.638	1.664	1.690
3	1.772	1.816	1.861	1.907	1.953	2.000	2.048	2.097	2.147	2.197
4	2.144	2.215	2.289	2.364	2.441	2.520	2.601	2.684	2.769	2.856
5	2.594	2.703	2.815	2.932	3.052	3.176	3.304	3.436	3.572	3.713
6	3.138	3.297	3.463	3.635	3.815	4.001	4.196	4.398	4.608	4.827
7	3.797	4.023	4.259	4.508	4.768	5.042	5.329	5.629	5.945	6.275
8	4.595	4.908	5.239	5.589	5.960	6.353	6.767	7.206	7.669	8.157
9	5.560	5.987	6.444	6.931	7.451	8.004	8.595	9.223	9.893	10.604
10	6.727	7.305	7.926	8.594	9.313	10.086	10.915	11.806	12.761	13.786
11	8.140	8.912	9.749	10.657	11.642	12.708	13.862	15.112	16.462	17.921
12	9.850	10.872	11.991	13.215	14.552	16.012	17.605	19.343	21.236	23.298
13	11.918	13.264	14.749	16.386	18.190	20.175	22.359	24.759	27.395	30.287
14	14.421	16.182	18.141	20.319	22.737	25.420	28.395	31.691	35.339	39.373
15	17.449	19.742	22.314	25.195	28.422	32.030	36.062	40.565	45.587	51.185
16	21.113	24.085	27.446	31.242	35.527	40.357	45.799	51.923	58.808	66.541
17	25.547	29.384	33.758	38.740	44.409	50.850	58.165	66.461	75.862	86.503
18	30.912	35.848	41.523	48.038	55.511	64.071	73.869	85.070	97.862	112.454
19	37.404	43.735	51.073	59.567	69.389	80.730	93.813	108.890	126.242	146.190
20	45.258	53.357	62.820	73.863	86.736	101.720	119.143	139.379	162.852	190.047
21	54.762	65.095	77.268	91.591	108.420	128.167	151.312	178.405	210.079	247.061
22	66.262	79.416	95.040	113.572	135.525	161.490	192.165	228.358	271.002	321.178
23	80.178	96.887	116.899	140.829	169.407	203.477	244.050	292.298	349.592	417.531
24	97.015	118.203	143.786	174.628	211.758	256.381	309.943	374.141	450.974	542.791
25	117.388	144.207	176.857	216.539	264.698	323.040	393.628	478.901	581.756	705.627
30	304.471	389.748	497.904	634.810	807.793	1025.904	1300.477	1645.488	2078.208	2619.936
40	2048.309	2846.941	3946.340	5455.797	7523.156	10346.879	14195.051	19426.418	26520.723	36117.754

TABLE A COMPOUND VALUE OF $1 (continued)

Period	31%	32%	33%	34%	35%	36%	37%	38%	39%	40%
1	1.310	1.320	1.330	1.340	1.350	1.360	1.370	1.380	1.390	1.400
2	1.716	1.742	1.769	1.796	1.822	1.850	1.877	1.904	1.932	1.960
3	2.248	2.300	2.353	2.406	2.460	2.515	2.571	2.628	2.686	2.744
4	2.945	3.036	3.129	3.224	3.321	3.421	3.523	3.627	3.733	3.842
5	3.858	4.007	4.162	4.320	4.484	4.653	4.826	5.005	5.189	5.378
6	5.054	5.290	5.535	5.789	6.053	6.328	6.612	6.907	7.213	7.530
7	6.621	6.983	7.361	7.758	8.172	8.605	9.058	9.531	10.025	10.541
8	8.673	9.217	9.791	10.395	11.032	11.703	12.410	13.153	13.935	14.758
9	11.362	12.166	13.022	13.930	14.894	15.917	17.001	18.151	19.370	20.661
10	14.884	16.060	17.319	18.666	20.106	21.646	23.292	25.049	26.924	28.925
11	19.498	21.199	23.034	25.012	27.144	29.439	31.910	34.567	37.425	40.495
12	25.542	27.982	30.635	33.516	36.644	40.037	43.716	47.703	52.020	56.694
13	33.460	36.937	40.745	44.912	49.469	54.451	59.892	65.830	72.308	79.371
14	43.832	48.756	54.190	60.181	66.784	74.053	82.051	90.845	100.509	111.119
15	57.420	64.358	72.073	80.643	90.158	100.712	112.410	125.366	139.707	155.567
16	75.220	84.953	95.857	108.061	121.713	136.968	154.002	173.005	194.192	217.793
17	98.539	112.138	127.490	144.802	164.312	186.277	210.983	238.747	269.927	304.911
18	129.086	148.022	169.561	194.035	221.822	253.337	289.046	329.471	375.198	426.875
19	169.102	195.389	225.517	260.006	299.459	344.537	395.993	454.669	521.525	597.625
20	221.523	257.913	299.937	348.408	404.270	468.571	542.511	627.443	724.919	836.674
21	290.196	340.446	398.916	466.867	545.764	637.256	743.240	865.871	1007.637	1171.343
22	380.156	449.388	530.558	625.601	736.781	866.668	1018.238	1194.900	1400.615	1639.878
23	498.004	593.192	705.642	838.305	994.653	1178.668	1394.986	1648.961	1946.854	2295.829
24	652.385	783.013	938.504	1123.328	1342.781	1602.988	1911.129	2275.564	2706.125	3214.158
25	854.623	1033.577	1248.210	1505.258	1812.754	2180.063	2618.245	3140.275	3761.511	4499.816
30	3297.081	4142.008	5194.516	6503.285	8128.426	10142.914	12636.086	15716.703	19517.969	24201.043

TABLE B PRESENT VALUE OF $1

Period	1%	2%	3%	4%	5%	6%	7%	8%	9%	10%
1	0.990	0.980	0.971	0.962	0.952	0.943	0.935	0.926	0.917	0.909
2	0.980	0.961	0.943	0.925	0.907	0.890	0.873	0.857	0.842	0.826
3	0.971	0.942	0.915	0.889	0.864	0.840	0.816	0.794	0.772	0.751
4	0.961	0.924	0.888	0.855	0.823	0.792	0.763	0.735	0.708	0.683
5	0.951	0.906	0.863	0.822	0.784	0.747	0.713	0.681	0.650	0.621
6	0.942	0.888	0.837	0.790	0.746	0.705	0.666	0.630	0.596	0.564
7	0.933	0.871	0.813	0.760	0.711	0.665	0.623	0.583	0.547	0.513
8	0.923	0.853	0.789	0.731	0.677	0.627	0.582	0.540	0.502	0.467
9	0.914	0.837	0.766	0.703	0.645	0.592	0.544	0.500	0.460	0.424
10	0.905	0.820	0.744	0.676	0.614	0.558	0.508	0.463	0.422	0.386
11	0.896	0.804	0.722	0.650	0.585	0.527	0.475	0.429	0.388	0.350
12	0.887	0.788	0.701	0.625	0.557	0.497	0.444	0.397	0.356	0.319
13	0.879	0.773	0.681	0.601	0.530	0.469	0.415	0.368	0.326	0.290
14	0.870	0.758	0.661	0.577	0.505	0.442	0.388	0.340	0.299	0.263
15	0.861	0.743	0.642	0.555	0.481	0.417	0.362	0.315	0.275	0.239
16	0.853	0.728	0.623	0.534	0.458	0.394	0.339	0.292	0.252	0.218
17	0.844	0.714	0.605	0.513	0.436	0.371	0.317	0.270	0.231	0.198
18	0.836	0.700	0.587	0.494	0.416	0.350	0.296	0.250	0.212	0.180
19	0.828	0.686	0.570	0.475	0.396	0.331	0.277	0.232	0.194	0.164
20	0.820	0.673	0.554	0.456	0.377	0.312	0.258	0.215	0.178	0.149
21	0.811	0.660	0.538	0.439	0.359	0.294	0.242	0.199	0.164	0.135
22	0.803	0.647	0.522	0.422	0.342	0.278	0.226	0.184	0.150	0.123
23	0.795	0.634	0.507	0.406	0.326	0.262	0.211	0.170	0.138	0.112
24	0.788	0.622	0.492	0.390	0.310	0.247	0.197	0.158	0.126	0.102
25	0.780	0.610	0.478	0.375	0.295	0.233	0.184	0.146	0.116	0.092
26	0.772	0.598	0.464	0.361	0.281	0.220	0.172	0.135	0.106	0.084
27	0.764	0.586	0.450	0.347	0.268	0.207	0.161	0.125	0.098	0.076
28	0.757	0.574	0.437	0.333	0.255	0.196	0.150	0.116	0.090	0.069
29	0.749	0.563	0.424	0.321	0.243	0.185	0.141	0.107	0.082	0.063
30	0.742	0.552	0.412	0.308	0.231	0.174	0.131	0.099	0.075	0.057
40	0.672	0.453	0.307	0.208	0.142	0.097	0.067	0.046	0.032	0.022
50	0.608	0.372	0.228	0.141	[illegible]	[illegible]	[illegible]	[illegible]	[illegible]	[illegible]

TABLE B PRESENT VALUE OF $1 (continued)

Period	11%	12%	13%	14%	15%	16%	17%	18%	19%	20%
1	0.901	0.893	0.885	0.877	0.870	0.862	0.855	0.847	0.840	0.833
2	0.812	0.797	0.783	0.769	0.756	0.743	0.731	0.718	0.706	0.694
3	0.731	0.712	0.693	0.675	0.658	0.641	0.624	0.609	0.593	0.579
4	0.659	0.636	0.613	0.592	0.572	0.552	0.534	0.516	0.499	0.482
5	0.593	0.567	0.543	0.519	0.497	0.476	0.456	0.437	0.419	0.402
6	0.535	0.507	0.480	0.456	0.432	0.410	0.390	0.370	0.352	0.335
7	0.482	0.452	0.425	0.400	0.376	0.354	0.333	0.314	0.296	0.279
8	0.434	0.404	0.376	0.351	0.327	0.305	0.285	0.266	0.249	0.233
9	0.391	0.361	0.333	0.308	0.284	0.263	0.243	0.225	0.209	0.194
10	0.352	0.322	0.295	0.270	0.247	0.227	0.208	0.191	0.176	0.162
11	0.317	0.287	0.261	0.237	0.215	0.195	0.178	0.162	0.148	0.135
12	0.286	0.257	0.231	0.208	0.187	0.168	0.152	0.137	0.124	0.112
13	0.258	0.229	0.204	0.182	0.163	0.145	0.130	0.116	0.104	0.093
14	0.232	0.205	0.181	0.160	0.141	0.125	0.111	0.099	0.088	0.078
15	0.209	0.183	0.160	0.140	0.123	0.108	0.095	0.084	0.074	0.065
16	0.188	0.163	0.141	0.123	0.107	0.093	0.081	0.071	0.062	0.054
17	0.170	0.146	0.125	0.108	0.093	0.080	0.069	0.060	0.052	0.045
18	0.153	0.130	0.111	0.095	0.081	0.069	0.059	0.051	0.044	0.038
19	0.138	0.116	0.098	0.083	0.070	0.060	0.051	0.043	0.037	0.031
20	0.124	0.104	0.087	0.073	0.061	0.051	0.043	0.037	0.031	0.026
21	0.112	0.093	0.077	0.064	0.053	0.044	0.037	0.031	0.026	0.022
22	0.101	0.083	0.068	0.056	0.046	0.038	0.032	0.026	0.022	0.018
23	0.091	0.074	0.060	0.049	0.040	0.033	0.027	0.022	0.018	0.015
24	0.082	0.066	0.053	0.043	0.035	0.028	0.023	0.019	0.015	0.013
25	0.074	0.059	0.047	0.038	0.030	0.024	0.020	0.016	0.013	0.010
26	0.066	0.053	0.042	0.033	0.026	0.021	0.017	0.014	0.011	0.009
27	0.060	0.047	0.037	0.029	0.023	0.018	0.014	0.011	0.009	0.007
28	0.054	0.042	0.033	0.026	0.020	0.016	0.012	0.010	0.008	0.006
29	0.048	0.037	0.029	0.022	0.017	0.014	0.011	0.008	0.006	0.005
30	0.044	0.033	0.026	0.020	0.015	0.012	0.009	0.007	0.005	0.004
40	0.015	0.011	0.008	0.005	0.004	0.003	0.002	0.001	0.001	0.001
50	0.005	0.003	0.002	0.001	0.001	0.001	0.000	0.000	0.000	0.000

TABLE B PRESENT VALUE OF $1 (continued)

Period	21%	22%	23%	24%	25%	26%	27%	28%	29%	30%
1	0.826	0.820	0.813	0.806	0.800	0.794	0.787	0.781	0.775	0.769
2	0.683	0.672	0.661	0.650	0.640	0.630	0.620	0.610	0.601	0.592
3	0.564	0.551	0.537	0.524	0.512	0.500	0.488	0.477	0.466	0.455
4	0.467	0.451	0.437	0.423	0.410	0.397	0.384	0.373	0.361	0.350
5	0.386	0.370	0.355	0.341	0.328	0.315	0.303	0.291	0.280	0.269
6	0.319	0.303	0.289	0.275	0.262	0.250	0.238	0.227	0.217	0.207
7	0.263	0.249	0.235	0.222	0.210	0.198	0.188	0.178	0.168	0.159
8	0.218	0.204	0.191	0.179	0.168	0.157	0.148	0.139	0.130	0.123
9	0.180	0.167	0.155	0.144	0.134	0.125	0.116	0.108	0.101	0.094
10	0.149	0.137	0.126	0.116	0.107	0.099	0.092	0.085	0.078	0.073
11	0.123	0.112	0.103	0.094	0.086	0.079	0.072	0.066	0.061	0.056
12	0.102	0.092	0.083	0.076	0.069	0.062	0.057	0.052	0.047	0.043
13	0.084	0.075	0.068	0.061	0.055	0.050	0.045	0.040	0.037	0.033
14	0.069	0.062	0.055	0.049	0.044	0.039	0.035	0.032	0.028	0.025
15	0.057	0.051	0.045	0.040	0.035	0.031	0.028	0.025	0.022	0.020
16	0.047	0.042	0.036	0.032	0.028	0.025	0.022	0.019	0.017	0.015
17	0.039	0.034	0.030	0.026	0.023	0.020	0.017	0.015	0.013	0.012
18	0.032	0.028	0.024	0.021	0.018	0.016	0.014	0.012	0.010	0.009
19	0.027	0.023	0.020	0.017	0.014	0.012	0.011	0.009	0.008	0.007
20	0.022	0.019	0.016	0.014	0.012	0.010	0.008	0.007	0.006	0.005
21	0.018	0.015	0.013	0.011	0.009	0.008	0.007	0.006	0.005	0.004
22	0.015	0.013	0.011	0.009	0.007	0.006	0.005	0.004	0.004	0.003
23	0.012	0.010	0.009	0.007	0.006	0.005	0.004	0.003	0.003	0.002
24	0.010	0.008	0.007	0.006	0.005	0.004	0.003	0.003	0.002	0.002
25	0.009	0.007	0.006	0.005	0.004	0.003	0.003	0.002	0.002	0.001
26	0.007	0.006	0.005	0.004	0.003	0.002	0.002	0.002	0.001	0.001
27	0.006	0.005	0.004	0.003	0.002	0.002	0.002	0.001	0.001	0.001
28	0.005	0.004	0.003	0.002	0.002	0.002	0.001	0.001	0.001	0.001
29	0.004	0.003	0.002	0.002	0.002	0.001	0.001	0.001	0.001	0.000
30	0.003	0.003	0.002	0.002	0.001	0.001	0.001	0.001	0.000	0.000
40	0.000	0.000	0.000	0.000	0.000	0.000	0.000	0.000	0.000	0.000
50	0.000	0.000	0.000	0.000	0.000	0.000	0.000	0.000	0.000	0.000

TABLE B PRESENT VALUE OF $1 (continued)

Period	31%	32%	33%	34%	35%	36%	37%	38%	39%	40%
1	0.763	0.758	0.752	0.746	0.741	0.735	0.730	0.725	0.719	0.714
2	0.583	0.574	0.565	0.557	0.549	0.541	0.533	0.525	0.518	0.510
3	0.445	0.435	0.425	0.416	0.406	0.398	0.389	0.381	0.372	0.364
4	0.340	0.329	0.320	0.310	0.301	0.292	0.284	0.276	0.268	0.260
5	0.259	0.250	0.240	0.231	0.223	0.215	0.207	0.200	0.193	0.186
6	0.198	0.189	0.181	0.173	0.165	0.158	0.151	0.145	0.139	0.133
7	0.151	0.143	0.136	0.129	0.122	0.116	0.110	0.105	0.100	0.095
8	0.115	0.108	0.102	0.096	0.091	0.085	0.081	0.076	0.072	0.068
9	0.088	0.082	0.077	0.072	0.067	0.063	0.059	0.055	0.052	0.048
10	0.067	0.062	0.058	0.054	0.050	0.046	0.043	0.040	0.037	0.035
11	0.051	0.047	0.043	0.040	0.037	0.034	0.031	0.029	0.027	0.025
12	0.039	0.036	0.033	0.030	0.027	0.025	0.023	0.021	0.019	0.018
13	0.030	0.027	0.025	0.022	0.020	0.018	0.017	0.015	0.014	0.013
14	0.023	0.021	0.018	0.017	0.015	0.014	0.012	0.011	0.010	0.009
15	0.017	0.016	0.014	0.012	0.011	0.010	0.009	0.008	0.007	0.006
16	0.013	0.012	0.010	0.009	0.008	0.007	0.006	0.006	0.005	0.005
17	0.010	0.009	0.008	0.007	0.006	0.005	0.005	0.004	0.004	0.003
18	0.008	0.007	0.006	0.005	0.005	0.004	0.003	0.003	0.003	0.002
19	0.006	0.005	0.004	0.004	0.003	0.003	0.003	0.002	0.002	0.002
20	0.005	0.004	0.003	0.003	0.002	0.002	0.002	0.002	0.001	0.001
21	0.003	0.003	0.003	0.002	0.002	0.002	0.001	0.001	0.001	0.001
22	0.003	0.002	0.002	0.002	0.001	0.001	0.001	0.001	0.001	0.001
23	0.002	0.002	0.001	0.001	0.001	0.001	0.001	0.001	0.001	0.000
24	0.002	0.001	0.001	0.001	0.001	0.001	0.001	0.000	0.000	0.000
25	0.001	0.001	0.001	0.001	0.001	0.000	0.000	0.000	0.000	0.000
26	0.001	0.001	0.001	0.000	0.000	0.000	0.000	0.000	0.000	0.000
27	0.001	0.001	0.000	0.000	0.000	0.000	0.000	0.000	0.000	0.000
28	0.001	0.000	0.000	0.000	0.000	0.000	0.000	0.000	0.000	0.000
29	0.000	0.000	0.000	0.000	0.000	0.000	0.000	0.000	0.000	0.000
30	0.000	0.000	0.000	0.000	0.000	0.000	0.000	0.000	0.000	0.000
40	0.000	0.000	0.000	0.000	0.000	0.000	0.000	0.000	0.000	0.000
50	0.000	0.000	0.000	0.000	0.000	0.000	0.000	0.000	0.000	0.000

TABLE B **PRESENT VALUE OF $1 (continued)**

Period	41%	42%	43%	44%	45%	46%	47%	48%	49%	50%
1	0.709	0.704	0.699	0.694	0.690	0.685	0.680	0.676	0.671	0.667
2	0.503	0.496	0.489	0.482	0.476	0.469	0.463	0.457	0.450	0.444
3	0.357	0.349	0.342	0.335	0.328	0.321	0.315	0.308	0.302	0.296
4	0.253	0.246	0.239	0.233	0.226	0.220	0.214	0.208	0.203	0.198
5	0.179	0.173	0.167	0.162	0.156	0.151	0.146	0.141	0.136	0.132
6	0.127	0.122	0.117	0.112	0.108	0.103	0.099	0.095	0.091	0.088
7	0.090	0.086	0.082	0.078	0.074	0.071	0.067	0.064	0.061	0.059
8	0.064	0.060	0.057	0.054	0.051	0.048	0.046	0.043	0.041	0.039
9	0.045	0.043	0.040	0.038	0.035	0.033	0.031	0.029	0.028	0.026
10	0.032	0.030	0.028	0.026	0.024	0.023	0.021	0.020	0.019	0.017
11	0.023	0.021	0.020	0.018	0.017	0.016	0.014	0.013	0.012	0.012
12	0.016	0.015	0.014	0.013	0.012	0.011	0.010	0.009	0.008	0.008
13	0.011	0.010	0.010	0.009	0.008	0.007	0.007	0.006	0.006	0.005
14	0.008	0.007	0.007	0.006	0.006	0.005	0.005	0.004	0.004	0.003
15	0.006	0.005	0.005	0.004	0.004	0.003	0.003	0.003	0.003	0.002
16	0.004	0.004	0.003	0.003	0.003	0.002	0.002	0.002	0.002	0.002
17	0.003	0.003	0.002	0.002	0.002	0.002	0.001	0.001	0.001	0.001
18	0.002	0.002	0.002	0.001	0.001	0.001	0.001	0.001	0.001	0.001
19	0.001	0.001	0.001	0.001	0.001	0.001	0.001	0.001	0.001	0.000
20	0.001	0.001	0.001	0.001	0.001	0.001	0.000	0.000	0.000	0.000
21	0.001	0.001	0.001	0.000	0.000	0.000	0.000	0.000	0.000	0.000
22	0.001	0.000	0.000	0.000	0.000	0.000	0.000	0.000	0.000	0.000
23	0.000	0.000	0.000	0.000	0.000	0.000	0.000	0.000	0.000	0.000
24	0.000	0.000	0.000	0.000	0.000	0.000	0.000	0.000	0.000	0.000
25	0.000	0.000	0.000	0.000	0.000	0.000	0.000	0.000	0.000	0.000
26	0.000	0.000	0.000	0.000	0.000	0.000	0.000	0.000	0.000	0.000
27	0.000	0.000	0.000	0.000	0.000	0.000	0.000	0.000	0.000	0.000
28	0.000	0.000	0.000	0.000	0.000	0.000	0.000	0.000	0.000	0.000
29	0.000	0.000	0.000	0.000	0.000	0.000	0.000	0.000	0.000	0.000
30	0.000	0.000	0.000	0.000	0.000	0.000	0.000	0.000	0.000	0.000
40	0.000	0.000	0.000	0.000	0.000	0.000	0.000	0.000	0.000	0.000
50	0.000	0.000	0.000	0.000	0.000	0.000	0.000	0.000	0.000	0.000

$£¢$£$£¢$£¢$£¢$£¢$£¢$£¢$£¢$£¢$£¢$£¢$£¢$£¢$£$£¢$£¢$£¢$¢$£¢

APPENDIX B

GLOSSARY

Accommodating (Compensating) Transactions Those transactions necessary to account or compensate for differences between international payments and receipts and used to eliminate international disequilibrium.

Accounting (Translation) Exposure Financial statement items to be exposed to foreign exchange risk whenever a change in exchange rates alters their value.

Advising Bank A bank which notifies the beneficiary of a letter of credit without adding its own commitment to that of the issuing bank.

African Development Bank (AfDB) A regional development bank for Africa established in 1964 and located in Abidjan, Ivory Coast.

Agency for International Development (AID) An office within the U. S. State Department established in 1961 to carry our nonmilitary U. S. foreign assistance programs.

Agreement Corporation A bank chartered by a state to operate in international banking under an agreement with the Board of Governors to the Federal Reserve System.

Appreciation A rise in the value of a currency against other currencies.

Arbitrage The purchase of something in one market and its sale in another market to take advantage of price differential.

Asian Development Bank (ADB) A regional development bank for Asia formed in 1966 by several Asian countries in partnership with the United States, Canada, and a number of European countries.

Autonomous Transactions Those transactions that occur due to self-interests. They include exports, imports, unilateral transfers, and investments.

Average Rate of Return The ratio of the average annual profit after taxes to the average net investment.

Balance of Payments A financial statement that records all transactions between a given country and the rest of the world during a specified period of time.

Balance Sheet Hedge A method designed to protect the value of a company's exposed assets. It involves the selection of the currency in which monetary assets and liabilities are denominated so that an exchange rate change would make exposed assets equal to exposed liabilities.

Bankers' Acceptance A draft accepted by a bank. When a bank accepts a draft, it promises to honor the draft at maturity.

Barter An exchange of goods and services between two countries without the involvement of finance.

Basic Balance In the balance of payments, the net balance of goods and services, unilateral transfers, and long-term capital flows.

Bearer The person who holds an instrument.

Bid Price The price at which a trader is willing to buy a given item such as foreign exchange.

Bill of Lading A shipping document issued to the exporting firm or its bank by a common carrier that transports the goods.

Blocked Funds Financial assets which cannot be repatriated because the local monetary authorities forbid their conversion into foreign exchange.

Bretton Woods Agreement An agreement signed by the representatives of 44 countries at Bretton Woods, New Hampshire, in 1944 to establish a system of fixed exchange rates.

Buy-American Policy A policy that requires the recipients of American aids to buy goods and services from American companies.

Capital Account In the balance of payments, the section that records the net changes in loans, investments, and other transfers of financial assets. The capital account consists of two major sections: long-term flows and short-term flows.

Capital Asset Pricing Model (CAPM) A theoretical model implying that the total risk of a security consists of systematic (undiversifiable) risk and unsystematic (diversifiable) risk.

Capital Budgeting The entire process of planning expenditures whose benefits are expected to extend beyond one year.

Capital Structure The combination of long-term debt, preferred stock, common stock, paid-in surplus, and retained earnings.

Capital Gains and Losses Gains and losses on sales of capital assets.

Cash Center A geographic location where all idle funds from the subsidiaries of a multinational company are maintained until they are needed.

Cashier's Check A bill of exchange (draft) issued by the cashier of a bank, for the bank, upon the bank.

CBD Cash before delivery.

Central Bank Banks' bank which has primary responsibility to control the growth of the money stocks in its country.

Certainty Equivalent Approach A method used to adjust for project risk. It adjusts for risk in the numerator of the net-present-value formula.

COD Cash on delivery.

Collecting Bank Any bank that handles an item for collection.

Common Market or European Economic Community (EEC) An organization formed in 1957 by France, Germany, Italy, Belgium, Netherlands, and Luxembourg to remove trade barriers among the member countries. The United Kingdom, Ireland, Denmark, and Greece joined later.

Comparative Advantage The relative advantage of a country in producing goods or services.

Confirmed Letter of Credit The letter of credit confirmed by a bank other than the opening bank. Thus, the confirmed letter of credit is a firm obligation of two banks.

Confirming Bank A bank that confirms a letter of credit issued by another bank.

Consignment The delivery of goods into the possession of another for the purpose of sale.

Consortium Bank A permanent group of banks to handle larger international loans.

Controlled Corporation A foreign corporation in which more than 50 percent of the voting shares are owned by U. S. shareholders.

Convertibility The ability to exchange one currency for another currency. The second currency must be convertible without restrictions.

Convertible Currency The currency which may be converted into other currencies without government restrictions.

Cooley Amendment Funds Local currency funds received in payment for agricultural products sold by the United States under U. S. aid programs.

Cost and Freight (C&F) The FOB (free on board) and the cost of transportation to the named point of destination.

Cost, Insurance, and Freight (CIF) The FOB value, the cost of transportation, insurance premium, and other costs incurred in connection with the shipment from the time of loading in the export country to their arrival at the named port of destination.

Cost of Capital The required rate of return that the company must earn on its projects for the market value of its common stock to remain unchanged.

Countervailing Duty An import charge used to offset an export subsidy by another country.

Covered-Interest Arbitrage Portfolio investment in a foreign country "covered" by forward sale of the foreign currency to eliminate foreign exchange risk.

Covering The purchase or sale of foreign exchange forward to protect a foreign exchange loss in the conversion from one currency to another.

Crawling Band A proposal for a trading band wider than two percent allowed under the Bretton Woods Agreement as well as 4.5 percent allowed under the Smithsonian Agreement.

Crawling Peg A proposal for regular change in the par value according to an agreed formula.

Credit Swap A hedging device that involves a simultaneous spot and forward loan transaction between a private company and a bank of a foreign country.

Credit Tranche The amount that a member country of the International Monetary Fund can borrow from the IMF above the gold tranche.

Cross Rate The exchange rate between two currencies when it is obtained from the rates of these two currencies in terms of a third currency.

Currency Swap An agreement made between parties to exchange one currency with another for a specified period of time and then exchange the latter currency with the former currency.

Current Account In the balance of payments, the section which includes merchandise exports and imports, earnings and expenditures for invisible trade items (services), and unilateral transfer items.

Debit In the balance of payments, the part of an international transaction that increases assets of a country and reduces liabilities or net worth of the country.

Depreciation A decrease in the foreign exchange market value of a currency.

Devaluation An official reduction in the par value of a currency by the government of that currency.

Development Bank A bank established to support the economic development of underdeveloped areas through long-term loans.

Direct Investment Equity investment such as the purchase of stock, the acquisition of an entire firm, or the establishment of a new subsidiary. The U. S. Department of Commerce defines direct investment as investment in either real capital assets or financial assets with a minimum of ten percent equity ownership in a foreign firm.

Dirty (Managed) Floating System A system in which exchange rates are allowed to change according to market forces but governments intervene to prevent undesired fluctuations. The monetary system since 1973 is sometimes called a dirty floating system because most industrial countries have permitted their currencies to fluctuate with frequent governmental intervention in the foreign exchange market.

Discounted-Cash-Flow Approaches Net-present-value and internal-rate-of-return methods which take into account the time value of money.

Documentary Draft A draft which accompanies such documents as bills of lading, commercial invoices, and other documents.

Division of Labor An economic theory which allows each person or nation to utilize any peculiar differences in skills and resources in the most economic manner. Division of labor is frequently called specialization of function.

Domestic International Sales Corporation (DISC) A subsidiary of a U. S. corporation which is allowed to defer its tax.

Double-Entry Accounting An accounting principle that requires each transaction to be recorded as debits and credits of an equal amount.

Draft (bill of exchange) An order written by a seller that requires a buyer to pay a specified amount of money at a specified time.

Drawee Bank A bank upon which a draft is drawn and which thus must pay. Such a bank is often called paying bank.

Drawer Bank A bank which draws (writes) a draft ordering payment.

Dumping A practice of selling a product in a foreign market at a price lower than that of the same product in the home market.

Economic Exposure Expected future cash flows whose real values may be changed because of exchange rate changes.

Edge Act Corporation A subsidiary of a U. S. commercial bank created under the Edge Act of 1916.

Efficient Exchange Market The exchange market where exchange rates reflect all available information and market prices adjust quickly to new information. In the efficient exchange market, market participants buy and sell foreign currencies in a way that eliminates all profits in excess of the minimum required to sustain their continued participation.

Elasticity The degree of responsiveness in one variable to changes in another. For example, in international trade the price elasticity measures the degree of responsiveness in exports or imports to changes in prices.

Equilibrium Exchange Rate The exchange rate at the intersection of the demand curve for and the supply curve of foreign exchange.

Eurodollars Dollar-denominated deposits in banks outside the United States. These banks may be foreign banks or foreign branches of a U. S. bank.

European Currency Unit (ECU) An artificial currency unit fixed in terms of the currencies of the nine EEC countries.

European Investment Bank (EIB) A regional development bank established in 1958 by members of the European Economic Community.

European Monetary System A complex exchange rate and intervention system adopted in 1978 by EEC countries to replace the snake.

Exchange Rate The price of one currency expressed in terms of another currency.

Export-Import Bank (Exim Bank) A U. S. government agency established to promote U. S. exports.

Factor A financial institution which buys a company's accounts receivable on a nonrecourse basis.

Fisher Effect An interest rate theory that states nominal interest rates in each country are equal to the required rate of return to the investor plus the expected rate of inflation.

Financial Assets Claims on such wealth as stocks, bonds, and other securities.

Financial Risks In international finance, those risks which may occur because of varying exchange rates, divergent tax laws, different interest and inflation rates, and balance-of-payments problems.

Fixed Exchange Rate An exchange rate which does not fluctuate or which changes within a predetermined band.

Flexible (Floating or Fluctuating) Exchange Rate An exchange rate which fluctuates according to market forces.

Foreign Base Company A corporation whose base or registration is in a country in which it does not conduct active operations.

Foreign Bond Bond sold outside the borrowing country but in the country of the currency in which the bond is denominated.

Foreign Credit Insuration Association (FCIA) An association of insurance companies in the United States which provide credit insurance to export sales.

Foreign Currency Swap An agreement between two parties to exchange local currency for hard currency at a specified future date.

Foreign Currency Translation The expression of balance-sheet items denominated in a foreign currency into a local currency.

Foreign Exchange Any currency other than the currency used internally in a given country.

Foreign Exchange Exposure The possibility that a firm will gain or lose due to changes in exchange rates.

Forward Exchange Rate An exchange rate for a currency to be delivered at a future date.

Free Alongside (F.A.S.) A price that includes the delivery of the goods along side overseas vessel within reach of its loading tackle.

Free on Board (FOB) The price of the goods to the foreign buyer which includes all costs, charges, profits, and expenses accruing up to the point where the goods are deposited on board the exporting vessel or aircraft.

General Agreement on Tariffs and Trade (GATT) An agreement signed in 1947 by 23 countries to liberalize world trade.

Geographic Arbitrage A practice which buys a currency in a market where its price is lower and then sells the currency in another market where its price is higher.

Gold Exchange Standard A system in which a country is prepared to convert its currency into gold.

Gold Tranche The amount that each IMF member country contributes in the form of gold as a part of its membership quota in the IMF. The gold tranche is usually 25 percent of a country's quota.

Group of Ten Ten major industrial countries which pledged in 1962 to lend their currencies to the IMF under the so-called General Agreement to Borrow. These ten countries are West Germany, France, Belgium, the Netherlands, Italy, the United Kingdom, Sweden, Canada, Japan, and the United States.

Group of Twenty The group of countries established to develop a proposal for reform of the international monetary system when the IMF felt that the Group of Ten countries did not sufficiently represent its entire member countries. The United States, the United Kingdom, West Germany, France, Japan, and India had individual representation in the Group of Twenty and 14 additional countries each represented a group of countries.

Group of Twenty-Four Twenty-four countries formed to ensure that interests and economic conditions of less-developed countries are taken into account in reform of the international monetary system. These 24 countries include eight countries each from Africa, Asia, and Latin America.

Gold Standard A system where a country uses gold as a medium of exchange and a store of value.

Hard Currency Currency that may be used in international trade.

Hedging Device An approach designed to reduce or offset a possible loss. For example, the multinational company may sell forward exchange or use other means such as credit swap to offset or reduce possible losses from exchange rate fluctuations that affect values of assets and liabilities.

Import Quota The maximum amount of a given product to be imported during a specified period of time.

Indexing The practice of adjusting assets, liabilities, or payments by some measure of inflation to preserve the purchasing power of the original amounts.

Inflation The overall rate of increase in prices for a group of goods and services in a given country.

Inter-American Development Bank (IDB) A regional development bank founded in 1959 by the United States and 19 Latin American countries to further the economic development of its member countries.

Interest Arbitrage The practice of lending or investing in another currency to take advantage of higher interest rates.

Interest Equalization Tax A tax imposed on U. S. residents who bought foreign securities between 1963 and 1974 in order to reduce after-tax yields on such bonds to the level of the yield on U. S. bonds.

Interest Parity Line A line that describes the equilibrium position for the relationship between interest differentials and forward premium or discount. Every point on the line represents a situation in which the interest differential equals the forward premium or discount.

Interest Parity Theory A theory stating that the difference between the spot rate and the forward rate equals the difference between the domestic interest rate and the foreign interest rate.

Internal Rate of Return The discount rate that equates the present value of expected net cash flows to the present value of the net investment.

International Bank for Reconstruction and Development (IBRD) The World Bank which is a companion institution to the IMF.

International Bonds Those bonds that are initially sold outside the country of the borrower.

International Development Association (IDA) An affiliate of the IBRD established to make long-term "soft" loans for development.

International Finance Corporation (IFC) An affiliate of the IBRD established to make development loans in forms which could be sold to other investors and converted into equity.

International Monetary Fund (IMF) An international monetary organization created at the Bretton Woods conference to make the new monetary system feasible and workable.

International Monetary System A system of such elements as laws, rules, institutions, instruments, and procedures which include international money.

Irrevocable Letter of Credit A letter of credit which cannot be revoked by the opening bank.

Issuing Bank The bank which issues a letter of credit, usually the importer's bank.

Joint Venture A business venture in which two or more parties (for example, a foreign firm and a local firm) have equity interest.

Kennedy Round The trade negotiations concluded in 1967 to reduce trade barriers between the United States and the EEC countries.

Less Developed Countries (LDCs) Normally, those countries with per capita income of less than $1,000.

Letter of Credit A document issued by a bank at the request of the importer. In the document, the bank agrees to honor a draft drawn on the importer if the draft accompanies specified documents.

Local Currency The currency of the country to which reference is made.

London Interbank Offer Rate (LIBOR) The arithmetic average of the interest rates offered by six major banks in London on six-month Eurodollar time deposits at a certain time during the morning.

Link Financing An arrangement that commercial banks in strong-currency countries help subsidiaries in weak-currency countries obtain loans by guaranteeing repayment on the loans.

M_1 The most common measure of money supply which consists of currency in circulation and demand deposits in commercial banks.

M_2 Another common measure of money supply which consists of M_1 plus time deposits in commercial banks minus large certificates of deposits (over $100,000).

Marshall Plan The European Economic Recovery Program established by the United States in 1948 to restore the productive capacity of European industry and agriculture destroyed during World War II.

Money Market Hedge A hedging device which involves a contract and a source of funds to carry out that contract. If an American firm has a German mark import payable in 60 days, it may borrow in dollars, convert the proceeds into German marks, buy a 60-day German Treasury bill, and pay the import bill with the funds derived from the sale of the Treasury bill.

Most-Favored Nation A nation which receives the most favored treatment in application of duties from another country.

Multinational Corporation (MNC) A corporation which operates in a number of different countries.

Negotiating Bank A bank which negotiates such things as discounts or purchases of drafts drawn by exporters.

Net Exposure The difference between exposed assets and liabilities.

Net Present Value The present value of future net cash flows minus the present value of the net investment for a project.

Netting A method designed to reduce the foreign exchange transaction cost of what would otherwise be a large number of crossing spot transactions. For example, if subsidiary A buys $1 million worth of goods from subsidiary B and B in turn buys $3 million worth of parts from A, the combined flows are $4 million. But on a net basis, subsidiary A would pay subsidiary B only $2 million.

Nontariff Barrier Restrictive practices in trade other than custom duties used by governments or by private firms. Nontariff barriers used by governments include import quotas, voluntary restrictions, exceptional customs valuation procedures, and health regulations. Nontariff barriers used by private firms include price control, division of markets, restriction of supplies, patent agreements, or control of technology.

Notifying (Advising) Bank A bank which notifies the beneficiary of the opening of a letter of credit.

Offer Price The price at which a trader is willing to sell a given item.

Office of Foreign Direct Investment (OFDI) A U. S. government agency created in 1965 to impose controls on U. S.-financed foreign direct investment. Its regulations were voluntary between 1965 and 1967 and became mandatory from 1968 until they were abolished in 1973.

Official Reserves Government-owned assets which consist of gold, SDRs, and convertible foreign exchange.

Offshore Funds Funds which use the currency of a country but are located outside that country for tax and other purposes.

Opening Bank A bank which opens a letter of credit.

Optimum Capital Structure The combination of debt and equity that yields the lowest cost of capital or maximizes the overall value of the company.

Organization for Economic Cooperation and Development An organization established in 1961 to replace the Organization for European Economic Cooperation (OEEC). The OECD includes Group-of-Ten countries, Austria, Denmark, Luxembourg, Norway, Switzerland, Finland, Greece, Iceland, Ireland, Portugal, Spain, Turkey, and Australia.

Organization of Petroleum Exporting Countries (OPEC) An organization established by a number of oil exporting countries to formulate uniform policies such as selling prices on their oil export sales. Full members with vote and veto include Algeria, Ecuador, Indonesia, Iran, Iraq, Kuwait, Libya, Nigeria, Qatar, Saudi Arabia, the United Arab Emirates, and Venezuela.

Outright Forward Rate A forward exchange rate expressed in terms of the amount of one currency required to buy a unit of another currency.

Overdraft A line of credit which permits the customer to write checks beyond deposits.

Overseas Private Investment Corporation (OPIC) A U. S. government agency established in 1969 to insure American overseas Investors against political risks.

Par (Mint) Value The value of a currency specified by the government of the currency.

Payback Period The number of years required for the net cash flows of a project to return its cost.

Payee The party to whom payment is made. The drawer may also be a payee of a draft.

Paying Bank The drawee bank on which a draft is drawn.

Planned Divestment The sale of majority ownership in foreign affiliates to local nationals during a previously agreed-upon period of time.

Portfolio Investment Investment in foreign financial assets without significant management control of the real assets.

Portfolio Theory A theory that indicates a company is often able to improve its risk-return performance by holding an internationally diversified portfolio of assets as opposed to a domestically diversified portfolio.

Possessions Corporation A U. S. firm engaged in business within U. S. possessions such as Guam and American Samoa. The possessions corporation obtains tax advantages if it meets certain requirements.

Purchasing-Power-Parity Theory An economic theory that in the long-run exchange rates reflect the relative purchasing power of currencies.

Recourse A right of an intermediary to claim reimbursement from a drawer of a draft if the drawee fails to pay.

Regulation M A regulation of the U. S. Federal Reserve System which requires U. S. banks to keep a stipulated percentage of their deposits at a Federal Reserve Bank or in vault cash.

Regulation Q A regulation of the U. S. Federal Reserve System which limits the interest rate that U. S. banks could pay on time deposits.

Required Rate of Return The minimum rate of return required by the investors.

Reserve or Official Reserve Account In the balance of payments, the section that represents the changes in official reserves such as SDRs and convertible foreign exchange.

Reserve Country A country whose currency is held as a reserve asset by central banks or governments of other countries.

Reserve Currency A currency held as a reserve asset by central banks or governments of countries other than the country of the currency.

Risk-Adjusted Discount Rate A rate which consists of the riskless rate of return plus a risk premium.

Risk Analysis An analysis of the different outcomes under different assumptions that each of these outcomes will occur.

Revaluation Either an upvaluation or a devaluation.

Safe Harbor A rule set in legislation which guarantees favorable treatment to the party.

Safeguard Clause A clause for conditions under which tariffs and nontarrif barriers may be reintroduced.

Short Position A situation in which the amount of liabilities held in a foreign currency exceeds that of assets held in that currency.

Sight Draft A draft payable on demand (at sight).

Smithsonian Agreement An agreement reached in December 1971 to widen the band up to 2.25 percent on either side of the par value.

Snake Within Tunnel A system that EEC countries agreed to allow their currencies to fluctuate a maximum of 2.25 percent against one another and permitted a 4.5 percent band against other countries. The tunnel disappeared in 1973 and the snake ended in 1978.

Sovereignty The power of a country to act as it wishes within its own borders.

Specific Duty A duty imposed as a fixed charge per unit, such as $2 per ton.

Special Drawing Rights (SDRs) A reserve asset created in 1967 by the IMF. SDRs are rights to draw on the IMF.

Spot Rate A foreign exchange rate paid for delivery of a currency within two days from the date of the trade.

Spread The difference between the bid and ask prices in a price quote.

Swap Loan A loan made by a local bank based on deposit of funds in offices of that bank in another country.

Switch Trading A practice where payments for exports to the East bloc and nonmarket countries are made through clearing units whereby sales are balanced with purchases from other countries.

Synergistic Effect A situation where the combined company is worth more than the sum of its parts.

Tariff A duty or tax imposed on imported commodities.

Tariff Harmonization The process of making tariffs more homogeneous by eliminating disparities in tariff rates on the same commodity.

Tax Haven A country which promises permanent tax inducements to attract multinational companies.

Tax Holidays The form of a complete tax exemption for the first few years given by a country when multinational firms invest their money in that country.

Third World A term used to mean those countries other than the industrial countries and with centrally planned economies.

Time Draft A draft payable a specified number of days after presentation to the drawee.

Transaction Exposure The possibility that gains or losses may result from the settlement of transactions whose terms are stated in a foreign currency.

Transfer Price The price of goods and services sold between related parties such as parent and subsidiary.

Unilateral Transfer In the balance of payments, the account which covers gifts by domestic residents to foreign residents, of gifts by the domestic government to foreign governments.

Upvaluation An official increase in the par value of a currency by the government.

Value-Added Tax (VAT) A sales tax assessed at one or more stages in the production process but only on the value added during that production stage.

Withholding Tax A tax collected from income to employees, stockholders, and others; it is collected before receipt of the income.

Yield The actual rate of return on a financial asset. It depends on the price paid for the security and the stated rate of interest or dividend.

INDEX

U

V

W

Z